Nursery Management

Administration and Culture

Nursery Management

Administration and Culture

Second Edition

Harold Davidson
Professor of Horticulture, Emeritus
Michigan State University
East Lansing, Michigan

Roy Mecklenburg
Director
The State Botanical Garden of Georgia
Athens, Georgia

Curtis Peterson
Assistant Professor
Michigan State University
East Lansing, Michigan

Prentice Hall, Englewood Cliffs, New Jersey 07632

Library of Congress Cataloging-in-Publication Data

Davidson, Harold (date)
  Nursery management.

  Bibliography: p.
  Includes index.
  1. Nurseries (Horticulture)—Management.
  2. Nurseries (Horticulture)—United States—
  Management. I. Mecklenburg, Roy. II. Peterson,
  Curtis, 1945–   . III. Title.
  SB118.5.D38   1988   635′.068   87-2238
  ISBN 0-13-627382-3

Editorial/production supervision and
  interior design: TKM Productions
Cover design: Wanda Lubelska
Manufacturing buyer: S. Gordon Osbourne

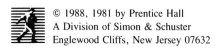 © 1988, 1981 by Prentice Hall
A Division of Simon & Schuster
Englewood Cliffs, New Jersey 07632

Printed in the United States of America

10 9 8 7 6 5 4 3 2 1

ISBN   0-13-627382-3   025

PRENTICE-HALL INTERNATIONAL (UK) LIMITED, *London*
PRENTICE-HALL OF AUSTRALIA PTY. LIMITED, *Sydney*
PRENTICE-HALL CANADA INC., *Toronto*
PRENTICE-HALL HISPANOAMERICANA, S.A., *Mexico*
PRENTICE-HALL OF INDIA PRIVATE LIMITED, *New Delhi*
PRENTICE-HALL OF JAPAN, INC., *Tokyo*
PRENTICE-HALL OF SOUTHEAST ASIA PTE. LTD., *Singapore*
EDITORA PRENTICE-HALL DO BRASIL, LTDA., *Rio de Janeiro*

*This book is dedicated to
nurserymen (men and women) of the United States
and to students of nursery management.
Both groups of people have taught us.
We trust that they, in turn, have learned
a small amount from us, the Profs.*

Contents

PREFACE   **xv**

Part I   General   **1**

1   BRIEF HISTORY OF THE NURSERY INDUSTRY   **1**

Early Eastern Nurseries   1
Early Midwestern Nurseries   4
Early Western Nurseries   6
Early Industry Observations   6
Legislation and the Automobile Affected Development   7
Early Garden Centers   8
Census Data on Nurseries   8
A Changing Industry   9
Summary   12

2   THE NURSERY INDUSTRY   **16**

Nursery Classification   16
Allied Areas   24
Trade Organizations   26
Specialized Associations   28
State, Regional, and Local Organizations   29
Centers of Production   29
Summary   35

Part II   Administration   **37**

3   MANAGEMENT APPLIED TO NURSERIES   **37**

Determining Goals   38
Planning   39
Organization   39
Control and Coordination   45
Employee Motivation, Evaluation, and Rewards   51
Summary   56

4   SELECTION OF A NURSERY SITE   **57**

Ecological Factors   57
Economic Factors   60
Sociological Factors   62
Biological Factors   62
Summary   63

5   ORGANIZATION AND DEVELOPMENT OF THE NURSERY   **64**

General Considerations   64
Specific Considerations   67
Planting Designs   69
Container-Production Areas   74
Production Programming   77
Estimating Plant Material Requirements   79
Estimating Space Requirements   80
Production Land Utilization   81
Summary   82

6   LAWS, REGULATIONS, AND CODES   **83**

Federal Laws and Regulations   83
State and Local Laws   92
Metric Equivalents   92

Codes   94

Summary   97

7   FINANCIAL MANAGEMENT   99

Function of Financial Records   99

Financing a Nursery Business   100

Evaluation of Alternative Investments   103

Negotiating a Loan   107

Assigning Value to a Nursery Crop in the Field   109

Information Needed about the Lending Institution   110

Computing the Future Cost of a Nursery Crop   111

Using Financial Information to Evaluate Management   112

Discretionary Spending   115

Determining Profit   116

Cost of Production   116

Accounts Receivable   127

Total Nursery Profits   127

Cash-Flow Analysis   129

Ratio Analysis   129

Summary   133

8   WHOLESALE MARKETING OF NURSERY CROPS   135

Specialization in Production Nurseries   136

Type of Nursery Crops Needed by Landscapers   136

Type of Nursery Crops Needed by Garden Centers   138

Type of Nursery Crops Needed for Mail-Order
Nurseries   139

Wholesale Nursery Sales Organizations   140

Standards   141

Standard Units of Nursery Stock   147

Shipping Agreements   148

Warranty   148

Nursery Crop Marketing Channels   149

Summary   157

9   NURSERY INVENTORY CONTROL   159

Plant Material Inventory   159
Equipment Inventory   164
Supplies   167
Summary   169

10   SHIPPING OF NURSERY STOCK   170

Plant Material   170
Buyer's Responsibilities   173
Seller's Responsibilities   174
Carrier's Responsibilities   179
Regulated Carriers   181
Summary   184

Part III   Culture   185

11   SOIL AND NUTRITION MANAGEMENT FOR FIELD-GROWN
     PLANTS   185

Essential Elements   186
Soil Reaction   188
Modifying Soil Reaction   189
Cation Exchange Capacity   198
Nutrient-Element Balance in Plants   199
Leaf Analysis   200
Soil Tests   201
Types of Fertilizers   202
Soluble Salts   206
Fertilizer Recommendations   206
Method of Application   212
Time of Application   214
Organic Matter   215
Soil Conservation   220
Soil Conservation Practices   221
Summary   222

12 MEDIA AND NUTRITION MANAGEMENT FOR CONTAINER-GROWN PLANTS 226

Functions and Criteria   226
Ingredients   230
Container Media   233
Chemical Supplements   237
Testing and Modifying   239
Media Sterilization   243
Post-Treatment   246
Summary   246

13 IRRIGATION OF NURSERY CROPS 249

Sources of Water   249
Water Quality   250
Soil Moisture Determination   251
Pumps and Power   253
Distribution Systems   255
Watering Field-Grown Crops   256
Watering Container-Grown Plants   259
Summary   272

14 MODIFYING PLANT GROWTH AND DEVELOPMENT IN THE NURSERY 275

Shoot Modification   275
Root Modification   285
Flowering and Fruiting   288
Winter Survival   293
Summary   297

15 CONTROLLING WEEDS, INSECTS, AND DISEASES 302

Weed Control   302
Insect Control   311
Disease Prevention, Monitoring, and Control   319
Summary   330

16 NURSERY CROP PRODUCTION   332

Planning the Operation   332
Liner Production from Seed   335
Liner Production from Vegetative Methods   335
Small Plant Culture   336
Field-Grown Crops   338
Container-Grown Crops   349
Harvesting Methods   356
Summary   359

17 NURSERY STORAGE FACILITIES   361

Storage Facilities   362
Additional Facilities   368
Factors Involved in Storage of Nursery Crops   370
Problem Areas   378
Storage of Chemicals   380
Summary   381

Part IV   Appendixes   385

A PARTIAL LIST OF BOOKS AND BULLETINS PERTAINING TO AREAS OF NURSERY MANAGEMENT   385

B ADDRESSES OF NURSERY-RELATED ORGANIZATIONS   388

C TRADE JOURNALS RELATED TO THE NURSERY INDUSTRY   390

D APPROXIMATE METRIC CONVERSIONS   392

E RATE PER 1000 FT² NOMOGRAPH   393

F RATE PER ACRE NOMOGRAPH   394

G FERTILIZER PROPORTIONER NOMOGRAPH, 100 PPM   395

H DETERMINING THE WEIGHT OF B&B PLANTS   396

I   AREA OF CIRCLES IN SQUARE FEET   399

J   VALUES FOR SELECTED RATES OF *i*   400

K   RELATIONSHIP BETWEEN T, RH, VP, AND VPD   402

L   APPROXIMATE WEIGHT OF B&B PLANTS   404

       INDEX   405

Preface

This book is intended as an introductory text for students and others interested either in starting or managing a nursery. The stimulus for writing the book came from both students and professional nurserymen requesting guidance in various areas of nursery management. The text is divided into four areas: (1) an introduction, (2) administration, (3) culture, and (4) an appendix. The two introductory chapters, the history of the nursery industry and the current status of the industry, are included to acquaint the reader with (1) the development of the nursery industry in the United States and how it has changed and will continue to change due to various forces, both internal and external to the industry. Some of the strongest forces of change have been, and will continue to be, economic, political, social, technical, and last but not least the weather; (2) the major centers of nursery production in the United States; and (3) the many types of organizations within the industry and the purpose for which they exist.

The two primary areas of the text are (1) administration and (2) culture. Within these areas the principles of business management and plant science as they pertain to nursery management have been interpreted by the authors as they viewed the state of the art in the mid-1980s. All topics have not been covered in detail, but hopefully they are presented in such a manner that the information will be useful to the reader. Where appropriate, additional readings have been suggested for those readers who may wish to pursue a subject in greater depth. The topics of plant propagation, garden center management, and landscape construction were deemed to be beyond the scope of this text. Readers are referred to Appendix A for references to these and related areas.

The fourth section of the book is the appendix. It contains lists of references, addresses of nursery organizations, nomographs, and other data that may be useful to a student of nursery management.

Since the nursery industry is very diversified, no single text can cover in detail all of the various aspects of the business. The information set forth in this text is intended to provide both general and specific information on topics related to nursery management which can be used in exercising sound management decisions. Young people would be well-advised to seek a period of ''intelligent employment'' within the industry prior to starting a nursery business. The production and marketing of quality plants are fascinating businesses, but both require considerable knowledge and skill if they are to be done productively and profitably.

Botanical names within the text conform to *Hortus Third,* which is an excellent dictionary of botanical nomenclature for nurserymen and others interested in the proper nomenclature for plants. The appendices contain various tables and nomographs that a nursery manager may find useful. Also included is a list of publications related to nursery management.

The authors solicit suggestions from both teachers and professional nurserymen as to how future editions can be improved in both content and manner of presentation.

ACKNOWLEDGMENTS

The authors wish to acknowledge the many authors of the technical articles on which much of this text is based. Without published results of their research, the science information relative to nursery production would be limited. Their names, along with the journals of publication, are listed in the references following the appropriate chapters. We also wish to express our appreciation to the many nurserymen who have been our teachers and who have provided information that has proven useful in writing this text. Individuals and/or companies who provided illustrations and photographs are mentioned in the appropriate legends. Special thanks go to the following individuals for supplying specifically-requested information or for offering critical reviews of various chapters: Richard H. Brolick, Martin J. Bukovac, Donald H. Dewey, David C. Farley, Harold E. Hicks, Ernest H. Kidder, John J. B. Light III, George W. Maentz, Alfred A. Manbeck, Paul E. Rieke, Richard A. Schroeder, Hugh Steavenson, Herman R. Struck, William R. Studebaker, and John G. Zelenka.

Finally, we acknowledge the patience and assistance of our wives, Martha, Ellie, and Brenda, in proofreading and critiquing the manuscripts, and we thank the staff at Prentice-Hall for their constructive, critical reviews.

Harold Davidson
East Lansing, Michigan

Roy Mecklenburg
Athens, Georgia

Curtis Peterson
East Lansing, Michigan

PART I   General

1 *Brief History of the Nursery Industry*

The American nursery industry undoubtedly began in Massachusetts Bay Colony, where the settlers grew young fruit trees as part of the general farm operation. As early as 1648, for example, according to a note in his journal, John Endicott traded 500 apple trees for 250 acres of land. Earlier, in a letter to Governor Winthrop in 1644, he stated:

> I humblie and heartilie thanck you for your last lettre of newes and for the trees you sent mee. . . . I haue not sent you any trees because I heard not from you, but I haue trees for you if you please to accept them whensoeuer you shall send. I thinck it is to late to sett or remoue. I could wish you to remoue in the latter end of the years your trees, and I pray you send mee what you want and I will supply what I can.

Since that time the industry has progressed steadily, although sometimes with difficulty. The short survey that follows comments on some of the historically important nurseries and nurserymen as well as modern ones (largely by regions) and discusses the major factors in the development of the industry. The chapter is summarized with a chronology of events from 1737 to 1985. For more details, the reader should consult the references and suggested readings at the end of the chapter.

EARLY EASTERN NURSERIES

The first major commercial nursery established in the United States was the Prince Nursery, also known for many years as the Linnaean Botanic Garden, at Flushing, New York. In 1737 William Prince started by cultivating a few trees to landscape his property. His success led him to commercial production, and shortly thereafter he published a catalog listing several hundred varieties. From it were stocked nearly all of the grafted apple, cherry, and pear orchards of New York, New Jersey, Massachusetts, and Connecticut. His nursery became so outstanding for its diversity of species, particularly fruit, that in 1777, following the battle of Long Island, General Howe made it a British protectorate.

Prince Nursery continued for over a century and introduced many outstanding foreign plants to the New World. By 1827 it contained over 100 species of plants from Australia alone, including *Eucalyptus* and *Banksias*. The nursery also experimented with plant breeding and introduced a number of new selections. As a result, its catalogs during the first half of the nineteenth century were considered the best in the trade. But Prince Nursery did more than grow trees: it also trained nurserymen, including Patrick Barry, one of the founders of the famous Mount Hope Nursery.

Another early nursery was Thomas Young's on Long Island. In 1768 Young was cited by the New York Society for the Promotion of Arts for having the largest number of apple trees (over 27,000) in rows. Other well-known Long Island nurseries started prior to 1900 were James Bloodgood's (1790), Andre Parmenter's (1825), Parsons's (1838), and Hicks's (1853). Mr. Parmenter, the first practitioner of the art of landscape gardening in America, frequently visited other parts of the country to lay out gardens and pleasure grounds for gentlemen of that century. By the early 1800s nurseries flourished in New York City. Michael Flay, for example, an immigrant from England, operated nurseries at the corner of Broadway and 12th Street and in Harlem. He was noted for the introduction of several very fine camellia varieties.

With the opening of the Erie Canal in 1825 and the development of a large orchard industry in western New York, a large nursery center developed near Geneva. According to Hedrick, David Thomas was the pioneer nurseryman of western New York; by 1830 he had the most extensive collection of fruit trees west of the Hudson River. One of the first nurseries in this area was founded by Reynolds and Bateman in 1830; it consisted of 6 acres about 1 mile from the center of Rochester. In 1839 they sold it to George Ellwanger and Patrick Barry, who established the Mount Hope Nursery. It was destined to become the leading nursery of the country during the latter part of the nineteenth century.

Patrick Barry was born in Ireland, emigrated to the United States when he was 20 years old, and obtained a job at the Prince Nursery in Flushing. After a period of "intelligent employment," he took part of his wages in nursery stock, moved to Rochester, and established a partnership with Ellwanger. Following a visit to the nursery in 1893, George Nicholson, curator of the Royal Gardens at Kew, England, noted that the cultivation of fruit trees had reached "enormous proportions," with 400 of the 600 acres devoted to the production of fruit trees. The Mount Hope Nursery was the primary source of liners, cuttings, and scion wood for the development of many of the nurseries in the Midwest. Another famous nursery near Rochester was Asa Rowe's, the oldest and most extensive in that area in 1841 and the source of stock and scions for many of the nurseries that developed in the Michigan territory.

The first nursery in Dansville, New York, was started in 1855 by O. B. Maxwell. After he and his brother Joshua inspected the site they were convinced that the soil and climate were well adapted to growing nursery stock. They were correct; by the early 1890s, Dansville—with 1200 acres of nursery products—was on a par with the great nurseries of Geneva and Rochester. George A. Sweet, the largest grower, had 125 acres in nursery stock; he was followed by J. B. Morly and T. Kennedy & Sons, with 75 acres each.

By 1850 western New York had become the nursery center of the nation, and the number of large nurseries increased rapidly. By about 1865, besides the previously mentioned nurseries, there was the W. & T. Smith Company; T. C. Maxwell and Brothers of Geneva; A. M. Purdy of Palmyra, known the country over as a specialist in small fruit; the Maloney Brothers Nursery; and Jackson and Perkins of Newark.

Jackson and Perkins began in 1864 as market gardeners, specializing in small fruits. About 1879 they began growing a few roses and hardy ornamentals. By 1894 they were producing about 175,000 roses yearly, and by 1900 they were known not only for their roses but for their outstanding collection of clematis, peonies, and other hardy ornamental plants.

One of the finest nurseries in New England in the late 1700s and mid-1800s was John and William Kenrick's of Newton, Massachusetts. John began his horticultural work by planting peach pits. Although he was acquainted with the art of grafting, he was not acquainted with ''inoculation'' (budding) as a method of vegetative propagation. When he learned the art about 1794, he began a commercial fruit production nursery that became the leading business of its kind in New England. About 1797 he added ornamental trees, including the Lombardy poplar, the most salable ornamental tree in New England at that time. After John died, William continued the nursery until his own death in 1870. William also experimented in silk culture, growing thousands of mulberry trees for his silkworms.

Another outstanding New England orchardist-nurseryman was Robert Manning of Salem, Massachusetts. In 1823 he began collecting, propagating, and offering for sale fruit varieties that were hardy in New England. Through his contacts with leading horticulturists, he obtained the best varieties available from Europe. By the time of his death in 1842, he had a collection of some 2000 fruit varieties, the largest ever assembled by an American up to that time. At one of the annual exhibitions of the Massachusetts Horticultural Society, he exhibited over 160 kinds of pears.

C. M. Hovey's 36-acre nursery in Cambridge also grew a remarkable number of varieties; besides 100 varieties of forest and ornamental trees, he sold 600 varieties of pears, 200 of apples, 100 of plums, 100 of cherries, 75 of peaches, and 50 each of grapes and gooseberries, as well as varieties of currants, apricots, raspberries, and strawberries. Hovey was also the editor of *The Magazine of Horticulture* and author of *The Fruit Trees of America,* a beautifully illustrated book on native and exotic fruits. Other early nurseries of New England were Ephraim Goodale's of Arlington, Massachusetts, and Benjamin and Charles Vaughan's in Hallowell, Maine.

One of the first nurseries in New Jersey was begun about 1794 by William Coxe in partnership with Daniel Smith. Coxe was an outstanding pomologist and wrote the first book on pomology (fruit production) published (1817) in this country. He collected all the best varieties of fruits available in the United States and from many parts of Europe and was one of the first to successfully graft the better varieties of grape onto the more vigorous stocks.

Philadelphia also had an extensive nursery area. Thomas Meehan & Sons was started in 1854 on 6 acres of land, and by 1908 there were 265 acres in production as well as good retail and landscape departments. Thomas Meehan popularized the planting of American trees so extensively that Nicholson refers to him as "the Nestor among American tree lovers and planters." By 1893 Meehan's nursery contained the largest collection of native American trees and shrubs to be found in any nursery in the world.

In 1897 the Conard and Jones Company of Pennsylvania pioneered the sale of seeds and plants by mail order. A few years later it became the Conard-Pyle Company, the producers of the famous "Star Roses." In 1920 Robert Pyle, who specialized in roses, introduced *Rosa hugonis* ("The Golden Rose of China") at the unheard of price of $5 per plant. Conard-Pyle is still the largest grower of roses in the eastern United States.

Bernard McMahon was another leading Pennsylvania horticulturist, with extensive plantings, nurseries, and greenhouses. McMahon received, propagated, and disseminated many of the plants collected by Lewis and Clarke on their expedition to the Northwest. The fine broad-leaved evergreen *Mahonia* now bears his name. Hoopes Brothers and Thomas, established in 1853 at West Chester, was also large, with 600 acres in production, and was widely known for its fine stock. Josiah Hoopes's *Book of Evergreens,* published in 1868, was a valuable contribution to the literature on conifers.

EARLY MIDWESTERN NURSERIES

The famous nursery production area of Lake County, Ohio, had its initial impetus in 1853, when Jesse Storrs, a farmer-nurseryman from Cortland, New York, located on 80 acres of farm land near the village of Painsville. In 1858 Storrs offered a partnership to J. J. Harrison, a skilled propagator, because in his opinion there was not room for two nurseries in the county. By 1970, however, the county contained more than 200 nurseries, with a combined acreage of over 5000 acres. The excellent climate of Lake Erie, the wide variety of soils, and the strategic geographic location within a developing nation all contributed to Lake County's success as a major nursery center.

Storrs and Harrison soon became the largest nursery in the country—about 1400 acres. Most of the land was worked with mules, but these were gradually replaced with Percheron draft horses. The firm grew not only woody plants but also large quantities of tropical plants, greenhouse crops, and vegetable seeds. Facilities included modern greenhouses as well as storage and packing houses, one large enough to accommodate several railroad cars.

Another famous nursery of Lake County was owned and operated by Henry Kohankie. Kohankie had been foreman of the ornamental department of Storrs and Harrison Company for 15 years before starting his own nursery in 1900. The nursery developed a nationwide reputation for its wide selection of high-quality ornamental plants, and for a long time its catalog was considered the ''bible'' of ornamental plants by many landscape architects.

Bloomington, Illinois, also became an important nursery center, since five important railroads intersected there and the soil and climate were well suited to all types of plants. The Bloomington Nursery, later the Phoenix Nursery Company, started in 1852 by Franklin K. Phoenix, grew a general line of nursery stock, and at one time was the largest in the country. Its packing houses, cold-storage cellars, and other buildings covered more than 20 acres.

The foundation of the famous nursery industry of Missouri was laid following the War of 1812, when young James (Judge) Stark moved from his home in Bourbon County, Kentucky, to the wilderness on the west banks of the Mississippi River. He came on horseback carrying fruit tree scions in old-fashioned saddlebags. In 1816 he started a small nursery, destined to become Stark Bros. Nurseries and Orchard Company. The judge was a great believer in advertising and used it unsparingly to promote the sale of his stock.

The horse also brought the nursery industry to Shenandoah, Iowa, in 1869. D. S. Lake, an employee of a nursery at Prairie City, Illinois, traveled the Midwest on horseback selling osage orange, hedge plants, and forest tree seedlings. In 1869 he and his wife moved to the Iowa frontier and started a fruit tree nursery on a few acres of land. One hundred years later it covered some 3000 acres, with about one-third in nursery stock. Because of the fine climate and soil, Shenandoah soon became one of the major centers of the country. Its nurseries pioneered in the development of mechanized equipment for field operations, storage, packing, and shipping.

Many of the fine nurseries of Ohio, Michigan, Illinois, Missouri, Iowa, and other midwestern states that were established in the mid-1800s had direct or indirect contact with the nursery centers of New York. One of the first nurseries established in Michigan was that of Z. K. and E. D. Lay near Ypsilanti in 1833. From Asa Rowe's nursery near Rochester, New York, they brought 25,000 cultivated trees, mostly of one season's growth. One year later Timothy W. Dunham of Orleans County, New York, came to Michigan to establish a nursery and brought with him ''a chest of drawers or shallow boxes filled with apple tree root grafts, about 3000 in number.'' Like the Lays, Dunham obtained most of his scions and plant material from Asa Rowe.

EARLY WESTERN NURSERIES

The development of the nursery industry in Oregon began with a load of nursery stock that was transported by prairie schooner from Salem, Iowa, to Milwaukee, Oregon, in 1847. In the spring of that year Henderson Lewelling (Luelling), a nurseryman, planted about 700 small trees and shrubs in stout wagon boxes filled with a compost of soil and charcoal. In April he hitched his nursery wagon to three yoke of cattle and began the long trip to Oregon. The hazardous journey across the plains and over the Rocky Mountains took about 9 months, but the following year he joined William Meek and together they established the first orchard-nursery of grafted trees in the Northwest. Their trees, along with others obtained from the nurseries of Ellwanger and Barry and A. J. Downing, shipped via the Isthmus of Panama, formed the nucleus of the nursery-orchard industry of the Northwest. Roots from seedling apples, sprouts from wild cherry, and roots of the wild plum supplied the first understocks for grafting, and good nurseries developed rapidly. About 1850, for instance, George Settlemeir began a nursery at Oregon City, later moved it to Mt. Angel, and soon had the largest variety of fruit and ornamental trees in the Oregon territory. The nursery business expanded chiefly because of the demand for quality apples, which sold for $12–15 per bushel.

Spanish missionaries, who undoubtedly began the California nursery industry before 1700, introduced most of the deciduous and evergreen fruiting plants. Unfortunately, according to Williamson, as a result of many unscrupulous, ignorant adventurers plunging into the production of fruit trees, the early California nurserymen were looked upon as little better than highwaymen. But once the ecological requirements of the newly introduced fruits were learned, the industry became stabilized.

The first commercial nursery of record in California was started by A. P. Smith of Sacramento in the early 1850s on land purchased from Captain John Sutter. By 1857 Smith had some 1200 roses of 200 varieties as well as many other plants. Like the nursery industry of the other states, the early California nurseries produced mainly fruit trees and grape vines to supply the heavy demands for these species.

EARLY INDUSTRY OBSERVATIONS

Most of the nurserymen of the late 1700s and the early 1800s were orchardists-nurserymen; that is, they produced fruit trees for their orchards and sold the excess. In later years nurserymen produced trees for sale and either planted or burned the excess. Initially, the primary method of propagation of fruit tree varieties was by grafting onto wild stocks; later, understocks obtained from France were used. Most of their trees were sold direct and delivered by oxcart, often over primitive roads or no roads at all. The large nurseries contained hundreds of acres—some over 1000—and catered to the wholesale trade and nursery agents.

The 1870s to the 1890s was the era of the itinerant nursery agents, many of whom were unscrupulous in their claims and careless about deliveries. Nevertheless, the results were not all evil. Traveling by horse and wagon, they sold nursery stock from farm to farm. They were responsible for the extensive plantings of elms and silver maples throughout the eastern and midwestern cities and for the familiar plantings of Norway spruce in the dooryards of most New York and midwestern farms.

Of course, not all nurserymen and agents were scalawags; most packed their goods carefully and labeled them accurately. Many nurserymen were held in high esteem, as the report of the orchard committee of the Michigan Pomological Society of 1873 testifies. When the committee evaluated the Ilgenfritz Nursery of Monroe in 1877, they stated that it had a "fine arrangement of packing houses and extensive cellars in which to heel-in stock. All the land upon which it is grown is thoroughly prepared and under-drained before planting is begun."

LEGISLATION AND THE AUTOMOBILE AFFECTED DEVELOPMENT

For the nursery industry 1912 was a significant year: the first national plant quarantine act was passed and parcel post went into effect. The Plant Quarantine Act prohibited the importation of certain plants into the country; and Plant Quarantine No. 37, effective in 1919, created a favorable economic situation for American nurserymen by severely restricting plant imports. In fact, American nurseries soon found it necessary to import skilled propagators from Europe.

Passage of the parcel post bill paved the way for various changes. First, it led to the rapid development of the mail-order business. Most of the major firms became established in the primary production areas, including: western New York; Lake County, Ohio; and Shenandoah, Iowa. This facet of the business, which relied heavily on the U.S. mail and on catalog, magazine, and newspaper advertising, prospered immediately. It is still a huge business, but when the "horseless carriage" arrived and as better roads were built and more people could afford automobiles, nurserymen also found it advantageous to develop retail outlets. Retail sales, in turn, led some of the more enterprising nurserymen to sell various types of soil amendments, garden tools and equipment, pesticides, garden ornaments, and outdoor furniture. This was the genesis of the modern garden center industry, which in 1972 accounted for more than $829 million in sales. California had the largest number of garden supply stores and recorded the greatest sales volume ($117 million); Pennsylvania, New York, Michigan, Texas, and Ohio each had sales in excess of $45 million.

EARLY GARDEN CENTERS

Garden centers started by way of seed houses, sometimes accidentally. Sometime around 1784, David Landreth established the seed house of David Landreth and Sons in Philadelphia. This was probably the first establishment of its kind in the United States. Another famous seed house was that of the Thorburns, for many years a center for horticultural interest in New York City. In 1801 its founder, Grant Thorburn, sold a rose geranium that he had placed in a pot on his grocery store counter to draw attention to the flowerpots he sold. From that insignificant beginning the establishment grew to a complete emporium of everything required in the practice of horticulture. A similar circumstance was responsible 150 years later for the formation of Frank's Nurseries of Detroit, which developed into one of the largest garden center, chain-store businesses in the country.

CENSUS DATA ON NURSERIES

The first special census of nurseries, conducted in 1890, revealed that 4500 nurseries occupied about 173,000 acres of land and employed more than 45,000 men, 2000 women, and 14,000 animals. Two-thirds of the nurseries were small (2–25 acres) and produced a variety of materials for local demand. Another group produced either a general line of nursery stock or specialized in a few items, such as small fruit, and relied on newspaper advertising and catalogs for their orders. They delivered by mail, freight, or express. A third group, the large producers, catered to the wholesale trade by issuing trade catalogs to other nurserymen, to extensive planters, and to nursery agents. Some of these nurseries were 1000 acres or more, shipped in railroad-car lots, and in the busy season, by the trainload. A fourth group produced a general assortment of stock and sold through salesmen who canvassed from house to house and farm to farm selling millions of plants. Total nursery production in 1890 was estimated to be approximately 3.4 billion plants, primarily fruit trees and small fruit plants. Major production was centered in New York, California, Illinois, Ohio, and Pennsylvania.

In 1974 these five states were still among the leaders in the production of nursery products, but their ranking had changed. California had become the leading state, with wholesale sales close to $130 million—almost seven times that of New York, the leader in 1890. The nursery center of the country was comprised of three southern California counties (Kern, Los Angeles, and Orange), with a combined production of $72 million. The 1985 *Nursery Business* survey reported that California was still the leading state in the production and sale of nursery stock, with sales in excess of $435 million. But Florida was a close second, with sales of $413 million. Texas, Pennsylvania, and Tennessee have also made substantial increases in their production over the past 10 years (Table 1–1). Ornamental plants have led all other categories of nursery products in total sales in the United States since 1950 (Table 1–2).

TABLE 1-1 Major Nursery Production States, 1985

Rank	State	Production (Millions of Dollars)	Total Acres	Total Nurseries
1	California	435	15,000	1,900
2	Florida	413	16,000	2,300
3	Texas	193	7,000	700
4	Pennsylvania	151	10,500	1,000
5	Tennessee	150	12,000	660
6	New York	140	8,800	1,506
7	Oregon	132	12,000	1,489
8	New Jersey	123	8,000	1,023
9	Ohio	116	8,700	1,109
10	Michigan	108	10,000	1,500
	U.S. total	2.934 billion	199 million	24 million

Source: Nursery Business 29(9); 30(10). This table is copyrighted material from Nursery Business and no further reprinting is allowed.

TABLE 1-2 Wholesale Value of Nursery Products, by Year (Millions of Dollars)

Nursery Product	1950	1960	1970	1979
Ornamental plants	57	125	233	759.4
Deciduous fruit and nuts	6	11	26	59.4
Lining-out stock	3	6	13	76.7
Citrus and subtropical fruit	2	7	6	19.9
Small fruit plants	3	4	6	29.5

Source: U.S. Census of Agriculture, 1969, 1979.

A CHANGING INDUSTRY

During the 1950s and 1960s, the total number of nurseries declined almost 50% in the 10 leading nursery states. Although the total acreage in nursery stock in seven of these states increased, three states, Florida, New York, and Texas, showed a decrease.

In addition to a change from fruit tree production to ornamental plant production, the nursery industry of the United States has experienced major changes in its methods of production and transportation. Machines, of course, have gradually replaced animals and reduced the need for hand labor. The introduction of hydraulic power made possible the development of mechanical planters, tree diggers, lifting and load equipment, and high-speed packaging and potting machines.

Changes in digging and root pruning illustrate the dramatic effect of machines and hydraulic power. Earlier all plants were dug by hand, and little, if any, root pruning was done. Even with the development of the "U-blade," root pruning and

Figure 1–1   Root pruning shade trees in the nursery with the aid of horse power in the 1800s. (Courtesy Isaac Hicks & Son, Westbury Nurseries.)

digging of bare-root plants needed 6–14 teams of horses (Fig. 1–1). The operation also required 6–18 people to drive the teams and operate the equipment. Beginning in the early 1900s, however, the steam engine gradually replaced horses. A large, 16-horsepower steam engine (Fig. 1–2) supplied the power for a double-barreled winch which pulled the cables attached to the U-blade. Currently, the power to root prune or dig bare-root trees is supplied by a 100-horsepower twin-engine high-clearance tractor operated by one worker (Fig. 1–3). A hydraulic tree spade, also operated by one person, can dig and lift, in a matter of minutes, a 20- to 40-ft tree with a soil ball 5 ft in diameter.

The development of selective chemical weed control agents, improved pesticides, and slow- or controlled-release fertilizers also changed cultural practices significantly. But the most pronounced change in the industry was the large-scale production of container-grown plants. Although the system of growing plants in containers was known for centuries, it was not adapted to large-scale production of small plants until after World War II. California pioneered in its development, but it soon spread to the other parts of the nation. The system allows nurserymen to grow, ship, and market their plants in the same container. It lends itself to a high degree of automation and eliminates the need to dig the crop just prior to sale.

The development of national highway systems in the mid-1950s and 1960s brought about another major change in the shipping of nursery stock. Rapid truck

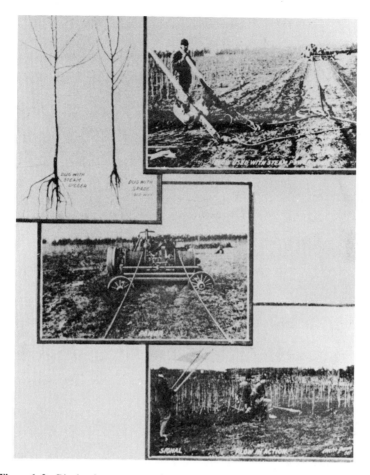

Figure 1–2 Digging bare-root trees in a nursery with the aid of a U-blade, double-barreled winch, and 16-hp steam engine. (From 1874 Catalog, Monroe Nursery.)

delivery permitted pick up at the site of production and delivery to the point of sale or of planting in the landscape. This eliminated the double and triple handling of plants shipped by railroad. Truck delivery has also contributed to greater specialization. Nurserymen now tend to produce only plants that grow well in their area. They may specialize in shade trees, evergreens, shrubs or ground covers, or even in a limited selection of shade trees or evergreens. Nurserymen who formerly produced a wide assortment of species may concentrate on only a few species and buy the balance of their catalog needs from other sources. The relatively low cost of truck transportation and the savings from reduced handling have been responsible for this. On the other hand, a significant increase in trucking rates could change this situation.

Figure 1–3   Digging bare-root trees in a nursery with the aid of a U-blade and high-clearance tractor. (Courtesy Bailey Nursery.)

SUMMARY

Some of the more significant events and developments in the brief history of the nursery industry of the United States are summarized in the following chronology.

Chronology of Nursery Industry of the United States

1737	Establishment of the first commercial nursery (Prince Nursery of Flushing, N.Y.) in the United States.
1847	The "Nursery Wagon" transported container-growing plants from Iowa to Oregon.
1869	Gypsy moth brought into the United States from Europe. This voracious pest was confined primarily to the New England states.
1870	San Jose scale accidentally introduced into this country from China on ornamental plants (via San Jose, California). This serious pest was widely distributed throughout the country in the late 1800s by interstate shipment of infested nursery stock.
1870	The first large tree-moving equipment developed by the Hicks Nursery on Long Island.
1873–74	A severe freeze throughout the Midwest caused the loss of thousands of plants and the failure of many nurseries.
1875	American Association of Nurserymen founded (incorporated 1921).
1881	California law passed to prevent distribution of the grape gall louse.

Chronology of Nursery Industry of the United States *(continued)*

1890–91	A blizzard killed millions of trees in nurseries and orchards throughout the country, causing serious financial loss to many nurserymen.
1891	*The Nursery Book* by Liberty Hyde Bailey was published.
1893	Publication of the *National Nurseryman*, a trade journal for the nursery industry.
1896	Maryland legislature passed the first law providing that all nursery stock being shipped into that state must be accompanied by a certificate, issued by an authorized official, stating that the stock was duly inspected and found to be free from indications of the presence of dangerously injurious insects and plant diseases (San Jose scale, peach yellows, rosette). Many other states soon followed this example and passed similar laws.
1896–98	A serious overproduction of nursery stock lowered prices; many nursery firms were forced out of business.
1898	Introduction of the white pine blister rust into New England. This disease was probably introduced on plants imported from Europe.
1898–99	A serious drought in the California area caused the loss of many plants, forcing a number of nurseries out of business.
1904	Discovery of chestnut blight on the grounds of the New York Zoological Park. This disease, which caused the demise of the American chestnut, was apparently introduced on plant material imported from China.
1912	Passage of the Plant Quarantine Act of 1912, the first federal plant quarantine designed to provide the necessary federal legislation to protect against the entry of dangerous insects and diseases on plants or plant products imported from foreign countries.
1912	Passage of the Parcel Post Act, which spawned the development of many mail-order nurseries.
1916	The Japanese beetle found in New Jersey was probably introduced by the importation of plants from Japan.
1919	Plant Quarantine No. 37 enacted into law.
1920	Photoperiodism recognized as an important factor in the control of growth and flowering of certain plants.
1929	The Dutch elm disease discovered in Cleveland, Ohio. This disease and its vector were most likely introduced into the United States on elm logs imported from Europe.
1930	Passage of the Plant Patent Law.
1934	Auxins, such as indoleacetic acid, recognized as having considerable practical value in stimulating the rooting of cuttings.
1936	DDT recognized as an insecticide of major importance in the control of insects.
1944	2,4-D first used as a selective herbicide in the removal of broadleaved weeds from lawns and for the control of selected weeds in nurseries.
1946	Development of garden center industry following World War II revolutionized the marketing of nursery stock.
1949	Container production of nursery stock developed on a large scale.
1949	Introduction of the first patented ornamental tree, "Moraine" honey locust (Plant Patent 836).
1956	Passage of Interstate and National Defense Highway Act, which led to rapid truck transport of nursery products.
1956	Introduction of hydraulic tree diggers revolutionized digging plants in nurseries. *(continuued)*

Chronology of Nursery Industry of the United States (continued)

1959	Development of selective chemical weed control for nursery crops.
1959	Drip or "spaghetti" irrigation methods developed for container production of nursery stock.
1960	Fertilizer injections introduced into the nursery industry.
1965	Federal Highway Beautification Act was enacted.
1967	Polyethylene film used to modify environment about nursery plants.
1975	Trickle irrigation introduced to field production of nursery stock.
1975	Photoperiod and light intensity used to control juvenile growth of woody plants.
1977	Nursery Marketing Council established.
1983–84	Disastrous freezes and citrus virus cause destruction of citrus groves and
1984–85	nursery plantings in Florida and other southern states.

REFERENCES

ANONYMOUS. 1908. A group of pioneer nurserymen and pomologists. Natl. Nurseryman 16(6):200–203.

————. 1908. The nurseries of Pennsylvania. Natl. Nurseryman 16(6):187.

————. 1908. The Storrs and Harrison Company. Natl. Nurseryman 16(11):361–364.

BAILEY, L. H. 1895. A century of American horticulture. Florist Exchange 7(17):387–394.

BARRY, W. C. 1894. The nursery industry of the East. Natl. Nurseryman 2(6):70.

COATES, L. 1908. The nursery business in California. Natl. Nurseryman 16:337.

DURUZ, W. P. 1941. Notes on the early history of horticulture in Oregon with special reference to fruit tree nurseries. Agric. Hist. 15(2):84–97.

GREENING, C. E. 1902. Evaluation of the nursery business. Michigan State Horticultural Society, E. Lansing, Mich., p. 91.

HALE, J. H. 1891. Nurseries. Bulletin of the 11th census. Michigan State Horticultural Society, E. Lansing, Mich., pp. 470–474.

HORTICULTURAL RESEARCH INSTITUTE. 1968. Scope of the nursery industry. HRI, Washington, D.C.

LEWIS, C. E. 1953. Hicks nurseries celebrate centennial. Am. Nurseryman 98(2):20.

MANNING, R. 1880. Sketch of the history of horticulture in the U.S. up to the year 1829. History of the Massachusetts Horticultural Society, 1829–1878.

MOREY, R. W., and W. A. GAMMEL, SR. 1984. Who are America's largest growers? Nursery Business 29(9):32–60.

————, J. MOREY, and C. MOREY. 1985. Nursery business 1985 Grower 100. Nursery Business 30(12):37, 39–42.

POTTER, C. H. 1965. Lewelling's legacy—the Oregon nursery trade. Am. Nurseryman 122(2):9.

THOMAS, J. J. 1873. Horticulture for the people. Michigan Pomological Society, E. Lansing, Mich., pp. 489–491.

THOMPSON, B. F. 1843. The history of Long Island. Gould, Banks & Co., New York, Vol 2, pp. 83–87, 239.

U.S. BUREAU OF CENSUS. 1967. Census of agriculture. Government Printing Office, Washington, D.C.

WILLIAMSON, R. 1893. Nursery business on the Pacific Coast. Natl. Nurseryman 1(8):95.

WOOD, J. 1900. Pioneer nurserymen. Natl. Nurseryman 8(3):27.

SUGGESTED READING

DAVIDSON, H. 1972. History of the Michigan nursery industry, MAN Yearbook. Michigan Association of Nurserymen, E. Lansing, Mich., pp. I–XII.

_____and D. A. SNELL. 1971. Growth and development of the garden center industry in the U.S. HortScience 6(1):12–15.

DOUGLAS, G., et al. 1947. The history of the Southern Nurserymen's Association. Southern Nurserymen's Association, Nashville, Tenn.

HEDRICK, U. P. 1950. A history of horticulture in America. Oxford University Press, Inc., New York.

VAN LAAN, G. J. 1982. A penny a tree—the history of the nursery industry of California from 1850–1976. California Association of Nurserymen, Sacramento, Calif.

2 *The Nursery Industry*

The nursery industry of the United States has grown from its embryonic beginning on Long Island in 1737 to a multimillion-dollar, nationwide complex of businesses today. It is composed of many interrelated parts, including nurseries that produce plants, landscape firms that use plants and related materials to develop attractive and functional landscapes, garden centers that sell plant materials and garden-related items, plus maintenance firms that specialize in maintaining plants and landscaped areas.

NURSERY CLASSIFICATION

A plant nursery is a place where hardy trees, shrubs, ground covers, vines, and herbaceous plants are propagated and grown. Nurseries in the United States are very diversified and may be classified and described according to four major criteria: (1) ownership, (2) function, (3) production system, and (4) type of plant material produced (Table 2–1).

Ownership

Nurseries are owned and operated either by private industry or by various governmental agencies and educational institutions. Within the private sector they may be either a proprietorship, a partnership, or a corporation. The advantages and disadvantages of these legal forms are discussed in Chapter 3. Government agencies operate nurseries to supply part or all of their plant material needs, to furnish planting stock for various reforestation and conservation programs, and for quarantine purposes. Educational institutions operate nurseries to support their many and diverse programs in research, teaching, extension, and to landscape their campuses.

TABLE 2-1 Classification of Nurseries

I. Ownership
  A. Private industry
    1. Proprietorship
    2. Partnership
    3. Corporation
  B. Government agencies
    1. County
    2. City
    3. State
    4. Federal
  C. Educational institutions
    1. Arboretia
    2. Botanical gardens
    3. Universities

II. Function
  A. Production
    1. Wholesale
    2. Retail
    3. Nonprofit
  B. Mail-order
  C. Landscape
  D. Wholesale plant materials distribution (also known as a rewholesale nursery)
  E. Quarantine
  F. Research

III. Production system
  A. Field production
    1. Bare-root
    2. Soil-balled
  B. Container production
    1. Above ground
    2. Below ground

IV. Product
  A. General, diversified, catalog; offering many types of hardy plants
  B. Specialty, limited catalog; specialty in one major class, but may offer some species from several subclasses
    1. Fruit
      a. General
      b. Tree fruits, including nuts
      c. Small fruits
    2. Ornamental
      a. General
      b. Shade and flowering trees
      c. Evergreens
        (1) Narrow-leaved
        (2) Broad-leaved
      d. Shrubs
      e. Roses
      f. Ground covers and vines
      g. Herbaceous perennials
      h. Indoor plants (house plants)
    3. Forest and conservation
      a. Reforestation
      b. Wildlife habitat
      c. Erosion control
    4. Propagation and liner materials
      a. Budded plants
      b. Grafted plants
      c. Rooted cuttings
      d. Seedlings
      e. Rootstocks

Function

Production nurseries propagate and produce plants for a variety of purposes, including fruit production, environmental quality improvement programs, conservation projects, and research and educational programs. Production nurseries may be either profit- or nonprofit-oriented. Those that are profit-oriented are in the private sector of the industry; the nonprofit production nurseries are operated by various governmental agencies and educational institutions. Those that are profit-oriented can be subclassified as either retail or wholesale production.

Retail production nurseries are generally small in size, commonly 50 acres or less, and sell their production directly to the ultimate user, in most cases homeowners.

Wholesale production nurseries are primarily large establishments that sell their plants in wholesale units to industry-related buyers (e.g., landscape contractors, garden centers). Wholesale production nurseries may specialize in a particular type of plant material and locate in areas where climate and soil are most favorable for production. In 1975 there were over 5000 wholesale nurseries in the United States, with combined sales in excess of $900 million.

Mail-order nurseries deliver the products that they merchandise via the U.S. mail, the United Parcel Service, or by bus. Their contact with customers is primarily through catalogs and literature sent directly to the customer, or advertisements placed with one or more of the mass communication media. Most of the material is herbaceous perennials, small fruit, or small trees and shrubs. Potted material is grown and shipped in a lightweight medium to reduce shipping costs.

Landscape nurseries design and construct attractive and functional landscapes utilizing the resources available within the organization. Modern landscape firms are staffed with designers that produce the landscape plans, growers that produce the plant material, and construction specialists who carry out the plans. Landscape nurseries produce woody ornamental plants that are larger than those available from most wholesale production nurseries. However, they seldom produce all their plant material needs and usually supplement their production by purchasing smaller, readily available material from other nurseries. Some landscape nurseries subcontract parts of a landscape project to other firms. For example, it is common to subcontract lawn work to a lawn specialist, and large pools, patios, and sundecks to a building contractor. In some states a builder's license is required to do this type of construction, especially if the construction is attached to a building.

A *plant material distribution center* (PMDC) is a nursery whose primary function is to locate, purchase, and assemble in a convenient location landscape plants which, in turn, are resold to landscape nurserymen or contractors. The PMDC takes title to the plant material and either holds it in a sales yard or grows it in a nursery to enhance quality prior to sale. The center may also stock for resale various items associated with planting (e.g., peat moss, tree wrap, mulch, etc.).

Quarantine nurseries are, as the name implies, nurseries where plants are held during a period of quarantine. They are operated by federal or state agencies charged with the responsibility of administering federal and state laws related to importation of plants.

Production System

On the basis of production systems, nurseries may be classified as either field production or container production. Field production nurseries (Fig. 2–1) may be subclassified by the method used in digging and processing their plants; they may be either bare-root or soil-balled. Plants that are dug bare-root have the soil removed from their roots as they are harvested, whereas soil-balled plants are dug with a soil

Figure 2–1   Field production of evergreens.

ball about their roots, which is then contained in some manner. The most common method used to contain soil-balled plants is to secure the soil ball with burlap, known in the industry as balled and burlapped (B&B). Other methods include boxing, potting, and basketing. Boxing is used for large plants, dug with large soil balls, shaped as an inverted, truncated pyramid, which is then contained with specially designed wood forms. Potting is used on small plants which are dug and lifted out of the ground with a soil ball and placed into pots. Basketing is a technique that has developed to containerize soil balls of plants that are dug with various types of tree diggers (Fig. 2–2).

Growing plants in containers has been practiced for centuries, but container production of plants in the nursery is a relatively modern practice (Fig. 2–3). Since the early 1950s it has evolved into a highly scientific and successful method of nursery production. It is an excellent example of nurserymen and scientists working together in solving problems and developing a highly effective and efficient system of growing and marketing plants in containers (Table 2–2).

In the early development of container production of plants, nurserymen used tin cans, tar-paper pots, or standard clay pots as the container, and the plants were grown above ground in an area fitted for handling plants in containers. The growing medium was whatever field soil was readily available. Fertilizer and irrigation system practices were adapted from field culture. Since container production, as a large

Figure 2–2 Digging B&B trees in a nursery with the aid of a hydraulic digging machine. Note the wire basket lined with burlap. (Courtesy Farley Bros. Nursery.)

commercial venture, began in the warmer parts of the country, there were few problems with overwintering of plants. But as the practice was adopted by nurserymen in the colder parts of the country, overwintering of plants in containers became a problem that had to be solved if the practice was to be successful for northern nurseries.

Since the 1950s major changes have been effected in the container production of plants. The containers are no longer the rusted food cans of the early years, but are designed and manufactured especially for the nursery industry. Metal containers are crimped so that they nest for shipping and storage, and are dipped in a rustproof paint so that they last for 2 or more years and make an attractive market container. Plastic containers may be obtained that serve various needs, including thin wall for inexpensive short-term crops and thick wall for long-term crops and for stacking during transport.

Various types and sizes of wood-fiber containers are also available. They are best used either for potting field-grown plants that will be shipped and then marketed within a few weeks or for plants that will be produced and marketed the same growing season by retail production nurseries. Fiber pots are structurally weak and should not be stacked when shipping the potted plants. Also, when they become wet they deteriorate. This can be either an advantage or disadvantage, depending upon the situation. In retail production it may be an advantage in that the exposed roots,

Figure 2–3   Container-grown evergreens in a production nursery. (Courtesy Monrovia Nursery Co.)

which grow through the walls of the container, can be used as an indication of a good vigorous root system. These plants must be carefully handled and planted without too much delay following purchase by retail customers. However, in wholesale production rapid deterioration of containers is undesirable, since it necessitates repotting, which is an added cost of production. Other types of containers used in nursery production include tar-paper pots, wood or wire baskets, thin-walled polyethylene bags, and polyethylene-lined baskets, pots, or boxes. Since the mid-1970s nurserymen have been using square pots in an attempt to minimize the development of circling root systems, common with round pots. Also, polyethylene bags are gaining in popularity for the production of small plants, especially liners.

TABLE 2-2   Advantages and Challenges of Producing and Marketing Plants in Containers

Production Advantages

1. More uniform plants. This is a result of providing optimum conditions for growth of the plants (e.g., medium, nutrition, water, light, spacing).
2. Provides a method of producing plants that are difficult to transplant.
3. Greater numbers of plants produced per unit area. Avoids need of land in rotation (cover crops) and reduces loss of plants due to cultivator injury.
4. Permits use of areas normally not usable for field production.
5. Avoids the digging operation.
6. Improves cash flow. Invested capital has a faster turnover rate.
7. Greater potential for mechanization of materials handling (e.g., potting [Fig. 2-4], pickup, and delivery to and from production site).

Figure 2–4 Potting machine aids in planting container-grown nursery stock. (Courtesy Cottage Gardens Nursery.)

Production Challenges

1. Total dependence upon artificial irrigation (offset by greater control of moisture levels).
2. Root development is limited by the size and shape of the container.
3. Need for repotting of plants if they are not used on schedule (potential for container-bound roots).
4. Need for winter protection in colder climates.
5. Greater need to supplement and monitor levels of chemical supplements.
6. Need to leach medium periodically (to avoid excess soluble salts).
7. Need for good water drainage. On some sites it is necessary to develop wastewater disposal systems.
8. Relatively high cost production system (offset with improved cash flow).

TABLE 2-2 *(continued)*

Marketing Advantages

1. Reduces transportation costs, due to lightweight medium.
2. Extends marketing season (both wholesale and retail).
3. Extends planting season.
4. Convenient prepackaged cash-and-carry item.
5. Relatively easy to maintain (water and fertilize) in sales area; no need to mulch or heel-in.
6. Better display of plants.
7. Less handling damage. Workers tend to carry plants in pots by the container rather than by their tops.

Marketing Challenges

1. Medium has a tendency to dry out faster, requiring greater attention to watering.
2. Plants in unsightly containers are unattractive to customers.
3. Difficult to remove plants from some types of containers, such as cylindrical metal containers.
4. Container-bound roots, if present, limit growth and life expectancy of plants in landscape sites.
5. Overcome landscape establishment problems with container-grown plants. (This is often related to culture in growing and planting.)

The root system that develops in the poly bag is more fibrous, due to root-tip pruning, caused by the folds at the bottom of the bag. However, larger plants grown in poly bags do not ship as well over long distances.

The growing medium is blended to specifications. By using various ingredients, nurserymen can obtain a medium that meets their particular production and market requirements. Soil fertility regimes are carefully planned and monitored to optimize growth and quality. Various types of slow-release and soluble fertilizers have been developed to aid in maintaining fertility levels at optimum. Irrigation practices are specifically designed for the effective and efficient use of water and water-soluble fertilizers. And container-grown plants can be overwintered in northern climates with a high probability of success if certain practices are followed relative to avoiding desiccation of the foliage, cold-temperature injury of the roots, and girdling damage by rodents.

Since the early 1980s a new system of growing plants in containers has been developed in an attempt to overcome the problems of winter injury to roots, and the poor success of growing trees in containers above ground. One system, developed in Minnesota, consists of an outer watertight container buried to its top in the ground. Drainage holes are drilled into the side of the container 2–3 in. from the bottom, creating a water reservoir for water pruning of the roots. Coarse gravel is put into the bottom of the container and covered with a fiberglass mat or other type of filter. An inexpensive sleeve is inserted into the outer container and a tree is planted into a porous growing medium. After one or two growing seasons, a well-developed, easy-to-transplant tree is produced.

A second below-ground system, developed in Oklahoma, utilizes 6-oz surpac-filter fabric bags. The developing roots grow through the fabric but are partially girdled, which induces root initiation, resulting in the development of a more fibrous root ball. The trees are easy to transplant any time when the ground is free of frost.

Product

Nurseries can also be classified and described on the basis of the types of plant material that they produce. Historically, the early nurseries of the nation produced fruit plants for the developing nation. Gradually, they included plants for landscaping, and as the need developed they produced seedlings of forest tree species for the forest industries and plants with special characteristics for conservation purposes and erosion control. When a nursery produces species from two or more of the foregoing categories, it is best classified as a general nursery, producing a catalog of diversified hardy plants. With the development of the railroads and especially with the advent of rapid truck transportation, large wholesale nurseries began to specialize in one or a limited number of species. Some wholesale production nurseries grow only one type of plant material, such as: shade trees, evergreens, shrubs, roses, or herbaceous perennials. Some specialize in one or two genera (e.g., *Rhododendrons* or *Taxus* and *Tsuga*). Other nurseries specialize in the production of seedlings for reforestation, conservation, and Christmas tree plantations. There are also nurseries that specialize in propagating materials for other nurseries. Their production may include dwarf rootstocks, grafted plants, rooted cuttings, seedlings, or shade tree whips. These firms are mostly located in the major nursery production areas or on sites that provide a major climatic advantage.

ALLIED AREAS

Within the industry there are a number of businesses that are closely allied to nursery production. They do not produce but buy, sell, and distribute plant material or provide a closely related service.

Landscape contractors perform the major construction operations associated with the development of large landscapes. Typical projects include shopping malls, industry-headquarters sites, industrial parks, golf courses, amusement parks, and so on. Landscape contractors purchase almost all of their plant material from nurseries that specialize in the production of large landscape plants. Arrangements for purchase and delivery of plants are often made through a nursery broker.

Nursery brokers are independent sales agents whose primary function is to arrange purchase-sales agreements between members of the nursery industry. They help to locate plants for the buyers and sell the products of the producers. Brokers may also arrange shipping and transportation schedules. They do not take title to the plant material but are paid a commission on sales booked with each nursery that they represent.

The *horticultural broker or distributor* is the primary supplier of the hard goods for the nursery industry. They purchase and stock for resale all types of tools, equipment, and supplies for the horticultural industries. Good horticultural brokers specialize in service to their customers by having the needed materials and supplying them when and where they are needed in the proper quantities.

The *modern garden center* is the outgrowth of the small retail nursery sales lot or fruit stand of the pre-World War II years. It is not only a retail center for plants, but it is the place where people come to purchase all their gardening supplies. Garden centers vary considerably in size, quality, and services offered. The larger, chain-operated garden centers are primarily self-service. Many operate on a low margin of profit based on a fast turnover and do a large volume of business, whereas the smaller, generally family-operated garden centers provide many special services, operate on a higher percentage markup, but do a lower volume of business. However, there are many variations between the two groups.

Sometimes the price of plants in a large garden center may be higher than those in smaller garden centers. And some fairly large garden centers offer special services to their customers. The marketing system varies with the philosophy of management and the level of competition in the market area. Most garden centers have found it necessary and profitable to broaden their product mix. Large investments in buildings, high rents for prime locations, and other high overhead costs make it necessary for garden center managers to be alert to various means of assuring sales during all months of the year, rather than being satisfied with only two peak sales periods, spring and fall, as was the situation in past years. Handicrafts, home decorations, garden furniture, pet supplies, and Christmas decorations are examples of items used to improve the cash flow at garden centers when plant sales are slow.

Landscape maintenance firms, as the name implies, specialize in maintaining the landscape plantings for individuals and businesses. Tree maintenance, as performed by the arborist, is a very specialized branch of the landscape maintenance business. The arborist is responsible for all types of specialized activities associated with large trees, including moving, pruning, and repairing damaged trees; bracing, spraying, and fertilizing living trees; plus the removal of dead or dying trees. Specialized training is needed to perform the functions of the arborist.

Although most home lawns and landscapes are maintained by homeowners, some are maintained by professional maintenance firms; in some parts of the country there are franchised lawn maintenance firms. Industrial and institutional landscape maintenance has become a relatively large business since the mid-1950s. There are also firms that rent and maintain plants for use in interior landscapes, including offices, malls, and public buildings.

Combination of Functions

Within the industry can be found many combinations of the foregoing groups or classifications. Some nurseries, for example, may produce plants by both field and container culture. Also, some businesses may be made up of two or more divisions. Many mail-order nurseries commonly operate garden centers. Some large nursery businesses operate a wholesale production nursery specializing in ornamental plants, a garden center, a landscape construction department, and a landscape maintenance department. In another situation the business may start as a small retail nursery and gradually develop over a period of years into a large wholesale production nursery with one or more allied businesses. At first it may be a proprietorship, which then becomes a partnership and finally a corporation. As a corporation it may be involved in producing evergreen seedlings for Christmas tree plantations and reforestation, ornamental evergreens and shade trees for landscape purposes (the latter produced by both field and container culture), and operating a garden center. Since the early 1980s a few of the larger corporations in the industry have also incorporated an environmental care division into their overall structure. These firms provide full service, including nursery production, landscape design, landscape construction, garden-center sales, and environmental care. The environmental care division can maintain the grounds of a small home or the property of a large industrial or university complex.

TRADE ORGANIZATIONS*

Trade organizations that serve the nursery industry are primarily oriented about the functional aspect of the business and to some degree about the type of plant material produced. But most of the trade organizations are organized on a geographic basis.

The *American Association of Nurserymen* (AAN) was first organized in 1875 as the National Association of Nurserymen, Florists, and Seedsmen. By 1883 the seedsmen and florists had organized their own trade association. Thus, the name was changed in 1884 to the American Association of Nurserymen and was incorporated as a nonprofit corporation in 1921. The AAN is active in many types of programs, including education, promotion, and legislation that enhance the efficient and economic progress of the nursery industry. They publish a nursery trade and supply directory, special AAN summaries on topics of current interest, and a quarterly magazine, *ALI*, with in-depth articles of concern to nurserymen.

The annual meeting of the AAN held in July is a forum for the discussion of industry problems and the dissemination of information. At the first meeting four topics were discussed: costs and inequities of freight rates, grades for nursery stock, statistics on the annual production, and condition of crops and postal rates. These topics have held priority in many meetings since and will undoubtedly have high priority at future meetings.

The AAN staff in Washington, D.C., provide the management and administrative staff for each of the next six trade organizations. They are the umbrella under which these organizations are united for economy of force and unity of purpose. The AAN also offers an opportunity to its members to subscribe to a group accident insurance program and to the Dodson Savings Classification Plan for workers' compensation insurance.

The *Horticultural Research Institute* (HRI) was organized in 1962 by a group of progressive nurserymen as a nonprofit, tax-exempt organization to plan and sup-

*See Appendix B for addresses.

port research for the nursery industry. Members of HRI are informed of all research results through the newsletter "Horizons." HRI also publishes special research reports on many topics of interest to the nursery industry. Examples of subjects addressed are antitrust, credit, estate planning, labor, wage-hour, tax accounting, truth in lending, and a technical glossary of horticulture and landscape terminology. Tax-deductible contributions can be made to HRI for the support of research programs.

The *National Landscape Association* (NLA) was founded in 1939 as the National Landscape Nurserymen's Association to promote better landscaping and to provide a means for the exchange of ideas and knowledge related to the profession. The association supports the publication of literature relative to landscape beautification and sponsors management clinics. In 1967 NLA came under the umbrella of the AAN for administration and promotion. Membership in NLA is open to nursery firms that do landscape work and are members of the American Association of Nurserymen.

The *Wholesale Nursery Growers of America, Inc.* (WNGA) was organized in 1964 with the major purpose of providing a forum for the exchange of ideas and information relative to the production of nursery products. The WNGA has developed a useful crop reporting system and has stimulated interest in and aided HRI in the conduct of a business analysis of the nursery industry. They are active in seeking scientific answers to problems of production and postharvest physiology of nursery crops. A quarterly newsletter contains information on technological advancements in growing and production, general business news pertaining to wholesale nurserymen, trend reports, and the latest developments in mechanization and transportation. Their meetings coincide with the annual summer meeting of the AAN and the midwinter meeting in Chicago. Membership is open to nurserymen engaged in the production of nursery stock at the wholesale level.

The *American Association of Nurserymen's Group Insurance Trust* is one of the oldest and most successful group insurance programs in existence. It is designed to provide life insurance and hospitalization with major medical insurance for the owners and full-time employees of AAN member firms. Members may select between two excellent life and health insurance plans, both featuring $100,000 major medical, double-life insurance option, and supplemental benefits to Medicare. It is composed of over 300 nursery firms and is managed by nurserymen trustees.

Garden Centers of America is the trade association for the garden center industry. It is management-oriented to give the nation's garden center operators the management information they need to operate a more profitable business. Garden Centers of America was organized in 1972 and functions under the AAN umbrella.

The *Nursery Marketing Council* (NMC) was established in 1977 to provide the nursery industry, through AAN, with a market research and analysis capability to produce advertising and public relations that ultimately will increase the use of plant materials and related products. Its activities benefit the entire nursery industry and are supported by voluntary contributions.

SPECIALIZED ASSOCIATIONS

The *International Plant Propagator's Society* (IPPS) was organized in 1951 to secure recognition for the plant propagator as a craftsman and to provide a forum for the dissemination of knowledge in this field. The society is divided into the eastern, western, and southern regions in North America, each division sponsoring an annual meeting. In addition, there is a region of Great Britain and Ireland, an Australian region, and a New Zealand chapter. The combined proceedings are published by the society, which also publishes *The Plant Propagator*, a quarterly magazine available to members only.

Mail-Order Association of Nurserymen, Inc. was founded in 1934 to promote the general interests of mail-order nurserymen by providing a forum for discussion of matters pertaining to the business. The association meets twice a year, in the summer with the AAN and in the winter at the Mid-America Trade Show.

All-American Rose Selections (AARS) was organized in 1938 in an attempt to bring some order out of the confusion that existed in the yearly introduction of roses. Prior to its inception, literally hundreds of inferior varieties of roses were introduced each year. Through its program of variety trials in selected test gardens, AARS has succeeded in establishing in the minds of home gardeners a high degree of confidence in its seal of quality. In 1976 All-American award winners comprised over 40% of all roses sold in the United States annually. This is a real tribute to All-American roses, since the award winners comprise less than 1% of the more than 8000 known named varieties of roses. The rose industry of the United States sells in excess of 40 million plants annually. AARS is a nonprofit organization whose sole function is to test new rose selections and to give recognition to those of merit in the form of an All-American award.

Landscape Material Information Service (LMIS), incorporated in January 1954 as a self-supporting, nonprofit association, was organized to act as a clearinghouse for the collection, evaluation, and dissemination of information pertinent to the interests of arborists, horticulturists, landscape contractors, nurserymen, various public agencies, and suppliers of landscape materials.

Members receive an updated plant materials availability list twice a year, a biweekly bulletin announcing contracted and planned landscape projects, and advice on the procurement of scarce plant material or other landscape supplies. Membership is centered primarily in the northeastern states.

The *Associated Landscape Contractors of America* (ALCA) was incorporated in 1961 as a nonprofit corporation (business league) to provide cohesion and coordination among industry members and to enhance the image of landscape contracting as a profession. The association publishes the monthly "ALCA Action Letter."

The *International Society of Arboriculture* was organized as the International Shade Tree Conference in 1924 (name was changed in 1975) to promote and improve the planting and preservation of trees and to assist in the beautification of the countryside. Its publications include *The Journal of Arboriculture*, the monthly *Arborists News*, and special publications and films issued on an irregular basis.

The *National Arborists Association*, founded in 1938, is an organization of commercial people engaged in arboriculture. It is interested in the business aspects of tree services and good public relations programs.

The *Nurserymen's Protective Association* provides credit information on other nurserymen (wholesale, construction, and retail) to its members.

National Association of Plant Patent Owners is a private trade organization whose members own one or more plant patents. The objective of the association is to keep its members informed on the rules and regulations of the Patent Office pertaining to filing for and the granting of plant patents. Its constant legislative arm is a vital force in protecting the plant patent system.

The *Garden Center Symposium* (GCS), organized in 1964, is a midwestern garden center trade association composed of small independent merchants who operate garden centers. The purpose of the symposium is to provide a means for the exchange of management information on garden center operations and a vehicle for gathering and disseminating data of value to garden center managers. The symposium compiles and maintains up-to-date lists of plants and supplies.

STATE, REGIONAL, AND LOCAL ORGANIZATIONS

In addition to the many national associations, most states have nurserymen's associations which embrace growers, contractors, landscape maintenance personnel, and garden center operators. The state associations promote and support legislation that affects the nursery industries within each state. They also conduct, in cooperation with state university extension services, educational meetings and demonstrations. Some of the larger state associations employ an executive secretary and publish a trade paper and buyer's guide.

In a few places, nurserymen within a geographic area have formed associations, either formal or informal, for the purpose of conducting seminars, sponsoring garden shows and trade shows, and supporting field demonstrations. These groups may be within the metropolitan area of a city (e.g., the Metropolitan Detroit Landscape Association), an area of the state (e.g., Long Island Nurserymen's Association), or they may involve a number of states (e.g., Southern Nurserymen's Association, a consortium of state nurserymen's associations in the South for the purpose of conducting a joint summer meeting at Atlanta, Georgia).

CENTERS OF PRODUCTION

The centers of nursery production in the United States have changed with the development of the nation and have tended to follow the westward migration. For many years Geneva, New York, was the primary center of production. But this gradually shifted to Lake County, Ohio, which became known as the nursery capital of the country in the late 1800s and in the early twentieth century. However, other areas were gradually developing: central Illinois; Shenandoah, Iowa; and Tyler, Texas. By the mid-twentieth century, the primary center of nursery production in the United States was in southern California.

In 1985 California was still the leading state in the production of nursery stock, with sales in excess of $435 million. But Florida was a close second, with sales reported in excess of $413 million. Texas, Pennsylvania, New York, and Oregon had sales between $130 and $190 million; and New Jersey, Ohio, and Michigan had sales in excess of $100 million but less than $130 million. For a yearly update on the leading nursery production states plus a list of the 100 leading wholesale growers, consult the trade publication *Nursery Business.*

California

If two words could characterize the nursery industry of a state, "container production" would do it for California. Growing plants in containers has become a science with California nurserymen. Soil has been replaced with mixtures of sand, peat moss, soil, and redwood sawdust. Plant nutrients are supplied by constant injection feed. Moisture control is obtained by "spaghetti" or overhead irrigation. Hand labor has been substantially replaced by machines. California nurserymen propagate, grow, and ship container-grown stock 12 months of the year. Most of the ornamental evergreens produced in southern and central California nurseries are shipped to eastern and midwestern markets. In 1969 California nurseries sold over 19 million ornamental plants in containers, almost one-half of the total U.S. production.

In addition to container-grown ornamentals, California is also the leading rose-producing area of the nation. Most of the rose growers are located in southern California, south of the Tehachoapi Mountains, but because of urban pressure, are gradually moving to the Bakersfield area.

California nurserymen produce large quantities of grapes and citrus and other fruit trees for the large fruit industry of the state. They grow palms, cycads, and various other subtropical plants in either container or field soils for use in interior and exterior landscapes. Production is increasing in bedding plants, ground covers, succulents, and cacti.

Florida

The nursery industry of Florida is centered in three distinct areas as a result of Florida's peninsular topography and its associated climatic zones. The lower-east-coast nurseries, located in Dade, Broward, and Palm Beach counties, produce most of the tropical and subtropical material used in Florida's beautiful tropical landscapes. The central region produces the hardier subtropical material, citrus, and foliage plants used for indoor landscaping. Apopka, located in the center of the state, is known as "The Foliage Capital of the Nation." In the northern region, particularly in Baker County, camellias and azaleas are produced as well as many of the hardier ornamental plants associated with the gracious landscapes of the South. Although the state plant board lists some 4000 certified nurseries, most of the state's $413 million wholesale nursery crop was produced by less than 20% of the nurseries and most of the production was container-grown foliage plants.

Texas

Texas is the third largest producer of nursery stock in the United States. In 1985 the wholesale dollar value was in excess of $190 million. Most of the production was container-grown woody ornamental and foliage plants. Roses are still produced in the field, but production has declined over the past two decades. Texas also produces broad-leaved evergreens, citrus, and nut trees which are marketed in the southern states. Texas has an excellent combination of land and climatic conditions for the production of nursery stock. Most land areas are well drained, and the soil is a slightly acidic sandy loam. There are between 300 and 320 growing days each year, and in most years there is a good distribution of rainfall.

Pennsylvania

The history of the Pennsylvania nursery industry dates back to the times of David Landreth (1784) and Bernard McMahon (about 1800), when these men were engaged in the seed and nursery business in Philadelphia. The nurseries with the largest production are located in the counties of Indiana, Erie, Butler, and Allegheny, which are situated west of the Allegheny Mountains, where there is a good distribution of rainfall, or they are located in the southeastern counties, Chester, Montgomery, Bucks, and Lancaster, close to major market areas.

The state is known for the production of ornamental plants, including conifers, broad-leaved evergreens, shade and flowering trees, and roses. The rose production is centered in the southeastern area near West Chester. The production of broad-leaved evergreens has increased considerably over the past few years because of the increased demand for such plants. Pennsylvania nurseries are favored by a mild climate and well-drained acidic soils. A number of the Pennsylvania nurseries are known for their quality production of seedlings and liners.

Tennessee

The central portion of Tennessee in the vicinity of McMinnville and Winchester, known as the Highland Rim area of Tennessee, produces a substantial amount of nursery stock, including coniferous and broad-leaved evergreens, ornamental trees and shrubs, nut trees, standard and dwarf fruit trees, ground covers, and vines. Tennessee is particularly well known for the production of flowering dogwoods *(Cornus florida)*. The area is favored with a long growing season, productive soils, and a good distribution of rainfall. Some 400 certified growers operate close to 15,000 acres in nursery production in this center of horticulture.

New York

Although New York state is best known for its skyscrapers and giant industries, it is also a major nursery production state. In the 1890 Census of Agriculture, New York ranked first in the nation in the value of all nurseries. Wholesale production nurseries are concentrated primarily in the central and western counties, including Wayne, Ontario, Livingston, Erie, Monroe, and Chautauqua and in Suffolk County on eastern Long Island.

New York produces a wide selection of nursery crops, but ornamentals account for nearly 90% of the total wholesale value. Fruit trees and grape vines, although a small part of the state's total production, represent a major contribution to the nation's fruit-plant production.

Oregon-Washington

The Oregon-Washington area is one of the major producers of nursery stock, bulbs, flower, and turf seed crops. The coastal area, west of the Cascade Mountains, particularly the Willamette Valley, has a maritime climate favorable to the production of shade tree whips, broad-leaved evergreens, and conifers. The inland area, east of the Cascade Mountains, has a less favorable climate, characterized by hot, dry summers and cold winters, and is thus limited to plants that are winter-hardy in that area. Many fruit tree nurseries are located on the eastern slopes of the Cascade Mountains.

Oregon and parts of Washington are also famous for their bulb production. Some 100 million bulbs are shipped from Oregon and Washington each year. Narcissus, tulip, and iris production is centered primarily in Washington, but lily and gladiolus production predominates in Oregon. Oregon is also a major producer of cut holly, which is sold for Christmas decorations. One of the large holly farms near Portland ships over 100 tons of berried holly branches each year to various parts of the United States.

New Jersey

The Garden State has been a major nursery area since colonial times. Major production centers are located in Middlesex and Monmouth counties, in close proximity to two major population centers, New York and Philadelphia, both important market areas for ornamental plants. In addition to a major market area, New Jersey also has a mild, maritime climate and some of the finest agricultural land in the nation, which make it a site that is ideal for the production of nursery stock. However, high land values and zoning laws unfavorable to agriculture, brought on by increased urbanization and industrialization, are limiting growth of nursery production in the central part of the state. Nursery production is almost totally directed to ornamental plants, including everything from ground covers up to 6-in.-caliper shade trees.

Ohio

The nursery center of the nation, prior to 1960, was considered by many to be Lake County, Ohio. In 1854 Jesse Storrs purchased a small farm in Lake County and soon founded the nursery firm of Storrs and Harrison, which became one of the largest nurseries of the late 1800s. By 1960 some 200 nurseries were producing a wide variety of nursery stock in a narrow belt 6–10 miles in width and about 20 miles long along the southern shore of Lake Erie. Because of the moderating influence of Lake Erie, plus a deep, rich, slightly acid soil, nurserymen grow ericaceous plants, narrow-leaved evergreens, shrubs, shade trees, roses, perennials, bulbous plants, and some fruit trees and small fruit plants.

Industrialization and urbanization of this area have caused some nurseries to move to locations in other parts of the state. Southwestern and central Ohio, which are less industrialized, but have good agricultural lands and a mild climate, may become the new center for nursery production in Ohio. Many nurseries are relocating in the Ohio River valley—an interesting trend, since the first nurseries of Ohio established in 1790 were located in the Ohio River area.

Michigan

Located in the heart of the Great Lakes area, Michigan has for over 100 years been a major producer of nursery stock. Most of the early production was directed toward supplying the rapidly expanding fruit industry. Even today, Michigan produces large quantities of fruit plants; however, more than 75% of its production is classified as ornamental plants. Michigan is a leader in the production of evergreen seedlings for reforestation and Christmas tree planting. The major production areas are located in the lower half of the southern peninsula, with the major nurseries located in the western, southwestern, and southeastern counties.

Illinois

Most of the major nurseries of Illinois are located in five counties (Cook, Lake, DuPage, Kane, and Iroquois) close to Chicago. They have the advantages of a relatively mild climate and rich loam prairie soil which favor B&B production, plus central geographical locations within the nation and many large rapidly growing urban centers within a radius of 300 miles.

Illinois nurseries, like most others that had their beginning with the opening of the West, were at first oriented toward the production of fruit plants. However, by the mid-1950s, production of ornamental plants dominated. Illinois nurseries are famous for the production of narrow-leaved evergreens, shade and flowering trees, and specimen plants for the landscape industry. The winter meeting of the Illinois State Nurserymen's Association (ISNA), held in Chicago in mid-January, gradually developed into the Mid-America Trade Show and is now jointly sponsored by ISNA, the Illinois Landscape Contractors Association, and the Wisconsin Landscape Federation.

Iowa

Shenandoah and adjacent Hamburg in southwestern Iowa are the center of a major nursery production area, producing fruit trees and ornamentals of all types. Large quantities of packaged and potted nursery stock are sold to garden centers, and bare-root material is sold to wholesale nurseries in other parts of the country. Shenandoah and Hamburg are major mail-order centers. Being centrally located in the nation, with good soils and a mild climate, accounts in part for the growth and development of Shenandoah as a nursery center.

New England Area

The New England states, particularly Rhode Island, Connecticut, and Massachusetts, are known for quality production of evergreens, especially *Taxus*, which seems to be ideally adapted to the climatic conditions along New England's southern coast. A 1959 survey of the Rhode Island nursery industry revealed that 78% of the nurseries were 3 acres or less in size, whereas 10.6% of the nurseries controlled 85% of the acreage under production. The small and large nurseries both concentrated in the production of relatively few species—the small nurseries because of space limitations and the large nurseries to gain production efficiency. The medium-sized nurseries grew a variety of plants, primarily for local retailing and landscape construction.

Oklahoma

Since the late 1950s a substantial nursery production area has developed in northeastern Oklahoma in the vicinity of Tahlequah. One large nursery specializes in container production of plants, whereas the others produce by field culture.

Southern States

The nursery industry of the southern states has expanded rapidly since 1969, growing from $75 million wholesale sales value to a value estimated at $280 million in 1984. Broad-leaved evergreens accounted for 40% of the total production of ornamentals in the southern nurseries, deciduous shrubs 34%, narrow-leaved evergreens 18%, and ornamental trees 8%. Mobile, Alabama, is a major production area for azaleas.

SUMMARY

The nursery industry of the United States is a highly dynamic, rapidly growing, changing industry. It is made up of nurseries that are very diversified in function and species produced. In the early development of the industry, most production centered about bare-root fruit trees, whereas currently the emphasis is on ornamental plants that are produced by various methods, including both field and container production. Many are sold as large B&B specimen plants, which are used to produce immediate effects in the landscape. Centers of production moved with the development of the nation. At first the major nursery centers were located in the East (New York, New Jersey, Pennsylvania), with a gradual shift to the Midwest (Ohio, Illinois, and Iowa), and finally to the West, with the major center located in southern California. The past 30 years have seen many production changes, which will be discussed in subsequent chapters.

REFERENCES

AMERICAN ASSOCIATION OF NURSERYMEN. 1977. Research summary: scope III of the nursery industry. AAN, Washington, D.C.

BOYER, C. A. 1952. Nurseries big business in Michigan. Am. Nurseryman 96(2):9.

CHADWICK, L. C. 1960. Nursery industry thrives in Ohio. Am. Nurseryman 92(1):19.

DAVIDSON, H., C. E. LEWIS, and R. A. MECKLENBURG. 1966. The Michigan nursery industry project 80. Mich. Coop. Ext. Serv. Rep. 43.

GARTNER, J., J. E. BREWER, and H. F. FLINT. 1959. The Rhode Island nursery industry. R.I. Agric. Exp. Sta. Misc. Publ. 50 rev.

GORTZIG, C. F. 1969. State of the trade in the empire state. Am. Nurseryman 130(2):18.

HUDSON, A. C., and H. B. SORENSON. 1957. The Texas nursery industry. Tex. Agric. Exp. Sta. MP222.

JARVESOO E. 1964. Nursery trade flourishes in Bay State. Am. Nurseryman 120(2):12.

LYLE, E. W. 1963. Roses, glamour crop of the Texas trade. Am. Nurseryman 118(2):9.

MEAHL, R. P. 1961. The Pennsylvania nursery industry. Agric. Ind. Adjustment Conf. Rep. Pa. State Univ.

PAULS, D. E., and A. H. HARRINGTON. 1960. The nursery industry of Washington. Wash. Agric. Exp. Sta. Circ. 372.

PELLETT, H. 1983. An update on the Minnesota system of container production. Am. Nurseryman 157(1):95.

POTTER, F. 1953. Nurseries play a major role in agriculture of New York state. Am. Nurseryman 98(2):9.

REIGER, R., and C. E. WHITCOMB. 1983. Grower can now confine roots to in-field containers. Am. Nurseryman 158(8):31–34.

SMITH, C. N. 1969. A fact book on the Florida wholesale woody ornamental nursery industry. Dept. Agric. Econ. Univ. Fla. Mimeo Rep. EC69–11.

SORENSON, H. B. 1963. The nursery industry of Texas. Am. Nurseryman 118(2):8

TECH. COMMITTEE SM-33. 1969. Marketing woody ornamentals. South. Coop. Serv. Bull. 143.

WHITCOMB, C. E. 1983. Container vs poly bags—which are better? Am. Nurseryman 157(1):101–103.

SUGGESTED READING

WHITE, R. P. 1975. A century of service. American Association of Nurserymen, Washington, D.C.

PART II Administration

3 *Management Applied to Nurseries*

There are many definitions of management, but the one that states it best is: **Management** is the bringing together of **men, money,** and **materials,** in a framework of time, for an economic or sociologic purpose. Simply stated, management brings together the three primary factors of production that managers use, places them together in a framework of time, and gives them a reason or purpose for being.

How do managers manage? What are their primary responsibilities? Naturally, a manager is a person and as such is subject to all the past, present, and future forces that have molded, are molding, and will mold the person into the individual that he or she is now and will be in the future. As a result, no two managers are exactly alike, and no two managers can be expected to manage exactly alike. Each will be different as a result of his or her individual personality and past experiences. But each manager by definition will have a purpose, the factors of production, and time. How a manager uses the factors of production and time determines how successful he or she will be in accomplishing the established objectives.

A manager's primary responsibilities are basically six in number: (1) determine goals; (2) plan; (3) organize and staff; (4) direct, control, and coordinate; (5) motivate; and (6) evaluate and reward.

These six responsibilities apply to all levels of management, from foreman to president. How they are applied depends upon the purpose or objective of the organization and the level of management. They are fully applicable in the management of nurseries.

DETERMINING GOALS

The purpose or goal is known by various names within a nursery. In the production department it is the production goal; in marketing it is the sales objective; in propagation it is the percent rooting or "take" in grafting; and to the average laborer it is the job. But to the owner or the stockholder, it is profit. In each situation, the purpose should be clearly understood. We will look at individual objectives in some detail under organization and staffing, but the overall objective of the nursery business should be clearly established and stated in such a manner that it gives direction to all units of the organization.

To arrive at the overall objective, management must give consideration to four integral questions: (1) what products or services are needed, (2) by whom, (3) at what price and quantity, and (4) does the organization have the interest and the ability to provide the products or services? For example, assume that a person or firm is thinking of producing shade trees. They may have heard that there is a shortage of shade trees, and they have some idle land from which they would like to derive an income. Assume that the land will produce the trees and that water is available. Now a series of questions must be asked to define the objective. What is the nature of the target market? Is it homeowners in a local area, garden centers in a limited geographic area, landscape contractors in a limited area or large geographic area, or other nurseries in a local or national market area? Or is the target market some combination of these?

If the market comprises homeowners or garden centers, the demand may be for small trees that can be transported in the family car. If it is landscape contractors, the demand will be primarily for large trees processed with a ball of earth. If it is other nurseries or a combination of markets, the demand may be for a combination of sizes. What species and cultivars does the market demand, and what price will the market support? Consideration must also be given to similar products and services currently available or to be available in the market area.

Following the market study, it is necessary to formulate and state the company objective in such a manner that it will give direction to the production and marketing effort needed to accomplish the objective. For example: objective A—to produce 1½- to 2-in.-caliper shade trees hardy in climatic zones 4 and 5 for the garden center market (Fig. 6–1). This objective limits size, geographic area, and type of market. It does not limit cultivar selection. Objective B—to produce large (3½- to 4-in. DBH) specimen trees for landscape projects. This objective sets the course for a long-time investment in trees of large diameter requiring powerful equipment for handling. It limits customers primarily to landscape contractors.

Either objective sets the direction for the production and marketing effort. In objective A, the production effort will be toward producing small shade trees as quickly and economically as possible. This will result in rotations of relatively short duration, relatively close spacing of trees in the nursery blocks, and a need to use practices and equipment that will meet the objective. The intended market is identified, and the merchandising program can be directed to reach the garden center market. The cash turnover is rapid, owing to the short rotations, which is an advantage when interest rates are high. In objective B, the production effort will be directed to producing large specimen trees which will require wide spacing and long rotations, and the need to develop techniques that will effectively produce high-quality trees for immediate effect in the landscape. It will require powerful equipment to move the large, heavy material. The marketing effort will be concentrated on contacting sources that have a need for large, well-developed trees, primarily landscape contractors, city park departments, golf courses, and so on. However, the cash turnover is delayed by a number of years, which is a disadvantage when interest rates are high.

Provision must also be made for modifying long-range objectives. Management must constantly evaluate the market and be responsive to trends. But all actions taken should be in keeping with the primary goal and the professional image of the nursery.

PLANNING

Planning is for the future, but it is based on past history. It is done to accomplish an objective, with the best expenditure of resources (personnel, money, materials), in the time period specified or implied. It should be a logical process of selecting the best course of action from a number of alternatives. Unfortunately, this is easier said than done. In some organizations decisions are made by default or without sound background information. When this happens too often, objectives are seldom attained and the organization fails.

When planning, a good manager consults with advisers. He or she will try to clearly define the problem to be solved or state the objective to be attained. The manager then encourages input from the staff. Depending upon the situation, it may require the gathering and evaluating of information by staff members, followed by the development of several possible courses of action. Upon an analysis of the situation and with the best possible information available, the manager must make a decision; this is one of management's responsibilities. The manager should not avoid it by trying to get a subordinate to make it; if the manager does this, especially if it is done too often, he or she will soon become ineffective. The decision should be clear and understood by the units involved in implementing the decision.

ORGANIZATION

The organization of a nursery business needs to be considered under three categories: (1) organization of the physical facilities, (2) the functional organization, and (3) the legal organization.

Organization of the physical facilities has to do with the physical relationship of production and administrative units one to the other and to the layout of propagation units and production fields for maximum efficiency. This information is discussed in Chapter 5.

Organization for function relates to developing the organization to maximize efficient use of people and their support systems: machines, facilities, supplies, and so on, to accomplish the various functions. It is the staffing and delegation of authority to accomplish an objective. In a group of workers, it is common that one will be more assertive than the others, and he or she becomes the leader. At that point the leader-follower organization is formed.

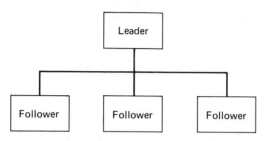

The leader-foreman is generally the most skilled in the particular physical skill that is being performed. He or she is expected to lead (manage) the others, and if a good working relationship exists with the followers, the job will get done. If not, there are problems and the leader will probably be replaced. This form of organization is limited by the span of control of the leader. Can he or she effectively control 3, 10, or 100 people?

The Bible (*Exodus*, 18:17–22) tells of Jethro's advice to Moses in 1450 B.C. when he was trying singlehandedly to lead the Israelites out of Egypt.

> What you are doing is not good. You and the people will wear yourselves out, you are not able to perform it alone. Listen to my counsel: You shall represent the people before God, and bring their cases to God; and you shall teach them the statutes and the decisions. . . . Choose able men from all the people, such as fear God, men who are trustworthy and who hate a bribe; and place such men over the people as rulers of thousands, of hundreds, of fifties and of tens. And let them judge the people at all times; every great matter they shall bring to you, but any small matter they shall decide themselves; so it will be easier for you, and they will bear the burden with you.

This passage from the Bible is the earliest known record of the principles of management and organization. By accepting the advice of his father-in-law, Moses created a simple, workable, line organization that accomplished the mission.

The *line organization* has been used for centuries in the functional development of organizations. It is the most common structural form found in most small-to medium-sized nurseries. When tailored to fit the needs of the nursery manager, it can be quite functional. The structure of an average, medium-sized production nursery can be represented as in Fig. 3–1. This structure illustrates the chain of responsibility for three basic functional areas: propagation, production, and sales.

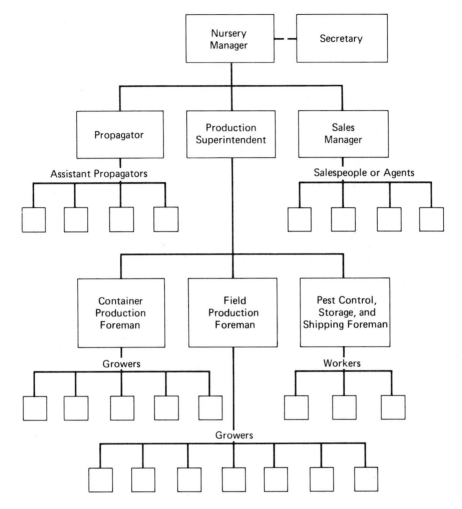

Figure 3–1 Example of line organization for a medium-sized nursery.

Since propagation is a specialized area, it is headed by a skilled propagator who has the responsibility (goal, mission) of propagating the materials needed for field production and the implied responsibility of keeping posted on new methods of propagation related to the type of plants being produced by the nursery.

The nursery superintendent has the largest division and is charged with the responsibility of meeting the production goals. This division is organized into three subsections and staffed accordingly. The sales division is responsible for marketing the products produced.

As an organization grows in size, its functional units increase. But the ultimate size of each unit is determined by the span of control of the individual leader (foreman or superintendent) in charge. At some point the business may become too large for the manager to control effectively without assistance; he or she then gradually obtains a staff, and the business is reorganized.

The *line and staff organization* (Fig. 3–2) is designed to accomplish this objective. The various staff people aid the manager in developing plans and coordinating the activities of the various functional units. In some situations it is desirable to add various service units that provide a service function (e.g., mechanical maintenance) to the overall organization.

The two most common staff positions are the comptroller, in charge of financial matters, and the personnel manager, in charge of labor relations. These two staff assistants aid the manager in the area of money and interior personnel management. If a customer relations director is added, his or her responsibilities should relate to exterior people relationships as opposed to interior. The position would have to do with public and government relations.

The research and development director is responsible for developing new products that the nursery might produce; testing new products that the firm might use; and developing, in cooperation with one or more of the functional units, new methods of operation. The mechanic heads the service unit and is responsible for keeping all mechanical equipment operational. It is important that the chain of com-

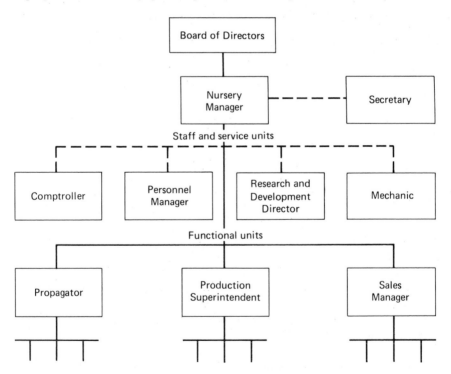

Figure 3–2 Example of line and staff organization for a large nursery.

mand be clearly established in a line and staff organization. Basically, staff members have no command control over the functional units. They are advisory to the manager, who alone directs and controls the functional units.

Sometimes the organization becomes too large for one person to maintain effective control over the functional units, at which time the manager delegates to the staff certain specific aspects of overall authority. When this is done, the business becomes an *executive organization* in which the manager is known as president and is assisted by a group of executive vice-presidents who have authority over functional units in their specific areas of responsibility.

In organizing and staffing a nursery, it is important to keep in mind the overall goal of the organization and the span of control of individual department heads, and to develop logical groupings of functional and staff units. Also, a nursery organization must be flexible and capable of meeting the constantly changing demands for labor as influenced by season, weather conditions, and the changing demands of the marketplace.

The organizing and staffing of a large production nursery is a challenging task. The demand for labor fluctuates with the season of the year and by operations within and between divisions. For many field-production nurseries, there is a maximum need for labor in the spring and fall, with a minimum need in the winter months. In early spring the demand is greatest in the areas of digging and shipping, followed in midspring by planting (Fig. 3–3) and June budding. Then during the summer the primary need is for cultivation and pest control, in August for fall budding operations, followed in the fall months by digging and storage operations.

Nursery managers need to develop good labor management techniques, since labor often accounts for 50% or more of the cost of production. Also, federal, state, and union regulations place specific restraints upon employers relative to conditions of employment and pay schedules.

The *legal form of organization* is another consideration in organizing the nursery business. The three commonly used legal forms of organization are the proprietorship, the partnership, and the corporation. Each form has advantages and disadvantages which should be evaluated prior to legally constituting the business, and periodically during the life of the organization.

The *proprietorship* is the easiest to form. Anyone who can acquire the land and wants to start a nursery can do so, as long as he or she complies with state and local laws related to zoning and taxation. In the proprietorship, responsibility is centered in one individual; there is no sharing of the profits. But the business is limited by the capabilities and limitations of the owner, and the business usually terminates upon the owner's death. This is a serious weakness of the proprietorship form of business. Many excellent small nurseries have failed to continue following the death of the owner, because no provision was made for continuation of the business.

The *partnership* is an agreement between two or more parties. It is easy to form, but at times it may be difficult to divest an undesirable partner or to market a share of a partnership. Partnerships in which the abilities of each partner comple-

Figure 3–3   Planting small flowering trees with the aid of a planting machine. (Courtesy Mechanical Transplanter Co.)

ment one another are generally more successful than those in which they duplicate each other. In the nursery industry one partner may be an excellent production worker and the other a salesperson. Or one partner may be excellent in landscape design and construction, whereas the other is an excellent garden center manager. Problems sometimes develop when both partners are growers and neither is good at administration or sales.

The major weakness in the partnership form of business relates to resolving problems that arise between partners or between the spouses of partners. It can be a very precarious legal form of business and should be constituted with considerable forethought. It is well to have the articles of agreement developed by a lawyer, following careful consideration by all parties. It is possible to develop limited partnerships and open-end-agreement contracts. The limited partnership allows some partners to limit their liability while at least one partner remains fully liable for the debts of the business. Open-end partnership agreements allow for taking in new partners and for the death, retirement, or resignation of partners.

The *corporation* is another legal form of business, designed to provide for the continuity of a business and to limit the liability of a stockholder. Many nurseries that start as proprietorships convert to a corporate form as they grow and develop in size. The corporation is limited by a charter that must be obtained from the state in which the business is incorporated. Also, the business must be managed by a board of directors, hold an annual meeting of stockholders, and file an annual report, generally with the secretary of state in the state of incorporation.

There are many ways that the corporation can be constituted, including public and private. In the public corporation, the stock is for sale to the general public, whereas in the private corporation (commonly referred to as subchapter S) the stock is kept within a closed, private group (commonly within a family). Many commercial nurseries are private (subchapter S) corporations. In general, the private form of corporation meets the needs of most nursery businesses. But when there is serious disagreement within the group and a stockholder wishes to divest himself or herself of one portion of the business, it may be difficult to obtain fair market value for the stock, since there may be a charter limitation on whom it can be sold to.

In organizing a nursery business, it may be desirable to have multiple forms of legal structure to gain the advantages of each. For example, it may be more desirable for a proprietor to own the land and structures, and lease these to the nursery. The production nursery may be a private corporation engaged in agricultural production, which in turn sells its product to another corporation, a sales-oriented organization, which markets it in interstate commerce. The two corporations remain smaller than one large corporation that owns all land and capital assets; this may provide a tax advantage. It limits restrictions placed upon businesses that engage in interstate commerce to only that corporation that is so engaged. It also reduces the size of capitalization, which may permit young people to buy into the nursery at considerably less equity than if the nursery owned all the land and capital assets. It also permits the landowner to sell or will his or her lands without consent of the corporation. This may present a problem to the production nurseries renting land, but by long-term lease arrangements it can generally be managed in an equitable manner. In any case, when developing a corporation or a combination of business forms, it is advisable to obtain the services of a lawyer who is familiar with the various legal and financial requirements, advantages, and limitations.

CONTROL AND COORDINATION

Control and coordination involves those activities that are needed to keep an organization headed on the course that it was assigned or that it chose to follow. Control relates to activities within a unit, whereas coordination relates to activities between units. In a small operational unit, control is direct and is accomplished primarily by voice; there is little need for written directives or written communication, but as an organization grows and the levels or echelons of management increase and the functional units are spread over a greater geographic area, control becomes indirect and must be accomplished by written directives or written communications, and direct control becomes minimal. One effective indirect means of obtaining control is to develop and publish a policy manual for standard procedures and policies. It is best

TABLE 3-1   Suggested Topics to Be Covered in Policy Manual for a Nursery

Administrative	Personnel
Mail handling	Affirmative action policy
Private use of facilities	Clothing and dress
Workers in administration area	Grievances
Equipment	Hours of work
Borrowing	Lost and found
Care and servicing	Lunchroom
Purchasing	Parking
Returning to storage	Promotion
Use	Safety
Finance	Sick leave
Insurance	Tardiness and absenteeism
Loans to employees	Termination
Medical benefits	Vacations
Overtime pay	Work rules
Paid holidays	Plants
Pay periods and paydays	Handling and care
Retirement programs	Sale to employees
Wage review	Supplies
	Obtaining within the nursery
	Purchases for the nursery
	Returning to storage

developed in cooperation with key employees and staff advisers. Some items that might be covered in the manual are tabulated in Table 3–1.

Another control mechanism is to set attainable goals for each functional unit. Depending upon the type of unit, the goals may be daily, weekly, monthly, seasonal, or yearly. For a digging crew, daily goals are in order, whereas for a propagator it may be x thousands of cuttings per month, season, or year; for the production and sales managers, the goal may be x number of plants/species/season; and for the general manager, the goal is dollars of profit.

Since there are objectives to be obtained, there must be some form of reporting. Records and reports are another means that managers use to gain control over their operational units. Records and reports should contain accurate, up-to-date information if they are to be valuable to the manager. Collecting and processing data that are not going to be used in making management decisions is a worthless practice that should be discouraged. But collecting data that, when processed, will be used for evaluation purposes and as a basis for future planning and management decisions is an implied responsibility of all levels of management.

Two excellent tools that can be used by management as a guide to labor productivity are: the reasonable-expectancy table (Table 3–2) for individual performance and the staffing table (Table 3–3) for crew performance. Both are developed from labor productivity records maintained by the production foremen. The data,

TABLE 3-2   Reasonable Expectancy for Labor-Hours

A. Digging evergreens by hand

Plant Size	Production System	Spreading (e.g., Yews, Mugho Pine)	Compact Upright (e.g., Yews)	Large Type (e.g., Spruce, Pine)
		Plants per Labor-Hour[a]		
12–15 in.	FP[b]	12.0		
12–15 in.	B&B	8.5		
15–18 in.	B&B	7.5	8.5	
18–24 in.	B&B	6.0	7.8	6.9
2–2½ ft	B&B		6.9	4.5
2½–3 ft	B&B		6.0	
3–4 ft	B&B			3.0
4–5 ft	B&B			2.0

B. Digging B&B trees by hand

Caliper (in.)	Trees per Labor-Hour[c]
1–1¼	24
1½–2	14
2½–3½	9
4	3.5

[a]Based on data from 6- to 10-worker digging crews. Includes carrying out and loading on pallets.
[b]Fiber pot.
[c]Based on data from 8-worker crew. Includes burlapping, topping, and tying tops.

Note: Data were obtained from a number of sources, and are not intended as a standard. Data and reasonable expectancy tables should be collected and developed individually for each nursery.

from records kept on the various functions performed within the nursery, can be processed into meaningful information that can be used in planning labor needs, estimating future cost of production and cash flow requirements for the business, and evaluating production. Table 3–3 is an example of how raw data can be converted into a more meaningful unit: average labor-hours per 1000 trees.

Digging and planting large trees varies considerably by the size of the ball and with the type of equipment used. Therefore, average labor-hours to dig and plant shade trees have been converted to graphs (Figs. 3–4 and 3–5) which can be used to estimate labor-hour requirements when digging and planting large trees.

Record taking and reporting must be made as simple as possible. Various types of forms are available or can be designed to obtain data on individual work performance, use of equipment and supplies, expenditure of funds, and so on. The uniform chart of accounts for use in financial management developed by the Horticultural Research Institute can be a useful management tool in this area. There are

TABLE 3-3 Nursery Staffing[a]

	Average Labor-Hours/1000
Planting in the Nursery	
Shade tree whips, 1½-in. caliper	
With tractor-drawn planting machine (V-shaped plow to open trench, plus closing disks and packing wheels), 8-worker crew	
Planted on 8-ft centers in rows $\bar{x} = 4000/10$-hr day	20.0
Shade tree whips, 1–1¼-in. caliper	
Hole marking and digging 10×10 ft (cleared land, experienced crew, good weather) $\bar{x} = 2100$ holes/134 labor-hours	64.0
Preplant pruning (remove from storage rack, prune roots and top, return to rack) $\bar{x} = 16$ trees/labor-hour	62.5
Planting by hand into predug holes; fill and water $\bar{x} = 5.4$ trees/labor-hour	185.2
Evergreen transplants	
With tractor-drawn mechanical transplanter, Model 2000, two-row, 10-worker crew, 9–10-in., spreading, BR	
Long rows $\bar{x} = 10,000/10$-hr day	10.0
Short rows (<1000 ft) $\bar{x} = 8000/10$-hr day	12.5
Pruning or Trimming	
Shade trees	
From the ground	
1–1¼-in. $\bar{x} = 5850$ trees/148 labor-hours	25.3
¾–1½-in. $\bar{x} = 300/10$-hr day	34.0
With pole trimmers, 1½–2½-in. $\bar{x} = 300/10$-hr day	34.0
With step ladders, 1½–2½-in. $\bar{x} = 200/10$-hr day	50.0
Evergreens cone-shaped 2–4-ft (i.e., Capitata yews)	
With long-bladed knife $\bar{x} = 10,000/10$-hr day	1.0
With power-pack hedge shears $\bar{x} = 4500/10$-hr day	2.2
With long-bladed hedge shears $\bar{x} = 2000/10$-hr day	5.0

TABLE 3-3 (*continued*)

	Average Labor-Hours/1000
Evergreens spreading 18–24-in. (i.e., Pfitzer juniper)	
With power-pack hedge shears (winter only for junipers) $\bar{x} = 7000/10$-hr day	1.5
With long-bladed hedge shears $\bar{x} = 4000/10$-hr day	2.5
Digging	
Evergreens	
By hand B&B	
15- or 18-in. spreading, 10-in ball $\bar{x} = 10$ workers: 450/10-hr day	220
4-ft upright 12–14-in. ball $\bar{x} = 10$ workers: 200/10-hr day	500
5–6-ft upright, 18-in. ball $\bar{x} = 8$ workers: 130/10-hr day	615
With Jiffy balling machine	
15–18-in. plants, digging and potting $\bar{x} = 8$ workers: 900/10-hr day	88.8
15–18-in. plants, digging and B&B $\bar{x} = 12$ workers: 800/10-hr day	100
Shade trees	
By hand (varies with size of ball, see Figs. 3-4 and 3-5)	
With tree-spade digging machine (includes tying branches, digging, packaging into burlapped wire baskets, secured, trunks wrapped) 10-hr day, from barn to digging area, minimum moving from field to field and back to barn at end of day	
66-in. Vermeer, truck-mounted $\bar{x} = 10$-worker crew: 25/10-hr day (2.8 labor-hr/tree)	2800
44-in. Vermeer, on tractor $\bar{x} = 7$-worker crew: 80/10-hr day (53 min/tree)	875
30-in Vermeer, on tractor $\bar{x} = 7$-worker crew: 150/10-hr day (28 min/tree)	467
28-in. Caretree, on Bob Cat (skid tractor) $\bar{x} = 10$-worker crew: 230/10-hr day (26 min/tree)	435

[a]Average labor productivity for selected nursery operations. Data obtained from a number of nurseries. Each nursery manager should develop tables for the particular set of conditions, methods of operation, machines, and work force.

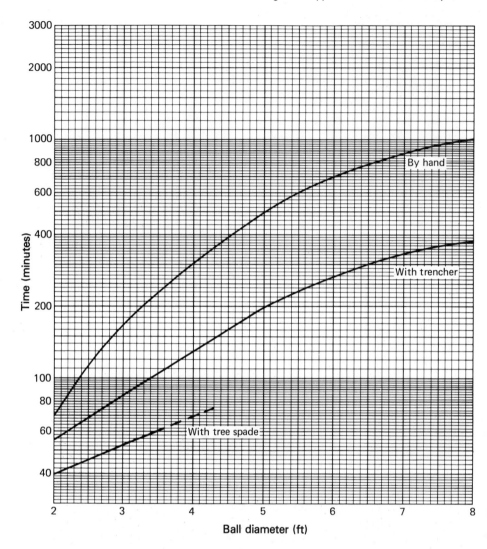

Figure 3–4 Average time for digging B&B trees. (The data in Figures 3–4 and 3–5 were obtained from a number of sources, and are not intended as a standard. Data should be collected and developed individually for each nursery.) (From Davidson and Speakman, 1969.)

charts for nursery production, landscape, and retail operations.

Each operational unit manager should establish contact with other operational units to coordinate activities, especially when an operation is highly dependent upon coordinated or sequential activities.

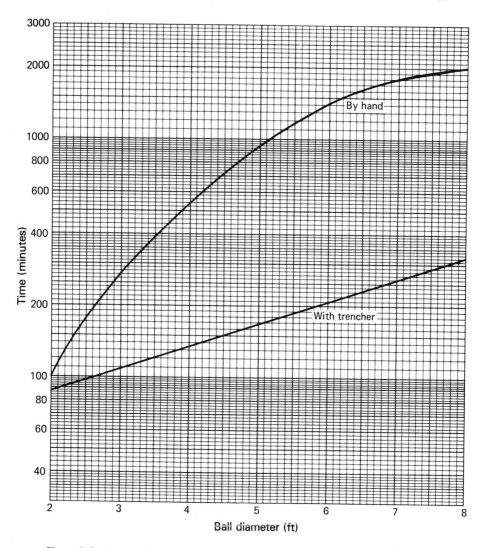

Figure 3–5 Average time for planting B&B trees. (From Davidson and Speakman, 1969.)

EMPLOYEE MOTIVATION, EVALUATION, AND REWARDS

Motivating, evaluating, and rewarding employees are important management functions. They sometimes do not receive the attention from nursery managers that they deserve. The three functions are closely interrelated. For example, a spontaneous statement such as "Well done," "A good job," or "Excellent" made by a manager as an evaluation of employee performance is one of the most appreciated rewards and one of the best positive motivators that is available to management. But all too often, its impact and value are overlooked. The proper and timely granting of employee rewards can have a major impact upon the success or failure of the business. Every employee is entitled to have his or her performance evaluated: to receive praise and advancement for work well done, rebuke for failure, and punishment for unacceptable behavior or performance.

A good nursery manager is cognizant of the fact that the most important factor of production relates to the employees. The manager must never forget that employees are people, and that they have needs, aspirations, skills, and ideas. It is how the manager perceives employees and satisfies these needs and skills that determines to a large degree the productivity of the employees and, ultimately, the success of the business.

Each person has a basic need for food, clothing, and shelter. And most people have a need to be with others. Human beings are social; they like to be with others of their own kind and enjoy the company of members of the opposite sex. People work to satisfy these physiological and sociological needs. However, people also have dreams and aspirations that go beyond these basic needs. They are called the ego or psychological needs: the need to be recognized as an individual and not just a statistic, the need to express and carry out ideas, and the need for praise and recognition.

When an employee is hired, he or she should be informed of his or her duties and responsibilities. The person should also be told the procedure for evaluation and reward. Communicating the job responsibilities varies with the position. For temporary, seasonal employees the communication may be verbal and rather specific. For top management the communication may be in writing, but general in nature. However, for middle management a detailed job description, in writing, may be in order, because it is necessary to clearly define the scope of the position and the limits of responsibility.

An application form should be used for most positions. The form serves a number of functions: to obtain (1) personal data on the applicant (name, address, date of birth, medical history, etc.), (2) pertinent information on the applicant relative to the position, (3) a history of previous employment, and (4) if applicable, a statement of the applicant's expectations. The form thus serves as the first step in the evaluation process. The form also screens out those applicants who do not wish to complete formal, written documents for one reason or another. A follow-up interview provides the nursery manager with a second opportunity to evaluate the potential employee. At this time the manager should also explain the unique characteristics and philosophy of the nursery and try to determine if the applicant has the desired qualifications for the position.

Once an employee has been hired, he or she should undergo training appropriate to the position and the person's background. All too often managers fail to train new employees properly. The initial period, after a person joins a nursery, is extremely important both to the person and to the nursery. New employees must learn what is expected of them and how far they can proceed on their own. Also, the employer must learn how to best motivate the new employee and how much responsibility can be delegated to the employee as he or she matures and develops as a productive part of the labor-management team.

Young people, especially those who have made a substantial investment in their education, by devoting two or more years of their lives to obtaining a college education, will need to obtain training in the work ethic. Unfortunately, people from urban areas have little opportunity to learn and practice the physical skills associated with the nursery industry. Academic institutions are not equipped to provide these, which are best learned on the job. They will need to serve a period of apprenticeship, learning the art and skills associated with the nursery industry. However, nursery managers have an obligation to these young employees, to the nursery industry, and to themselves to provide this period of internship. By doing so, they will be making an investment in a human resource that will pay substantial dividends in the future.

It has been said that a good supervisor is someone who can get people to do what he or she wants done, the way he or she wants it done, when he or she wants it done by people who want to do it. How is this accomplished? By incentives. Incentives will vary with individuals, groups, and situations. Some of the most common incentives are commendation, pay, time off, titles, and various fringe benefits. But one of the best incentives is participation. When people are asked for their advice relative to achieving an objective, they feel a part of the organization. They feel personally involved and have a sense of importance. Employees, especially in the middle-management positions, must feel that they are essential to the organization meeting its objective. A manager who solicits advice must be prepared to utilize that advice and provide appropriate recognition (reward) when it is deserved.

For the applicant the evaluation process commences at first contact with the employer. The applicant should be sure the contact is appropriate for the position. A letter should be neatly typed and supported by a vita sheet or completed application form. At the interview the applicant should be clean and dressed appropriately for the position.

After working for a predetermined period, the new employee should be evaluated. The evaluation should not be made too quickly or on insufficient evidence of performance, but slowly and deliberately. The employee should be commended for his or her accomplishments and counseled in areas or skills that could be improved upon. Also, when appropriate, an increase in salary should be given, since incentive pay is an important means of rewarding good performance.

Most new employees begin as *hourly workers* whose primary function is the performance of physical skills. Although they work with materials, the skills employed require little technical knowledge. They may include such jobs as digging holes to plant trees, digging and lifting plants, packing, or making cuttings. Hourly workers can be evaluated on the basis of quantity and to some degree the quality of production. In most nurseries, standards of quality are set by management. In some establishments the quality standards are high and must not be sacrificed for quantity, whereas in other establishments, by design, the standards of quality are somewhat lower, in the interest of obtaining quantity of production. Nevertheless, the objective set for the worker is generally some type of daily goal, and the compensation is wages paid at an hourly rate. In establishments where quality of performance is appreciated, superior performance should be provided with additional rewards, such as a rate of pay greater than the average or a bonus paid at the end of a season or at some other predetermined time period. However, in addition to these standard methods of earned or contractual rewards for labor, management should also be cognizant of other methods of reward appropriate to the age level, social background, and the desires and expectations of the workers. Young people hoeing weeds in the nursery will often work better and faster if they know they will be rewarded with time off with pay. Most people will do a better job if they know that their work is appreciated and will be rewarded accordingly. Hourly workers usually move up to "skilled workers" when they have acquired a degree of technical knowledge and the appropriate skill level.

Skilled workers also work with materials, but the jobs are more demanding of technical knowledge and ability. Examples are budding and grafting; application of fertilizers and pesticides; and operating equipment, such as tree diggers. Skilled workers are evaluated both on the quantity and quality of their performance. Their earned rewards may include in addition to a higher wage rate such fringe benefits as days off with pay, paid vacation, and health insurance. Various supplementary rewards may be expense-paid trips to professional meetings or an opportunity to obtain additional training at company expense.

Foremen are the first level of management. They are charged with the responsibility of getting a job done; this is most commonly accomplished by managing people and materials. Therefore, one of the foreman's responsibilities is to motivate, evaluate, and reward the workers. However, foremen are evaluated by their superiors on how well they get the job done. Since the foreman's job is a management position it includes the responsibility of maintaining records on the use of the resources (workers and materials) over which he or she has responsibility. A simple but meaningful system is one that accounts for both the workers and machine-hours that go into each job, plus a record of the materials that were expended. In a nursery the job may either be plant-production-oriented or it may be nonproductive, such as maintenance of roads, digging a pond, and so on. Nevertheless, it is important to management to obtain data on productivity to evaluate the crews' performances. The data can also be used to develop reasonable expectancy and staffing tables, in estimating cost of production, and for cash flow analysis.

The foreman's earned rewards are similar to those of the skilled laborer: higher salary, various fringe benefits, and so on. In addition, there should be certain supplementary rewards for jobs that are well done, particularly under adverse situations: weather, time, shortage of personnel. These supplementary rewards might be a cash bonus or a gift appropriate to the person and the situation. Care must be exercised in giving a bonus on a regular basis; it can easily become an expected, earned reward. Foremen should seldom, if ever, be evaluated on a monetary productivity basis, although this is done in some nurseries or landscape construction firms. A couple of examples will illustrate the point.

In a landscape construction firm, a job is bid at a monetary value, and the foreman who is assigned to the job is sometimes evaluated on how much money was made on the job. If the job is profitable, the foreman may share in a bonus, whereas if the job lost money, the individual may be reprimanded or even be discharged. But foremen in most firms, either landscape or nursery, have control over only two factors of production—workers and materials; they should be evaluated only on their ability to use these two factors effectively. If they bid the job or have a degree of financial control, it is reasonable to evaluate them on profitability of the job.

A foreman in charge of a digging crew in a nursery is provided with a mechanical tree digger, a crew of workers, and the needed materials, such as burlap, wire baskets, pinning nails, twine, and so on. The job is to harvest a certain number of trees per day (week or season). Implied within the objective is that the trees be firmly balled and that no damage be done to the trees being dug or to the trees that remain in the block to grow on to larger sizes. If this objective is attained (assuming that it was attainable), the reward is a good monthly salary. However, if performance is above average—the trees are well balled, there is no damage to the trees, the job was done in less than average time, and the customers of the nursery are pleased with the quality of the product—the foreman should be given a supplementary reward, generally praise and possibly a bonus. The foreman, in turn, should praise the workers and share a portion of the bonus with them.

In making the evaluation of the crews' performances, various means are utilized: visual observation of the crews on the job, comments from customers on the quality of the product, and digging records of the number of trees dug and the labor-hours utilized to accomplish the job. From the digging records, the nursery superintendent or the nursery manager will obtain the data needed to arrive at average times to dig and process trees of various size classes and to estimate costs to harvest plants of various sizes. Since management has the data on wage rates and costs of supplies, equipment, and so on, they are in a position to make the necessary calculations to evaluate the economic productivity of the system and to make the appropriate rewards or effect changes in the system.

Similar types of evaluations can be made for all the divisions of the nursery if the goals or objectives are clearly defined. In propagation the goal is output of young plants, seedlings, cuttings, grafts, and so on. In the nursery it is the production of salable plants to meet a market objective, and digging crews are evaluated and rewarded on the basis of productivity and the quality of their performance.

The goal of top management is to produce a profit for the organization. Therefore, management is evaluated on the basis of profitability and is rewarded accordingly. This topic is discussed in Chapter 7.

SUMMARY

Although the management process can be divided into and discussed as six component parts—(1) setting goals, (2) planning, (3) organizing and staffing, (4) directing, controlling, and coordinating, (5) motivating, and (6) evaluating and rewarding—it is a unified process with each part dependent upon all others. Successful managers constantly evaluate and seek ways to improve the use of their resources. Managers must keep abreast of changing demands in the marketplace and changing methods of production in order to make sound management decisions relative to the long-range goals of the organization. Changes in goals or in methods of production will of necessity affect the organizational structure, which in turn will modify methods of control, coordination, motivation, and so on. And once the new structure is developed to meet the newly developed objectives, the process starts over again. Management is a never-ending process. It is a logical process that good managers understand and practice in a successful manner. Poor managers either fail to understand the process or fail to practice one or more of the parts that make up good management.

For additional information on management, the reader should consult one or more books on the topic; a few are listed as Suggested Reading. Another source of good management information is the Small Business Management Series, published by the Small Business Administration and sold by the Superintendent of Documents, Washington, D.C. 20402.

SUGGESTED READING

CARROLL, S. J., JR., and H. L. TOSI, JR., 1973. Management by objectives. Macmillan Publishing Co., Inc., New York.

DALE, E. 1973. Management: theory and practice. McGraw-Hill Book Company, New York.

DAVIDSON, H., and T. SPEAKMAN. 1969. Time study for planting trees. Weeds, Trees, Turf. 8(8):18.

DRUCKER, P. F. 1977. An introductory view of management. Harper's College Press, New York.

PETERS, T. J., and R. H. WATERMAN, JR. 1982. In search of excellence. Warner Books, Inc., New York.

PINNEY, J. J., and R. D. PINNEY. 1985. Beginning in the nursery business. American Nurseryman Publishing Company, Chicago.

STRONG, E. P. 1965. The management of business. Harper & Row, Publishers, Inc., New York.

4 Selection of a Nursery Site

The selection of a site for a nursery should be done with considerable care and thought, since location will have a major effect on the overall success of the organization. Soil, water, and environment are factors of paramount importance in the selection of a site for a production nursery, whereas for a garden center the important considerations are population density, social customs, and traffic patterns. However, each factor should be considered and evaluated for the effect it will have on the overall success of the business. The factors are grouped into four convenient categories for discussion: ecological, economic, sociological, and biological.

ECOLOGICAL FACTORS

Climate

For the production of nursery stock, either field-grown or container-grown, a mild climate with a long growing season and an even distribution of rainfall is most desirable. Areas with extremes in temperature, especially rapid fluctuating temperatures, or those that are subject to wind, hail, or ice storms should be avoided. Sites should be selected that afford protection from drying winds, and alternate freezing and thawing. Within a large geographic area, there are sites to be found that have a favorable microclimate for the growth of plants. Sites close to a large body of water are often temperature-moderated by the lake effect up to 2 or more miles from the shoreline.

Topography

The land for efficient operation should be relatively level; steep slopes should be avoided, but rolling land can be terraced. Sites that are subject to flooding or are known to be frost pockets should be avoided. Areas with large outcroppings of rock and large stones are less desirable as sites for a field-production nursery than those that are free of such obstructions, which impede many operations associated with modern nursery practices.

Soil

The media for container-grown plants are generally artificially blended (Chapter 12). Therefore, the native soil is not an important site factor for a container-production nursery. But it is an important consideration relative to drainage and trafficability. Container-production nurseries need a dependable source of supply for sand, peat moss, water, fertilizer, containers, and so on, and these materials should be available at reasonable prices.

The selection of soil type for a field-production nursery will vary with the type of nursery stock to be produced. Seedlings and bare-root plants can be produced best when grown on sandy or sandy loam soil because (1) it does not crust over following rains or irrigation, allowing better seedling emergence; (2) it exhibits less tendency to heave, minimizing injury due to lifting of the plants out of the ground when the ground thaws in the spring; (3) it can be worked earlier in the spring and sooner after rains; (4) it requires less power for cultural operations; and (5) plants can be removed from it with less damage to the roots. Plants that are marketed with a soil ball about their roots are best produced in either a silty loam or a clay loam soil.

Soils for the production of quality nursery stock must have good structure and porosity. These characteristics have a strong influence upon air-water relationships, nutrient availability, the activity of microorganisms, and ultimately upon plant growth and development. Soils with a granular or crumb structure make excellent soils for field-production nurseries. These soils have good drainage characteristics while retaining adequate moisture for plant growth. They contain a balanced supply of clay minerals and soil colloids, which function as adsorption sites for plant nutrients. And they permit digging operations even in wet seasons.

The optimum soil reaction (pH) for the production of most woody plants is between 5.0 and 7.2. Therefore, it is desirable that the proposed nursery site have a pH within or close to this range. Soils with a pH greater than 7.2 should be avoided because it is difficult and costly to lower their pH. Acid soils can be corrected fairly easily with lime.

Although it is desirable that the soil have an optimum level of fertility, it is not an absolute requirement, since the intensity and balance of most elements can be modified fairly readily with commercial fertilizers. However, soils that test high in calcium and magnesium should be avoided as sites for the production of woody species, since high levels of these two bases will induce trace element deficiencies. Soils for field-production nurseries should contain 2–5% organic matter and must be free of pests, including noxious weeds, nematodes, insects, disease organisms, and herbicide residue, which might restrict the growth or impair the quality of nursery crops.

A valuable guide in selecting a site for a field production nursery is the past agronomic history of the site. A soil that is currently producing or recently produced a productive agricultural crop is to be desired over one that has a past history of low productivity. In addition, the native vegetation of the area can be a clue to the productive potential of the site. Assistance in evaluating potential nursery sites may be obtained from the U.S. Soil Conservation Service, county agricultural agents, the state department of agriculture, and soil, insect, disease, and horticulture specialists located at the state university. The Soil Conservation Service has available, upon request, excellent soil maps that can be of considerable value in selecting sites for a nursery.

Water

An ideal nursery site, with respect to water, would be one where there is good rainfall distribution throughout the planting and growing season, with a minimum of rain (or snow) during the digging and shipping season. Since this is almost impossible to find, it is best to locate a site where there is access to a dependable supply of quality water. The delivery capability will vary from a few hundred gallons per minute to many thousands of gallons per minute, depending on the size and type of nursery to be established (see Chapter 13).

Water can be obtained either from a municipal water system or from streams, rivers, ponds, lakes, or wells. It should be free of alkalies, excessive salts, or industrial wastes that might be detrimental to plant growth. Irrigation water for use on seedlings and young transplants should have less than 200 parts per million (ppm) of dissolved solids. Whereas, the water used on larger field-grown or container-grown plants may have from two to three times this amount. A Solu-bridge can be used to estimate this value. A reading of 0.3 millisiemens (ms) per centimeter at 25°C is equivalent to 200 ppm of dissolved solids. Irrigation water that contains calcium in excess of 500 ppm is likely to raise the pH of the soil, which in time could have an adverse effect upon the growth of the plants (see Chapters 11 and 13).

In some areas of the country, sodium and boron can cause problems in the propagation and production of young plants. The sodium absorption ratio of the irrigation water should be less than 10 and the boron content less than one-half part per million (ppm). In addition to a supply of water for the nursery stock, a source of safe drinking water must be available for employees. Prior to making the final selection of the site for a nursery, consult with the state geologist or with the state department of natural resources relative to state laws pertaining to water rights.

Air

Air pollution is a problem to be considered in selecting a site for a nursery. Air that is polluted with sulfur dioxide (SO_2), fluorides (e.g., hydrogen fluoride [HF]) photochemical smog, and ozone (O_3) should be avoided. These phototoxic pollutants are produced primarily by industry, motor transportation, and by the generation of electricity. Therefore, it is undesirable to locate either downwind from an industrial site that could be a potential source of pollution or in a confined geological area where photochemical smog concentrates due to poor air circulation.

ECONOMIC FACTORS

Cost of Land

The initial cost of the land will often determine if a nursery establishment can be started on a given site. Generally, it is thought that a production nursery engaged in extensive production cannot afford to produce plants on high-priced land. On the other hand, nurseries engaged in intensive production, landscape nurseries, or garden centers can afford higher-priced land provided that other factors do not limit productivity or sales. In addition to land costs, the annual taxes and property assessments will affect the net return on the investment and may in some cases preclude the operation of a nursery on the site. Many fine nurseries have closed or are closing operations on certain sites as a result of increased taxes caused by higher land values, brought about by urbanization.

One solution to high land costs is for an individual to own the land and lease it to the nursery on a long-term lease. This allows an individual to capitalize on appreciation of land values but permits a nursery to program production. In some states tax advantages can be obtained if the land is committed by contract to long-term (at least 10 years) agriculture. Information on these contracts can be obtained from the Cooperative Extension Service in the various states or from real estate agents who specialize in farm properties.

Labor

Since nurseries rely on considerable hand labor to perform much of the work associated with production and landscape construction, a supply of manual labor must be available. Field-production nurseries, because of the seasonal nature of their operations, experience periods of peak demand for labor followed by periods where there is little need for labor. This seasonal need for unskilled labor is met in part by the employment of migrant laborers. However, with the passage of labor laws, many nurseries are finding it difficult to obtain seasonal labor. Some have solved this problem by employing high-school students, off-duty firemen, retirees, homemakers, and so on, on a part-time basis, whereas others are contracting for the employment of laborers from the various territories of the United States. Still other nurserymen are either contracting out some of the production operation (e.g., digging and packaging) or they are mechanizing many of the traditional hand operations associated with the nursery industry. In addition to manual laborers, nurseries also need individuals capable of performing various skilled operations (e.g., propagators, pesticide applicators) and others who have abilities as foremen or managers.

Facilities

Power is needed by most nurseries; some need only one form while others may require many forms. Electric power is needed for lighting and the operation of equipment, including irrigation pumps, refrigerators, potting machines, computers, typewriters, and so on. Three-phase electric power is desirable to operate certain types of machines (e.g., soil mixing, potting, packaging, and computers). If the three-phase lines are not close to the site, it can be costly to have the power brought to the site. This cost might be avoided by careful selection of the site or by using alternative sources of power, such as diesel-powered generators.

Oil, gas, or coal is necessary for the operation of the heating plant. Since the energy crisis of the mid-1970s, it is necessary to check on the availability of a dependable, noninterrupted supply of heating fuel at a cost that the business can afford. Gasoline is needed in large quantities to power trucks, tractors, cars, and other equipment used in the nursery. This should be contracted for delivery to the nursery so that the business can take advantage of bulk rates and submit the associated charges for a federal tax credit, which is permitted for off-the-road use.

Good transportation facilities are necessary for most nurseries. A high percentage of the nursery stock shipped in the United States is transported by motor truck. However, substantial amounts are also transported by railroad, particularly from the Northwest, and some is transported by airplane. Since motor freight is the primary means of transport, nurseries should locate so that trucks carrying heavy loads may have access without restriction. This is particularly important for nurseries located in the northern parts of the country, where weight limitations are often imposed on county roads during the spring-thaw period.

A garden center located on a road or highway that affords easy access is much more desirable than one located on a superhighway or on a second-class or unpaved road, where access is difficult. In some situations a site located on the right-hand side of the road for people going home from work in large urban areas may be more desirable than one located on the left side.

Competition

Competition should always be evaluated before starting a new business. This is particularly true when the establishment will serve a limited clientele or market in a limited geographic area. The number of similar establishments and the progressiveness of each should be carefully considered. An elementary question that should be answered prior to starting a new business is: "What can I produce (product or service) that is superior to my competition, is needed by others, and can be sold for a profit?" However, competition is not a problem in selecting a site for a production nursery that will have a large market area (e.g., many states or the nation). In fact, the presence of other nurseries in the area may be an asset. Nurserymen often cooperate with each other on the use of specialized equipment, human resources, and in shipping arrangements.

SOCIOLOGICAL FACTORS

Many sociological factors have influenced and will continue to influence the development of the nursery industry just as they influence many other segments of the economy. Increased population, wealth, and leisure time all point to a greater demand for nursery products. But these factors vary considerably between communities, and it behooves enterprising nurserymen to know these trends. The mode of life and the ethnic background of the people may also influence the acceptance of the products and services to be offered or the manner by which they can be merchandised.

City or township clerks should be contacted relative to zoning restrictions, building codes, permits, and business licenses prior to buying land to develop a nursery or prior to improving the present facilities. Local zoning laws may prohibit or restrict the development of a nursery, landscape construction firm, or a garden center on a given site.

The availability and quality of the schools, churches, hospitals, civic associations, and cultural centers are also important considerations for all segments of the nursery industry. Communities that support these facilities are prone to support good landscapes and are therefore good sites for garden centers and landscape nurseries. The availability of these facilities will indirectly affect a wholesale nursery's ability to attract and keep good personnel.

BIOLOGICAL FACTORS

Various biological factors should also be investigated prior to selecting a site for a nursery, including the presence of any serious insect, disease, or weed pests. In addition, in some parts of the country deer can be a serious pest, causing extensive damage to nursery stock. County agricultural agents can often provide information on the presence and seriousness of these pests in their counties. Extension specialists, located at land-grant universities, can provide information on the control and eradication of pests. The Department of Natural Resources or a related agency can provide information on deer populations (including seasonal patterns), deer management programs, fence construction, and advice on site selection.

SUMMARY

Establishing a successful nursery, landscape operation, or garden center is not a simple matter. It requires a large investment in land and facilities, familiarity with the laws and restrictions on all levels and units of government, and the assembling of a cohesive, productive group of people to accomplish the goals of the organization. Therefore, prior to selecting the site, all factors should be considered and evaluated. Advice from specialists in the area of real estate, soil science, horticulture, entomology, pathology, water resources, and associated areas should be solicited and evaluated. Considerable assistance may be obtained from county agricultural agents, soil conservation service, and extension specialists located at land grant universities. And it is highly desirable to have worked in the industry for a number of years prior to starting a nursery business. There is no substitute for experience.

REFERENCES

DAVIS, D. D. 1973. Air pollution damages trees. USDA Forest Service.

ENGSTROM, H. E. 1941. Nursery practice for trees and shrubs suitable for planting on the prairie plains. USDA Misc. Publ. 434.

HAMILTON, D. 1980. Consider crop, economic and environmental factors when selecting a nursery site. Am. Nurseryman 151(5):10.

MCANINCH, J. B., et al. 1983. Deer damage control in N.Y. agriculture. N.Y. State Dept. Agriculture and Markets, Div. of Pl. Ind.

PETERSON, G. W., and R. S. SMITH, JR. 1975. Forest nursery division in the U.S. USDA Agric. Hand. 470.

RICHARDS, L. A. 1954. Diagnosis and improvement of saline and alkali soils. USDA Agric. Hand. 60.

STOECKELER, J. H., and G. W. JONES. 1957. Forest nursery practice in the Lake States. USDA Agric. Hand. 110.

————, and P. E. SLABAUGH. 1965. Conifer nursery practice in the prairie plains. USDA Agric. Hand. 279.

5 *Organization and Development of the Nursery*

The organization and development of a nursery site should be done with considerable care and forethought to maximize efficiency of production and to minimize loss of time. Some thought should also be given to future expansion and ways of attaining long-range goals. A detailed planometric map (Fig. 5–1) of the site, locating all existing facilities, natural or man-made, should be developed. Then with the aid of overlays, plans can be made to develop the site, including the location of production areas, irrigation facilities, shipping-receiving-storage areas, administrative headquarters, residences, circulation and parking, windbreaks, and beautification. A separate overlay should be made diagramming the location of all underground utilities, including depths, location of valves, and so on.

GENERAL CONSIDERATIONS

The actual size and location of the individual units within the nursery will vary with the size and type of the operation, topography, soil type, cultural practices, equipment and extent of mechanization, availability of labor, and various economic factors.

The *best sites* in a field-production nursery should be allocated to the production areas, since soil is one of the major production assets. When possible, irrigation facilities should be centrally located within the production area to minimize the length of main lines and laterals.

Shipping-receiving-storage facilities are best located at a site that will be easily accessible from a major highway. The area should include adequate parking and turnaround area, elevated docks, adequate assembly areas, and restroom facilities for employees and truck drivers.

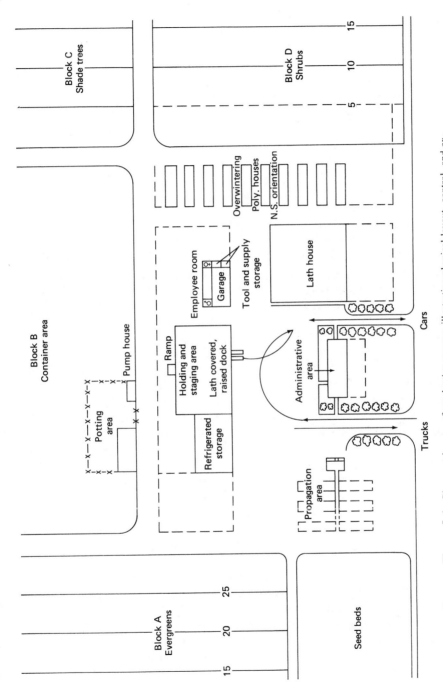

Figure 5–1 Planometric map of production nursery illustrating physical layout, control, and expansion potential. Dashed lines indicate areas for expansion.

The *administrative headquarters* should be located to provide centralized control over production, shipping, and sales. In planning the building, consideration should be given to the interrelationship and coordination required by the various departments that will be housed in the headquarters. Adequate parking and convenient access to the sales area need to be provided for customers. If residences are to be constructed on the property, they should be located away from the commercial areas but conveniently connected to them.

Circulation and parking are important considerations in the development of nurseries and garden centers. Access and parking for customers should be made as easy and as convenient as possible. Preferably, these facilities should be blacktopped. Roads to the shipping-receiving-storage areas should also be readily accessible, about 30 ft in width, with no sharp-angle turns. In parts of the country where snow is a problem, it is advisable to locate the facility close to a major roadway to minimize snowplowing. Also, space at the sides of roads and parking areas must be available for piling of snow. Roads within the production area can be of crushed stone or gravel. They should be between 20 and 30 ft in width, but the gravel area can be confined to a 12- to 15-ft strip in the center. Roadways within the production area often serve as turnaround areas for field-operation equipment.

Windbreaks, if used, are planted on the windward side of seed beds and young transplant areas to reduce the dehydrating, eroding, and abusive effects of strong winds. Unfortunately, as the plants in the windbreak grow, so do their roots, which soon compete with the nursery crops for the available water and nutrients. Windbreaks that support vegetation 6 ft or more in height can materially reduce the yield of crops immediately adjacent to and up to several feet from the windbreak. The distance is roughly proportional to the height of the windbreak. Also, plants in the windbreak can harbor insects, diseases, and mammals that could be injurious to the nursery crops. If windbreaks are planted, avoid species that are known to be an alternate or primary host to a disease or insect that is a pest of nursery crops. Two good uses of evergreen plantings in a nursery are for protecting outdoor propagation areas with sheared hedges and the screening of storage room walls from the heating rays of the sun. These plantings can also serve as a source for seed or cuttings if the appropriate species or cultivar is planted. In areas where a permanent natural windbreak is undesirable, it could be advantageous to construct a windbreak out of snow fencing or to interplant with an annual crop such as corn between every two or three seed or liner beds.

In developing the overall plan for the nursery, consideration must also be given to constructing storage areas for equipment, tools, fertilizer, pesticides, and other materials. Container production nurseries will need storage areas for the basic ingredients of their growing media (sand, peat, bark, and so on); a holding area for containers; and special storage tanks for fertilizer concentrate.

Employee facilities, such as parking areas, locker rooms, lunchrooms, restroom facilities, and foremen's offices, should be carefully planned and properly constructed and maintained. Clean, neat facilities for employees are important in maintaining morale, which will have a direct effect upon production efficiency.

Public areas of the nursery should be planned and landscaped. Mature, well-maintained specimen plants can be developed into attractive synoptic plantings, which will aid in selling smaller nursery plants.

SPECIFIC CONSIDERATIONS

Production areas of nurseries include propagation greenhouses, seed beds, cold frames, liner beds, and the blocks or container yards. In most nurseries, production is centered on one farm, but in large nurseries production is often distributed over a number of farms. When a nursery offers a diverse product mix, it is desirable to organize the production effort either by method of production (field vs. container) or by plant type (herbaceous vs. woody; evergreen vs. deciduous; trees vs. shrubs vs. ground covers; etc.) When a number of farms are utilized, it is good management to concentrate compatible plant types onto one farm to gain production efficiency.

Seedbed areas are best situated on level, well-drained sandy loam or silty loam sites with a moderate level of nutrition and the pH appropriate to the crop (Chapter 11). The beds should be oriented in an east-west direction if a lath or snow fence is to be employed for shade, so that the lath strips will be oriented in a north-south direction. This orientation produces a moving sun-shade pattern during bright sunny days, which will prevent sunscalding of the seedlings or newly rooted cuttings beneath, which could occur if the lath strips were oriented in an east-west direction.

The width of the seedbeds is generally determined by the width of equipment used in working the area. The wheels of all heavy equipment should be confined to pathways between the beds. Some commonly used widths are 36, 42, and 48 in. Prior to planting, it is highly desirable to obtain a soil analysis to determine levels of nutrients and presence or absence of nematodes. In many situations, it is also desirable to fumigate or sterilize the soil prior to planting to assure freedom from diseases, weeds, and other pests.

Liner beds are areas of the nursery where young plants are grown under intensive culture for a period of 1–2 years prior to planting, either in the field or in containers. The liner beds may be open fields exposed to the elements, or they may be protected by shade houses (Fig. 5–2). Shade houses are utilized to temper the climate to produce better-quality plants for transplanting.

Plantings in the liner area are either in beds or in long, narrowly spaced rows. The spacing between the rows is determined primarily by the equipment utilized to plant, care for, and dig the plants. Spacings of 3, 4, 5, and 6 in. between rows are common. The actual spacing in the rows is determined by species, growth rate, and desired size of the transplants. Where beds are utilized, the width is adjusted to accommodate the equipment, but a 3½- or 4-ft bed with 10-in. pathways is common (Fig. 5–3). A 100-ft liner bed, 42 in. wide, planted to eight 5-in. rows with plants 4 in. in the row would support a population of 2520 plants. If the offset system of planting is utilized, that is, four rows are mechanically planted at a time followed by

Figure 5–2   Young evergreens planted in liner beds, protected by a shade house. (Courtesy Zelenka Nurseries.)

four additional rows interplanted between the others, the width of the pathway may have to be increased by one row width to accommodate the offset of the equipment.

Prior to planting of liner areas, the land must be properly prepared, including plowing, disking, leveling, sterilizing, or preplant weed control and subsoiling if necessary. The soil should be prepared to a depth of at least 6 in., although deeper preparation is needed for tap-rooted species. Moisture is critical to producing optimum growth in this intensive production area. Therefore, a readily available source of good quality water is an essential factor in the proper management of the area.

Field-production areas of large nurseries may consist of one or more farms designated by name. Each farm is subdivided into blocks and rows. For ease of management, some form of designation is assigned, generally letters for the blocks and numbers for the rows. Two standard systems are used for labeling plant material

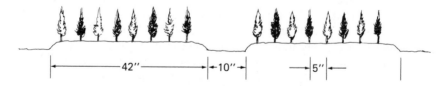

Figure 5–3   Liner beds 52 in. on centers.

within production nurseries. In propagation beds, small field-production areas, and in container-production nurseries, the most common method of labeling is from left to right and from front to rear (Fig. 5–4). In large field-production nurseries, especially when planting is done mechanically, the labeling system conforms to the direction in which the rows were planted (Fig. 5–5).

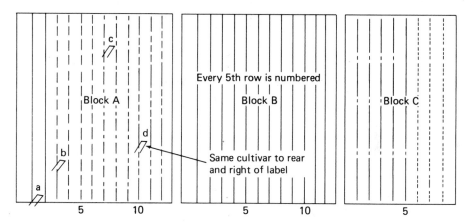

Figure 5–4   Designation of blocks and rows in a field-production nursery.

PLANTING DESIGNS

The organization or design of nursery production areas varies from area to area of the country and from nursery to nursery. The primary designs are the row, square, offset square, rectangle, equilateral triangle, interplanting, or a combination of two or more systems. The determining factor in organizing production areas should be production efficiency. When land is expensive, intensive cropping systems may be warranted. When land is relatively inexpensive, the use of wider spacing may be justified. However, a balance is desirable, particularly with the use of large equipment currently employed in planting, maintaining, and harvesting nursery stock.

The *row* is the oldest and simplest method of planting nursery stock on level terrain. However, on hilly, well-drained sites, the straight row can still be used, whereas on hilly, poorly drained sites, the row is modified to follow the contour. The row is used primarily in the production of bare-root plants such as herbaceous perennials, roses, shrubs, and small-diameter trees. The spacing between rows is determined by the width of equipment used in planting, maintaining, and harvesting the crops. The standard width between nursery rows in many field-production nurseries is 42 in., but this is modified to fit production methods. Long nursery rows can be planted, cultivated, and harvested much more efficiently than a series of short rows, since less time is spent in turning around at the end of the rows.

The *square design* (Fig. 5–6) is commonly used for the field production of B&B material such as large trees and specimen evergreens. It is also used exten-

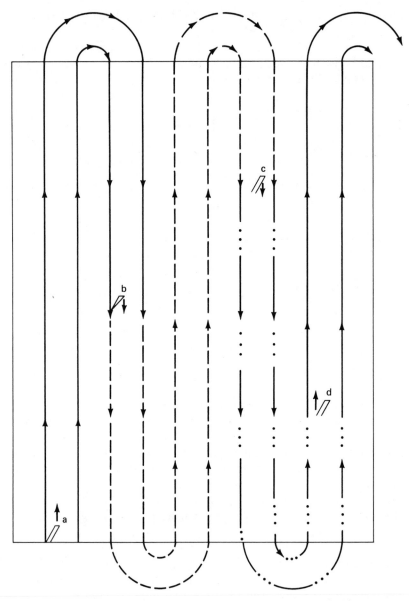

Figure 5–5 Labeling of nursery rows, conforming to the direction in which the rows were planted in large field-production nurseries using multirow planting machines.

sively in the placement of containers within the beds of container-production nurseries. It allows for cross cultivation in the maintenance of field-production nurseries and lends itself to harvesting on the diagonal (Fig. 5–7) for thinning of the field block or container bed when harvesting a crop of small plants for early market. The spacing between plants following harvesting is the diagonal of the former square.

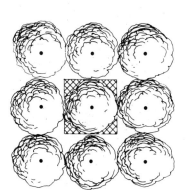

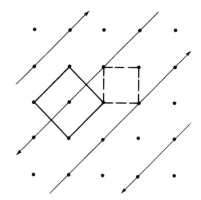

Figure 5–6 Square design.

Figure 5–7 Digging on the diagonal.

This can be calculated by use of the Pythagorean theorem: $c = \sqrt{a^2 + b^2}$. The square design is used where land costs are relatively low because it efficiently utilizes only 78% of the land, but this disadvantage is partially compensated for by its advantages.

The *offset square* is used in some nurseries. This is where the plants in even-numbered rows are offset between the plants in the odd-numbered rows. However, this system gains little advantage over the square, since the distance between plants in the row remains the same. It also sacrifices the advantages of cross cultivation and harvesting on the diagonal. It is used, sometimes, when planning a marketing program, incorporating three times of harvest. When this is done, every other row is dug, followed a year later by every other plant in the remaining row, and finally the widely spaced plants are harvested.

In the *rectangular design* (Fig. 5–8), the distance between rows is greater than the distance in the row. It is the least efficient in space utilization (less than 78%), but it is employed where land is relatively inexpensive or where larger mechanical equipment is utilized in maintaining and harvesting operations.

A modification of the rectangular design is the *rectangle-square system* (Fig. 5–9). It is used to decrease loss of space but still allows for the movement of large digging equipment between every two double rows. Another modification is the *interplanting system* (Fig. 5–10), employed where wide spacing is used for a long-

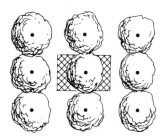

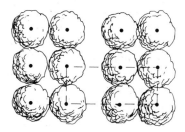

Figure 5–8 Rectangle design.

Figure 5–9 Rectangle-square design.

Figure 5–10 Interplanting design.

term crop. In this system, a short-term crop is interplanted to gain a quick cash return. However, it has the disadvantage of different cultural requirements, and if not properly cared for and harvested on time it can lead to problems in management. In some situations the interplanted short-term crop could be a quick cash crop (e.g., vegetables). It is desirable to integrate the cultural programs for the two crops prior to planting to assure compatibility.

A variation of the interplanting system that is used in the production of field-grown shade trees requiring large-sized digging equipment for harvest is to plant two rows of rapidly maturing plants between every two, three, or four rows of shade trees. The open alley, produced by early harvest of the interplant crop, allows easy access of the heavy digging machines for harvesting of the large shade trees.

The *equilateral triangle-hexagon design* (Fig. 5–11) should be used when it is desired to maximize the utilization of space (Table 5–1). It is most commonly used in container-production nurseries where land is expensive and maximum production per unit area is desired, but it can also be used in field-production areas where land is expensive. In this design 91% of the space is utilized when the plants reach their maximum size. The rows are offset from the square but the between-the-row distance is 15% less than the spacing between plants in the row. However, plants in the ground cannot be cross-cultivated and harvesting time is critical.

A space-efficient design for shade trees, which permits easy access of equipment into the blocks, is to plant the trees in four- or five-row units, utilizing the equilateral triangle design, with a wide alley between each unit. This is for access of the large equipment used in maintenance and harvesting. The alley can be seeded to a sod to allow equipment to function during periods when the soil is wet. The area in plants can either be clean-cultivated or sod strips can be established between the rows with clean cultivation in the rows. Herbicides can be used to aid in maintaining the planted areas in a weed-free condition (Fig. 5–12).

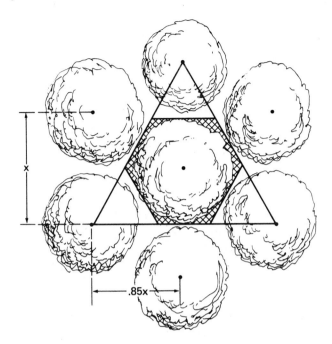

Figure 5–11 Equilateral triangle-hexagon design.

Economic and Cultural Considerations

The physical organization of the plantings within a nursery will vary with the situation, but the following economic and cultural factors should be considered.

1. *The efficient use of land.* The equilateral triangle produces the most efficient use of space; the square-rectangle is the least efficient.

2. *The size of plant for the market objective.* If the market objective is for small plants, the spacing can be relatively close, but if the objective is to produce large, landscape-sized plants, the spacing must be wide to accommodate the crown of the plant.

3. *The cultivar.* If the cultivar has a narrow, upright habit of growth, the spacing can be close, whereas if the cultivar is widespreading or of a weeping habit, the spacing must be wider.

4. *Equipment use in maintaining and harvesting.* When the horse and mule were used for cultivation, the spacing between rows was fairly narrow. But with modern equipment of high horsepower, it is necessary to increase the spacing between the rows to permit entry and movement of the equipment.

5. *Economic return on investment.* Although many agricultural enterprises, including container-production nurseries, measure return on investment per acre of land, it is more appropriate for a field-production nursery to evaluate a total produc-

TABLE 5-1   Plant Density for Various Spacings in the Nursery

Spacing (ft)	Square feet/Plant, $l \times w$	Area/Plant, $0.7854d^2$	Number/ 1000 ft^2	Number/Acre	Number/ Equilateral Triangle[a]
2 × 2	4	3.14	250	10,890	12,620
2 × 3	6	3.14	167	7,260	
2 × 4	8	3.14	125	5,445	
2.8 × 2.8[b]	8	6.28	125	5,445	
3 × 3	9	7.07	111	4,840	5,600
3 × 4	12	7.07	83.3	3,630	
3 × 6	18	7.07	55.5	2,420	
4.2 × 4.2[b]	18	14.14	55.5	2,420	
4 × 4	16	12.57	62.5	2,722	3,150
4 × 6	24	12.57	41.7	1,815	
4 × 8	32	12.57	31.3	1,361	
5.7 × 5.7[b]	32	25.13	31.3	1,361	
5 × 5	25	19.64	40.0	1,742	2,018
5 × 6	30	19.64	33.3	1,452	
5 × 8	40	19.64	25.0	1,089	
5 × 10	50	19.64	20.0	871	
7.1 × 7.1[b]	50	39.27	20.0	871	
6 × 6	36	28.27	27.8	1,210	1,400
6 × 8	48	28.27	20.8	907	
6 × 10	60	28.27	16.7	726	
8.5 × 8.5[b]	72	56.55	14.1	605	
8 × 8	64	50.27	15.6	680	785
11.3 × 11.3[b]	128	100.53	7.8	340	
10 × 10	100	78.54	10.0	435	500

[a]Distance between rows = 0.85 in-the-row distance.

[b]Spacing resulting from removing diagonal rows.

tion system, including land, spacing, maintenance, and harvesting to maximize return on total investment, not only on land. Land use is one input into the system, and it should be used efficiently. But materials handling is the major cost input in the production of nursery products, and if machines make labor more effective, it may be necessary to redesign the production areas to obtain the most effective materials-handling system, even though it calls for less efficient use of land.

CONTAINER-PRODUCTION AREAS

The design of container-production areas is strongly influenced by a number of factors, including irrigation and drainage, materials handling, cultural and maintenance requirements of the plants, size of the containers, and the costs involved. *Irrigation* is an absolute requirement in the development of container-production

Figure 5–12 Shade trees growing in a nursery with grass sod between the rows. Rows are treated with a selective herbicide. (Courtesy Manbeck Nursery.)

nursery areas, since plants in containers are totally dependent upon a supply of water. Container-grown plants should be grouped according to their water requirement to obtain maximum benefit from the irrigation system (Chapter 13).

Drainage is the companion factor to irrigation and must be considered in the development of the container area, since large volumes of water are applied to the plants throughout the growing season, and much of this water falls outside the containers or drains through them. It is necessary to remove this excess water from the area to assure drainage of the media within the containers, and to carry on various plant maintenance and materials-handling operations. If the site is not well drained, it will have to be graded and a drainage system developed. Excess water should not be drained back into a pond used for irrigation of nursery stock, since it may be high in soluble salts or contaminated with weed seeds, herbicides, or spores of various fungi, any of which have the potential of causing plant production problems. In most situations excess water is disposed of via county or municipal drainage facilities. However, in recent years, some communities have enacted ordinances prohibiting the disposal of water contaminated with excess soluble salts into these facilities.

This necessitates developing other means to dispose of the excess water. Two alternatives are to construct holding ponds or to install "French" drains at various sites within the area if the soil profile permits. The water collected in the holding ponds might possibly be reused within the nursery if it is of acceptable quality. However, in most situations it is either used to irrigate agronomic crops or is allowed to evaporate into the air. If the water can be reused, the ponds should be constructed fairly deep with a relatively small surface area, whereas if the water cannot be reused, the ponds should be constructed fairly shallow with a large surface area. French drains are simply deep holes or trenches dug through low-porosity topsoils into high-porosity subsoils. The trenches are then filled with rocks or crushed gravel. These drains allow the excess water to percolate into the soil and recharge the underground water supply. The area about the beds is graded to channel the water to the drains.

Materials handling is probably the most significant factor in the development of the area. Plans need to be developed and the area designed to expedite the efficient handling of materials through the various phases of production, including media preparation, potting, setting out of containers, pickup of containers for shipping or rearrangement for overwintering, and loading for shipping. A well-planned design should provide for a logical rotation of crops through the production cycles so that double handling of the containers is kept to a minimum. The design of the area must also provide for the space needs of machines, especially transport equipment, used in the operation of the nursery.

The cultural and maintenance requirements of the plants will also influence the design of the container area. Plants that have special requirements are best grown together in areas where their special needs can be met most efficiently. Also, plant maintenance requirements such as fertilizing, pest control, pruning and training, and spreading for growth increase, must be provided for, although in some situations the planted containers are spaced when set out to meet their spacial needs throughout the production cycle. This is done to minimize handling, but it sacrifices water efficiency if the plants are watered by an overhead means.

In areas of the country where it is necessary to provide winter protection for container-grown plants, overwintering structures (see Chapter 17) must be planned for in the development and organization of the site. When such facilities are to be constructed, they should be designed and located so that plant material can be moved into and out of the facility with efficiency. Also, the structure must be oriented and built in a manner to withstand the force of wind in areas where winds are a problem.

Size of containers is another parameter that affects the overall design of the container area. Containers are best grouped by size to aid in providing for the water requirements, ease of handling, and maintenance. The various areas might include small (1 and 3 gal), medium-sized (5, 7, 15 gal), and large (20 gal or larger) containers. Within each area the containers can be subgrouped into beds by species. The size and arrangement of the beds is influenced by the growth habits of the plants, the rotation program, and the size and physical limitations of the area.

For maximum utilization of space within the beds, containers are set touching one another in offset rows. As the plants grow and require additional space, the containers are spaced and rearranged, commonly utilizing the equilateral triangle-hexagon design. In some situations, the interplanting (understory) design is utilized. In this design shade-tolerant species are grown under the canopy of taller-growing plants. Where space is not a factor or where either physical requirements of the plants or the physiography of the area impose limitations, other designs are utilized.

The cost of developing container-production areas should be carefully researched prior to construction. This includes the raw materials for plant production (e.g., ingredients for the medium, water, fertilizers, containers, etc.); the cost of land leveling, irrigation, drainage, and so on; and the costs of operating the facility. In some situations the initial cost of development could be a limiting factor in effecting a successful cash flow except at low interest rates (see Chapter 7), whereas in other situations the development or expansion of a container production facility may be a desirable capital investment for nurseries that are expanding, especially when reinvesting income derived from previous crops.

PRODUCTION PROGRAMMING

It is extremely difficult to efficiently produce a wide range of plant material. Growing a wide variety of species, each requiring its special method of propagation and field culture, does not lend itself to production efficiency. In order to gain a greater degree of management control over production, it may be desirable to specialize either by type of plant or by method of production. Limiting production to plant groups that have similar production requirements and are compatible with production capabilities is one means of gaining production efficiency. Also, with increased mechanization of routine production operations there is greater need for standardization of techniques. Specialization and standardization permit managers to plan and control production, thus ensuring a greater chance of success in the business. But nursery managers must be careful not to become too specialized, since monoculture is very vulnerable to disaster should there be a major change in weather conditions, plant pests, or market demand. It is seldom desirable that one genus or one class of plant material make up more than 20–25% of the total production effort.

Production programming must begin with a market analysis to determine if there is a market for the product, the potential demand, in what size and form, and how many plants per year would meet the production goal. Information must be obtained on production requirements related to propagation, soil and water requirements, general culture in the nursery, and pest problems. An estimate must be made of the resources that will be needed, the production efficiency or mortality that can be expected, and the costs involved. The production requirements are summarized, in part, in Fig. 5–13.

Up-to-date technical information should be collected and summarized so that

Species _____   Size class _____

Sales or market   Previous sales _____
  information
                                          Projected sales
_____   Garden center _____
_____   Wholesaler   _____
_____   Landscape   _____
_____   Other   _____
Technical data   Projection for planning _____
_____
Propagation: method and times _____
_____
Soil and water _____
_____
Plant requirements _____
_____
Pests _____
_____
_____
Expected growth performance _____
_____
_____
Additional data _____
_____

Resources needed
_____

Space:
  Propagation bench space_____ sq.ft
  Liner beds   _____ sq.ft
  Fields   _____ acres

Materials:
  Fertilizer _____
  Pesticides _____
  Other   _____

Labor inputs _____
_____

Estimated losses:
  Through replacements _____
  Through grade-out   _____
  In-the-field   _____
  In liner beds   _____
  In propagation   _____

Equipment needs _____
_____
_____
_____

Cost estimates _____
_____
_____

Notes _____
_____
_____
_____

Figure 5–13 Nursery production information.

the manager, propagator, and grower will have available, in abstract form, the details needed for planning the best production system and timing of operations. This information should be updated periodically with practical, relevant experience data as they are accumulated within the production nursery. (See Chapter 16 for details on production programs.)

ESTIMATING PLANT MATERIAL REQUIREMENTS

Once a production quota has been established for the end product, it becomes necessary to calculate the quantity of cuttings to be stuck, grafts to be made, or seeds to be sown in order to produce the transplants and ultimately the liners that will either be field-planted or planted in containers in order to meet production quotas. In each step of the operation there is a mortality that can be expected plus a loss of material at grade-out for some classes of plant material, and a factor for replacements. These data may be available from past records or an estimate can be made based on information obtained from other sources.

Estimates for subsystem quotas are obtained by working backward from the estimated production or sales figure. The calculation is made for each step in the production cycle by dividing the production quota of that phase of production by its estimated return percentage (Table 5–2). This is obtained by subtracting the percent mortality from 100%. For example, if 10,000 is the production goal, 10,000 represents 100%; if replacements are 5%, 10,530 plants must be produced to meet sales plus replacements ($10,000 \div 0.95 = 10,530$). Combining percentage loss figures to calculate the material needed to start the production cycle results in a figure less than what is actually needed.

TABLE 5-2   Estimate of Plant Material Requirements

Species:	Taxus 'Hicksi'
Class:	B&B 3–4 ft
Rotations:	Field 5–1; linear 2–1
Propagation:	Evergreen cuttings, Dec.–Apr.

Estimated Goal for:	Plants
Sales objective	10,000
Replacements 5%[a]	
First revision	10,530
Grade-out (if applicable)	
(not applicable with B&B material)	
Field mortality 15%	
Second revision (liners needed)	12,400
Liner loss 10%	
Third revision (transplants needed)	13,770
Propagation loss 25%	
Fourth revision (cuttings to stick)	18,350

[a]Percentages must be obtained from past experience. These are for demonstrative purposes only.

ESTIMATING SPACE REQUIREMENTS

Space requirements can be estimated for propagation, liner production, and either field or container production. When a perpetual production system is designed, it is necessary to know the rotation system that will be employed in addition to the planting densities that will be used in the field- or container-production areas, the liner area, and the propagation bench. This information can then be used in planning for and adjusting the space needs for the total operation.

Using this information, the various department heads (propagation, field, container, storage, shipping, etc.) can plan and program their space, labor, and material requirements. For example, the propagator can assemble all the production programs for the current season and plan his or her material, space, and labor requirements.

TABLE 5-3   Propagation Space Needs and Allocation Chart

Group	Priority	Space Needed (ft²)	Weeks	Adjusted Square Feet	Weeks
A	2	500	45–5	—	—
B	3	1000	40–5	B_1: 500	40–5
				B_2: 500	5–17+
C	2	500	5–15	500	10–20+
D	1	1500	42–10	—	—

After the individual species to be propagated have been classified by method of propagation and a priority index assigned (Table 5–3), the space and time requirements can be estimated and adjusted to fit the limitations imposed by the available bench space (Fig. 5–14). In the example here, group D has priority 1 and is plotted first, followed by groups A and C. Group C must be delayed by 5 weeks due to space limitations, but group A is programmed according to schedule. Group B, with priority 3, is split into two groups, B_1 stuck on time and B_2 delayed until week

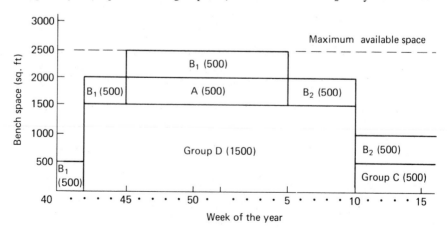

Figure 5–14   Propagation space availability diagram.

5; the cuttings can be held in storage until space is available. Similar estimates can be made by other department heads, who coordinate their activities with each other under the overall control of the production manager

PRODUCTION LAND UTILIZATION

Field-Grown Crops

Land used in the production of field-grown stock is generally occupied for several years. In addition, the land may be out of production, either lying fallow or in a cover crop, for a period of time that will vary from a few months to a number of years prior to replanting. One salable acre of nursery crops will require a number of non-salable acres to support the program. Table 5–4 lists estimated acreage requirements for selected classes of field-grown nursery stock.

Management practices will vary with type of nursery and production objective. Therefore, the estimated acreage requirements should be used only as a guide where individual data are not available. Another land requirement that must be added to these figures is the land needed for turnaround and service areas. It is estimated that these requirements may vary between 5 and 10% of the production requirement.

Container-Grown Crops

Land used in the production of container-grown crops is occupied for only a few months for crops with a rapid production cycle, up to 1–2 years for species with longer production cycles. This is one of the major advantages for container production—shorter rotation time—leading to faster turnover of invested capital. The actual space requirement varies with the market objective, the climate, various cultural practices, and spatial arrangements.

If the market objective is to produce small plants in small containers on a

TABLE 5-4 Estimated Acreage Requirements for Field-Grown Nursery Stock

Class[a]	Average Age at Sale	Years in Rotation	Land Required per Acre of Annual Sale
Broad-leaved evergreens	3.5	0.8	4.3
Range	2.6–4.5	0.5–1.4	3.5–5.0
Narrow-leaved evergreens	3.5	0.9	4.4
Range	2.4–5.3	0.5–1.3	3.3–5.8
Deciduous shrubs	2.7	1.3	4.0
Range	1.8–4.4	0.5–3.2	2.4–5.8
Ornamental trees	4.4	0.7	5.1
Range	2.1–8.2	0.2–1.9	3.3–8.8

[a]Range = shortest to longest period reported.

Source: Data from *South. Coop. Ser. Bull.* 143 (1969).

rapid rotation, 1 acre of land may produce two to three crops per year, so that only 0.5 or 0.33 acre of space is required per area of annual sales. However, for large plants on a 2-year rotation, it may take as much as 2 acres of land or as little as 1.5 acres per acre of annual sale. Climate and various cultural operations will influence growth rates, which will affect turnover rates. Nurseries located in southern latitudes have longer growing seasons and are capable of producing crops in a shorter period than nurseries located in northern climates. Also, plants that are produced under optimum cultural conditions of light, nutrition, moisture, and pest control can be produced on a shorter production cycle, which will reduce the time that each container-grown plant occupies space in the nursery. Finally, the space needs will be influenced by the spatial arrangement of the containers through the production cycle.

Container-production nurseries that are operated on a profit basis must be cognizant of utilizing space efficiently and minimizing rotation time when planning the development of a production system. By careful planning, many container-production nurseries can increase their production efficiency on both an acre basis and on invested capital.

SUMMARY

The organization and development of the land areas within a nursery should be carefully planned prior to development. The best sites should be reserved for plant production. Each unit should be located and developed to produce optimum growth of plants and to maintain their quality following harvest but still permit efficient use of labor in each phase of the production, maintenance, and marketing effort. The time spent in carefully planning the layout and development of the nursery site is well worth the effort in the efficiency that can be gained in the use of the other factors of production.

REFERENCES

DAMBACH, C. A. 1948. A study of the ecology and economic value of crop field borders. Graduate School Stud. Ohio State Univ. Bio. Sci. Ser. 2.

GILFORD, J. C. 1974. Some thoughts on production planning. Proceedings of the 9th Refresher Course for Nurserymen, Pershore College of Horticulture, Pershore, England, pp. 34–43.

STOECKELER, J. H. 1957. Forest nursery practice in the lake states. USDA Agric. Hand. 110.

WIANT, H. V., JR. 1973. Efficiency of regular spacing planting designs. Tree Planters Notes 24(3), p. 31.

6 Laws, Regulations, and Codes

The nursery industry, like other major industries, must comply with certain laws and regulations. The laws and regulations are promulgated by government primarily for the protection of people. Federal laws and regulations, other than tax laws, that are of concern to the nursery industry include (1) Federal Social Security and Unemployment Compensation, (2) Fair Labor Standards Act of 1938 as amended, (3) Occupational Safety and Health Act of 1970, (4) Migrant and Seasonal Agricultural Worker Protection Act of 1983, (5) Plant Pest Acts and Quarantines, (6) Federal Environmental Pesticide Control Act of 1972, (7) Federal Warranty Act of 1975, (8) Federal Price and Services Act of 1936, (9) Plant Patent Act of 1930 as amended, (10) workers' compensation, and (11) Trade Practice Rules for the Nursery Industry. In addition, various state and local units of government have laws that affect the nursery industry.

FEDERAL LAWS AND REGULATIONS

The following is a synopsis of federal laws and regulations as they affect the nursery industry. For specific details and up-to-date information on these laws and regulations, since they are amended periodically, the nursery manager should contact the American Association of Nurserymen or a lawyer. The AAN is in a position to provide member firms with useful information on all federal regulations and legal decisions relative to the nursery industry.

The 1935 *Federal Social Security Act* provided for federal-state cooperation in an old age assistance and unemployment insurance program. The Old Age and Survivors Insurance (OASI) program is designed to provide an income in the worker's old age and to assure some income for dependents after his or her death. The cost of the program is borne by both employers and employees. Every employer who employs one or more persons is liable for this tax. Employers pay a tax on each employee's wages up to a base amount (which changes with time). The employee pays a similar tax. However, the employee's share of the tax is deducted by the employer at the close of each pay period and forwarded to the Director of Internal Revenue. As of January 1, 1986, the wage base was $42,000 and the tax rate was 7.15%, paid equally by employer and employee. Current information on OASI and the necessary forms are available from the district director of the Internal Revenue Service.

Federal Unemployment Compensation became effective for agricultural workers January 1, 1978. Under the federal law the tax, paid by the employer, is 6.2% of the first $7000 of wages (percentage and base change with time). If employees are covered by a state unemployment compensation law, the employer receives a credit against the federal tax. Since the wage base and tax percentage vary with the individual states, it is suggested that nurserymen contact their state unemployment compensation agency for specific data. Most states impose substantial penalties for late payment or failure to pay unemployment compensation taxes.

The *Fair Labor Standards Act* of 1938 (referred to as the Federal Wage-Hour Law) established 25 cents as the minimum pay for 1 hr of labor. But the law was limited to firms engaged in interstate commerce, and agriculture was exempted from coverage under the law. Over the years minimum pay has increased and coverage has been extended with fewer exemptions. As of January 1977, the only agricultural exemption was for an employer who used less than 500 worker-days of agricultural labor during the preceding calendar year. Also, overtime (not less than 1.5 times the employee's regular rate) must be paid for hours worked in any week in excess of 40.

For many years agriculture had a seasonal exemption, but as of January 1977 there was no seasonal exemption. Within a nursery organization, the only personnel exempt from the minimum pay and overtime requirements are executive, administrative, or professional employees, each of whom must meet the test for exemptions as required by the latest regulations.

Nurserymen must comply with the Federal Wage-Hour Law's equal-pay provisions. The law requires equal pay, regardless of sex, for equal work on jobs that require equal skill, effort, and responsibility, and are performed under similar conditions. Exceptions to the law are payments made because of a seniority system, a merit system, a system that measures earnings by quantity or quality of production, or a differential based on any factor other than sex.

Employers found in violation of the law can be required to pay the difference in back wages for 2 years as well as increase the pay of the employee(s) who had been paid the lesser amount. An employer cannot reduce the wage of other employees in order to come into compliance with the act.

Time and payroll records must be maintained for 3 years. The records must show daily and weekly hours worked by all nonexempt employees. Also, the records must show overtime payments separately from straight-time payment, total earnings, deductions, and net pay.

The latest amendment to the law also contains a number of new provisions and penalties to the child labor portion. The law prohibits the use of oppressive child labor in interstate commerce or in the production of goods for interstate commerce. The law limits the use of child labor by age group and type of activity.

Individuals 18 years of age or older may be employed in any occupation without regard to the time of day or the number of hours worked. But minors under 18 years of age may not be employed in occupations declared to be hazardous by the Secretary of Labor. Examples of hazardous occupations within the nursery industry are operation of a tractor of over 20 PTO horsepower; operation of power-driven posthole digger or driver; operating or assisting in operation of trencher, earth-moving machine, forklift, power-driven saws; driving a vehicle transporting passengers; working on a ladder or scaffold of over 20 feet; and handling or applying agricultural chemicals classified under the Federal Insecticide, Fungicide or Rodenticide Act as category I and category II.

Minors under 16 years of age may be employed in agricultural occupations, except those which have been declared to be hazardous. But their employment is not permitted during school hours. All minors must be paid minimum wage unless certificates are obtained for the employment of full-time students at 85% of the minimum.

Employers must maintain records on the employment of all individuals under 19 years of age. Such individuals should be required to furnish either an age or employment certificate (obtained from local school authorities) or a copy of their birth certificate as proof of age.

The Williams-Steiger *Occupational Safety and Health Act* (OSHA) of 1970 was enacted by Congress "to assure so far as possible, every working man and woman in the nation safe and healthful working conditions and to preserve our human resources." This act covers all employers with 11 or more employees.

The general duty clause of the act states: "Each employer (1) shall furnish to each of his employees a place of employment free from recognized hazards that are causing or are likely to cause death or serious physical harm to his employees; (2) shall comply with the occupational safety and health standards promulgated under this act." However, the act also places some responsibility on employees. The general duty clause also states: "Each employee shall comply with occupational safety and health standards and all rules, regulations and orders issued pursuant to this Act which are applicable to his own actions and conduct."

Landscape contractors are subject to the general construction safety and health standards, which include first-aid services, provisions for medical care and consultants, wearing of hard hats, eye and face protection, and so on.

If growing horticultural commodities is the primary activity of the establishment, it is considered agriculture; thus most safety and health standards do not apply. However, the general-duty clause is applicable to employees of the establishment. Nurserymen should obtain a copy of subpart J, Regulations 1910.141 through 1910.148, for regulations and standards that apply to nurseries.

As of September 1976, five federal standards apply to nurseries, including SMV emblem, housing in labor camps, anhydrous ammonia, tractor-rollover protection, and PTO guards. The SMV (slow-moving vehicle) emblem must be displayed on all slow-moving equipment operating on public roads. The emblem must be kept clean and be replaced when faded.

Nurserymen who operate labor camps must obtain a license, generally from the department of health in the state where the camp is located. Requirements for licensing are based on a 1968 U.S. Department of Labor standard on housing agricultural workers. The standard covers environmental aspects of temporary housing for employees, such as building construction, sanitation, water, refuse disposal, and so on.

The anhydrous ammonia standard requires that equipment used in applying anhydrous ammonia meet certain standards. Nurserymen should ask suppliers to certify in writing that their equipment meets OSHA standards.

The rollover protection standards as published by OSHA require that all tractors of more than 20 engine horsepower manufactured after October 25, 1976, must be equipped with rollover protective structures and a seat belt. Employers must instruct employees on operation practices and ensure the use of seat belts when operating tractors with rollover protective structures.

Safety standards on guarding of farm equipment, effective October 25, 1976, require power-takeoff (PTO) drives to be guarded. Also, signs must be placed at prominent locations on tractors and PTO-driven equipment specifying that PTO safety shields must be kept in place.

Record-keeping requirements are very specific. They are contained in the booklet entitled ''Record Keeping Requirements Under the Williams-Steiger Occupational Safety and Health Act of 1970.'' Every nurseryman should obtain a copy from a district office of the U.S. Department of Labor. Employers who violate the law can be assessed costly penalties.

OSHA provides that states may develop their own safety and health laws and assume most of the enforcement processes. But the state program must be at least as effective as the federal program. Most states have developed and are enforcing programs in safety and health.

To assure compliance with this far-reaching piece of legislation, nursery managers may wish to organize an OSHA committee within the nursery. The committee, chaired by a key employee, should be responsible for advising the manager on matters pertaining to safety and health, keeping informed on all state and federal requirements, and seeing that nursery employees comply with all applicable standards.

The Migrant and Seasonal Agricultural Worker Protection Act of 1983 (MSAWPA) replaced the Farm Labor Contractors Registration Act (FLCRA) of 1964. The purpose of this act is to remove the restraints on commerce caused by activities detrimental to migrant and seasonal agricultural workers; to require farm labor contractors to register under this act; and to assure necessary protection for migrant and seasonal workers, agricultural associations, and agricultural employers. MSAWPA eliminated the requirement for nurserymen, or their employees, who employ migrant and seasonal agricultural workers to register as farm labor contractors and to be fingerprinted. Totally exempt from any aspects of the act are employers hiring less than 500 man-days of labor in any calendar quarter in previous year. Also exempt are those who hire or transport workers within a 25-mile radius of their permanent residence and for not more than 13 weeks a year. Family businesses owned or operated by members of same immediate family are exempt provided that a member of same family does recruiting. Nurserymen hiring migrant and seasonal agricultural workers, beyond the exempted states, must do so through a registered farm labor contractor. It is the contractor's responsibility to arrange all the details of employment and to assure compliance with MSAWPA.

The *Plant Pest Act of 1912* and the *Plant Pest Act of 1957* are the basic laws of plant quarantines in the United States. Prior to 1912, there were no laws protecting the United States from the entry of foreign pests or to prevent and control their distribution within the country. The 1912 Act, as amended by Congress, gave authority to the Secretary of Agriculture to regulate by quarantine the importation and interstate movement of nursery stock, other plants, and plant products that may be vectors of foreign plant pests.

There are three levels of quarantine that affect nurserymen, depending upon their sources of materials and the geographic distribution of their products:

1. *Foreign quarantines* affect the movement of plants and plant products between nations. But in general, few nurserymen are concerned with foreign quarantines, except as they affect shipments to and from Canada and Mexico. Nurserymen wishing to import or export plants or plant products should obtain a copy of "Foreign Quarantine Notices," Title 7, Chapter III, Part 319, from the Animal and Plant Health Inspection Service (APHIS), USDA, and obtain a special permit, which can be obtained in most states through the state department of agriculture or from APHIS. There are some plants and plant products that cannot be imported into the United States from certain foreign countries. Details are contained in "Foreign Quarantine Notices," which is updated periodically.

Canadian quarantine regulations limit shipping of all clonally produced fruit trees and ornamental stock of the genera *Malus, Prunus, Cydonia, Chaenomelles,* and *Vitis* to Canadian nurseries holding valid permits to import this type of plant material. Details of the regulation are available from the AAN. In addition, nonfood nursery stock must be certified Japanese beetle free for export to Canada after the following treatment: B&B, containerized, and potted nonfood plants are dipped in a dip solution containing 32 oz (2 lb) of chlorpyrifos (active ingredient) per 100 gal of water. The plants are to remain in the dip solution until bubbling ceases. Upon removal from the dip solution, plants must be allowed to drain until the soil is reasonably dry, but not less than 3 days. Plants held for more than 3 days must be protected from reinfestation. (Chlorpyrifos is produced by Dow Chemical Co. as Dursban 4E.)

2. *Interstate quarantines* are of major concern to nurserymen engaged in interstate shipment of plants. These may be federal or state quarantines. The general

policy in the enforcement of interstate quarantines is to permit unrestricted movement of all plant products within the regulated area and to restrict shipments beyond the quarantined area to uninfested products and plants. Examples of domestic quarantines include golden nematode, Mexican fruit fly, citrus blackfly, pink bollworm, imported fire ant, witchweed, and schleroderris canker. A number of states impose exterior quarantine requirements on nursery plants moving in interstate commerce. Nurserymen in states where Japanese beetles are known to exist must have their production land treated so that the plants can be certified as free of Japanese beetles when they are shipped into states imposing the quarantine. Copies of federal regulations may be obtained by writing: Plant Protection and Quarantine Program, APHIS, USDA, Federal Building No. 1, Hyattsville, MD 20782.

3. *Intrastate quarantines* or regulations are authorized by state legislation and are imposed and administered by the state agency in charge of plant pest regulation, generally a part of the state's department of agriculture. These regulations are designed to prevent the spread of specific pests within the state and as a means of preventing other states or the USDA from restricting the movement of plants and plant products from the entire state rather than from just the infested portion of the state.

A quarantined area is usually a civil boundary such as national, state, or county. In order to move regulated products out of a quarantined or restricted area, they must be inspected or subjected to some pest-destroying treatment and carry a certificate assuring their freedom from the pest upon which the quarantine is placed. All states have laws pertaining to the inspection and movement of nursery stock. Nurserymen should be familiar with these laws and comply accordingly. The AAN publishes a quarantine wall chart and maps of quarantine areas. All nurserymen shipping nursery stock interstate should have up-to-date copies of the chart and the selected maps to post in the shipping area of the nursery. But nurserymen should invite inspection, since the plant inspector can help identify plant pests and suggest control measures before they become serious problems.

A state license is required in all states of persons, partnerships, or corporations growing and/or desiring to sell nursery stock. The license is obtained from the director of agriculture, but in some states it may be available from the secretary of state. Also, all nursery stock must be inspected and found free of serious pests before it may be sold or moved from place to place. Nurserymen are required to make application for inspection and are often assessed a fee, usually on the acreage of salable stock. Nurserymen must comply with all federal and state quarantines, rules, and regulations.

Nurserymen shipping nursery stock out of state have been required to file a nursery inspection certificate with the state department of agriculture in the various states into which stock was shipped. However, since 1974 many states have accepted a current list of certified nurseries and nursery stock dealers in lieu of the individual certificates. This change was recommended and adopted by the National Plant Board in 1974. An up-to-date list of states accepting the list in lieu of certificates is generally available through the Department of Agriculture, Plant Industry Division, within each state.

The *Federal Environmental Pesticide Control Act* (FEPCA) of 1972 (amendments to Federal Insecticide, Fungicide and Rodenticide Act [FIFRA]) were enacted to protect people and the environment from the hazards of dangerous pesticides. The act classifies pesticides and pesticide applicators, and it limits the application of pesticides according to the applicator's training and certification. The act is administered by the Environmental Protection Agency (EPA).

Pesticides are classified into two categories: general use and restricted use. General-use pesticides are those which when applied in accordance with directions for use will not generally cause unreasonable adverse effects on the environment. Restricted-use pesticides are those which when applied in accordance with directions for use may cause unreasonable adverse effects on the environment, including injury to the applicator. The misuse of pesticides, including use, that is "inconsistent with label directions" is in violation of FIFRA and is subject to a fine.

The EPA is responsible for classifying and updating the classification of pesticides. Anyone can purchase and apply general-use pesticides, but since October 1977, only certified pesticide applicators can purchase and use restricted-use pesticides. The law requires that individuals who use or supervise the use of restricted-use pesticides be certified either as a private applicator or as a commercial applicator. They must keep a record of all restricted-use materials used for 3 years.

A private applicator is a person who uses or supervises the use of restricted-use pesticides for the purpose of producing an agricultural commodity on property owned or rented by the applicator or his or her employer, or on the property of another person if applied without compensation (other than trading of personal services between producers of agricultural commodities).

A commercial applicator is a person who uses or supervises the use of any pesticide that is classified for restricted use for any purpose or on any property other than as provided for by the private applicator classification.

To be certified, a person must be determined to be competent with respect to the use and handling of pesticides. States can develop their own programs for training and certifying applicators, subject to the approval of the federal EPA administrator. In most states, the state department of agriculture administers the certification and licensing of pesticide applicators. Two pesticide applicator manuals are available from the Superintendent of Documents, U.S. Government Printing Office, Washington, DC 20402: "A Guide for Private Applicators" for those applying pesticides only on their own or rented crop land, and "A Guide for Commercial Applicators" for those applying pesticides on other people's property for hire. The manuals are helpful to those who wish to become certified as pesticide applicators. For up-to-date details on classification of pesticides, procedures for certification, liabilities, and so on, nurserymen should contact their state department of agriculture or the agriculture agents of their local county Cooperative Extension Service.

The Magnuson-Moss *Warranties Act* of 1975 supplements the Uniform Commercial Code (UCC) in force in all states except Louisiana. The act requires that written warranties on all "consumer products" manufactured after July 4, 1975, and costing more than $10 must be designated either "limited" or "full" and that the warranty designation must be made clearly and conspicuously. A "consumer product" is "any tangible personal property, including nursery products, which is to be distributed in commerce and which is normally used for personal, family or household purposes."

The act, administered by the Federal Trade Commission (FTC), does not require the seller to grant warranties, but if a warrant is offered, the law is applicable. To qualify as a "full warrant" under the act, the seller (nurseryman) must warrant that he will remedy (repair, replace, or refund) without charge in a reasonable time in the event of a defect or failure of the product. A full warrant includes the cost of replanting if the plant was planted by the nurseryman. However, a nurseryman is not under obligation to fulfill a warrant if it can be shown that the plant died or was damaged as a result of storms, animals, or by the warrantee's (customer) failure to provide reasonable and necessary maintenance. Nurserymen not wishing to be obligated by the full-warranty requirements may grant a "limited warranty," in which they state the limitations of the warrant.

The FTC, through the publication of regulations, will clarify and particularize the seller's obligations under the act. The act does not regulate state laws related to contracts which also govern laws of warranty. Therefore, nurserymen offering written warranties may wish to consult an attorney familiar with the laws and regulations pertaining to warranties to ensure that their warranty complies with both state and federal laws. Current information on the latest federal regulations on warranties can be obtained by writing to one of the regional offices of the FTC or the AAN. Information on state laws can be obtained from the office of the state attorney general or from state nursery associations.

The Robinson-Patman *Price and Services Act* of 1936, an amendment to the antitrust act of 1914, prohibits a seller from discriminating between his or her business customers in price and service and prohibits a buyer from knowingly receiving illegal favors or services. The act applies to the sale of tangible goods in interstate commerce and is enforced by the FTC. In essence, the act requires that a seller treat all commercial customers equally with regard to the price of the same product and service offered. The simplest way for nurserymen to comply with the act is to sell from a price list (catalog) which is uniform for all customers competing for the product, in wholesale units.

The Towsend-Purnell *Plant Patent Act*, an amendment to the general patent law, was passed by Congress in 1930 and amended slightly in 1954. The significant portion of the statute states, "Whoever invents or discovers and asexually reproduces any distinct and new variety of plant, including cultivated sports, mutants, hybrids and newly found seedlings, other than a tuber-propagated plant or plant found in an uncultivated state, may obtain a patent, therefore. . . ." Characteristics that may distinguish a new variety (cultivar) of a plant for patent consideration include, among others, habit of growth; color of stems, leaves, flowers, or fruit; resistance to cold, drought, heat, or disease; productivity or lack of productivity of flowers or fruit; fragrance; storage qualities; and ease of asexual propagation.

The plant patent is a grant by the federal government to the inventor (or his or her heirs or assignee) the right to exclude others from asexually propagating the plant or selling the plant so reproduced for a period of 17 years from the date of issue. Application for a plant patent may be obtained from the Commissioner of Patents, Washington, D.C. 20231. Nurserymen wishing to patent a plant may wish to discuss the topic with a current holder of a plant patent and to contact an attorney or agent registered with the patent office. A copy of ''Directory of Registered Patent Attorneys and Agents'' is available from the Commissioner of Patents.

Workers' compensation insurance (WCI) must be carried by employers who hire one or more employees that work in a hazardous occupation (listed in section 3, workers' compensation law) and by all employers who employ three or more employees. If coverage is not required by law, an employer may obtain workers' compensation insurance on a voluntary basis. The insurance may be obtained from any private insurance company authorized to transact the business of workers' compensation insurance within each state.

Rates for WCI vary according to the type of employment, the hazards involved, and the personal injury history of the company. Insurance groups working through trade associations (e.g., AAN) offer special WCI savings plans. These plans are designed to provide dividends on WCI premiums, depending upon the claim experience of policyholders within the group. Nurserymen are advised to consult their state or national trade association or Dobson Insurance Group, P. O. Box 559, Kansas City, MO 64141, for details of the plan.

Trade practice rules for the nursery industry as promulgated by the FTC in 1956 and amended in 1979 as *Guides for the Nursery Industry* are designed to foster and promote the maintenance of fair competitive conditions in the interest of protecting industry, trade, and the public. In general, the rules consider it an unfair trade practice to sell, offer for sale, or distribute industry products by any method, or under any circumstance or condition, which has the capacity and tendency or effect of deceiving purchasers or prospective purchasers as to quantity, size, grade, kind, species, age, maturity, condition, vigor, hardiness, number of times transplanted, growth ability, growth characteristics, rate of growth or time required before flowering or fruiting, price, origin or place where grown, or in any other material respect.

Among practices prohibited by the foregoing are direct or indirect representations: (1) that plants have been propagated by grafting or bud selection methods, when such is not the fact; (2) that industry products are healthy, will grow anywhere without the use of fertilizer, or will survive and produce without special care, when such is not the fact; (3) that plants will bloom the year round, or will bear an extraordinary number of blooms of unusual size or quality, when such is not the fact; (4) that an industry product is a new variety, when in fact it is a standard variety to which the industry member has given a new name; (5) that an industry product cannot be purchased through usual retail outlets, or that there are limited stocks availa-ble, when such is not the fact; (6) that industry products offered for sale will be delivered in time for the next (or any specified) seasonal planting when the industry member is aware of factors that make such delivery improbable; (7) that the appear-ance of an industry product as to size, color, contour, foliage, bloom, fruit, or other physical characteristic is normal or usual when the appearance so represented is in fact abnormal or unusual; (8) that the root system of any plant is larger in depth or diameter than that which actually exists, whether accomplished by excessive pack-ing material, or excessive balling, or other deceptive or misleading practice; (9) that bulblets are bulbs; and (10) that an industry product is a rare or unusual item, when such is not the fact.

All commercial nurseries should have a copy and be familiar with the trade practice rules for the nursery industry. Copies of the rules may be obtained from the FTC.

STATE AND LOCAL LAWS

Most states have laws related to (1) environmental pesticides; (2) labor standards; (3) liens; ((4) licenses; (5) occupational safety; (6) pest control, including diseases, insects, and vertebrates (deer, rodents, birds, etc.); and (7) sales taxes.

In some states wholesale nurserymen are required to collect a sales tax on gross in-state sales unless they are presented with a copy of a resale certificate, a farmer's exemption certificate, an exempt use certificate, an exempt organization certification, a direct payment permit, or identification of the purchaser as a govern-ment agency. Out-of-state customers are exempt from the tax except when the plants are delivered to a point in or picked up in the state of sale.

Municipal laws affecting nurserymen generally relate to licenses, property zoning, and road limitations. Information on these laws and regulations can be ob-tained from state nurserymen's associations, the state department of agriculture, and various units of local government, especially the city or township clerk.

METRIC EQUIVALENTS*

The United States is the one remaining major nation in the world that has neither adopted the metric system nor established a time schedule for conversion. Neverthe-less, nurserymen who do business with foreign countries need a conversion table to convert imperial units to metric units or metric units to imperial units. Table 6–1, listing approximate metric units, is suggested for use in grading nursery stock either by caliper, height, spread, or size classes.

*See Appendix D for metric conversions.

TABLE 6-1   Metric Conversions for Nursery Stock Graded by Caliper, Height, Spread, and Size Class

			Nursery Stock Size Classes	
Imperial	Metric	Approx. Metric	Imperial	Approx. Metric
Inches	Centimeters	Centimeters	Inches	Centimeters
0.5	1.27	1.5	3–6	8–15
1	2.54	2.5	6–9	15–25
1.5	3.81	4.0	9–12	25–30
2	5.08	5.0	12–15	30–40
2.5	6.35	6.0	12–18	30–50
3	7.62	8.0	15–18	40–50
3.5	8.89	9.0	18–24	50–60
4	10.16	10.0		
4.5	11.43	11.0		
5	12.70	13.0	Feet	
5.5	13.97	14.0		
6	15.24	15.0	2–2½	60–80
6.5	16.51	16.0	2–3	60–90
7	17.78	18.0	2½–3	80–90
8	20.32	20.0	3–3½	90–100
10	25.40	25.0		
12	30.48	30.0		
15	38.10	40.0		Meters
18	45.72	50.0		
			3½–4	1.00–1.25
			4–5	1.25–1.50
			5–6	1.50–1.75
Feet			6–8	1.75–2.50
			8–10	2.50–3.00
2	60.98	60.0	10–12	3.00–3.50
2.5	76.20	80.0	12–14	3.50–4.00
3.0	91.44	90.0	14–16	4.00–5.00
			16–18	5.00–5.50
			18–20	5.50–6.00
	Meters	Meters		
3.5	1.07	1.00		
4	1.22	1.25		
5	1.52	1.50		
6	1.82	1.75		
7	2.13	2.00		
8	2.44	2.50		
9	2.94	2.75		
10	3.05	3.00		
12	3.66	3.50		
14	4.27	4.00		
16	4.88	5.00		
18	5.48	5.50		
20	6.09	6.00		

CODES

Various codes, including numbers, colors, and letters, are used in the nursery and landscape for many purposes.

Numbers are used by many nurseries that use electronic data processing equipment to code the plant material by species, cultivar, and grade, to expedite processing. The order forms of some firms are specially designed to simplify ordering and to speed processing. Prepunched IBM cards can be rapidly assembled into an "order deck" to rapidly and accurately prepare the necessary documents to process the order.

Climatic zones within the United States and Canada are designed by number (Fig. 6–1). These zone numbers are used by nurserymen to designate areas of the country where their plants are expected to be hardy and where the plants will make optimum growth. However, these zones of hardiness do not apply to plants growing in containers since the root systems are exposed to ambient air temperatures which can at time be greater than or lower than cardinal temperature that results in death of root tissue. The zones are also used in planning shipping schedules for spring and fall deliveries.

Zip-code numbers are used by mail-order nurserymen when processing their mailings to gain financial advantages by bulk mailing.

Numbers are also used to identify or code orders, estimates, employees, equipment, and prices. Where orders are identified by number, a convenient practice is to combine the order number and the date received or processed into a date-order number by year, month, day, order (e.g., 87-07-20-333). This not only provides immediate identification of the order but provides a rapid means by which sales or purchases can be analyzed by any desired time period.

Prices can be coded by numbers to fit the needs of the nursery. One effective method is to designate that the last digit of a number series be the number of dimes and all previous digits indicate the number of dollars. For example, a price code 176 means that the wholesale price is $17.60, and the code 100 means that the wholesale price is $10. Various modifications can be made to this system.

Seedlings and transplants are commonly coded by number to indicate the number of years in a seed or transplant bed (e.g., 2–1 indicates 2 years in seedbed, 1 year in transplant bed; 2–0 indicates 2-year seedling).

Color is used to aid in the rapid identification of items. Colored tapes or flagging are used to identify specific plants in the nursery that have been selected by or for a customer. It is a good practice to reserve one color tape (e.g., red-striped) for use in identifying plants that are to be rogued from the nursery or a landscape planting. This specific tape should never be used for any other purpose. Colored tape is used to identify female plants of a dioecious species (e.g., holly). This aids in identifying female plants when they are not in flower or fruit.

Colored labels can be used to identify size classes to expedite the assembling of orders by inexperienced help. They have also been used by bedding plant grow-

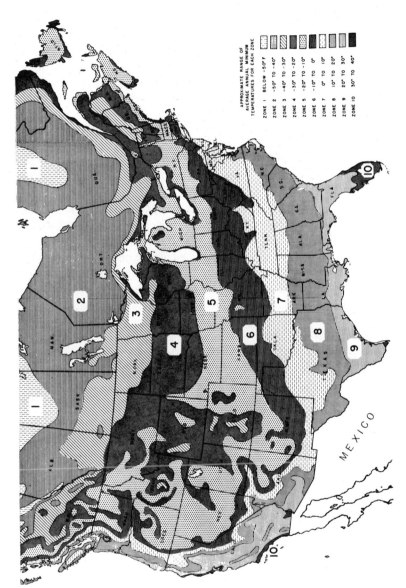

Figure 6–1 The Plant Hardiness Zone Map illustrates the expected minimum temperatures of most of the horticulturally important areas of the United States (excluding Alaska and Hawaii) and Canada. It shows 10 different zones, each of which represents an area of winter hardiness for certain ornamental plants. (From USDA Agric. Res. Serv. Misc. Publ. 814.)

ers to identify plants of a certain price. For example, plants priced at $2.50 per flat may have a blue label, whereas plants priced at $3.00 per flat may have a red label, and so on.

Another use for color coding is for the identification of clones, particularly of deciduous species during the dormant period. Color codes can be used to excellent advantage in coding scion wood and understocks, especially when a number of different clones are involved, as in the grafting or budding of fruit tree varieties on clonal understocks. Color-coded fruit trees are appreciated by orchardists, who must make large plantings with inexperienced help. The color codes are best applied with spray paint.

Some nurseries, particularly landscape nurseries, use distinctive colors to identify their tools and equipment to avoid loss while working on jobs with other contractors. Distinctive colors are also used to identify special equipment that should be used for only certain jobs, such as sprayers to apply 2,4-D-type herbicides.

Colored forms or tabs can be used to expedite the processing of orders or messages within the office. Many nurseries use specifically designed color-coded order forms for this purpose. The various colored sheets within a set of forms aid in identifying the action to be taken. For example, a wholesale nursery may use a yellow form for the shipping and the receiving copy, a white form for the office copy, pink for order acknowledgment, and green for use by the shipping department. A landscape firm can use various colored forms to control and coordinate landscape sales (e.g., white—sales record, orange—nursery division, green—construction division, pink—record division, etc.)

Certain *abbreviations* are used as standard practice in the nursery industry, although there is some variation between nurseries. Some of the more common abbreviations are:

B	Budded
B&B	Balled-and-burlapped
B&P	Balled-and-potted
BR	Bare-root
C	Cutting
CAL	Caliper
CG	Container-grown
COLL	Collected plants from native stands
DBH	Diameter Breast Height
FP	Field-potted
FR	Field row or field run
G	Grafted
HT	Hybrid tea

PB	Peat-balled
RP	Rose pot or root-pruned
S	Seedling
SPEC	Specimen
Std	Standard
T,TT	One for each time transplanted
X, XX, XXX	Used to designate degree of heavy grades; some nurseries use this symbol to indicate number of times transplanted

An example: *Picea pungens* Moerheim, G, 10–12, 4 yr, TT. This is a Moerheim blue spruce that was grafted, transplanted twice, is now 4 years old, and averages 10–12 in. in height.

SUMMARY

Nurserymen must comply with a number of federal, state, and local laws and regulations. These have been summarized briefly within this chapter. Since laws and regulations are subject to modification with time, it is desirable that nursery managers keep informed of changes that will affect their nurseries. This is best accomplished by maintaining membership in the AAN as well as in various state and local nursery associations. Codes, including numbers, colors, and abbreviations, are used within the industry for many reasons. Where standard codes exist, they should be utilized.

REFERENCES

AMERICAN ASSOCIATION OF NURSERYMEN. 1975. The Federal Warranty Act. ALI 2(4):4.

_____ . 1975. Buyers and sellers beware. ALI 2(4):16.

_____ . 1979. Guides for the nursery industry. Federal Register 44(40):11,177–11,179.

FLEMING, W. E. 1972. Preventing Japanese beetle dispersion by farm products and nursery stock. Agric. Res. Serv. USDA Tech. Bull. 1441.

LEVERETT, E. J., JR., and J. H. PADGETT. 1972. Complying with the occupational safety and health act. Am. Nurseryman 135(11):10.

MOREFIELD, K. R. 1972. OSHA and nurseries. Am. Nurserymen 136(4):28.

_____ . 1974. Wage hour laws. ALI(1):5.

PUBLIC LAWS 1912. An act to regulate the importation of nursery stock. U.S. Statutes at Large. 62nd Congress. Vol 31, part I, pp. 315–319.

PUBLIC LAWS 1930. Plant Patents Act. U.S. Statutes at Large. Vol. 46, part I, Chapter 312, p. 376.

PUBLIC LAWS 1935. Social Security Act. U.S. Statutes at Large. 74th Congress. Vol. 49, part I, pp. 620–648.

PUBLIC LAWS 1938. Fair Labor Standards Act. U.S. Statutes at Large. 75th Congress, 3rd Session. Vol. 52, pp. 1060–1069.

PUBLIC LAWS 775. 1954. Plant Patents. U.S. Statutes at Large. Vol. 68, part I, Chapter 1259, p. 1190.

PUBLIC LAW 85–36. 1957. Federal Plant Pest Act. U.S. Statutes at Large. 85th Congress. Vol 71, pp. 31–35.

PUBLIC LAW 91–596. 1970. Occupational Safety and Health Act. U.S. Statutes at Large. 91st Congress. Vol. 84, pp. 1590–1620.

PUBLIC LAW 92–516. 1972. Federal Environmental Pesticide Control Act. U.S. Statutes at Large, 92nd Congress. Vol. 86, pp. 973–999.

PUBLIC LAW 97–470. 1983. Migrant and Seasonal Agricultural Worker Protection Act. U.S. Statutes at Large, Vol. 96, pp. 2583–2600.

SIMPSON, R. C. 1973. Understanding quarantine effects. (Reported by H. G. Tilson.) Am. Nurseryman 137(10):74.

U.S. DEPARTMENT OF COMMERCE. 1970. Plant patents. Superintendent of Documents, Washington, D.C.

SUGGESTED READING

MANWELL, J. P. 1984. Warranties. Part 1. What you should know about. ALI 11(3).
———— 1984. Warranties. Part 2. ALI 11(4).

7 *Financial Management*

Proper management of money and the effective evaluation of sources of money are a major part of the long-range development and operating plan of a nursery and are essential to the life of any business. The growth of a nursery results in increasingly complex financial management. It is as essential for the manager to understand financial management as it is for the manager to understand production techniques, marketing, and all the other factors of the business. To develop and manage the financial aspects of a nursery business properly, nursery managers should have the services of a lawyer and an accountant and understand the appropriate management use of the information provided by these professionals. They advise. The manager makes decisions and, therefore, must understand financial management.

FUNCTION OF FINANCIAL RECORDS

The importance of financial management cannot be overemphasized. Money is used to purchase labor, materials, and in some cases the management and technical expertise necessary to start and operate a nursery. Financial statements and records are used (1) to evaluate the current financial health and past accomplishments of the nursery firm, (2) to determine the appropriate income tax liability, and (3) to assist in securing the additional financial support needed for a growing business. They may also be used to help predict the growth potential of the nursery and to help identify those divisions of the nursery with the greatest potential for profit. Financial records are one of the major sources of information needed in the management of a nursery. Their accuracy and historical nature, however, can be misleading, and they should not be the only factor used in making decisions. Financial records are not to be used as a substitute for good judgment and experience in nursery production, marketing, and personnel management.

FINANCING A NURSERY BUSINESS

Money is needed to finance the purchase of equipment, land, structures, supplies, and labor necessary to begin to produce nursery crops. A nursery manager usually has three potential sources of funds needed to establish and operate a nursery business (Fig. 7–1):

1. *The owner's personal savings.* The owner's investment of personal savings demonstrates his or her commitment to the business and ability to earn and save, both of which are important in developing the proper personal and business credit ratings needed to obtain future financing.

2. *Funds generated in the nursery through profit and depreciation accounts.* The sale of products and services in a business produces money needed for general payment of taxes, cost of bad debts, interest and loan repayment, profit, and depreciation. Depreciation allowances are charged against sales income each year to purchase and replace the equipment, buildings, and facilities when they have worn out and are no longer functional. In rapidly expanding and profitable nurseries, capital needs may frequently rise more rapidly each year than can be provided by profits and depreciation allowances from the nursery.

3. *Borrowed funds.* Borrowed funds are used both to initiate and, in most cases, to operate a nursery. There are a variety of sources of borrowed financing available to the nursery manager, including partnerships, contract growing, and loans from a variety of financial institutions.

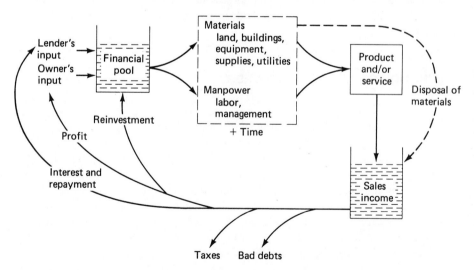

Figure 7–1 Business cash-flow cycle.

Partnerships

Partnerships can be developed for the purpose of obtaining additional funds for capital investments. This normally involves sharing management decisions and profits with all full partners. A successful business partnership usually requires that the partners have separate and well-defined management responsibilities. A partner supplying only financial resources may become less desirable when at a later date these financial resources are no longer needed. This problem is alleviated by developing limited partnerships for a specific investment in a crop. Limited partnerships permit the principal partner to retain almost complete management control at all times. Limited partners may invest in a specific crop which the nursery plants, maintains, harvests, and markets for the partnership. The terms of the partnership agreement should specify the yearly investments required of the limited partner, the services provided by the nursery, the terms of marketing, and the distribution of profits. Limited partnerships are difficult to develop for a new firm, because the investor considering a limited partnership is usually relying on the principal partner's demonstrated nursery management ability, as well as detailed production cost analyses, as partial security for the investment. Certain income tax advantages can be provided to the limited partner, which may make this type of investment appealing to the investor. Limited partnerships may also be developed to allow key employees or individuals with valuable technical expertise to become involved in the financing and management of a division of the firm. In this case the primary purpose of the partnership may be to obtain expertise or to retain and motivate a valuable employee rather than to obtain financing, even though the employee invests funds in the firm and shares in the profits derived from the limited partnership.

Contract Growing

Another source of funds, called *contract growing,* involves using capital obtained from other firms which are involved in marketing nursery stock. A manager may contract to produce a specific crop at a specified price for another firm in return for receiving the financing necessary to produce the crop. In some cases the marketing firm may provide the plants, supplies, and equipment needed to produce the crop. The firm loaning the money receives the benefit of having the entire crop at a specified price (a hedge against inflation) to complete the range of nursery products it markets, whereas the nursery receives the benefit of the financing and a guaranteed market for the crop. Contract growing agreements generally require that the nursery manager producing the crop share some of his management control in return for capital financing.

Borrowing from Financial Institutions

A nursery manager may also borrow money from a number of traditional financial institutions. Borrowing from a financial institution involves obtaining capital to be repaid with interest on a specified schedule in an agreement or note signed by the nursery manager and the creditor. One of the advantages of borrowed funds is that the nursery manager does not share management control with creditors as is usually the case with contract growing or partnerships.

In most cases, buildings, land, nursery stock, equipment, or other assets which are owned either by the nursery or by the owner of the nursery are placed as security or collateral for the loan. If the loan is not repaid as agreed, the ownership of these assets or property is transferred to the financial institution and can be sold to repay the loan. The value of the assets or property identified as collateral must be such that the loan can be repaid even if the assets are under an unfavorable forced-sale condition. Since creditors have a prior claim on the income and assets of the nursery, they will usually accept a relatively lower rate of interest in comparison to contract growing agreements. The identification of the amount, duration, and purpose of the loan (Table 7–1) plus a knowledge of the nursery's ability to repay the loan allows for a better understanding and evaluation of the credit status by both the owner and the lender.

TABLE 7-1   Classification of Business Loans

   I. Time

       A. Short-term loans (up to 1 year): used to finance working capital during short periods of high expense and low income. Bankers will generally lend up to 80% of accounts receivable.

       B. Intermediate loans (1–5 years): used to finance equipment. Bankers may supply up to 90% of the value of the equipment being purchased.

       C. Long-term loans (5 years or more): used to finance land, buildings, and other capital improvement or expansion. Bankers may supply up to 60–70% of the assessed value (not market value) of property and real estate.

  II. Security provided

       A. Real estate

       B. Crop

       C. Stocks and bonds

       D. Equipment

 III. Type of lender

       A. Banks

       B. Government agencies

       C. Finance companies

       D. Private individuals

       E. Private businesses

 IV. Purpose of loan

       A. Purchase real estate, such as additional land; greenhouses; storage facilities; lath or shade facilities; install drainage for production field; and so on

       B. Purchase lining-out stock, fertilizer spray materials, equipment, and so on

       C. Pay labor and management

Source: Murray and Nelson (1960).

EVALUATION OF ALTERNATIVE INVESTMENTS

The nursery manager must determine the best expenditure for the limited capital available before approaching financial institutions or any other source of funds. Not all of the potential capital investments that can be outlined by a nursery manager can or should be financed. Capital investments must be thoroughly evaluated by the manager to ensure the sound financial management of the nursery. The evaluation procedure has a number of logical steps, each of which is essential if the proper management decisions are to be made.

The initial step is a thorough search within the nursery for all possible profitable investments for the available capital. A nursery manager has alternative crops to produce, requiring different types of production and harvesting equipment, storage and packaging facilities, and labor requirements. These alternative investments must be described in detail. The total capital required and the added earnings expected (cash flow) should be forecast for each alternative investment. Once this information is available, a realistic estimate can be made of the economic benefit of each investment. Profit may not be the only factor considered; the impact of income taxes and other taxes, as well as the future growth and ability to provide a stable future income, may play a major role in the selection of an investment. The actual decision must be based, at least in part, on the economic forecast for each potential investment in a crop, type of equipment, or facility.

There are a number of methods for measuring or comparing the potential economic benefit for alternative nursery investments. These methods of analysis vary considerably in their complexity and reliability. It should be kept in mind, however, that detailed methods of comparison are no substitute for realistic estimates of potential earnings, costs, and a complete consideration of all the alternatives. No decision can be any better than the reliability of the data used in making that decision.

Urgency Analysis of Alternative Investments

Some nursery managers, particularly in the early stages of the growth of the firm, tend to evaluate a potential investment in a crop or type of equipment only when presented with a crisis deadline. For example, a nursery manager may discover that as a result of overproduction, rooted juniper cuttings must either be sold substantially below cost, planted in the nursery's own production fields, or destroyed. The decision must be made within a few weeks or the sales and planting season will be past and the plants will be worthless. The urgency of the decision and involvement in the sales and planting activities frequently precludes consideration of long-term management goals and alternative crops that might be produced. The decision to plant the rooted cuttings is frequently made even though the manager is aware that they may well be beyond his or her current and projected ability to profitably market them.

Not all investment decisions based on how urgently the investment is needed are unprofitable, nor are they necessarily less profitable than decisions that may be made with other criteria. Some decisions must be faced without taking the time to consider alternatives. For example, if a tree-digging machine breaks down during the digging season and is beyond repair, a replacement must be purchased immediately to allow harvesting to proceed. Making an investment based on urgency may be necessary, but may be inappropriate for long-term investments and is an inappropriate substitute for good financial management.

Payback-Period Analysis of Alternative Investments

A second method of capital investment analysis involves the determination of the payback period for alternative investments. The *payback period* is the time it takes for earnings from the investment to pay back the entire initial investment. For example, a nurseryman might have the opportunity to produce and market 4 ½-in. caliper shade trees. The manager could either buy 2- to 2 ½-in. caliper trees or buy 6- to 8-ft whips, to begin to produce the trees. Purchasing 6- to 8-ft whips might require a 10-year production period with additional investments each year in cultural care and land cost. The 2½-in. caliper trees might require only a 5- to 6-year production period, with yearly investments for cultural care for only a 5- or 6-year production period. Since no earnings are received until the 4 ½-in. trees are sold, the planting of 2 ½-in. caliper trees has the shortest payback period (5 or 6 years versus 10 years). Payback period, however, may be unrelated to the potential profit that could be earned with the alternative investment proposals. Tree whips might be purchased for $5.00 each, and the same variety at a 2 ½-in.-caliper size might cost $27.50 each. Not only are the 6- to 8-ft tree whips substantially cheaper to purchase, they would cost less to ship and plant and might have a higher survival rate after planting. The 6- to 8-ft whips could produce a greater profit even though they require a longer investment period.

The payback period method measures how quickly an investment can be converted to cash and is, therefore, a measure of the firm's liquidity (the relative ability to convert assets into cash) or financial flexibility rather than profit. There may be management advantages in having increased flexibility provided by shorter-term investments as compared to long-term investments, but this advantage should not be confused with the profitability of a potential investment. It is also more difficult to forecast the marketability of a nursery crop many years in the future for a long-term crop investment, increasing the risk involved.

Simple-Rate-of-Return Analysis
of Alternative Investments

A third method for analyzing alternative investment opportunities is to compare the *simple rate of return* on an average yearly basis. Consider the following investments. An investment in tree-digging machine A of $25,000 will produce additional earnings (savings in labor) of $7500 per year. The depreciation is $5000 per year over an expected machine life of 5 years. The simple rate of return for machine A is:

$$\frac{\text{additional earnings } - \text{ depreciation}}{\text{total investment}} = \text{percentage annual rate of return}$$

$$\frac{\$7500 - 5000}{\$25,000} \times 100 = 10\% \text{ rate of return}$$

Ten percent is the average annual rate of return for this particular investment. An alternative investment could be made in a more efficient machine, B, which could only be leased. This machine would cost $6400 per year and provide a savings of $8000 in labor per year. The simple rate of return would be

$$\frac{\$8000 - 6400}{\$6400} \times 100 \text{ or } 25\%$$

Therefore, even though machine B would produce only $500 more per year in earnings than machine A, its simple rate of return on invested money would be 25%, as compared to 10% for machine A. The simple rate of return indicates which investment would provide the largest added earnings on a yearly basis.

The simple rate-of-return analysis, however, is not really comparable to interest rates on borrowed funds, because the total investment is not made for the life of the machine. The entire $25,000 investment in Machine A is not utilized for the full 5-year period. In fact, during the last (or fifth) year of use, the remaining investment is only $5000 and the additional earnings are $7500.

Discounted-Cash-Flow Analysis
of Alternative Investments

A *discounted-cash-flow analysis* (DCF) accounts for the size of investments, their length, and the date they are made, as well as the amount and date that income occurs. The profit from a potential investment in the nursery is compared by DCF analysis to the profit that could be derived by investing the same sum at a fixed rate of interest in a bank or elsewhere.

DCF analysis allows for the direct comparison of two nursery investments that have different investment schedules, differing rates, and dates of earning income. For example, a $1000 income at the end of 5 years is not comparable to a $200 income per year of 5 years, even though they both provide $1000 in income for a 5-year investment. Incomes and investments can be directly compared only if they can be adjusted in value to the present time. For example, the present value of a $1000 income to be earned 5 years from now can be viewed as the amount of money that must be invested now in order to grow to $1000 at a compound interest rate (using the current rate of interest offered by banks). The amount of money that must be invested to obtain a specific income in 5 years can be obtained by multiplying the income by a discount factor for compound interest rates. (Discount factors are available in table form for a variety of interest rates and years; see Appendix K and Aplin and Casler [1973].) The discount factor for 7.5% interest for 5 years is $1/(1 + 0.075)^5$, or 0.6966. Multiplying the 5-year 7.5% interest discounting factor of 0.6966 times $1000 produces a present value of $696.60.

$$Pv = \$1000 \times 0.6966 = \$696.60$$

Another way of saying the same thing is that a present investment of $696.60 at an annual 7.5% interest will produce $1000 in 5 years.

An income of $200 per year for 5 years can be assigned a present value in a similar manner. Each $200 annual income is adjusted to present value by multiplying times the appropriate discounting factor (percent interest and years). These present values are added to determine the present values of the $200 per year for 5 years (Table 7-2). Thus, the present value (Pv) of an income of $200/year for 5 years is worth $809.17; as calculated by DCF analysis.

TABLE 7-2   Discounted-Cash-Flow Analysis of the Present Value of
$200 Income per Year for 5 Years

Year	Income	Discounting Factor	Present Value
1	$200	0.9302	$186.04
2	200	0.8653	173.06
3	200	0.8050	161.00
4	200	0.7488	149.75
5	200	0.6966	139.32
			Total: $809.17

The same answer can be obtained by using the formula for present value of an annuity:

$$Pv = \frac{a\,[1 - (1 + i)^N]}{i}$$

$$Pv = \$200 \times 4.04588 = \$809.18$$

where Pv = present value
     a = periodic investment
     i = interest rate
    N = years

This results in the same answer (1 cent variation due to rounding) as the previous calculation.

Break-Even-Point Analysis

Investment analysis may also be used to answer the question: What is the most efficient rate of production? A *break-even analysis* is based on the fact that in each nursery operation there are fixed costs which do not change (within certain limits) as the volume of production either increases or decreases. These costs might include the cost of capital invested in equipment, buildings, and land. Variable costs, on the other hand, are directly tied to the volume of production and sales, increasing and decreasing in direct proportion to increases or decreases in volume. A break-even analysis requires the graphic display of fixed selling costs, cost of goods sold, variable selling costs, and net sales at two different volumes or rates of operation. Figure 7–2 shows a break-even analysis of a nursery having the following financial data at two different rates of production:

Total sales	$30,000	$95,000
Fixed costs	− 15,000	− 15,000
Variable costs	− 23,000	− 70,000
Net profit	$ − 8,000	$ + 10,000

The break-even point (intersection of total sales and total costs lines in Fig. 7–2) of these two programs is gross sales of $56,000, which occurs at a production of 2750 units. The assignment of a nursery selling cost as either fixed or variable is to some degree the result of management judgment. The costs illustrated in Fig. 7–2 approximate straight-line functions only for a narrow range of sales volume in a real nursery organization.

Sound financial management requires (1) a thorough search for alternative profitable investment opportunities, (2) an accurate forecast of investments required and potential economic benefit, and (3) the use of an appropriate investment analysis method. The final decision should be based on the investment analysis, as well as the manager's experience in production, marketing, personnel management, estimate of the potential growth in the demand for nursery stock, and good judgment.

NEGOTIATING A LOAN

Successful financial management usually requires the borrowing of funds from a variety of potential lending institutions. Most lenders will want financial data from the nursery, audited by a certified public accountant, as well as information con-

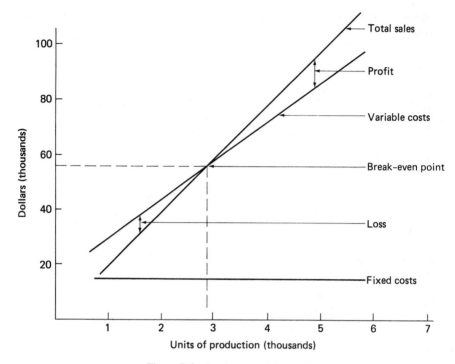

Figure 7–2   Break-even-point analysis.

cerning the ownership and management and the objectives of the proposed financing. The extent of information required will, in part, depend on the size and nature of the financial commitments.

Lending institutions are interested in the nature of the business organization (e.g., incorporation documents, corporate or business by-laws, lease agreement, and long-term contracts) and the history of the business requesting financing. They will also want to know as much as possible about the management of the firm; their personal and family backgrounds; biographical data, including relevant training and experience; evidence of personal character; and the financial status of owners and management. They will be interested in the possible replacement of key management personnel with other employees should they become incapacitated. The lending institution may be interested in the type of accounting system used, a current balance sheet (Table 7–3), a profit and loss statement (Table 7–4), the relevant financial ratio analysis comparisons (Table 7–7), and the long- and short-range financial outlook of the entire nursery industry. They may also wish to see an audit of the accounts and past financial records of the firm.

The lenders will be interested in the objectives of the loan; the payback schedule, the projected budget (how the money will be used), and the resulting schedule of the investment. It may be beneficial to indicate alternative payback options that might be available as a result of changing the schedule of production, harvest, and sale of the nursery crop. The proposed budget should indicate the payback options of all other financial commitments in addition to the one being negotiated. The lenders will also be interested in the nature of proposed collateral, particularly an estimate of its forced liquidation value as well as the liquidity of all the assets of the nursery business. Other assets would include the volume and history of accounts receivable, owner's personal assets, and the value of equipment, vehicles, land, and buildings. The use of nursery stock as security or collateral for a loan requires that the nursery stock in the field be given an estimated forced-liquidation value. The forced-liquidation value can be very low if the rate of construction of new homes, for example, drops dramatically and, therefore, very conservative estimates should be used.

ASSIGNING VALUE TO A NURSERY CROP IN THE FIELD

There are at least three ways to assign value to a nursery crop in the field. One system begins with the wholesale price of nursery stock of a similar size and grade, then subtracting a harvesting and selling cost to arrive at an ''in-the-field'' value. A manager might estimate that harvesting and marketing a particular nursery crop contributes 25% to the total cost of the crop. The in-the-field value of the crop would be 75% of the wholesale price. This method will include profit in the value assigned to the crop. A second method, based on costs of production, totals all production expenses, including labor, equipment, supplies, cost of land, taxes, and plants involved in developing the nursery crop to its present stage. This method will overestimate the value of the nursery crop when it is very young because the planting and cultural care may be substantial for the first 1 or 2 years, during which relatively little growth occurs (Fig. 7–3). Just before harvest, the crop is growing at a maximum rate and the cultural care tends to be at a minimum, making its sale value greater than production costs. However, if harvest is substantially delayed, the sale value of the crop may not continue to increase, because of reduced growth and quality resulting from crowding. An estimating method based on costs of production does not include profit in the estimated value of the nursery crop in the field, and could be very erroneous for recently planted crops.

A third method for assigning value to a nursery crop uses an outside consultant to provide a professional appraisal of what the specific nursery crop would sell for in a forced sale. The value would be reduced by the auction sale expenses to develop an in-the-field value for the crop.

A reduction in the value of a nursery crop estimated by any of the foregoing methods may be taken to provide a conservative estimate of what the crop might be worth as a result of a forced sale. Nursery crops or any other item of collateral should be precisely defined, since the nursery would be turning over control of that crop to the lending institution if and when the terms of the loan were not met. Each block of nursery stock to be assigned as collateral should be inventoried and the block described by a surveyed description.

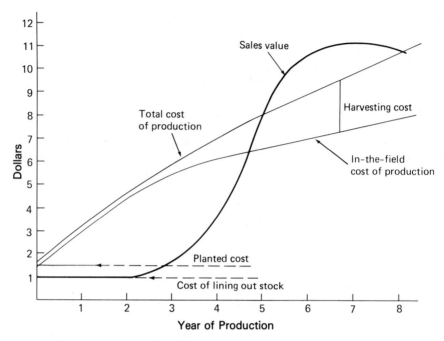

Figure 7–3   Cost of production versus sales value for field-grown nursery crops.

INFORMATION NEEDED ABOUT THE LENDING INSTITUTION

The successful negotiation of a loan also requires that nurserymen know as much as possible about the lending institution. In many cases, the refusal of a loan has little to do with the quality of the firm and management requesting the loan, but is the result of regulations and limits set by the lending institution. A business manager requesting substantial financing should know the lending institution's loan limits (the maximum loan that can be made to one customer and the maximum length of time it will be loaned). Financial needs exceeding the institution's loan limit or time limit may require that the lender collaborate with other lending institutions.

The board of directors of the lending institution determines the broad guidelines and nature of the loans it will make. Each lending institution has more information about and greater confidence in specific types of businesses and is more inclined to make loans to these types of businesses than to others. The preparation of information and negotiation of loans is a time-consuming process, particularly for large, long-term, nursery-business loans. It would be desirable to work with a stable lending institution which does not frequently change its loan guidelines and has remained interested in loans to agricultural businesses for a long period of time.

Those lending institutions having strong ties with agricultural industries will quite likely be more confident in making nursery-business loans.

It will save time and effort if the nursery manager knows the limits of the loan authority given to the individual representing the lending institution. Lending institutions usually have a loan committee that limits the amounts and length of time of loans granted by its employees. Potential loans beyond the limits, both in time and dollar amount, must be reviewed and authorized by the loan committee. The nursery manager will want to know how frequently the loan committee meets in order to estimate the time necessary to obtain financing.

In negotiating a loan, it is usually most productive for the business manager to present the general purpose and nature of the financing needed and the supporting business information and documents. The specific terms of the loan should be negotiated rather than requesting the lending institution to accept or reject a single specific proposal.

As in any business transaction, it is well to compare the financial services of competing lending institutions. The effective interest cost of the loan, the amount of collateral required, as well as other conditions should be compared to the conditions offered by other financial institutions. Lending institutions vary considerably in their willingness to lend money to a specific type of business, and it is well worth the time spent in finding the institution most favorable to your business.

COMPUTING THE FUTURE COST OF A NURSERY CROP

A number of simple formulas can be used to calculate the return of a nursery crop investment. For example, 5000 *Taxus media* 'Hicks' are to be grown for 5 years. Assume that the transplants will cost 35 cents each and that it costs $150 to plant them. The annual cost of caring for these plants will be $500 for labor, $75 for materials, and $500 for overhead. All costs will be financed at 10% per year:*

$$5000 \text{ plants} \times 35 \text{ cents} = \$1750$$
$$\text{planting cost} \qquad\qquad = \underline{150}$$
$$\$1900$$

The future value (in 5 years) of this investment at 10% interest can be calculated using the formula for *future value of invested capital:*

$$C_n = C_o(1 + i)^n$$

where C_n = value of the invested capital at year n

  C_o = invested capital at year 0 (beginning of investment)

  n = number of years of investment

  i = interest rate per year

$$C_n = \$1900 \ (1 + 0.10)^5 = \$1900 \ (1.61051) = \$3059.97$$

*Rates used are for illustrative purposes only. Actual rates may vary with time and circumstance.

The annual investment in caring for these plants are: labor, $500/year; materials, $75/year; and overhead, $500/year; or $1075/year for 5 years. Projecting these annual costs forward 5 years with the future-value-of-annuity formula:

$$Fu = \frac{a[(1 + i)^n - 1)]}{i} \qquad (a = \text{periodic investment})$$

$$5940 = \frac{1075\ [(1 + 0.10)^5 - 1]}{0.10}$$

The maintenance costs equal $5940. The total investment in the plants after 5 years is $3059.97 + $5940 = $8999.97 or $1.80 per plant.

There is usually little reason to assign all assets of the nursery to the lending institution, even if the loan is substantial. The ratio of assets to loan value should be negotiated to allow for future financial flexibility. As the value of assets changes, increasing as in the case of growing nursery stock, it should be part of the loan agreement that some of the assets can be removed from the loan security. At certain times of the year, a nursery may have the opportunity to invest with the bank for relatively short periods of time when a positive cash flow condition exists. These investment opportunities could be part of the overall loan arrangements with the financial institution.

USING FINANCIAL INFORMATION TO EVALUATE
   MANAGEMENT

Evaluating the management of most nurseries is a very difficult task because of the complexity of nursery operation. In the United States there are relatively few production nurseries that produce only one product by a single system and sell their product to a single buyer at one time. Therefore, it is extremely difficult to determine the actual cost of production. Management is evaluated on how effectively they have managed all three factors of production and primarily on how much profit is generated. Two of the most valuable financial documents for evaluating management are a balance sheet and a profit-and-loss statement.

Balance Sheet

Sound financial management of a nursery requires the periodic evaluation of the financial well being or status of the firm. The operation of a nursery results in a constant change in the firm's assets, liabilities, and net worth (the difference between assets and liabilities). A *balance sheet,* prepared periodically by an accountant, is a statement of the financial status of the nursery on the date the balance sheet was prepared. By itself, it does not indicate the rate of change or even the direction of change of any of the assets or liabilities of the firm. Balance sheets are usually issued on a regular basis—monthly, quarterly, or annually—and are of greater

TABLE 7-3 Balance Sheet Items

Assets	Liabilities
Cash assets	Current liabilities
Checking and savings balances	Accounts and notes payable
Receivable assets	Accrued liabilities
Accounts receivable	Interest payable
Reserve for bad debts	Federal income and other taxes
Inventory assets	Royalties owed
Plants	Long-term liabilities
Hard goods	Mortgages and loans
Prepaid expense assets	Equity liabilities
Expenses paid prior to due date	Total received for common and
	preferred stock
Equipment and facilities asset	Undistributed profits
Land and improvement to land	Total owed owners
Equipment, furniture, and fixtures	
Production, shipping, and warehousing	
facilities	
Sales and administration facilities and	
equipment	
Depreciation allowance assets	
Improvement to land	
Equipment, furniture, and fixtures	
Production, shipping, and warehousing	
facilities	

significance when compared to similar reports for the same period of previous years.

The assets and liabilities recorded on the balance sheet are divided into current and long-term entries. If the item can be converted into cash within 1 year, it is considered current. This distinction helps to predict the current year's financial position as distinct from the long-range financial position of the firm. An example of the accounts that might be included in a production nursery business balance sheet are shown in Table 7–3. The Horticultural Research Institute (HRI) has developed a uniform chart of accounts which is suggested for use by the entire nursery industry. The widespread use of a uniform chart of accounts would make the comparison of industry-wide financial ratio analysis (discussed later in the chapter) more reliable and efficient.

Profit-and-Loss Statement

One of the prime concerns of a nursery manager—the potential profit from the operation of the nursery—is not displayed on a balance sheet. An *income statement* or *profit-and-loss statement* combines the total sales over a period of time (month, quarter, or year) and subtracts the total expenses for the same period of time showing the profit or loss developed by the firm (Table 7–4). This is one of the most

TABLE 7-4   Items Normally Included in a Profit-and-Loss Statement

Income	Operations
Income from production operations	Contract labor
Sale of green goods—plants	Royalties
Sale of hard goods	Travel
Sale of services offered	Utilities
Service charges	Gas and electricity
Other income	Water and sewer
Gain on sale of fixed assets	Telephone
Rental income	Heat
	Shipping and warehousing expense
Expenses	Employees
Production expenses	Wages
Cost of goods	Fringe benefits
Cost of plants used in production	Insurance
Cost of plants purchased for resale	Taxes
Cost of materials used in production	Supervisory salaries
Insurance expenses	Equipment, furniture, and fixtures
Taxes	Cost to purchase or rent
Employees	Cost to maintain
Wages	Insurance
Fringe benefits	Taxes
Taxes	Depreciation
Supervisory salaries	Facilities
Equipment, furniture, and fixtures	Cost to purchase or rent
Cost to purchase or rent	Cost to maintain
Cost to maintain	Insurance
Insurance	Taxes
Taxes	Depreciation
Depreciation	Operations
Facilities	Shipping supplies and materials
Cost of greenhouses, overwintering, and	Automation costs
shade houses	Utilities
Depreciation	Gas and electricity
Insurance	Water and sewer
Maintenance and repair	Telephone
Taxes	Heat

important statements provided by an accountant. If the nursery is to survive for any length of time, it must show a profit. Management decisions to expand or change production, as well as the ability to obtain financing, will be influenced substantially by a profit-and-loss statement. To a creditor, the profit-and-loss statement will indicate the potential ability to pay back existing liabilities as well as additional loans.

Since profit, the reward for the risk of operating a commercial enterprise, is a measure by which a commercial nursery is evaluated, it is important to have an understanding of the various concepts of profit. The concept of what constitutes a profit varies with the accounting system, the age of the business, the age of the owner(s), and the legal type of organization of the business.

The interpretation of a profit-and-loss statement as well as other financial statements depends upon the type of accounting system used by the firm. Most production nursery accounting systems are on a cash basis. Some of the larger production nurseries may be on an accrual basis in order to more effectively be managed as part of a much larger corporation. Expenses in a cash-basis accounting system are recorded at the time payment is made, and income is recorded at the time of receipt. The nursery production cycle (the length of time between the initial planting of a crop and the date of harvest) is usually much longer than the accounting period of a balance sheet or profit-and-loss statement. The accounting period may be quarterly, or more commonly 1 year, whereas the production cycle may range from a few weeks to 6 years. The cash basis system of accounting is misleading if the nursery is changing rapidly by expanding or contracting the volume of nursery crops planted each year. The cash expenses involved in buying the lining-out stock and caring for an increasing volume of nursery stock in the ground could very well be greater than the income from the sale of the relatively small volume of mature harvested nursery stock. In a cash basis accounting system, the inventory of nursery crops in the ground is not assigned a value until it is sold, so the profit-and-loss statement will show little, if any, profit, since income has been used to increase nursery crop inventory. However, this has been a common accounting practice in the nursery industry.

An accrual-basis accounting system will include the value of unsold inventory and plants under production. This provides a more realistic indication of the potential health of the business and reflects an increase or decrease in production volume. However, an accrual-basis accounting system presents a financial picture of the nursery which is subject to dramatic change by the loss of inventory plants by winter kill, disease or insect attack, and changes in the market demands.

DISCRETIONARY SPENDING

Net receipts in a nursery operation will also vary considerably with discretionary spending. By what amount will expenditures for capital assets (land, buildings) be increased as the nursery grows? What amount will be invested into new growing inventory? What will be invested in new equipment? These decisions will dramatically affect the net profit of a business.

When a nursery business is young, and particularly if the management is young, there is a strong tendency to reinvest profits into land, growing inventory, and related facilities to expand the business. Under the cash system of accounting, the value of an expanding field inventory is not adequately reflected in the standard financial records that are maintained by most nurseries. An expanding nursery will appear to be unprofitable under a cash accounting system. As the owners of the nursery grow older and, to some extent, as the business ages, there is a desire to maximize personal income. This can be done in a number of ways that will affect net profit. The most common are a reduced rate of expansion, increased salary, and fringe benefit programs. Another is improved office facilities and modes of transportation. They are all rewards for financial success. None of these rewards, however, necessarily reflects a true evaluation of the nursery business. Much of the financial success of many older nurseries may be due to an economic increase in land value due to urbanization or potential recreational use.

The 1976 Tax Reform Act requires corporate farms to use accrual accounting and to assign values to unsold nursery stock inventories. However, it contains the following exemption: "This section shall not apply to the trade or business of operating a nursery." In an accrual basis of accounting, "changes in resources and obligations including those resulting from the generation of revenues and the occurrence of expense are recorded as they occur (or nearly so)" (Edwards et al., 1974). The inventory of unsold nursery stock in the field or in containers would be assigned a value in an accrual basis of acccounting. The increase in value of unsold plants each year would be considered as income in accrual accounting. Production costs including harvesting would be considered expenses only in the year they occur. This dramatically changes potential tax liability. In March 1979 the IRS advised that accrual-basis accounting can be changed to cash bases and that nurseries continuing to use accrual-basis accounting need not maintain inventories.

DETERMINING PROFIT

One of the ways to evaluate the success of an investment in nursery stock is by determining the costs of the various factors of production in a realistic manner and determining the true profit when these costs are deducted from the sales income. True profit is calculated as the effective rate of interest returned on the investment made in the production of the crop or crops during the production period.

When planning the production system for a nursery, after it has been determined what species of plants are going to be produced, it becomes necessary to determine the specific inputs that will be required, some of which are (1) how many plants must be grown to meet a specific market objective; (2) how long the production cycle is and how much land is needed; (3) how much manpower and skill will be required to carry out the various physical operations required in the production cycle; (4) what facilities, equipment, materials, and supplies will be required; (5) how much money will be invested during the production cycle; and (6) how the various factors (labor, machines, land, and other facilities) can be synchronized to produce the best production system. Once this has been done and the production goal is clearly defined, it will be feasible to evaluate the accomplishments.

COST OF PRODUCTION

Since plants are the marketable product of the nursery which are sold to produce income, a system must be developed to determine the money inputs that are invested to produce the plants. However, most production nurseries produce many species of plants to make up the salable product mix. Each species has its own special input requirements in the way of material and labor skills, so that it becomes almost impossible to accurately determine the dollar inputs into their production. However, if the species are grouped into larger categories, such as shade trees, flowering shrubs, and so on, it does become possible to determine average costs of production.

It is impossible to place a true value on plant material growing in a nursery. This is because the plants gain a true sales value only when a buyer consummates an offer to buy. Up to that point plants in a nursery have only a potential or an estimated value in-the-ground which could be substantially reduced by various economic, biological, or climatic factors. A slowdown in the national economy, or periods of high interest rates which reduce the rate of housing construction, can be quickly reflected in the public demand for plant material; this was dramatically seen in the great depression of the late 1920s and early 1930s and the period of high interest rates in the 1980s.

In the winter of 1873–1874 a severe freeze throughout the Midwest caused the loss of thousands of plants and the failure of many nurseries; and the blizzard of 1890–1891 caused serious financial loss to many nurserymen. A beautiful block of shade trees that might have a potential value of many thousands of dollars could be reduced to a worthless jungle by a brief but devastating hail or sleet storm. Also, a severe drought, such as the one that affected the midwestern United States in the mid-1930s and the one that devastated parts of Europe in 1976, can seriously reduce any potential value that nursery stock might have. But nursery stock either in the ground or in containers does have potential value. Certainly, the nurseryman who owns the stock must place a value on the plants, a value for which he would be willing to sell the plants at a profit, and a forced-sale value which might be the dollar value that he would be willing to accept for the plants, in situ, if he were forced to sell. The forced-sale value most likely would be close to the actual dollar costs that he has invested in the production of the plants, but would not reflect a profit. Therefore, cost-of-production information is needed to determine how much is invested in the plant material in order to estimate an in-the-ground value. Cost-of-production information is helpful in providing nurserymen with factual information to make better management decisions relative to production scheduling and pricing. It is also valuable in evaluating changes in cultural methods and productivity of labor. Without production records, including costs, the nursery manager cannot fully evaluate production efficiency. It is very likely that without production cost records, plant material could be priced at a level below the actual total cost of production and be sold at a net loss without the manager being aware of it.

The first step is to determine what data are to be collected, how they are to be collated and processed into usable information, and how much time and money will be budgeted to accomplish the goal. It is pointless to collect data if there are no plans to use the data, and a waste of time and money if there are no predetermined objectives for the use of the information that is generated upon processing the data.

Nurseries that produced relatively few species or types of plant material or that specialize in a limited product mix can develop and operate relatively simple systems for obtaining production cost data. Nurseries that produce a wide selection of species or a diverse product mix, on the other hand, will need more elaborate systems. However, they need not be complex, and it may be more practical to begin obtaining cost-of-production data within broad plant categories such as outlined in Table 9–1, and later by individual varieties or cultivars.

Systems for Estimating the Cost of Production

Two systems are available for estimating the long-term costs of producing nursery stock. The first system involves obtaining direct costs (obtained from daily time sheets and material records) on labor and material inputs, whereas the second system involves estimating inputs of labor from staffing tables developed over a period of years. In both systems a method is suggested for estimating costs of land, facilities, various overhead expenses, and interest charges. For management purposes it might be desirable to calculate an in-the-ground cost of production based on field data including direct labor and material inputs only, whereas a price-list cost of production would also include overhead and interest charges. The in-the-ground cost would represent the average total cost of production (investment) up to a given point in the production cycle.

Planting, Maintaining, and Harvesting Costs

One convenient and meaningful system for production nurseries is to collect and process the data within three categories: planting, maintaining, and harvesting, the three primary functions in the production cycle. Figure 7–4 illustrates the system. The dollar values used in the example are for illustrative purposes only. Each manager must collect and process his or her individual data. In year zero, 4000 young shade trees were purchased. Cost includes plants and transportation. The average cost was $6.73/plant. The direct labor and material costs (obtained from daily time sheets and material records) for planting and maintaining the first year were $3720 and $1840, respectively. Unit values can be calculated for comparative analysis if desired. This information is tabulated for both the in-the-ground value and the price-list cost.

Overhead Costs

Overhead is the total of all costs of production that cannot be charged directly to the blocks of plant materials, including such things as rent for use of land and facilities, administrative and management salaries, taxes, and so on. There are various ways of determining overhead and equating it to the various factors of production. One method commonly employed in nurseries is to equate total overhead to total direct labor (DL) and to calculate a percentage factor. Overhead is applied as a function of labor cost because many overhead costs are related to labor more directly than to other functions of production costs. This value may vary from a low of

Figure 7-4 Example of cost-of-production schedule for field-grown shade trees.

	Year 0				Year 0+1		
	Units	Cost/unit	In-the-ground cost	Price list Cost	units	Cost/unit	In-the-ground cost
Cost of plants	4000	$6.73	$26,920	$26,920	3950		32,480
Labor: planting		.42	1,680	3720			960
: maintaining		.51	2,040	W 3720		.24	
Materials: planting		.36	1,452	W 1,840			525
: maintaining		.10	388	32,480		.13	W 33,965
			W 32,480	3720			
Overhead (100% D.L.)				W 36,200			
Interest (7.0%)				2534			x̄ = 8.69
Total			x̄ = 8.22	W 38,734	-39		
Plants lost	-50			9.81	3911		
	3950						
Plants sold							
Labor: harvesting							
Materials: harvesting							
Overhead: harvesting							
Plants remaining / costs outstanding							

(continued)

119

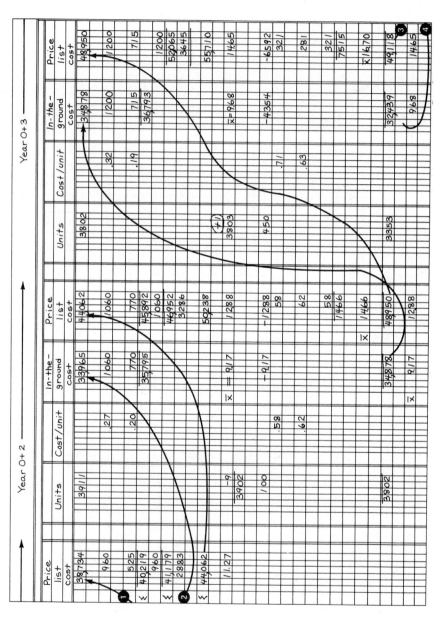

Figure 7–4 (*continued*)

120

Year 0+4 ———→   Year 0+5 ———→

Units	Cost/unit	In-the-ground cost	Price list cost	Units	Cost/unit	In-the-ground cost	Price list cost
3353	.45	32439	491118	11197		12379	29194
		1500	1500		1.00	1200	1200
	.20	650	650		.38	450	450
		34589	1500			14029	1200
			52768				23044
			3694				1613
			54462				24657
-6/3347		x̄=1033	1687	-4/1193	1.23	x̄=11.76	2067
2150	1.04	-22210	-36271	1008		-11854	-29835
			2236		.73		1240
	.64		1378				736
			2236				1240
			42121				24051
			x̄=12.59				x̄=23386
1/1197		12379	29194	785		2175	3822
		1034	16687			11.76	2067

③
④

Figure 7-4 (continued)

50% of DL to a high of 150% of DL. In the example, 100% of DL was used throughout. Nurserymen are cautioned to calculate the value of their own services and to include all indirect costs of production.

Interest on invested capital is another factor that should be included, since money invested in plants could have been placed into a bank or other interest earning investment. A 7.0% interest charge is used in the example. The rate will vary with years, but a fair value prevailing within the community should be used. Note the significant increase in cost of production when overhead and interest on invested capital are included. Maintenance data are collected and processed in a similar manner for the ensuing years, and the average cost of production is calculated. At the end of each year an actual inventory count is taken of the plants within the block, and an average cost-of-production value is calculated.

When plants are sold, harvesting data are collected and processed. All these data are tabulated under price-list cost, since the plants are being removed from the site. No interest is charged to cost of production. However, it may be charged in the sales division if the sale is on credit. Once the plants are sold, their average value must be removed from the ledger. The sale and removal of some of the plants in a block will result in a much higher unit cost for maintenance, and a lower total value of plants remaining on the site, with a higher individual unit value per plant. At some point the resulting higher individual unit value of plants may exceed the average obtainable selling price, necessitating a decision by management as to the prudence of maintaining the few remaining plants. Hopefully, by keeping up-to-date, accurate records, the decision to remove all plants from a block can be made before they cost more to keep than their increased potential selling price.

Determining Profitability with a Cost-Sales Analysis

From the estimated cost of production records and from the records for sales, a cost-sales analysis can be prepared to fully evaluate the profitability of having grown the 4000 trees for a period of time extending over 7 years. One method of evaluation is to determine the future value of all inputs and income through the production cycle and to determine if there was a positive cash flow (Fig. 7–5). In the example, with 7% interest rate, a 100% direct overhead, and estimating sales costs at 10% of the selling price, there was a positive cash flow of $15,607.

A somewhat better tool to employ for this evaluation is discounted-cash-flow analysis, equating all finances back to year zero and determining an interest rate that results in a zero (or close to zero) net cash flow. All of the yearly financial inputs, less interest, and all yearly net sales are tabulated and the net cash flow determined by years (Table 7–5). These values are then discounted to year zero by using various interest rates (Table 7–6). This can be done fairly rapidly with the aid of a computer and in a few minutes with the aid of a desk calculator. A partial set of interest rates is tabulated in Appendix K. For more detailed rates, consult interest tables contained in a handbook related to mathematics.

#	Yr.	Production inputs	1 Current value	2 Selling costs (est. 10%)	3 7.0% Interest factor	4 Future value 0+6 yrs.
1	0	Plant costs	26920		1.5007	$40400
2						
3		Labor, direct costs				
4	0		3720		1.5007	5583
5	1		960		1.4026	1347
6	2		1118		1.3108	1465
7	3		1521		1.2250	1863
8	4		3738		1.1449	4279
9	5		2209		1.0700	2364
10	6		1000		0	1000
11					≤	17900
12						
13		Material costs				
14	0		1840		1.5007	2761
15	1		525		1.4026	736
16	2		832		1.3108	1090
17	3		996		1.2250	1220
18	4		2028		1.1449	2322
19	5		1187		1.0700	1270
20	6		700		0	700
21					≤	10100
22		Overhead costs				
23		(100% direct labor)				17900
24					≤ ≤	86300
25						
26		Sales income		Selling costs		
27	0			(est. 10%)		
28	1					
29	2	100 @ $18.00	1800	- 180 X	1.3108	2123
30	3	450 @ 21.00	9450	- 945	1.2250	10418
31	4	2150 @ 25.00	53760	- 5375	1.1449	55385
32	5	1008 @ 30.00	30240	- 3024	1.0700	29121
33	6	180 @ 30.00	5400	- 540	0	4860
34						
35					≤	101907
36						
37						
38		Profit =	101,907	- 86,300	=	$15,607
39						
40						

Figure 7–5 Plant materials cost-income analysis.

When evaluated at an interest rate of 15%, the example project generated a negative cash flow, but at 12% the cash flow was positive, in excess of $1700, indicating that the project earned a profit in excess of 12% but less than 15%. If outside sources of funding were used to finance the project, it would be necessary to subtract the effective rate of interest from the profit percentage to determine the per-

TABLE 7-5 Net Cash Flow

Year	Input	Net Sales	Net Cash Flow
0	− 36,200	0	− 36,200
1	− 2,445	0	− 2,445
2	− 3,068	+ 1,620	− 1,448
3	− 4,038	+ 8,505	+ 4,467
4	− 9,504	+48,385	+38,871
5	− 5,605	+27,216	+21,611
6	− 2,700	+ 4,860	+ 2,160
			+67,109
			−39,893
			+27,216

centage of net profit in order to truly evaluate management for organizing and directing the enterprise.

Discount analysis of the project points out an important point relative to cash flow. When the discount rate is high, a faster turnover of cash flow is much more desirable, since the present value of long-term future income declines rapidly. Note the rapid drop in discount factors for 15% compared to 12%. Also, depending upon the amount of return on investment that is desired and the rate of turnover in cash flow, the value of the last remaining plants in a block of nursery stock may become a significant factor. In the example, if 15% were desired, it becomes important to sell the last 185 plants, whereas if 12% is a satisfactory rate of return, the last 185 trees could be sacrificed without significantly affecting the rate of return on the investment. Naturally, other factors must be considered, namely, land cost and the projected sales income from other uses of the land. In the example, the projected

TABLE 7-6 Discounted-Cash-Flow Analysis

Year	Net Cash Flow	12% Factor	12% Value	15% Factor	15% Value
0	− 36,200	1.0000	− 36,200	1.0000	− 36,200
1	− 2,445	0.8929	− 2,183	0.8696	− 2,126
2	− 1,448	0.7972	− 1,145	0.7561	− 1,095
3	+ 4,467	0.7179	+ 3,215	0.6575	+ 2,937
4	+38,871	0.6355	+24,702	0.5718	+22,226
5	+21,611	0.5674	+12,262	0.4972	+10,745
6	+ 2,160	0.5066	+ 1,094	0.4323	+ 934
			+41,273		+36,842
			−39,528		−39,421
			+ 1,745		− 2,579

income was relatively low. Also, in the total financial evaluation of the business, the sale of the last remaining plants may become a source of supplementary income rather than direct income from the project, provided that the land cannot be programmed for some more productive use. In many production nurseries, the last remaining plants may not be salable or must be sold at less than full market value.

Another System for Estimating Cost of Production

Another system for estimating the cost of production is a method proportioning the various financial inputs by land, capital assets, direct materials, estimated labor inputs, and overhead expenses. Many of the financial inputs to start a nursery are for land and capital assets, such as propagation structures, storage facilities, and so on. It is difficult to equate a fair cost of the use of these facilities to plant production cost, since they are not direct costs. Nevertheless, they are costs of production and must be included.

One method is to own and develop these facilities under a proprietorship, which then rents them to the nursery, which may be a corporation or a partnership. For example, it may require 10 acres of land at $100 per acre for 7 years to produce 4000 trees. Land costs for the production of the trees would be $1000 per year for 7 years. This would be posted to cost of production as noted in Table 7–7. Similar estimates can be made for the use of other capital assets. Materials that go directly into the production of the plants can be fairly accurately estimated either on an acre basis (e.g., fertilizer, pesticides, etc.) or on an individual plant or per 1000 plant basis, whichever is most desirable. The data are then converted to the number of plants being costed (in the example, 4000 trees).

Supplies to develop the land and facilities are charged to the owners and are reflected in the rent charges. Equipment charges may either be rent, if owned by a proprietor and leased to the nursery, or they may be calculated as an overhead cost, depending upon which is the most equitable approach to the problem. Over a period of time management should develop production tables that reflect the average productivity for the equipment or for the labor-machine combination used to accomplish the various jobs in the nursery (e.g., digging, planting, packaging, etc.; Figs. 3–3 and 3–4).

Labor skills that are directly related to the production of the plants should be charged accordingly. This is best done on a unit basis (generally per 1000); but for large balled and burlapped shade trees the costs may be equated to a single tree, although for some labor skills the actual production may be determined on the number of units produced per hour. Labor skills not directly related to plant production and those that span many categories (supervisors, administrative staff, and management) are best equated as an overhead cost. All overhead costs, those that are not directly related to plant production, can be equated to either direct labor or material costs. In most nurseries, they are applied as a percentage of direct labor, as noted in the previous example.

TABLE 7-7 Estimated Cost-of-Production Schedule and Cash-Flow Analysis for 4000 Trees

A. Production Costs and Cash Flow

Year	Rent ($100/acre)	Storage Facilities ($50/1000 ft³)	Materials, Estimated to Nearest $100	Direct Labor, Estimated to Nearest $100	Overhead, 50% of DL	Total Yearly Investment	Net Sales Income[a]	Net Cash Flow
0	$1,000	—	$28,800	3,000	1,500	−34,300	0	−34,300
1	1,000	—	500	1,000	500	−3,000	0	−3,000
2	1,000	50	800	1,500	750	−4,100	+1,620	−2,480
3	1,000	150	1,000	1,500	750	−4,400	+8,500	+4,100
4	1,000	100	2,000	4,000	2,000	−9,100	+47,250	+38,150
5	1,000	50	1,500	2,000	1,000	−5,550	+27,000	+21,450
6	1,000	50	800	1,000	500	−3,350	+5,000	+1,650

B. Sales Income

Year	Plants	Price	Income	Sales Expense	Net Sales Income
0	0		0		0
1	0		0		0
2	100	18	1,800	180	1,620
3	450	21	9,450	945	8,500
4	2100	25	52,500	5,250	47,250
5	1000	30	30,000	3,000	27,000
6	200	30	6,000	600	5,400

C. Discounted-Cash-Flow Analysis

Year	Net Cash Flow	12%		15%	
		Factor	Value	Factor	Value
0	−34,300	1.0000	−34,300	1.0000	−34,300
1	−3,000	0.8929	−2,680	0.8696	−2,610
2	−2,480	0.7972	−1,987	0.7561	−1,870
3	+4,100	0.7179	+2,940	0.6575	+2,700
4	+38,150	0.6355	+24,240	0.5718	+21,810
5	+21,450	0.5674	+12,170	0.4972	+10,660
6	+1,650	0.5066	+840	0.4323	+710
			+40,190		+35,880
			−38,960		−38,780
			+1,230		−2,900

[a] From Table B.

It requires money to pay for the materials, the labor skills, and the rent for land and facilities. The money may be obtained from outside sources or from within the nursery organization. But regardless of where it comes from, it should earn a fair rate of interest. This must be reflected in the discount rate as well as the profit due management for the risk involved in producing the nursery stock. If management could put the finances available into low-risk bonds that earn 7.5%, this might be the interest rate that should be charged for the use of the financial input. If management desires an additional 7.5% for the additional risk of investing in the nursery as compared with investing in low-risk bonds, the suggested discount rate might be 15%. In the example, it can be seen (Table 7–7C) that the potential net cash flow earns a positive cash flow at 12%, but a negative cash flow at 15%, making the venture questionable from the start. At the desired 15% discount rate, either the income from sales is delayed too long or is not great enough, or the amount invested the first year is too great. A reevaluation of the production system is warranted.

ACCOUNTS RECEIVABLE

Accounts receivable are the uncollected bills the nursery has on its financial records for nursery stock it has sold. This is probably the most difficult area of financial management for most nurseries. The credit policy established by a nursery for its customers must reflect the cost of borrowing money, the credit policies of competing nurseries, and the individual customer's current credit rating. Wholesale nurseries in a common market area will frequently establish informal exchanges of credit information on their customers who have unpaid bills. This practice tends to limit the total debt a customer can develop in a market area and encourages customers to pay up long-standing bills.

TOTAL NURSERY PROFITS

Profitability of the nursery must be measured by the cost involved and the sales income generated by the total product mix. An evaluation must be made to determine if the various production systems within the nursery are in balance to maximize productivity of the business. Once the basic assets (land, buildings, equipment, permanent labor force) are assembled, it becomes obligatory that management utilize the assets to its best advantage. Certain fundamental questions must be answered and reevaluated on a continuing, periodic basis: Is the product mix the best for the potential sales market? Are the production facilities being used to optimum capacity? Are the various labor skills being employed most effectively? What changes can be made in the production system to maximize returns on investment?

The product mix is the combination of plants that are being or could be produced by the nursery. Over a number of decades, nursery production has gradually shifted from emphasis on the production of fruit trees to the production of woody ornamental plants. Even within nurseries, there has been a shifting to the production of those species that grow well within a given climate. But once a production nurseryman has determined the primary species of plants to grow and has developed the facilities and assembled the labor skills to accomplish the production goals, he or she needs to determine if nursery income could be supplemented by producing selected supplementary species with the facilities and labor skills available. It may be that the current production systems are not fully utilizing the existing facilities, or that at certain times of the year the full-time labor force is not fully productive. All too often the propagation and storage facilities of large production nurseries are empty when they might be used in a supplementary manner. It might be possible to modify current production practices in order to maximize the effective and efficient use of expensive greenhouse space and plant storage facilities.

In some situations the production of supplementary species may require additional inputs in the way of labor. However, the small labor input, coupled with essentially "free" use of existing facilities, may be well worth the investment. Management is evaluated and rewarded on the productive utilization of all three factors of production (materials, personnel, and money). Thus, management must be constantly evaluating all factors of production and trying to put together the most productive and profitable system.

Nursery managers are in a position to use computers to evaluate their production systems. By programming a computer with data relative to cultural practices, labor productivity, and cost information, the manager will be able to simulate various types of nursery production systems and cycles and test their potential worth by discount analysis. Nursery managers have a very powerful tool at their disposal; it awaits their use.

Taylor et al. (1986a,b) have developed a cost model for both a small container nursery and a field nursery which would be appropriate for plant hardiness zones 5 and 6. The model is based on the Columbus, Ohio, area using cost data from nurseries in the north central United States during 1984–1985, and assumes that both of these operations were new installations and that all supplies, land, and so on, had to be accounted for in the cost analyses. Both the field and container nursery cost analyses indicate that a comparison of the cost of producing plants with the income from the sale of plants at wholesale catalog prices produce a loss in most cases. Selling costs are not included. These analyses indicate that starting a new, profitable nursery in the north central United States would be very difficult. Existing nurseries could remain competitive because they had purchased land, buildings, and equipment at lower prices and because they may share buildings, equipment, and management with other enterprises. Both of these studies dramatically demonstrate the necessity for accurate cost analysis for both existing and proposed nursery production operations.

CASH-FLOW ANALYSIS

One of the financial problems common to all types of nursery businesses is the highly seasonal nature of the annual sales cycle. It is not uncommon to find production nurseries that develop 50% of their annual sales during one quarter of the year. Cash-flow problems result because expenditures precede sales and do not occur in a similar annual cycle. In many cases the major labor input in harvesting nursery stock (which requires substantial cash) occurs almost completely before the nursery stock is paid for by the consumer. Table 7–8 illustrates a typical monthly sales distribution for wholesale nursery growers in the north central United States. A few nursery firms have been partially successful in their efforts to develop other products or services that provide income and productively use labor during the periods of the year when nursery income and labor needs are minimal.

TABLE 7-8   Percentage of Annual Sales

Dec.	4.2	Mar.	14.9	June	5.4	Sept.	6.3
Jan.	3.9	Apr.	26.0	July	3.0	Oct.	6.4
Feb.	6.0	May	13.0	Aug.	3.7	Nov.	7.2
	14.1		53.9		12.1		19.9

Source: WLRHRI operating cost study, 1971.

The fluctuation in income and expenses during the year requires short-term financing during the periods of the year when expenses exceed income. A projected cash-flow budget should be prepared based on past cash-flow data and the future payment and income projections. The cash-flow analysis should be prepared at least once a year in monthly increments (possibly weekly) and might be required more frequently in cases where projections are altered by dramatic shifts in marketing or production. The total cash expenses and the total income from all sources are tabulated on a monthly basis, and positive or negative cash flow for each month is recorded (Table 7–9). A cumulative positive or negative cash flow developed for each month or week will indicate the necessity for short-term loans well in advance, allowing for proper financing. A cash-flow budget also indicates opportunities for short-term investment of surplus funds for some periods of the year.

RATIO ANALYSIS

A very useful management tool has been provided by WLRHRI (Wholesale Landscape and Retail Horticultural Research Institute) in the publication of an operating cost study for the various segments of the industry. This study and others like it provide average financial data from participating nursery firms that a manager can use as a comparison in evaluating the performance of a nursery. An operation cost

TABLE 7-9   Cash-Flow Statement

From January 1 to December 31[a]

	Jan.	Feb.	Mar.	Apr.	May
Cash balance first of month	$2,000	$2,000	$ 1,000	$ 2,400	$ 6,900
Funds provided:					
Receipts from customers	$5,000	$1,000	—	$15,000	$20,000
Bank operating loan		$5,000	$10,000		
Total funds provided	$5,000	$6,000	$10,000	$15,000	$20,000
Total funds to be accounted for	$7,000	$8,000	$11,000	$17,400	$26,900
Funds applied					
Salaries	$1,400	$1,400	$ 1,500	$ 1,500	$ 1,400
Hourly payroll	1,000	1,000	4,000	6,000	4,000
Commissions					1,000
Installment payments	250	250	250	250	250
Purchases for resale					
Freight out					500
Packaging supplies		2,000	1,000		2,500
Purchases of liners					
Manure, peat, and fertilizer					1,000
Rent expense					
Advertising and promotion			500	500	500
Other operating expenses	2,350	2,350	1,350	2,250	1,850
Bank operating loan repayment					5,000
Distribution of profit					
Total funds applied	$5,000	$7,000	$ 8,600	$10,500	$18,000
Cash balance end of month	$2,000	$1,000	$ 2,400	$ 6,900	$ 8,900

[a]Figures are taken from the cash receipts journal and the cash disbursements journal.
Source: Smith et al. (1970).

study, such as the one provided by WLRHRI, becomes increasingly more useful as the number of participating firms increases and as additional years of data accumulate. A manager can compare financial trends over a number of years in the nursery industry to the trends in the nursery being evaluated.

A number of financial ratios, uniquely suited to the nursery industry, have been developed. G. S. Perkins, working with Florida production nurseries, evaluated nursery production (production area turnover) by dividing the total acreage of nursery crops that were harvested in the nursery each year by the total acreage the

TABLE 7-9 (*continuued*)

			From January 1 to December 31[a]				
June	July	Aug.	Sept.	Oct.	Nov.	Dec.	Total
$ 8,900	$ 5,900	$4,900	$ 1,900	$ 3,900	$ 8,900	$10,000	
$21,000	$ 5,000	$3,000	$10,000	$15,000	$10,000	$ 5,000	$110,000
							$ 15,000
$21,000	$ 5,000	$3,000	$10,000	$15,000	$10,000	$ 5,000	$125,000
$29,900	$10,900	$7,900	$11,900	$18,900	$18,900	$15,900	$127,000
$ 1,400	$ 1,400	$1,400	$ 1,400	$ 1,400	$ 1,400	$ 1,400	$ 17,000
3,000	2,000	2,000	3,000	2,000	2,000	1,000	31,000
1,000							2,000
250	250	250	250	250	250	250	3,000
3,000				2,000			5,000
1,500				1,000			3,000
				500	1,000		7,000
2,000							2,000
					1,000		2,000
500						500	1,000
			500				2,000
1,350	2,350	2,350	2,850	2,850	2,350	1,850	26,100
10,000							15,000
						7,000	7,000
$24,000	$ 6,000	$6,000	$ 8,000	$10,000	$ 8,000	$12,000	$123,100
$ 5,900	$ 4,900	$1,900	$ 3,900	$ 8,900	$10,900	$ 3,900	$ 3,900

nursery had in production. The production-area turnover highlights fast-growing and/or fast-moving crops and illustrates the efficiency resulting from efforts to keep nursery production areas producing and to eliminate vacant production space. For 1971 Perkins reported an average value of 47.7% production-area turnover for participating Florida nurseries. It should be kept in mind, however, that slow-moving or possibly slow-growing nursery crops may produce low production-area-turnover percentages and high profits. Production-area turnover values are similar to an investment analysis which compares the payback period discussed earlier in this chapter.

An additional indication of nursery productivity is provided by the dollar volume of plants sold per acre of nursery production. An average of $28,120 per acre was reported for Florida production nurseries in 1971. WLRHRI, in its 1972 operating cost study, reported an average of $2000 as nursery crop sales per acre. The higher values reported in Florida ($28,120) probably reflect the difference in sales volume per acre of container production versus field production. Production costs and sales volume per acre are much higher in container-production nurseries than the cost of production and sales volume per acre in field-production nurseries. Ratios and nursery operation cost comparisons are only valid when comparing firms with similar production systems. A high dollar value of nursery crops sold per acre of nursery production indicates productivity but may be unrelated to profitability of the operation.

Ratio analysis can also be used to determine the efficiency and productivity of nursery labor. Perkins reported that the average value of nursery crops produced per full-time employee was $15,243. An additional labor productivity ratio can be developed by dividing annual production labor cost by the annual volume of crops sold. This percentage is the labor cost per dollar of nursery crop sold, assuming that there is no expansion or contraction in the firm's volume of production. Both labor productivity ratios would illustrate increased labor efficiency through mechanization and alterations of cultural practices as well as more effective motivation and management of nursery labor. Landscape construction and garden center labor efficiency can also be compared by dividing total annual sales by the number of full-time employees. Ratio analysis can also be useful in evaluating the productivity of equipment (volume of annual sales/annual equipment depreciation and maintenance costs).

A number of ratios can be used to evaluate various aspects of the financial management of the firm and allow for the comparison of one nursery to others as well as to firms unrelated to the nursery industry. The ratio of goods sold by a garden center to total capital measures the proportion of invested sales that is returned in sales each year. The higher the ratio of sales to invested capital, the sooner the invested capital will be turned over. This factor indicates at least in part how efficiently the capital investments are being utilized in the firm. The solvency of a nursery firm can be approximated by developing the ratio of total debts to total net worth. This ratio indicates the relative amount of money supplied by creditors compared to the amount of money the owners have invested in the firm. The ratio of current assets to current liabilities (current ratio) is of interest, particularly to creditors, because it provides an indication of the firm's ability to meet its current liabilities. The median current ratio reported by the WLRHRI operating cost study in 1972 was 63:1 for production nurseries and 31:1 for landscape firms.

The return the owner receives on the capital invested in the nursery can be evaluated by calculating the ratio of profit (before taxes) to net worth. The 1972 WLRHRI operating cost study indicated that production nurseries reported a median value of 22.3%. Perkins suggested that the goal of production nursery management should be a profit percentage return on capital that is at least twice the current annual interest rate charged for borrowed funds. The usefulness of any ratio analysis or operating cost study involving profit data depends (as was discussed earlier in this chapter) on the type of accounting system, the value assigned to nursery crop inventories, and the manager's discretionary spending of gross profits. Discretionary spending consists of those expenditures which are frequently made by management based on how these expenditures will influence the taxes paid by both the owners and the firm rather than how they will influence gross profits. The common manipulation of discretionary spending by nursery management makes ratio analysis involving profit data of questionable utility.

The use of any ratio analysis is limited to comparisons with similar firms and with ratios of past years' financial data for the same firm. Ratios and operating-cost data, even those most specifically related to the nursery industry, serve only to identify areas where a firm differs from other firms or past years. Ratios do not indicate whether these differences are healthy or unhealthy. The median ratios of the nursery industry are not absolute standards that must be approximated. The goals of the firm (growth, profit, quality of product, stability, etc.) should not include the creation of financial ratios that approximate the median for the industry.

SUMMARY

Financial management makes use of financial records to document the growth potential, profitability, and the value of the assets of a nursery to obtain capital for operation and expansion of the firm. These records can also be used to help decide what kinds of expansion, production, purchases, and so on, will be most beneficial. The cost of production can be documented by financial records indicating the profitability of various types of nursery products and practices. Financial records and proper financial management are essential to start, manage, and evaluate the success of the nursery. Financial management is the core of the nursery business, and all aspects of the business are affected by it.

REFERENCES

AMERICAN ASSOCIATION OF NURSERYMEN. 1979. Update, a report to the Allied Landscape Industry. AAN, Washington, D.C.

AMERICAN NURSERYMAN. 1976. Tax Bill Exemption. Vol. 144, No. 8, pp. 110–111. American Nurseryman Publishing Company, Chicago.

APLIN, R. D., and G. L. CASLER. 1973. Capital investment analysis: using discounted cash flows. Grid Publishing, Inc., Columbus, Ohio.

EDWARDS, J. D., R. H. HERMANSON, and R. F. SALMANSON. 1974. Accounting I, 3rd ed. Richard D. Irwin, Inc., Homewood, Ill.

HORTICULTURAL RESEARCH INSTITUTE. 1971. Uniform chart of accounts for nursery production, landscape, and retail operations. HRI, Washington, D.C.

MURRAY, W. G., and A. G. NELSON. 1960. Agricultural finance. Iowa State University Press, Ames, Iowa.

PERKINS, G. S. 1973. The economics of ornamental nursery management. Fla. Agric. Exp. Sta. Univ. Fla. J. Ser. 5180, pp. 411–415.

SMITH, E. M., G. C. HIMES, and H. HOLLAR. 1970. A method of utilizing accounting for nurseries producing field grown stock. Coop. Ext. Serv. Ohio State Univ. Bull. 520.

TAYLOR, R. D., H. H. KNEEN, D. E. HAHN, and E. M. SMITH, JR. 1986a. Calculating the bottom line for a small container nursery. Am. Nurseryman, February.

———— , H. H. KNEEN, D. E. HAHN, E. M. SMITH, JR., and S. UCHIDA. 1986b. Calculating field nursery costs. Am. Nurseryman, February.

TOWER, R. B. 1962. A handbook of small business finance. Small Business Management Series 15 (Small Business Administration). Superintendent of Documents, Washington, D.C.

WHOLESALE LANDSCAPE AND RETAIL HORTICULTURAL RESEARCH INSTITUTE, INC. 1972. Operating cost study. WLRHRI, Washington, D.C. (1965–66, 1967, 1968, 1969 are also available.)

8 *Wholesale Marketing of Nursery Crops*

The wholesale marketing of nursery crops can be discussed from a number of viewpoints, depending on how one views the marketing process. The retail garden center manager, the mass merchandiser, landscape architect-designer, landscape contractor, wholesale salesman, production nurseryman, and so on, are all involved in wholesale marketing, and each has very personal requirements and interests in the process. Each of these individuals will define the marketing of nursery crops differently. Each will also positively or negatively evaluate the current nursery crop marketing process in relation to how well it satisfies his or her own needs. Marketing, as defined by Kohls, is "the performance of all business activities involved in the flow of goods (in this case nursery crops) and services from the point of initial agricultural production until they are in the hands of the ultimate consumer." Owing to a lack of space in this text, only the wholesale marketing of nursery crops to retailers such as garden centers, landscapers, and mail-order nurserymen will be considered.

The flow of nursery crops from the producer to the retailer is quite complex, in part because of the vast variety of nursery crops, the rapid expansion of the nursery industry, and the long distances that nursery crops are shipped from producer to consumer. A study of the nursery industry in Michigan revealed that approximately 75% of the nursery stock sold at the retail level was produced out of the state. Nursery crops were shipped into Michigan from a majority of the states in the continental United States. At the same time, many wholesale production nurseries in Michigan sell 75% or more of their crops out of the state. A similar marketing pattern would be expected in most of the major nursery market areas in the United States except California, where imports are limited by local competition and stiff import regulations.

SPECIALIZATION IN PRODUCTION NURSERIES

There are a variety of reasons for the long-distance shipments of nursery stock in the United States. A specific nursery crop may be more economically produced in one section of the country because of a more optimal climate and soil, lower land and labor costs, greater availability of technically trained employees, lower-energy requirements, longer growing season, and possibly more progressive nursery management. Many production nurseries also specialize in the type of consumer they serve as well as in the nursery crops they produce, and therefore serve a broader geographic area. The same species and cultivar of shade tree, for example, will be grown, pruned, harvested, packaged, and labeled quite differently, depending upon whether the tree will be merchandised through a garden center in early spring as a packaged plant, or through a landscape contractor as a balled and burlapped plant in late summer. The production nursery manager frequently makes irreversible cultural, harvesting, and packaging decisions which commit the nursery crop to a specific type of marketing channel and consumer. The same variety of plant produced in a similar manner will be needed by different retail markets in different stages of growth, different quantities, delivery schedules, labeling, prepricing tags, types of cultural care information, and reorder potentials. State laws in some states dictate part of this.

Most production nurseries, to obtain the benefits of specialization, have directed their nursery crop production to serving a relatively narrow segment of the market. In this way the management of a nursery can more efficiently provide the nursery crop and the necessary services needed by a specific type of retail marketing firm. Developing a successful, profitable wholesale marketing program for a nursery crop begins with an understanding of the needs and nature of the customer. Too often a marketing program begins with a specific product that must be sold. A marketing program should not be a crisis-solving activity. It is an essential part of the nursery management process and must be considered as the first step in the planning and organization of a production nursery.

TYPE OF NURSERY CROPS NEEDED BY LANDSCAPERS

A landscape nurseryman has specific plant needs and will usually want larger plants than will retail garden centers. The nursery stock will usually be B&B, boxed, or container-grown, with very limited quantities purchased as bare-root plants. This in part reflects the reduced maintenance and extended transplanting and sales season, as well as improved transplantability of B&B, boxed, or container-grown plants compared to bare-root plants. If the landscaper is buying plants for a landscape project, specific plants and sizes may be called for by the architect, which in some cases may be produced by a limited number of nurseries or, at times, may be unavailable. Landscape architects are, therefore, a prime source of information in planning the specific plants and sizes in the production system.

Timing Deliveries for Landscapers

During the past 30 years, the landscape planting season has gradually expanded into the summer and winter seasons as a result of cultural and technical innovations. Landscape planting can now be carried out most of the year, except for certain types of tender landscape plants. However, the ability of workers and equipment to function properly under existing weather conditions will reduce efficiency during the winter season in the northern United States. A landscaper therefore has a more constant need for plants throughout the year than do garden centers, which have pronounced spring and fall seasons.

The landscaper may want to schedule the delivery of plants to a landscape site on a specific day or in some cases at a specific hour of the day to improve efficiency of costly leased equipment and labor and eliminate the damage to plants resulting from reloading and excessive handling.

Landscapers may frequently purchase rather large quantities of the more commonly used nursery stock which they plan to hold in their own lath, shade area, or temporarily plant in their own fields until needed in a future landscape project. This provides a convenient, inexpensive, immediately available source of landscape plants. Some will produce larger trees which are expensive to ship long distances and unusual specimen plants which are difficult to find in production nurseries. Other landscapers will purchase only those plants needed on a current landscape project.

Price Quotations for Bidding

Some landscape projects are bid months or even years before the landscape project begins. The production nursery may need to guarantee a price, 1, 2, or even 3 years before delivery in order for the landscaper to submit a bid. Wholesale nursery catalog prices are usually valid for only part of the year; therefore, special price quotations are needed from the wholesale nursery. Large production nurseries supplying quotations will usually want to know the name of the project the landscaper is bidding, particularly if the landscape project is large enough to approach exhausting the regional supply of one size or variety of landscape plant. A number of landscape contractors obtaining prices and guaranteed delivery for the same project will create the illusion of a shortage, which drives prices up and prevents other landscapers from preparing a competitive bid. A production nursery can supply price quotations and guarantee delivery to many landscapers if they are bidding the same landscape project. This keeps the prices down for the landscapers and increases the chances of the production nursery supplying the plants for the project being bid. Production nurseries also may want the opportunity to supply all the plant needs for the project, providing a more efficient shipment to the site and volume discounts on plant material.

Services Provided by the Nursery Broker

In the larger market areas, an independent broker may buy in large quantities and maintain nursery stock on a sales lot in order to wholesale it to retailers. The nursery broker may also provide the service of finding and procuring unusual specimen plants needed by the landscape contractor. Other nursery stock brokers may not handle or store landscape plants, but in effect serve as sales representatives for a number of production nurseries. This type of broker may be asked by the landscaper to obtain prices for all plant needs, saving considerable time and expense for the landscaper. The broker may arrange for the digging and delivery schedules if needed. Because of the volume handled by a broker and knowledge of the availability of nursery stock and the availability of transportation, the broker may be able to arrange efficient, combined order shipments with a reliable trucker, realizing substantial savings in the cost of plants and transportation for the landscaper.

TYPE OF NURSERY CROPS NEEDED BY GARDEN CENTERS

In contrast to landscapers, retail garden center managers are usually not interested in a broad selection of rare or unusual landscape plants and have short, high-volume spring and fall sales periods. A large northern chain of retail garden centers, Frank's Nursery Sales, Inc., reported 11.3% of their sales in the first quarter of the year, 39.1% in the second, 20% in the third, and 29.4% in the fourth quarter of the year. The fourth-quarter sales (October, November, and December) are primarily Christmas-related items. The dominance of the second quarter (April, May, and June) spring plant sales in retail garden centers is a serious challenge for garden center managers. Well over half of the plant sales in most garden centers will occur during the second quarter of the year. Garden centers in mild climates will have more uniform sales throughout the year as a result of a longer growing season.

A garden center's merchandising program often begins in winter with the sale of indoor plants, bird seed, pet supplies, and crafts. Spring sales begin with the display of fertilizers, grass, vegetable and flower seeds, dormant packaged bare-root perennials, deciduous plants such as roses and fruit trees, and flowering shrubs. In the northern United States, this sale begins with the first comfortable spring days. Dormant plant sales will be followed by B&B or containerized plants and bedding plants. Peak sale opportunity for landscape plants such as flowering shrubs and trees may be only the week or two that the plant is in bloom in the community. The garden center manager will usually develop an advertising program which is fixed weeks or even months in advance of the sales period. This program will be timed to promote those types of plants that attract the interest of the consumer. Advertising programs might also feature sale-priced items called *loss leaders,* specifically chosen to increase traffic in the store.

Timing Deliveries for Garden Centers

The timing of nursery stock deliveries for retail garden centers is one of the most important challenges for the production nursery specializing in serving garden centers. Many garden center managers will buy only from those production nurseries that demonstrate the ability to deliver their products consistently when requested. Consumers are interested in purchasing nursery stock the first few warm days in spring, particularly if they occur on a weekend. This does not allow sufficient good weather for a local nursery to harvest plants from the field, package, and deliver nursery stock to the garden center in time for early spring sales. Southern nurseries have a distinct advantage in providing early deliveries for northern garden centers. Many northern nurseries utilize a variety of different storage facilities to hold nursery stock harvested and packaged during the preceding fall and winter (see Chapter 17). This allows the northern production nursery to ship fall harvested nursery stock in early spring before the local climate would permit field harvesting.

The sale of nursery stock in garden centers is highly dependent upon the weekend weather. A rainy cold weekend will almost stop sales, whereas a warm sunny weekend will stimulate demand substantially. A production nursery specializing in providing nursery stock for garden centers must be able to respond to a good-weather weekend by accelerating deliveries. The production nursery must also be able to deliver nursery stock according to the retailer's scheduled advertising program. A garden center loses not only the potential sale but customer confidence when an advertised plant is not available as a result of limited supplies. The short duration of garden center sales requires that every available display space be filled with plants, and that a maximum effort be made to restock as soon after sales as possible.

TYPE OF NURSERY CROPS NEEDED FOR MAIL-ORDER NURSERIES

The mail-order nursery uses a sales catalog as well as other forms of advertising to sell nursery stock that will be delivered for the most part via parcel post or a parcel service. Mail-order catalogs are usually mailed in mid- to late winter, but early fall catalogs specializing in fall planted bulbs are also common. This industry is particularly sensitive to parcel post rates and makes every effort to reduce the bulk and weight of its nursery products, packaging, and catalogs. Most mail-order items are either bare-root dormant plants or are grown in small, lightweight soil and containers. Nursery stock is usually dug in the fall, processed during the winter, packaged, and shipped in early spring. Bare-root dormant plants are usually moistened and wrapped in moisture-proof material, frequently sealed in polyethylene bags, and packed in cardboard containers. The mail-order catalog has been the single most important public source of information and sales motivation for the entire nursery industry, including garden center sales and landscape plantings.

Timing Deliveries for Mail-Order Nurseries

The scheduled shipment of mail-order nursery stock is usually based on the estimated time of optimal planting weather for the particular area to which it is being shipped. Shipments may also be limited by the chances for freezing damage to plants during delivery. The entire marketing area (frequently a major segment of the continental United States) will be divided into zones having the same optimal planting dates. A mail-order nursery frequently limits shipping season to only a few months to allow the consumer to plant nursery stock at the best time of year for plant survival.

WHOLESALE NURSERY SALES ORGANIZATIONS

A variety of different types of nursery sales organizations and agreements with nursery salespersons can be found in the industry. Some production nurseries will hire their own staff who work on a salary and/or commission to sell the nursery's products. The nursery's market area might be divided into districts so that each is the exclusive area for one salesperson. The sales actually booked by the salesperson as well as orders made directly by customers that were originally contacted by the salesperson are his or her accounts and contribute to sales commissions. The sales staff frequently spends a great deal of time personally visiting each customer in the district, providing marketing and management information. It usually takes a number of years of travel before the salesperson can develop the maximum sales potential in the district.

Some nurseries have a separate sales division which markets the nursery's products and, as mentioned earlier, may market plants and related items not produced by the parent nursery. This provides a more complete line of products and services and makes for a more efficient sales organization. Nursery brokers sometimes called representatives or ''reps'' operate their own independent sales organizations, selling on commission products from a number of production nurseries. These individuals will only book orders. The shipments will originate from the production nursery. A rep will, in most cases, be able to provide a complete line of nursery crops and related products as well as arrange for special shipment, delivery, and other services. The rep receives a commission on all orders personally booked and all orders direct to the production nursery from customers the broker originally contacted. A rep can sell a more complete line than most salespersons representing a single nursery (and the rep usually will write larger orders in a smaller territory than will most salespersons). Both brokers and salespersons will frequently provide assistance in developing advertising programs, display patterns, delivery timing, loss-leader sales, and so on, for retail garden center managers. They may provide data on the previous years' orders, delivery dates, and reorders to assist the buyer in developing this year's purchasing decisions. They are also excellent sources of nursery industry information as a result of their travel and experience with the industry.

Selling nursery stock to discount or department stores with garden center sections usually involves dealing with a head buyer in the home office before the salesman has the opportunity to contact the manager of each store. The buyers for some discount chains will know little about the nursery business but a great deal about merchandising. Frequently, the time, quantity, and nature of the initial shipment is established by the buyer in the home office, and subsequent reorders originate with the store manager. The nursery sales force may have to contact each of the individual store managers as well as the head buyer. Many discount or department stores and some garden center managers want large color tags with the botanical and common names and a picture to help identify and sell the plant, and some will want the nursery stock prepriced.

Buyers may also directly contact production nurseries in order to gain more information on the price, quality, and availability of nursery crops. Many buyers for mail-order, garden center, and landscape firms will periodically visit production nurseries searching for new sources of plants as well as new types of plants. Buyer trips to production nurseries are one of the best ways to evaluate the quality and availability of common as well as unusual types of landscape plants, and are encouraged by production nurseries. Some production nurseries will host open houses or field days for landscape architects, municipal arborists, and landscape contractors. Many landscape architects will make extensive searches for unusual, high-quality plant material to add variety and interest to their landscape designs.

STANDARDS

American Standard for Nursery Stock, sponsored by the AAN, is the recognized standard for nursery stock in the United Staates and is designed for the improvement and standardization of nursery products. The standards have been very effective in establishing grades for deciduous shade and flowering trees, deciduous shrubs, coniferous and broad-leaved evergreens, roses, vines and ground covers, fruit trees, small fruits, lining-out stock, seedlings, bulbs, corms, and tubers. The standards apply to harvesting of field-grown plants by all three methods—ball and burlap, ball and potted, and bare root—and to container-grown plants. In addition, they set standards for the minimum size of root system for ornamental plants of all types. The standards are used by most buyers and sellers of nursery stock, but they should be used only for the minimum acceptable size and quality of plants.

Where minimum–maximum size ranges are stated, an average size is required. That is, when one hundred 6- to 8-ft trees are ordered, the plants should average about 7 ft, not just make grade at 6 ft. Since it is almost impossible to establish standards for quality of living products, it is necessary to rely on the integrity of the individual nurseryman, and where this is not forthcoming, to seek other sources of supply.

The standards are reviewed and updated periodically to meet the requirements of the American National Standards Institute. The latest edition may be obtained from the AAN office in Washington, D.C.

Deciduous Trees

Caliper of the trunk shall be the determining measurement in grading decidu-ous shade and flowering trees. The measurement is made 6 in. above ground level for trees up to and including those 4 in. in diameter. Above this size the measure-ment is to be made 12 in. above the ground (Fig. 8–1). Caliper is stated in ¼-in. units up to 2-in. size, in ½ in. units up to 4-in. size, and in 1-in. units above 4 in. (e.g., 1 ¼–1 ½ in., 2–2 ½ in., 5–6 in.). The standard recognizes four major types (standard shade trees, slow-growth shade trees, small upright trees, and small spreading trees) and suggests optimum and maximum heights and minimum root spread for trees of various caliper within each type. Height is quoted in single-foot units up to 6 ft and in double-foot units over 6 ft (e.g., 5–6 ft, 6–8 ft).

Deciduous Shrubs

Deciduous shrubs are graded by height and number of canes or stems (Fig. 8–2). The height classes for dwarf or semidwarf shrubs is stated in inches up to 24 in. (3-in. units up to 18 in., 6-in. units between 18 and 24 in.), and ½-ft units over 6 ft (e.g., 12–15 in., 18–24 in., and 2–2 ½ ft). Height classes for strong-growing shrubs is stated in 6-in. series up to 24 in., single-foot units between 2 and 6 ft, and in double-foot units above 6 ft (e.g., 12–18 in., 4–5 ft, and 6–8 ft). The standards suggest a minimum root spread and indicate that the average height of a grade is close to the mean of the height class (e.g., size of plant, 4–5 ft; minimum root spread, 14 in., and average height, 4 ½ ft).

Evergreens

Evergreens (Fig. 8–3) are divided into narrow-leaved and broad-leaved plants, and each group is subdivided into types based on habit of growth. The types include:

1. Conifer (Narrow-leaved plants)
   a. Creeping or prostrate
   b. Semispreading
   c. Broad spreading, globe, and upright dwarf
   d. Cone (pyramidal)
   e. Broad upright
   f. Columnar

2. Broad-leaved plants
  a. Spreading
  b. Semispreading
  c. Globe and dwarf
  d. Broad upright
  e. Cone

The height or spread in each group is stated using 3-in., 6-in., 1-ft, and 2-ft intervals. The interval varies with type, but the following intervals are fairly standard.

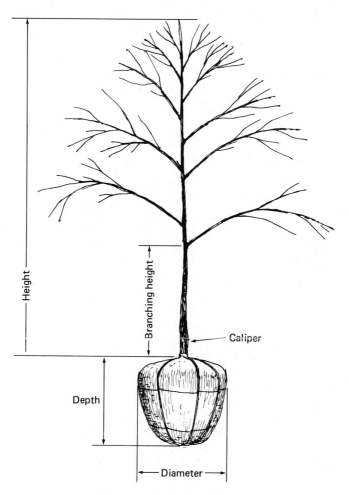

Figure 8–1 Caliper measured 6 in. above ground level if 4 in. or less; if more than 4 in. measure at 12 in.; caliper determines size of rootball (see Table 8–1). (From American Association of Nurserymen, 1986.)

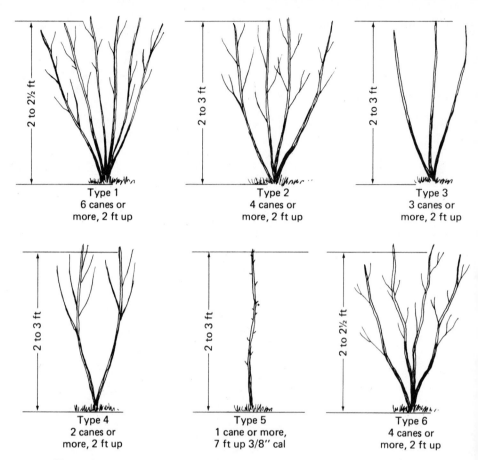

Figure 8–2 Comparisons in the various types of deciduous shrubs. (From American Association of Nurserymen, 1986.)

3-in. intervals up to 18 in.	12–15 in.
6-in. intervals between 18 in. and 4 ft	2½–3 ft
1-ft intervals from 4 ft up	5–6 ft

Measurement of height is determined from where the branches start, not at ground level, if the plant is leggy. It also stops where the main part of the plant ends, not at the tip of a shoot.

Christmas Trees

Nurserymen interested in standards for Christmas trees should write to the Consumer and Marketing Service, U.S. Department of Agriculture, Washington,

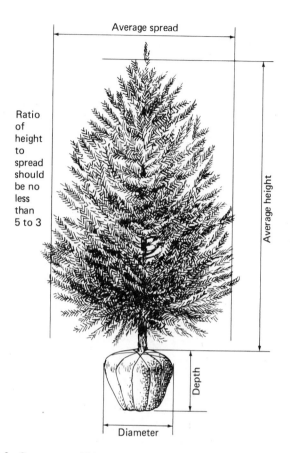

Average spread

Ratio
of
height
to
spread
should
be no
less
than
5 to 3

Average height

Depth

Diameter

Figure 8–3 Cone or pyramidal-type evergreen. (From American Association of Nurserymen, 1986.)

DC 20250, and request a copy of "United States Standards for Grades of Christmas Trees."

Rose Grades

Rose standards apply only to 2-year-old field-grown roses when sold either bare-root or individually wrapped and packaged or in cartons. Roses are graded by size, number, and length of canes. Consideration is also given to weight and caliper of canes, depending upon grade and variety. The basic rose grades are No. 1, No. 1 ½, and No. 2. Each grade must have a minimum number of strong canes, generally 3, of a certain length and in each case branched not higher than 3 in. above the bud union (Fig. 8–4). All No. 1 and No. 1 ½ grades shall be tied 10 to a bundle and No. 2 grades 20 to a bundle, with two printed variety labels and a grade specification label on each bundle.

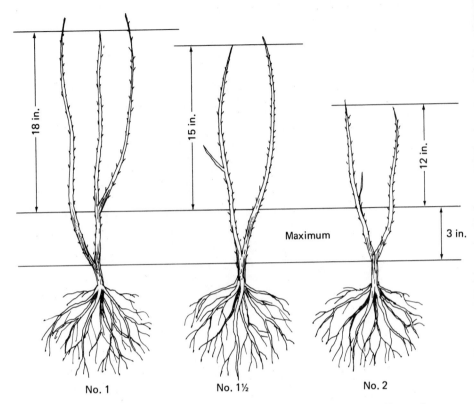

Figure 8–4 Comparisons of No. 1, No. 1½, and No. 2 Hybrid Tea, Tea, and Grandiflora roses. (From American Association of Nurserymen, 1986.)

Fruit Tree Grades

Caliper is the basic standard for fruit trees and is taken 2 in. above the collar or bud. It is generally stated in sixteenths of an inch; classes being stated in the odd-number series (e.g., 5/16 to 7/16, 9/16 to 11/16). In the three West Coast states, 1-year-old standard fruit tree stocks are commonly graded in intervals of ⅛ in. Trees should have reasonably straight stems, and all grades 5/16 and larger (except 1-year sweet cherries) should be branched and well rooted. Fruit trees are tied 10 or 20 to a bundle, depending upon size, and identified with two printed labels.

Balling and Burlapping

Balling and burlapping (B&B) or boxing of trees and shrubs is one means of packaging plants for market. It is a practice associated with large trees and with evergreens of various sizes. Although some plants can be successfully transplanted without a large ball of earth, it has become an accepted practice to transplant large trees B&B or boxed.

American Standards for Nursery Stock recommends minimum sizes of balls for five general plant types (Table 8–1). Although the recommendations are for plants that have been field-grown under favorable conditions, it is recognized that the root system of plants varies with species, soil conditions, and cultural practices, and that the ultimate size of the ball depends largely upon the integrity of the nurseryman. However, ball sizes should always be of a diameter and depth large enough to obtain the fibrous roots necessary to assure successful transplanting. The depth of the ball may vary with tree species, soil type, and the area of the country where the tree grows. The diameter/depth ratios in Table 8–2 can be used as a guide in balling plants.

TABLE 8-1   Recommended Balling and Burlapping Specifications for Four General Types of Plants

Spreading Conifer and Broad-leaved Evergreens		Cone and Broad Upright Conifers and Broad-leaved Evergreens		Columnar Evergreens		Standard Shade Trees	
Spread (ft)	Diam. (in.)	Height (ft)	Diam. (in.)	Height (ft)	Diam. (in.)	Caliper (in.)	Diam. (in.)
1½	10	1½	10	1½	10	1¼–1½	18
2	12	2	12	2	12	1½–1¾	20
2½	14	3	14	3	13	1¾–2	22
3½	18	5	20	4	14	2	24
4	21	6	22	5	16	2½	28
5	24	7	24	6	18	3	32
6	28	8	27	7	20	3½	38
7	32	9	30	8	22	4	42
8	36	10	34	9	24	4½	48
		12	38	10	27	5	54
		14	42	12	30	6	60
		16	46	14	33	7	70
		18	50	16	36	8	80
				18	40		

Source: American Association of Nurserymen, 1986.

TABLE 8-2   Ball Diameter/Depth Ratios for B&B Plants

Diameter of Ball (in.)	Depth of Ball
<20	Not less than 3/4 of diameter
20–30	Not less than 2/3 of diameter
31–48	Not less than 3/5 of diameter

Source: American Association of Nurserymen, 1986.

STANDARD UNITS OF NURSERY STOCK

Wholesale nursery stock is usually priced in no more than four or five of the following units: 1, 10, 25, 30, 50, 100, 250, 500, and 1000. The unit price may reflect the savings resulting from not having to break bundles or pallets in storage and the savings involved in processing a few large orders as compared to many small orders. The pricing by unit discounts may also be as much the result of traditional practice as it is a reflection of current actual costs. Some nurseries give a discount on total sale rather than numbers of plants. Some wholesale catalogs may indicate that different plants in unit quantities may be combined as one order to receive an even better unit price. In some cases no unit price under 10 or 25 is listed or accepted, or an additional charge may be made for units of less than 10 or 25 of one item. Prices for orders substantially in excess of the 1000 rate are usually negotiated. A wholesale buyer such as a landscape designer or contractor may want to personally select the plants in the production field in order to obtain a specific shape or form. Some nurseries will indicate that this is possible only with an additional 20% charge for the special service to cover the additional cost of selling and the additional cost of digging a specific plant within a row.

SHIPPING AGREEMENTS

All wholesale prices are listed in the catalog as FOB (free on board) the production nursery. The buyer bears the shipping cost. In some cases the production nursery will operate its own trucks and is fully responsible for any damage during shipment. In most cases nurseries arrange shipment for the buyer, but the sale is still under the standard FOB terms (see Chapter 10). Additional boxing, packaging, or bailing beyond that normal for harvesting the crop is usually done by the production nursery for an additional charge at cost.

WARRANTY

In many cases a wholesale catalog contains the statement that no warranty is expressed or implied as to the description, productivity, quality, viability, or any other matter of the nursery stock sold, and that the nursery will not be responsible for the result secured upon transplanting. However, most nurseries warrant their plants to be true to name and in a healthy condition when shipped. The survival of nursery stock, as well as the subsequent growth and production of flowers, fruit, and so on, is to a large degree the result of the care the plant receives during storage and after transplanting. It is not reasonable for the production nursery to be responsible for the performance of the plant. Wholesale catalogs may also indicate that the production nursery accepts no responsibility for the warranty the buyer may give to his customers, including any governmental department or agency.

NURSERY CROP MARKETING CHANNELS

Nursery marketing channels, as mentioned earlier, reflect the nature and location of the consumer, the optimal production environment, and to some degree the existence of management expertise and availability of labor. The marketing channels for nursery stock sold by retailers in the northeastern United States were documented by E. Jarvesoo in 1969. It is very probable that some of the plant materials in this survey were purchased from a specific area but not grown there. Materials are often purchased from the other production nurseries and wholesaled again in order to provide a more complete line of nursery stock. As shown in Fig. 8–5, over one-half (51%) of the shade trees sold in the northeast were shipped in, Tennessee (34%), Oregon (8%), and Ohio (6%) being the largest suppliers. Approximately one-third (35%) of the deciduous ornamental trees (flowering trees) were shipped into the northeast, with the majority coming from Oregon (18%), Ohio (7%), and Tennessee (4%). It is interesting to note the change in rank of Oregon and Tennessee when comparing shade trees and flowering trees.

In contrast, evergreen trees, narrow-leaved evergreen shrubs, and broad-leaved evergreen shrubs were predominantly purchased in the northeast. This could be expected because the northeastern states are a major production area of evergreen trees and narrow-leaved and broad-leaved evergreen shrubs for the states east of the Mississippi River. Approximately one-fifth (19%) of the deciduous shrubs and one-half (40%) of the roses retailed in the northeast were shipped in (Figs. 8–6 and 8–7).

Surveys in other major market areas would be expected to yield similar relationships reflecting the production advantages available in various areas of the continent. The growth of housing and commercial construction in the sun belt has stimulated an east-to-west movement of landscape plants. As a general rule, production areas will supply nursery crops to market areas and garden centers having a more severe climate and a later spring than the area of production. This is not always a north-south relationship, but might reflect the climatic protection provided by the lake effect, such as the Great Lakes or maritime climates along the coasts. The warmer-to-colder climate shipment of nursery crops reflects the advantages offered by longer growing season, reduced winter injury, and overwintering costs as well as the ability to spring-harvest field-grown nursery stock and deliver it to a retail outlet for the first spring sales. In some cases the development of spring growth and flowers can be delayed in common cold storage in order to time flowering for maximum sales in northern retail market areas.

Selling Southern Grown Nursery Stock
in Northern Markets

There appear to be limits to how much milder or warmer the production climate may be in relation to the consumer's climate. Most of the northeastern retail outlets surveyed by Jarvesoo did not report the purchase of woody nursery crops

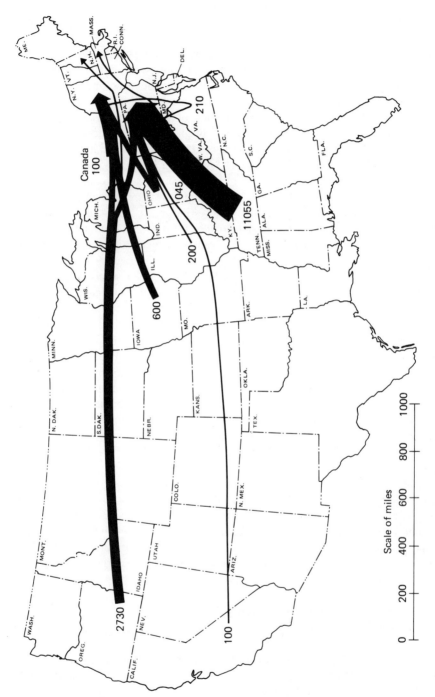

Figure 8–5 Sources of supply and main destinations of deciduous shade trees, northeast, 1963.

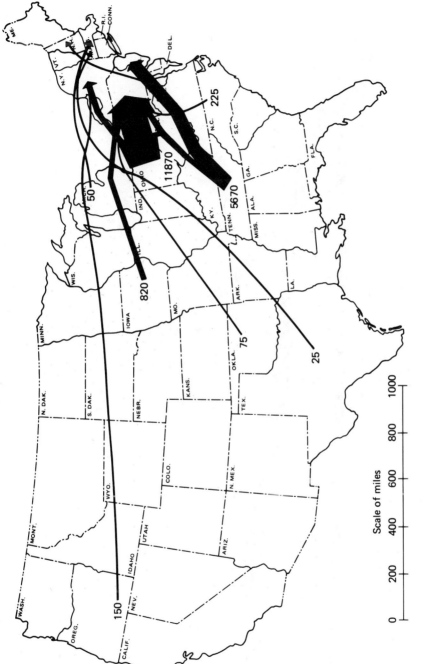

Figure 8–6 Sources of supply and main destinations of deciduous shrubs, northeast, 1963.

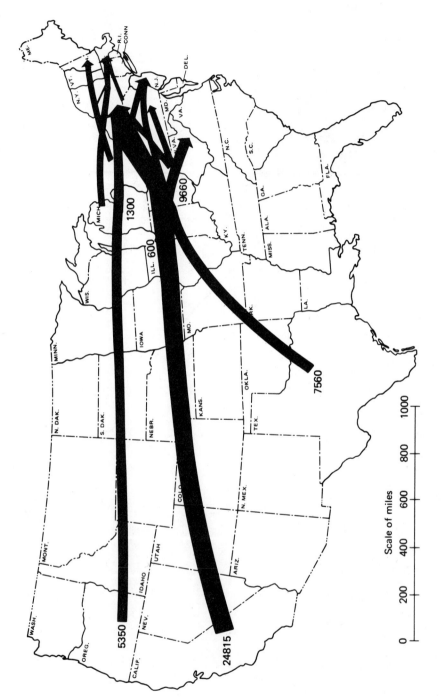

Figure 8-7 Sources of supply and main destinations of roses, northeast, 1963.

Scale of miles

0   200   400   600   800   1000

(with the exception of roses) in 1963 from zones 8, 9, and 10 (Figs. 8–5, 8–6, and 8–7). It would seem apparent that many outdoor nursery crops moving from warmer to cooler climatic zones (Fig. 8–5) are rarely shipped to a climatic zone more than 20°F colder (mean annual minimum temperature). Exceptions to this relationship include roses and some juniper and arborvitae species. A number of reasons for the limitation in movement of nursery crops to colder climates can be proposed. The distances involved may make freight costs prohibitive. However, as shown in Figs. 8–5 through 8–7, substantial quantities of nursery crops are shipped from the west to the east coast of the United States. Plants grown more than two climatic zones warmer may be in full growth during early spring shipment and be vulnerable to frost damage. The cost of delaying growth and flowering by cold storage to avoid frost damage may be prohibitive. Many nursery crops adapted to northern climates have specific cold-exposure requirements for breaking dormancy and specific day-length requirements for vegetative growth, flowering, and the development of low-temperature hardiness. Plants best adapted to cooler northern climates may be unable to resist the high summer temperatures and humidities in some southern climates. These requirements of plants adapted to northern climates may preclude their efficient growth in production climates more than two climatic zones warmer.

A number of nursery crops, such as *Cornus florida* and *Cercis canadensis*, can be found growing in native stands over a range of four climatic zones. However, these native stands have developed into ecotypes that are adapted to a specific habitat and are not necessarily capable of surviving over the entire range for the species. This has been found true with almost every species of native woody plant that has been studied. If a specific plant variety is genetically adapted to the climate of a northern market, the fact that it has been grown for a number of years in a much milder climate will not alter that genetic potential. It will be able to develop its full genetic potential for low-temperature hardiness when grown for one growing season in the northern climate to which it is genetically adapted. This is also true for plants having the genetic potential for high temperature and/or high humidity tolerance and produced in cooler or dryer climates. Many nursery crops are reproduced vegetatively as new varieties and few data are available concerning the climatic limitations of these new varieties. If information is lacking concerning the climatic limitations of a new variety, it might be advisable to purchase these nursery crops from production nurseries in a similar climatic zone. The flow of nursery crops from the site of production to the ultimate consumer is quite complex and is changing with the development of new technology, new nursery crops, and the changing costs of transportation versus production.

Obtaining Marketing Information

The degree of specialization in marketing channels results in a considerable challenge for both the buyer and seller of nursery crops. The American Association of Nurserymen publishes an annual booklet *Sources of Plants and Related Supplies* (see Appendix A), which lists production nursery sources for more than 1600 varieties of commercial nursery crops and related supplies. A similar service, available in *Nursery Report,* is provided by the Landscape Materials Information Service, Callicoon, New York. The botanical name of each variety of nursery crop is followed by a listing of production nurseries offering it for sale, with size and quantity of the nursery crop. This booklet provides a broad base of current information for the wholesale buyer of nursery crops and is financed by membership dues of those firms listed as well as those firms obtaining the published listings.

Many state nursery trade associations provide listings of the production nurseries in that state producing various categories of crops, such as shade trees, deciduous shrubs, fruit trees, indoor foliage plants, ground covers, and so on. Additional information for the buyer is available in both the classified and unclassified advertising in nursery trade journals and trade association publications such as the *American Nurseryman, Nursery Business, Home and Garden Supply, Southern Florist and Nurserymen, Pacific Coast Nurserymen, The Voice of MAN,* and others (Appendix C). In many cases the production nursery's advertisement in a trade journal is very brief, providing only the name, address, telephone number, and the type of crops produced. The wholesale buyer may obtain the production nursery's current catalog by contacting the nursery. The wholesale nursery catalogs provided by production nurseries are the most detailed and accurate source of information concerning the availability of nursery crops.

Marketing at Nursery Association Meetings

Trade association meetings provide an additional opportunity for buyers to contact production nursery salespersons and to become aware of the availability of various types of nursery crops. These contacts may be informal discussions between buyers and salesperson or may be the result of an exhibit in a formal trade show. Most state, regional, and national nursery trade association meetings are partially financed by fees charged for exhibit space in the trade show rooms and are a major attraction for the meeting. A broad range of plants as well as pesticides, fertilizers, specialized landscape construction equipment, supplies, tools, and production nursery equipment are on display at most nursery trade shows. The trade fair is certainly one of the most effective opportunities for production nurserymen and wholesale buyers to meet. The actual sales booked at the trade exhibit are commonly less important than the subsequent sales made as a result of the contacts made during the trade exhibit.

Booking Wholesale Nurseries Crop Orders

There has been a gradual change in the purchasing practices for nursery crops. A number of years ago most orders were booked 3–5 months before spring delivery, and the traditional state and regional annual trade meetings, held during the winter season, provided an ideal time for ordering plants. Orders for nursery crops, particularly from garden centers, are currently placed well before the winter season.

Some of the newer regional trade exhibit meetings are scheduled in summer or early fall, allowing orders to be booked 6–9 months before spring delivery. The dates for state and regional meetings are usually consistent from year to year to eliminate conflict between meetings.

A number of regional trade shows have become major sales events for the industry: the Western Association of Nurserymen, Trade Show and Meeting, Kansas City, Missouri; the Garden Living Industries of the Eastern United States, Kiamesha Lake, New York; Mid-America Trade Show, Rosemont, Illinois; Mid-Atlantic Nurserymen's Trade Show, Cockeysville, Maryland; Southern Nurserymen's Association Trade Show, Atlanta, Georgia; TAN-MissLark Regional Convention, Nursery and Garden Supply Show, Houston, Texas; Pacific Horticulture Trade Show, San Diego, California; and others. In some cases the regional trade shows have an educational program in addition to the trade exhibit.

Almost every state having a substantial market for nursery crops has a state nurserymen's association meeting with a trade fair. This places a substantial burden on the wholesale nursery marketing to 8–10 states, particularly if it is expected that the nursery exhibit and, thereby, support the association in each state. The state meetings, in many cases, have strong educational programs in conjunction with the Cooperative Extension Service and their land-grant university. Members of the state nurserymen's association are encouraged to buy from those nurseries exhibiting in the trade show, and by doing so, support the association. These meetings are important because they deal with the issues and challenges facing the nursery industry, including relations with state legislature and various regulatory agencies.

Pricing Nursery Stock

The pricing of nursery stock is primarily based on supply and demand. Pricing of nursery stock is limited by production costs, plant quality, and the service and reliability of that service provided at delivery. The changes in prices for nursery stock are not at a uniform rate for all types of plants. The reported mean cost of the same plant material for 1972 and 1974 in an NLA bidding exercise illustrates this point:

Plant Material	1972–1974 Change in Price (%)
2–2½-in. shade trees	+61
2–2½-in. flowering trees	+70
18–24-in. spreading evergreens	+11
2¼-in. potted ground covers	+14

Two methods are commonly used to establish the current price. A production nurseryman may use the current wholesale catalog from another large nursery serving the same marketing area. The nurseryman will set his or her price using the nursery catalog as a guide. The other method is based on an evaluation of the future supply-and-demand relationship for that particular nursery crop. Obviously, the cost of production will provide the lower limits of wholesale prices, particularly if that crop is going to continue to be produced. The sales organization, commission salespersons, and brokers are a valuable source of information concerning the supply and demand anticipated for specific nursery crops and marketing channels.

Projecting Future Sales

Changes in the supply and demand for a specific plant will reflect adverse growing conditions such as winter damage or drought in a particular production area, changes in consumer demand, and the national economy. The garden center industry tends to expand, at a somewhat greater rate, increasing demand for garden-center-type plants during periods of general economic recession. Apparently, when consumer earnings decrease, the consumer spends more time and effort on "do it yourself" gardening and landscape projects. The demand for plants used in landscape construction, on the other hand, is influenced by public building programs, such as highway landscaping, low-income housing, educational facilities, medical complexes, shopping centers, and so on, as well as major industrial complexes. Changes in the volume of landscape construction are commonly found 2–3 years or more after changes in the volume of building construction. Landscaping is usually accomplished 2–3 years or more after the beginning of general construction on the project. The relative demand for plants used in landscape construction such as shade trees and sod can be estimated by noting changes in construction starts and allowing sufficient time for the delay between construction starts and landscape planting. Unfortunately, the 3- to 6-year or longer crop cycle from propagation to harvest of shade trees is, for example, too long in most cases to take full advantage of reliable economic predictions and changes in the construction industry.

The future demand for nursery stock can be enhanced by a number of other procedures. The development of a patented landscape plant allows the production nursery to control production and therefore the supply of that plant to the consumer. The number of patented landscape plants has dramatically increased in the past 10–15 years, for a variety of reasons. Advertising patented plants to both wholesale and retail consumers is more obviously rewarding to the nursery owning the patent because it develops demand only for those specific nursery crops produced by the nursery. The ability to create demand through advertising and to control supply has stimulated the investment in breeding and selection programs for patented landscape plants.

The demand for the entire spectrum of nursery crops could be stimulated by the growth of a coordinated national advertising program such as the nursery industries National Marketing Council (NMC). NMC provides a common nationwide advertising theme and materials which can be used by a local retail nursery. In 1986, NMC offered to fund 50% of approved advertising up to a total of $2000 for qualified private businesses or state, regional, or local associations. Wholesale growers financially support NMC, which distributes themes, advertising artwork, as well as materials for radio, direct mail, television, transit advertising, and in-the-store merchandising aids equally to landscape firms and retail garden centers.

A well-coordinated cooperative advertising program of sufficient size could have a major impact on the nationwide demand for nursery crops and the growth of the entire nursery industry.

A mandatory marketing-research program was approved by the Ohio nursery industry in 1986 to advertise and promote the sale of nursery stock in Ohio and to conduct research on the production and sale of nursery stock. Anyone who sells nursery stock, including growers, retailers, landscapers, and mass merchandisers, with plant sales of over $10,000 is required to contribute 1/4 of 1% of gross receipts to the Ohio Department of Agriculture. The program is to be administered by a 15-member committee from the nursery industry. This program is the first of its kind in the United States. A similar program is being considered by the state of Michigan at the time of publication.

Developing a Marketing Program

The development of a wholesale marketing program for a production nursery begins with an analysis of the needs of the customers: garden center buyers, land-scape contractors, city foresters, and other nurserymen. These needs reflect, in part, the needs of the ultimate customers. The market analysis is followed by a produc-tion study of species to be produced, cultural requirements, production methods, rotations, costs, and so on. These data are then evaluated against an estimate of potential income from future sales and against product competition to determine an estimate of probability for success of the program.

A successful marketing program for nursery products requires the input of as much factual production and marketing data that are available, matched with the best estimates of future demands, price structure, and potential product competi-tion. Management must integrate all of this information and continually modify pro-duction and sales programs to remain economically sound in a constantly changing market environment.

SUMMARY

Wholesale marketing of nursery crops is rapidly changing as a result of many fac-tors, especially changes in market demands, production technology, and modes of transportation. In recent years, the marketing phase has quite possibly changed more than any other aspect of nursery management. The nursery industry of the United States continues to expand, creating many new opportunities for profitable marketing. Because of its relatively small size as compared with other industries, it is difficult for nursery managers to obtain good market information. Currently, the best information is obtained through various trade associations, trade journals, and from attendance at trade shows and meetings. Hopefully, the Nursery Marketing Council, established in 1977, will serve as the major source of market information for the industry.

The growers' ability to anticipate market demands is a limiting factor in the growth of the nursery industry and poses one of the most significant marketing challenges for the nursery industry of the future.

REFERENCES

AMERICAN ASSOCIATION OF NURSERYMEN. 1986. American standard for nursery stock. AAN, Washington, D.C.

————. 1979. Partners for profit. Nursery Industry Cooperative Advertising Program. AAN, Washington, D.C.

————. 1973–74. Sources of plants and related supplies, an Allied Landscape Industry Service, AAN, Washington, D.C.

BENDER, F., and V. BENSEN. 1968. Marketing channels of floricultural products and ornamentals in Maryland. Agric. Exp. Sta. Univ. Md. Misc. Publ. 642.

FRANK'S NURSERY SALES, INC. 1975. Ann. Rep. 6399 E. Nevada, Detroit, Mich. 48234.

JARVESOO, E. 1969. Procurement and sales practices of retail outlets for ornamental nursery products. N.J. Agric. Exp. Sta. Rutgers Univ. Bull. 824.

LANDSCAPE MATERIALS INFORMATION SERVICE. 1967. Twenty-ninth nursery report. LMIS, Calicoon, N.Y.

NURSERY INDUSTRY AND FLORICULTURE, PROJECT '80 RURAL MICHIGAN NOW AND IN 1980. 1966. Agric. Exp. Sta. Coop. Ext. Serv. Mich. State Univ. Res. Rep. 43.

U.S. DEPARTMENT OF AGRICULTURE. 1965. Plant hardiness zone map. USDA Agric. Res. Serv. Misc. Publ. 814.

9 *Nursery Inventory Control*

An inventory or stock control system is needed in all phases of nursery production and merchandising in order to maintain control of plant materials, equipment, tools, and supplies. Numerous systems are available, from the very simple to the complex. The following systems can be used effectively to maintain control of materials within nurseries.

PLANT MATERIAL INVENTORY

A plant inventory system is designed to provide management with data that can be used for making management decisions. An inventory of plants is needed to plan a sales campaign and project future trends. By maintaining an up-to-date sales inventory, management can minimize overselling or leaving plants unsold, thus assuring a higher percentage of satisfied customers. A knowledge of the plant inventory can be the basis of planning work schedules, labor needs, storage requirements, and land use. Inventory data are needed when planning production programs, calculating production costs, and making pricing decisions. Plant inventory systems can also provide information to evaluate cultural practices. To accomplish these ends a nurseryman must know how many plants of each variety (cultivar) are available, in each size, within the nursery. The actual system of plant inventory control will vary with the size and type of nursery and with the degree of sophistication desired by the nurseryman. Plant inventory systems vary from a daily update available from a computer to little, if any, control. For a small nursery or a large nursery specializing in one genera, such as rhododendrons, or one type of plant material, such as selected shade trees, the system can be relatively simple. But for a large, general nursery growing a wide selection of plants, the system can be rather complex. A com-

**TABLE 9-1   Grouping of Plants for Inventory
and Production Cost Analysis**

1. Shade trees	6. Fruit trees
2. Small or flowering trees	7. Small fruits
3. Large evergreens	8. Container stock
4. Small evergreens	9. Bed material
5. Deciduous shrubs	10. Propagation

mon technique is to inventory and obtain cost of production data by plant groups (Table 9–1).

Taking of the physical inventory is facilitated by an integrated layout of the nursery using planting blocks and standard labeling of rows (see Chapter 5). The count is made by trained individuals using calipers and measuring sticks (Fig. 9–1) to obtain diameters of trees and heights or spread of shrubs. Another handy device is a template tree grader, designed to caliper trees up to 3 in., by sizes, as recommended by *American Standards for Nursery Stock.* An aid in measuring height and

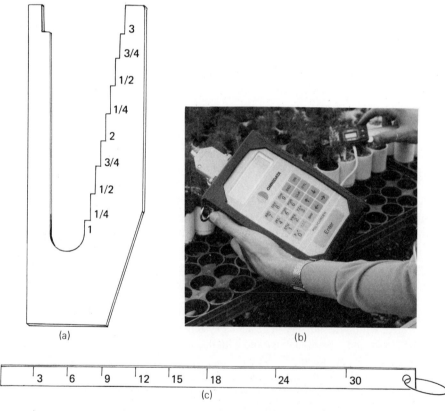

Figure 9–1   Equipment used for grading trees and shrubs in nurseries. (a) Template-type tree grader; (b) Polycorder; and (c) measuring stick shrub grader.

spread of shrubs is a stick marked in size classes. For tabulating the actual count in the field, a clipboard equipped with a series of mechanical counters is most commonly used.

Automatic recording of tree caliper measurements is possible through the use of a Polycorder and a Fowler caliper (Fig. 9–1). Measurements can be taken over a range of 0–8 in. (0–200 mm) with an accuracy of 0.001 in. (0–0.3 mm). The components of this system include the Polycorder (a portable, electronic notebook), a Fowler Max-Cal electronic caliper, and Omnidata's model 565F interface cable. With the use of an electronic notebook the problems commonly associated with data collection are eliminated. The Polycorder is programmable and the data can be transferred directly to a computer.

Other measurements, in addition to caliper, can also be made and recorded in the Polycorder, including soil moisture readings from soil moisture blocks, weights from an electronic balance, and tree and shrub heights and diameters with the aid of electronic measuring tapes.

Nurserymen generally count and measure all trees and specimen plants, whereas representative samples—portions of rows, or small plots—are used to estimate the inventory of seedlings, small evergreens, deciduous shrubs, roses, and so on. A complete inventory is taken in most field-production nurseries at the end of the growing season and periodic inventories are made as needed. In large container production nurseries the inventory is updated daily, weekly, or monthly. The data are recorded onto the *field inventory data collection form* (Fig. 9–2). In some nurseries this may be the extent of the plant inventory, but in others these field data are processed into more meaningful information for use by management.

In some larger nurseries the field inventory data are posted to an *inventory flow sheet* (Fig. 9–3) together with new planting and sales data. By proper posting of the flow sheets, it is possible to determine fairly accurately the status of the plant material within the nursery by type and location. If accurate data are collected, it is possible to determine plant losses and to estimate growth rates. This information can also be used to pinpoint problem areas and to check on cultural practices. The inventory flow sheets should be designed to fit the needs of the nursery manager. Figure 9–3 is an example of a form designed for a nursery specializing in the production of shade trees. The columns headed "Est. unit sales" and "Est. end. inv." are for the manager's best estimate of sales and final inventory. If they are not needed by management, they can be omitted from the form.

Data from the flow sheets or from the field inventory forms are used to post the *sales inventory*. This is generally done at the end of the growing season but prior to the sales period for field-production nurseries. However, for container-production nurseries the sales inventory is posted with new data (plants for sale) on a daily, weekly, or monthly basis. The sales inventory, maintained by the sales department, can be posted either to a *sales inventory card* (Figs. 9–4 and 9–5) or it can be entered into the inventory file of a computer. Sales data must be posted promptly if the system is to be effective. Notation is made of the buyer and the sales posted by use of the sales inventory fraction, the numerator being the number of trees removed

Block ___17___

Rows or parts of rows	Species	Size	Date 11/17/80		Date		Date	
			REG	PG	REG	PG	REG	PG
30-31 ↑ N	Acer rubrum 'Red Sunset'	NS	2	1				
		2-2½	54	0				
		2½-3	107	5				
		3-3½	16	1				
		3½-4	3	1				
		4-4½	1	0				
		4½-5	—	—				
31-32	Acer rubrum 'October Glory'	NS	14	1				
		1¾-2	73	—				
		2-2½	115	3				
		2½-3	76	—				
		3-3½	14	1				

REG = Regular Grade   Initials: _AFD_ _____ _____
PG = Park Grade (less than standard quality)
NS = Not Saleable

Figure 9–2   Example of a field inventory data collection form.

from inventory and the denominator the number of plants remaining. The summary column provides quick reference as to the total balance remaining within the size class. At the time of posting the sales inventory cards, the block number where the plants are to be dug can also be noted. The production manager can precode the cards if he or she desires that the blocks be cleared on a priority basis. The data are filed alphabetically either by botanical names or by common names within plant

Acer rubrum 'Red Sunset'

Var. / Year		N Units sold	N End inv.	N Est. unit sales	N Est. end inv.	N+1 Units sold	N+1 End inv.	N+1 Est. unit sales	N+1 Est. end inv.	N+2 Units sold	N+2 End inv.	N+2 Est. unit sales	N+2 Est. end inv.	N+3 Units sold	N+3 End inv.	N+3 Est. unit sales	N+3 Est. end inv.
Pg. N	Planting year — NP		(100)														
	NS		100				97				19						
	1¼" or 4'																
	1½"										45				15		
	1¾"										29				38		
	2"														25		
	2½"													10	5	30	
	3"																
	3½"																
	Total		100				97				93			10	83		
	Loss					3 u	3%			4 u	4% 7 %B			0 u	0% 7 %B		

Var. / Pg. N+1		N Units sold	N End inv.	N Est. unit sales	N Est. end inv.	N+1 Units sold	N+1 End inv.	N+1 Est. unit sales	N+1 Est. end inv.	N+2 Units sold	N+2 End inv.	N+2 Est. unit sales	N+2 Est. end inv.	N+3 Units sold	N+3 End inv.	N+3 Est. unit sales	N+3 Est. end inv.
	Planting year — NP						(60)										
	NS						60				45				16		
	1¼" or 4'																
	1½"										13				20		
	1¾"														13		
	2"														9		
	2½"																
	3"																
	3½"																
	Total						60				58				58		
	Loss					0 u	0%			2 u	3.3% 3.3 %B			0 u	0% 3.3 %B		

Var. / Pg. N+2		N Units sold	N End inv.	N Est. unit sales	N Est. end inv.	N+1 Units sold	N+1 End inv.	N+1 Est. unit sales	N+1 Est. end inv.	N+2 Units sold	N+2 End inv.	N+2 Est. unit sales	N+2 Est. end inv.	N+3 Units sold	N+3 End inv.	N+3 Est. unit sales	N+3 Est. end inv.
	Planting year — NP										(100)						
	NS										100				36		
	1¼" or 4'																
	1½"														58		
	1¾"																
	2"																
	2½"																
	3"																
	3½"																
	Total										94				94		
	Loss									4 u	4% 4 %B			2 u	2% 6 %B		

	N Sub total				N+1 Sub total				N+2 Sub total				N+3 Sub total			
Page totals	100				157				247				235			
Sub total loss					3 u				10 u				2 u			
Total																
Total loss																

Use for 2 or more pages

ABBREVIATIONS

NP = number planted
NS = not saleable
U = units
%B = percent of base planted

NOTES

Units sold: obtain from sales records
End inventory: obtain from field inventory
Est. unit sales: manager's best estimate
Est. end. inventory: estimated end inventory

Figure 9–3 Growing inventory flow sheet. (Courtesy Studebaker Nurseries, Inc.)

groups (Table 9–1). The sales inventory can also be posted with current price information as an aid in quoting prices to customers during the selling season.

Each nursery manager must adjust the plant inventory system to the situation and develop it to provide the control and information necessary to make sound man-

Species: Acer rubrum		Cultivar: 'Red Sunset'										
Sales inventory card	Size		2″			$\frac{165}{350}$			$2\frac{1}{2}$″		550*	
	Blocks	10	17	96	$\frac{10}{**}$	17	⩽					⩽
'80 Date / Buyer	No	4	20	5	1	1	31					
1/10 Cot Gard	10		$1\%_0$				21					
3/11 D&L Land	15		$10\%_0$	$5\%_0$			6					
3/16 Lan. P.D.	2				$\frac{1}{0}$	$\frac{1}{0}$	4					

*Price code: Last digit is number of dimes; previous digits are dollars: e.g. 165 = $16.50, 550 = $55.00.
**Underlined numbers are park grade classification.

Figure 9–4 Example of a sales inventory card.

agement decisions. Electronic computers (Fig. 9–6), particularly those equipped with video readout screens, are ideal for the rapid and efficient processing of sales data within large nurseries. They can be used to provide an immediate update of sales inventory. They can be programmed to provide an analysis of sales, by variety, customer, geographic area, and by salesperson. In addition, the computer can be used to update sales books, prepare price schedules, and with the input of field inventory data, can be programmed to estimate potential sales inventory.

EQUIPMENT INVENTORY

A considerable financial investment is made in equipping and maintaining a production nursery. Equipment needed for the many and varied operations within a modern nursery includes cars, trucks, tractors, and wagons; tillage, planting, and potting machines; fertilizer spreaders; pumps; injectors and irrigation equipment; sprayers; digging machines; and storage equipment. Besides the large equipment, many types of hand tools, such as axes, digging spades, shovels, pruning equipment, knives, sharpening stones, towing chains, drafting equipment, and so on, are also needed. Some form of management control must be maintained over the equipment if the organization is to function efficiently. The primary means of gaining control of equipment is to maintain a physical inventory of all equipment and to develop plans for security, proper use, and maintenance.

Species: _Ilex crenata_
'Green Thumb'

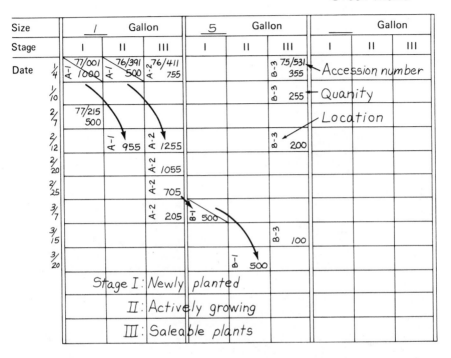

Size	/	Gallon		5	Gallon		___	Gallon	
Stage	I	II	III	I	II	III	I	II	III
Date 1/4	77/001 A-1 1000	76/391 A-1 500	76/411 A-2 755			75/531 B-3 355	Accession number		
1/10						255 B-3	Quanity		
2/7	77/215 500						Location		
2/12		A-1 955	A-2 1255			200 B-3			
2/20			A-2 1055						
2/25			A-2 705						
3/7			A-2 205	B-1 500					
3/15						100 B-3			
3/20				B-1 500					
	Stage I: Newly planted								
	II: Actively growing								
	III: Saleable plants								

Figure 9–5 Example of an inventory form for a small or medium-sized container-production nursery.

When major pieces of equipment are purchased by the nursery, they should be given an inventory number. A code number combining year of purchase, functional unit, and purchase can be used. For example, if the 34th purchase of the year was a tractor purchased in 1987 for use primarily by the production division (Division A), it would be identified as 87A34. This number should be painted or stamped onto the equipment and then entered into the inventory and maintenance records. The equipment inventory, either a card file or a computer file, is kept in the business office as a record of purchase with name of supplier, purchase price, depreciation schedule, and other related information. The maintenance card, with proper identification number, name, year, and model, is sent to the mechanic to record all maintenance and repair data. Equipment purchases should be limited to as few manufacturers as is feasible to reduce the inventory of parts that need to be maintained by the mechanic. Knowing which parts are stocked by a local supplier can reduce the nursery's spare parts inventory.

Some nurseries find it desirable to maintain a "use log" on some equipment (tractors, trucks, diggers, etc.) to determine the efficiency of the equipment. For efficient use and security, all equipment should be assigned to responsible individu-

Figure 9–6 Computer used for inventory control and for other business records. (Courtesy Monrovia Nursery Co.)

als and the individuals properly instructed in its use and maintenance. Company policy pertaining to use and maintenance of equipment should also be clearly stated in a policy manual of the nursery. Painting equipment, especially small items and hand tools, in a distinctive color can aid immeasurably in preventing loss. The use of distinctive markings can also minimize the mixup of equipment among divisions of a nursery or among crews in a landscape company.

Valuable equipment should be stored in a locked facility that also provides protection from the weather. Company policy should provide the necessary guidelines for the cleaning and storing of equipment. By establishing and maintaining a good equipment inventory and management system, it is possible to gain a high degree of control over the equipment, and at the same time assure its effective and efficient use.

SUPPLIES

Nurseries also have large financial investments in supplies. Management can gain
control over the use and expenditure of supplies by maintaining an inventory control
system, providing appropriate areas for storage, and by establishing security methods. Table 9–2 is an example of a supply inventory system for a production nursery.
The items are classified by phases of production (propagation, planting, har-

TABLE 9-2 **Inventory of Supplies for a Production Nursery[a]**

Class	Item	Units
Propagation		
Budding and grafting	Strips, 0.016 gauge, ¼ × 5 in., 1200/lb	lb
	Ties, no. 4 fruit	M
	Tape, ½ in. wide	roll
	Wax	lb
Containers	Pot, clay	
	2½ in.	ea.
	3 in.	ea.
	4 in.	ea.
Labels	Pot, wooden, painted	
	3½ × ⅝ in.	M
	10 × ⅝ in.	M
	Plant, plastic,	M
	5½ × ½ in.	
Media	Sand	yd^3
	Peat moss	bale
	Perlite, 50 lb	bag
Rooting	Hormone, IBA, 0.2%	lb
Planting and maintenance		
Containers	Fiber, 6 × 6	ea.
	Poly, 2 qt, 600 per	case
	Zarn	
	6 qt, 160 per	case
	3 gal, 100 per	case
Fertilizers	18–9–9, 50 lb per	bag
	10–6–4, 40 lb per	bag
	0–20–0, 50 lb per	bag
Fungicides	Captan, 50 wp, 5 lb per	bag
	Karathane, 25 wp, 3lb per	bag
	Truban, 25 EC	qt
Herbicides	Casoron, 4 G, 5 lb per	bag
	Princep, 80 wp, 5 lb per	bag
	Roundup, 5 gal per	cont.
Insecticides	Chlordane, 10 G, 50 lb per	bag
	Guthione, 50 wp, 2½ lb per	bag
	Sevin, 5 dust, 50 lb per	bag
Media	Sand	yd^3
	Bark, hardwood	yd^3

(continued)

TABLE 9-2 *(continued)*

Class	Item	Units
Polyethylene film	Std.	
	Clear 4 ml, 40 × 100	roll
	White, 4 ml	1000 ft^2
Shade cloth	Saran, 63% shade	1000 ft^2
Soil fumigants	Dowfume, six 1½-lb cans per	carton
Harvesting		
Baskets	Wire	
	24 × 20 in., 100 per	ea.
	30 × 24 in., 100 per	ea.
Burlap	Untreated, 36 × 36 in., 500 per	bale
	Treated, 36 × 36 in., 500 per	bale
Containers	Fiber, 10 × 10 in.	ea.
Nails	Pinning	
	6D oval head	
	350 per lb, 45 lb per	carton
Tape	Plastic tagging, ⅝ in., 12 rolls per	box
Tree wrap	4-in. width, 50 yd/roll, 12 rolls per	carton
Twine	Sisal, 3-ply, 6 balls per	bale
	Jute, 4-ply, 10 lb per	ball
Storage and shipping		
Containers	Shipping, cardboard	ea.
Media, packing	Peat moss	bale
	Shingletoe	bale
Tarps	Shade, poly, 15 × 20 ft	ea.
Equipment maintenance		
Antifreeze	Prestone	gal
Fuels	Gas	
	Leaded	gal
	Unleaded	gal
Lubricants	Slip grease	lb
Oils	10–W–40, 9 qt per	case
Physical plant		
Heating	Oil	gal
Paper	Stationery, 500 sheets per	box
	Hand towel, 16 rolls per	box
	Toilet, 100 rolls per	box

[a]Example of selected items, not a complete list.

vesting), equipment maintenance, and physical-plant supplies. Each stocked item is described along with the common unit of purchase. In addition, it is desirable to list sources of supply, price per unit, and pertinent comments. These data, commonly kept on file cards, can also be put into a computer for rapid video display of supply information as well as an electronic means of supply inventory control.

Supplies for the divisions of the nursery should be purchased primarily by the business office. But provision should be made for a responsible employee to make purchases for the nursery in an emergency or in the best interests of the business.

Supplies should be stored in proper facilities and when appropriate under proper security. Packaged supplies such as fertilizer and peat moss should be stored in covered sheds to minimize destruction by wind and rain, whereas inorganic materials such as brick or stone may be left exposed. All chemicals should be stored in their original containers and marked with the year of purchase and used in order of purchase date. Poisonous chemicals should be stored in a specially marked storage cabinet and flammable materials kept in fire-resistant containers. Only usable quantities of supplies should be kept in work areas with the balance in a locked supply-storage facility.

A periodic inventory (monthly, quarterly) of supplies should be taken to determine use rates and to prepare orders for bidding. In some nurseries, considerable quantities of material (gas, oil, containers, plastic, soil, peat, etc.) are used, and competitive bids from three or more suppliers are worthy of consideration. If the use rate exceeds the normal rate as determined by past history or by logical estimates of use, the manager should review the situation with his key supervisors and determine if corrective measures are needed.

SUMMARY

Inventory data on plants, equipment, and supplies must be collected and processed in a meaningful manner if the nursery is to attain its objective. However, it should be remembered that few people like to collect data and to keep records. All forms should be as simple as possible, and methods of recording data should be carefully worked out to make certain that it can be done expeditiously and correctly. Steps should be taken to explain the need for record keeping to everyone involved and to make the process as painless as possible. Recording, filing, and analyzing data requires time and is expensive. Do not record too many data; this can be as bad as recording too few; record only what can and will be used. A well-planned and carefully monitored system of inventory control can provide management with an effective tool for maintaining control over materials.

10 *Shipping of Nursery Stock*

The shipping of nursery stock is the operation in the nursery-to-market chain that is most vulnerable to loss of plant quality; control of the plant material usually passes from the seller to the buyer via a third party, the carrier (Fig. 10–1). Considerable forethought, planning, cooperation, and coordination by all three parties are needed to prevent losses. Each of the parties has a vested interest in the operation and should take the necessary positive actions to ensure that the products ordered are delivered in the best possible condition, in the right quantities, grades, varieties, and at the right time.

PLANT MATERIAL

Nursery stock is a perishable product. Because it is living material, it has moisture and temperature requirements that must be provided for during shipping. The variety of plant material shipped by nurseries ranges from dormant seedlings to large shade trees in full leaf weighing many tons. This necessitates considerable variations in the methods of packaging and means of transportation. Most small plants are dug bare-root during the dormant season and are shipped in packages or in large nursery boxes; the roots must be kept damp and the plants maintained in a dormant condition. Damp, aged shingletow, or similar material spread about the roots during packaging provide the needed moisture. Temperatures of 35–40°F to maintain dormancy during shipping are obtained by using a carrier equipped with refrigeration. If delivery can be effected in 5 days or less, the temperature can range between 30 and 65°F without serious injury to the plants. However, either a long delay enroute or exposure to a temperature below freezing or above 80°F could result in injury to the plants.

Figure 10–1 Staging area for loading and shipping of nursery stock. (Courtesy Monrovia Nursery Co.)

Large plants are typically dug B&B with plain, treated, or plastic burlap about the soil ball. Some nurserymen support B&B stock within wire baskets. In some parts of the country, the root ball is contained within a wooden box. In the past, most large trees were transplanted during the dormant season, but with the development and proper use of mechanical tree diggers, they can now be moved in full leaf. The plants should be taken from the field immediately after digging and placed in a cool, humid area and the root balls and foliage watered to minimize water stress.

Plants in full leaf must be shipped at a temperature above freezing but as low as practical to reduce transpiration. Shade trees in full leaf, nondormant evergreens, and container plants transported in open trucks should be protected with a strong, Saran tarpaulin during shipping. The Saran tarpaulin (90% shade) provides a barrier to the sun's rays and excessive wind damage but allows heat to escape. Spraying deciduous plants in full leaf with antitranspirants is a beneficial practice when the RH of the ambient atmosphere is above 85%. The film remains effective for several weeks. However, at low RH the antitranspirant film cracks and peels from the surface of the leaf within 2–3 days following treatment; its long-term effectiveness is minimal. When transporting large trees on open carriers, the trees and tarpaulins must be tied down securely to avoid wind whip and possible physical damage when the vehicle passes through a tunnel or under a low bridge. Some of the positive actions that can be taken to help ensure the viability of plant material during shipping are summarized in Table 10–1.

Desiccation during shipment can be minimized by watering the plants prior to digging and utilizing rapid methods of transport. When delays in transport happen, the plants are subject to drying out. When possible, keep the plants in a cool, humid area; ventilate if in a closed van, and water balled or containerized stock. Plants that arrive in a wilted condition should be placed in shade and watered immediately. If the critical wilting point has not been reached, the plants can be saved. Balled and burlapped plants should be misted or watered with the aid of a root feeder. Dormant bare-root plants will benefit either by being immersed into a tank of cool water or by being buried in a moist medium (sawdust, wood chips, soil) for several days to allow the buds to absorb water.

TABLE 10-1   Suggested Moisture Control, Temperature, and Other Actions to Ensure Successful Shipping of Plant Material

Class of Plant Material	Moisture Control	Temperature (°F)	Notes
Dormant			
Bare root (roses, shrubs, fruit trees, shade trees, and small fruit trees)	Damp, aged shingletow about roots or poly liner within container	35–40	Shipped in nursery boxes
Packaged (roses, shrubs, fruit trees, and small fruit)	Damp medium in package about roots	35–40	Individually packaged; shipped in nursery boxes
Perennials (flowering, strawberry plants)	Poly liner within container	28–35	Shipped in nursery boxes
Balled and burlapped			
Shade trees			
Dormant		30–50	Tipped and tied
In leaf	Water[a] prior to digging; store in cool area with high humidity	40–60	Tipped and tied
Evergreens			
Dormant		30–50	Stacked on balls; tarp if in open truck
Nondormant	Moisten soil[a] prior to shipping	40–60	Stacked on balls; tarp if in open truck
Containerized			
Small sizes (1–5 gal)	Watered and drained[a] prior to shipping	40–60	Decked or stacked 3–5 high on cans
Large sizes (barrels)	Watered and drained[a] prior to shipping	40–60	Tipped and tied Saran tarp if in open truck

[a]Water adds considerable shipping weight, 8.34 lb/gal. Root ball should be damp, never dry, and seldom wet to field or container capacity.

Freezing damage can be avoided by selecting rapid methods of transportation and avoiding shipment when low temperatures are predicted for the proposed route or by using carriers with heated trucks. The greatest cause of cold temperature injury to nursery stock during shipping is delays with railroad cars during winter months. Plant material that arrives with frost on the foliage may not be injured, provided that the low, critical temperature for the species was not reached (Table 17–1). Frosted shipments should be placed in a cool area (35–40°F) and allowed to thaw gradually prior to handling.

BUYER'S RESPONSIBILITIES

The buyer of nursery stock initiates the transaction by completing a purchase order which lists varieties, size, quantity, and price per unit. It is also the buyer's responsibility to specify shipping instructions, including shipping dates, means of transportation, and any special handling procedures. Orders should be placed as early as possible, and a confirmation of the order obtained from the seller to assure a contractual obligation. Dates of delivery should be stated so that plant material will arrive on time. Avoid the use of ''will advise'' for time of shipment. The seller will hold such orders in the inactive shipping file until advised to ship by the buyer. It is better to supply the seller with a delivery schedule that allows the grower some flexibility in his or her digging and shipping program, but assures timely delivery of quality stock. When time of delivery is important to meet a deadline in a planting program or material is being advertised in a garden center merchandising program, this information must be communicated to the seller so that he or she can take the necessary steps to assure timely delivery. A lead time of 2 weeks is usually the minimum required to process a large order.

In addition to the shipping date, the buyer should clearly indicate where to ship the plants, particularly if the plant material is to be shipped to a place other than to his or her place of business. This is especially true for plant material being shipped to a landscape construction site. In some cases the hour of delivery may be important. Landscape contractors may want to specify the hour of delivery to assure that workers and equipment will be available to unload large B&B trees.

If a specific means of transportation is desired, this information should be provided to the seller, or the buyer must arrange for the necessary transportation. When shipping instructions are not provided, it is left to the best judgment of the shipper who acts as an agent for the buyer, since most purchases are FOB the seller's nursery. If the buyer sends a truck to pick up the plant material, he or she should have some concept of the size and weight of the load (see Appendix H) and supply a vehicle that will accommodate it. It is also his or her responsibility to provide the necessary tarps, ropes, and materials to protect the plants and to secure the load.

The buyer should become acquainted with the seller. A visit to the nursery will help to determine the quality of the plant material and to become acquainted with the total production and shipping operation. Details of the purchase agreement should be discussed and agreed upon. Many large wholesale production nurseries have a minimum total order in dollars that will be accepted, and in some cases a minimum quantity within a size class (e.g., 10 BR shrubs, 5 B&B trees, 20 1-gal containers, or 5 5-gal containers). Handling procedures should be discussed and agreed upon to assure a maximum degree of quality control. The buyer should make the necessary financial arrangements with the seller and provide a number of credit references if he or she is a new customer.

Unloading and servicing of the plant material upon delivery is the buyer's responsibility. He or she should have an appropriate area available to receive, store, and protect the plants. In most situations the plants will need water, and if bare root, the material will have to be heeled-in to protect the root system from desiccation or exposure to freezing temperatures. One-year-old wood chips make an excellent mulch for this purpose.

Special equipment is needed for unloading large B&B trees. The practice of rolling B&B plants off the truck-bed can break the balls and result in premature death of the plants. A forklift, a tractor equipped with a front-end loader, or a small crane is much more effective and less damaging to the plant material.

The plant material should be inspected and counted immediately upon arrival and any discrepancies from the order as booked should be brought to the attention of both the seller and the carrier. The buyer has the right to open damaged cartons and examine the contents prior to signing the delivery receipt. A detailed description of damage, if any, should be noted on the delivery receipt, dated, and endorsed by consignee and carrier. This information should be sent to the seller within a 10-day period of receipt of the order. Failure to do so is tacit acceptance of the order as delivered. Plants that arrive in a frozen, dried, or pest-infested condition should be called to the attention of the state plant inspector to obtain a professional judgment on the quality of the nursery stock.

SELLER'S RESPONSIBILITIES

The seller has the responsibility of digging, assembling, packing, and shipping the order. All stock shipped shall be of the size, grade, quantity, and quality specified in the order and should conform to the latest edition of *American Standard for Nursery Stock*. The seller's responsibility begins upon receipt of the order.

One of the first decisions that the seller must make is to accept or reject the order. First, is the plant material available for sale, and second, does he wish to make a contractual obligation with the buyer? If the customer is new to the nursery, he or she should check credit references and discuss financial arrangements. The stock records should be checked for inventory count by variety and size to either confirm the order or to communicate the necessary adjustments to book the order. Upon acceptance, the appropriate quantities are deducted from inventory for sale. The invoice (Fig. 10–2) is typed and copies sent to appropriate individuals for action, with a copy to the buyer, which confirms the order. In small to medium-sized

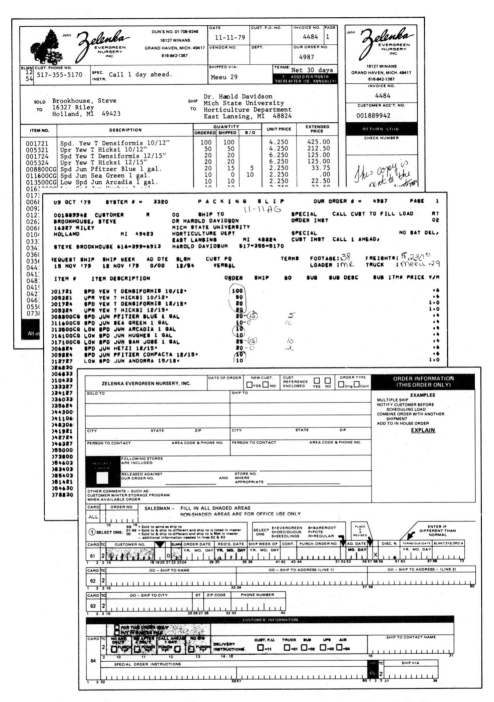

Figure 10–2 Examples of forms used to process an order by a large wholesale-production nursery. (Courtesy Zelenka Nurseries.)

nurseries, most of this paperwork is accomplished by a staff of trained clerks employing standard forms and following standard operating procedures. Larger firms accomplish much of the paperwork for booking, invoicing, and inventory control by the use of computers (Fig. 9–6).

The process of assembling, packing, and shipping of the order requires considerable coordination within the nursery and with the carrier. Nurseries that operate on a seasonal basis with a peak shipping season in the spring generally designate a key employee as shipping clerk, whereas nurseries that are shipping 10–12 months of the year employ or contract for a traffic coordinator.

The traffic coordinator or shipping clerk is responsible for arranging the most dependable, rapid, and economical means of transportation. He also coordinates assembling and packing of the order. Upon receipt of the order in the shipping department, it should be keyed to a shipping date. Orders that must arrive at the buyer's site on a specific day or hour of the day should be noted on the shipping schedule to assure timely delivery.

The traffic coordinator can select from a number of means of transportation, each with advantages and disadvantages. Air freight is fast but expensive and is generally utilized for lightweight shipments needed in a hurry. Bus freight and United Parcel Service (UPS) are used for small, lightweight shipments (less than 50 lb/package) that can be delivered within a 2- to 5-day period. Both of these require that the shipper bring the material to the terminal and the buyer pick it up at a terminal, although UPS will deliver. Railroad boxcar, a common method of shipping nursery stock in the past, is now used only on a limited basis. The railroad boxcar takes from 6 to 10 days for direct shipment from coast to coast, but at times delays of 3 weeks or more are encountered. The charge is based on 100-lb units/mile, with a minimum shipping charge that is often two or three times the 100-lb rate. Although most wholesale nurseries that ship via railroad boxcar are equipped with a railroad loading dock, few buyers have railroad siding and docking facilities, necessitating double handling at the receiving end.

Motor freight is the most common means of shipping nursery stock. Direct motor freight can pick up plant material at the production site and deliver directly to the seller, avoiding multiple handling and delays often experienced when material moves by common carrier and passes through various terminals enroute.

When it is necessary to ship less than a truckload (LTL), the traffic coordinator can arrange a pooled or split load if two or more orders are to be delivered in the same geographic area of the country. Pooled loads require more coordination to assemble and are more costly, since a stopover charge is added to each order. But pooled loads are less expensive and are generally delivered faster than LTL shipments. Motor freight is charged on a mileage basis per trailer. Thus, it is advantageous to obtain a full load or to split-load rather than employ LTL shipments.

Bare-root plants are normally packaged in the storage area and delivered to the loading dock. Containers for shipping nursery stock should be sturdy; preferably only those that can withstand a 250-lb test should be used. This is to prevent breakage during shipping and crushing of containers that are on the lower layer. Overwatering plant material prior to boxing for shipment in fiberboard-type containers soaks and weakens the container, contributing to breakage and damage to plant material.

Containerized and B&B material are picked up at the growing or storage sites and delivered to the loading dock. Many forms of mechanical equipment are utilized in packaging and loading. Automatic bundling, tying, and strapping machines (Fig. 10–3) aid in packaging bare-root orders. Forklift trucks lift and transport heavy

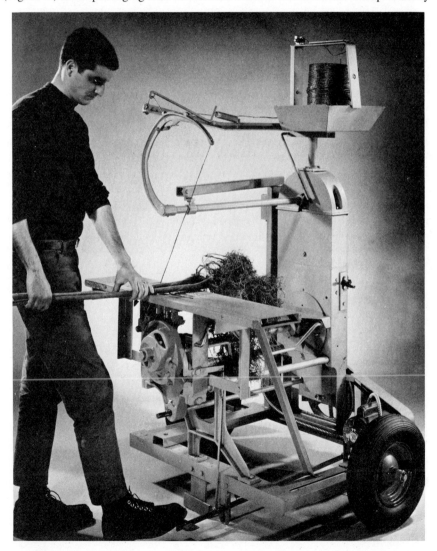

Figure 10–3 Automatic nursery stock tying machine. (Courtesy Saxmayer Corporation.)

loads about the nursery and into the carrier (Fig. 10–4). Some nurseries employ self-tracking lowboy trailers or electric carts to transport container material. Where possible, pallets of various types and endless belt units are employed to expedite the movement of plant material in the loading process.

Plant material loaded into railroad cars or motor freight trailers must be carefully stacked to avoid damage to the plants, and shifting of the load during transport. At the same time, maximum advantage of the total space available can be taken. Small B&B plants and those in metal containers are generally stacked three to four tiers high, whereas plants in nonmetal containers are generally shelved to avoid breakage of the containers. B&B trees in wire baskets require that the trunks be protected with some form of padding to avoid injury during loading and transport. Split loads shipped in closed vans can be divided with a barrier to aid in unloading and to minimize loss of plant material destined for the next stop enroute.

Accurate records must be maintained. A careful count of plants and packages must be made at the time of loading to assure that the buyer receives what was ordered and that the seller bills the customer for the material shipped. The seller is under obligation to conform to the most current issue of *American Standard for Nursery Stock*. All stock must be correctly labeled; in some states plants must be tagged with their botanical name. Following loading, the seller must provide the carrier with a copy of the invoice and other appropriate information. In split loads, it is advisable to place the invoices in separate envelopes and to mark them with information that the driver will need to expedite delivery. This information generally includes buyer's name, place of delivery with any special directions, time of deliv-

Figure 10–4   Forklift aids in loading nursery stock. (Courtesy C. E. Lewis.)

ery if applicable, and telephone numbers of people to contact in the event of a delay. At the time of departure, the shipping clerk should notify the buyer, either by telex or by telephone, of the expected time of arrival and the name of the carrier.

In addition to shipping records, it is desirable that the party who arranges for the shipping maintain an up-to-date file on each carrier hired to haul plant material. The file should contain copies of the carrier's certificate of insurance and permits to operate a motor vehicle in the various states enroute. The certificate of insurance is needed to assure fiscal responsibility in the event of an accident, and up-to-date permits assure transit within the various states.

It is desirable for the seller to obtain cargo insurance when arranging shipments by exempted carriers not booked through a trucking broker. The seller holds title to the plant material until it is delivered either to the buyer or to a common carrier. Nurserymen who hire trucking firms are advised to contract their trucking needs through a reliable trucking broker who will arrange the necessary details and carry the appropriate cargo insurance.

Most traffic controllers maintain an order board, updated twice daily, so that sales and administrative staff can quickly respond to inquiries relative to shipping of orders.

CARRIER'S RESPONSIBILITIES

The carrier is responsible for transporting the plant material from the seller to the buyer. In most situations the carrier (railroad, motor carrier, bus, UPS, or U.S. mail) is a third party, but in some situations the buyer may send a truck to pick up the plant materials or the seller may deliver in one of his or her own trucks. Nevertheless, it is necessary for the carrier to comply with local, state, and federal laws pertaining to the operation and maintenance of motor carriers. The Interstate Commerce Commission (ICC) is the agency of the federal government that regulates motor carrier transportation interstate and across international boundaries. The ICC regulates motor transport by various economic regulations, which apply only to commercial carriers who do hauling for hire; nurserymen who do their own trucking, under a farm license, are exempt from the economic regulations. However, truck safety regulations, administered by the U.S. Department of Transportation (DOT) apply to all owners of trucks operating in interstate commerce. These regulations are contained in *Federal Motor Carrier Safety Regulations* published by the DOT, available from the Superintendent of Documents in Washington, D.C. Topics contained in the regulations are qualification of drivers, driving of motor vehicles, parts and accessories necessary for safe operation, notification, reporting and recording of accidents, hours of service of drivers, inspection and maintenance, and driving and parking rules. Every employee who does interstate trucking should be provided with a copy of the regulation, be required to read and understand the regulations, keep an updated driver's log, and turn it in for inspection on a regular basis.

Although nurserymen are exempt from the economic regulations of the ICC, they are subject to the federal highway use tax. This tax is imposed on all motor vehicles or vehicle-trailer combinations having a taxable gross weight of more than 26,000 lb. The Internal Revenue Service (IRS) publishes a schedule showing taxable gross weight for various motor vehicles and vehicle-trailer combinations. The tax must be reported and paid to the District Director of the IRS.

In addition to the federal regulations, many states and local communities have laws or regulations pertaining to the operation of motor vehicles. Nurserymen who transport nursery stock into other states should be acquainted with the applicable laws and regulations. A book that covers laws and regulations that drivers need to know is *Professional Truck Drivers Handbook*. Order copies from Private Truck Council of America, 2022 P Street, NW, Washington, DC 20036.

Interstate truckers are subject to the economic regulations of the ICC under the Federal Motor Carrier Act. They must obtain a license from the commission, which also regulates rates, territories, routes, insurance coverage, and so on. However, Congress has exempted agricultural and horticultural commodities from the act, thus allowing truckers who haul plant material for nurserymen greater flexibility in service and rates. The exemption holds only if exempted commodities are carried in the truck or trailer combination at any one time. If a trucking firm transports a mixed load of exempt and nonexempt material, it is subject to the economic regulations. Table 10–2 lists some of the exempted horticultural commodities. As a result of this special exemption, many for-hire truckers devote a major portion of their effort to servicing nurseries and other agricultural industries.

Since drivers are primarily responsible for the operation of their vehicles and loads, they should supervise loading and tie-down to assure proper weight distribution and securing of loads (Fig. 10–5). To avoid economic penalties for overweight, a weight estimate of the load should be made at the time of loading (Appendix H).

TABLE 10-2   Partial List of Horticultural Commodities Exempted from Coverage under the Federal Motor Carrier Act

Bark
Bulbs
Christmas trees
Containers, crates, boxes (used to move exempted commodities or being returned for reuse)
Flowers, cut or growing
Grass seed
Greenery
Humus
Leaves
Manure, natural or dried
Nursery stock
Peat moss, dried, shredded, baled
Plants: flower and vegetable
Roots, asparagus, mint, rhubarb, etc.
Seeds
Trees
Wreaths (natural with small amounts of foundations or decorative material)

Figure 10–5 Shade trees loaded and tied for shipping. (Courtesy Studebaker Nurseries, Inc.)

Most truckers can estimate the weight of the load by the pull on the engine as they leave the loading dock. To obtain an accurate weight, the trucker can have the load weighed at a local business (grain elevator, foundry, etc.) that is equipped with the necessary scales.

REGULATED CARRIERS

Some nursery stock, primarily boxed and packaged material, is shipped via regulated motor carriers. They charge rates regulated by the ICC and can transport only within the geographic area specified in their certificate of operating authority. Long-distance shipments can pass through a number of terminals and be transported by a number of carriers enroute to the consignee, which can result in delays and possible injury to the plant material. To avoid delays, buyers can request "through routing" from the carrier that will make the final delivery. This information should then be communicated to the seller, who will make the necessary arrangements. If the buyer cannot obtain through routing, he or she should request the shipper to select the best routing available. However, many shippers select "open routing," which passes the responsibility to the carrier to route the shipment; this often results in delays.

Regulated carriers must issue a bill of lading for each shipment received for transport. The bill of lading provides a description of the product (contents, number, weight, size, etc.). The product should be described in wording that conforms to the motor carrier's classification requirements. To do otherwise can result in higher rates. For example, a shipment of bare-root shrubs boxed and marked "dormant nursery stocks'' or ''perishable nursery stocks'' would cost more to ship than the same shipment boxed and marked ''shrubs, other than balled in earth, tops tied and roots wrapped.'' The latter wording conforms to the motor carrier's classification. Also, some carriers refuse to handle perishable shipments. To avoid this possibility, nurserymen should avoid the use of ''Perishable'' but mark the bill of lading ''Do Not Delay! Early delivery requested.'' When possible, labels on containers should be in large, easy-to-read print and placed on the front and back of the container rather than being typed and placed on top of the container. Only the name and destination of the buyer need to be on the outside of the container. The bill of lading contains all other necessary information.

Upon delivery the regulated carrier must present a freight bill covering the shipment, listing rates assessed; total charges to be collected; special charges (with details); and the route, including name of carriers that participated in the shipment and terminals through which the shipment moved. This information is needed in the event a claim or lawsuit should be filed against a carrier for damages to the plants suffered while in transit.

If it should become necessary to file a claim for damages or overcharges against a carrier, nurserymen should engage a traffic service agency. The traffic service agency will also audit freight bills for overcharges and provide assistance in tracing and expediting shipments that are lost or delayed in transit.

Freight Charges

Freight charges are based on a rate per mile for truck and trailer of a given size. Many nurseries, especially those that produce container-grown plants, provide a schedule of shipping charges. These charges are established for zones of delivery, at various distances from the production site. The charges are stated either as truckload or LTL-zone rates (Table 10–3).

Pooled deliveries are also booked on a rate per mile plus a stopover charge for each partial loading. If all customers are in the same geographic area, the charge per customer can be proportioned either by weight or space. However, where there is considerable difference in mileage between stops, a more equitable basis for proportioning charges is the adjusted LTL charge. This charge can be obtained by first calculating a LTL reduction factor, which is applied against the LTL charge for each customer. The LTL reduction factor is obtained by dividing the total freight charges for a pooled load by the total charges for LTL delivery to each customer. The factor is then used to adjust the LTL charge to each customer. For example, LTL charges to three customers are $400, $600, $800, whereas the total pooled cost is $1400. The LTL reduction factor is 0.78 and the adjusted charges are $310, $470, and $620. With the aid of a simple desk calculator, these calculations can be made rapidly and accurately.

The traffic coordinator or shipping clerk can estimate cost of shipments with

TABLE 10-3 Example of Shipping Charges from Container-
Production Nursery to 10 Delivery Zones[a]

A. Truckload rates [Maximum load: 6500 1-gal containers or equivalent (1
5-gal = 2 3-gal = 4 1-gal)]

Zone	Price
1	$ 200
2	250
3	300
.	.
.	.
.	.
10	1500

B. Less-than-truckload rates

	Price		
Zone	1 gal	5 gal	3 gal
1	$0.05	$0.25	Double 1-gal rate
2	0.10	0.50	
3	0.14	0.60	
.	.	.	
.	.	.	
.	.	.	
10	0.25	1.40	

[a]Each distal zone increases by a radius of approximately 100 miles.

the aid of official state highway maps, a Rand McNally road atlas, or a mileage guide for major cities available from the Household Goods Carrier's Bureau.

Many individual truckers give allowances to nurserymen who load or unload LTL shipments aggregating 10,000 lb or more in one calendar day. Firms that load or unload LTL shipments totaling 10,000 lb or more should negotiate with truckers for the "Loading/Unloading Allowances." Although the allowance may be only a few cents per 100 lb, in the course of a year the amount can be sizable, particularly to heavy-volume shippers or receivers.

Shippers should consider executing a "no-recourse clause" on bills of lading on collect shipments. Failure to do so leaves the shipper liable to pay any uncollected freight charges that the carrier is unable to collect from consignee. Executing the no-recourse clause could save the shipper from having to pay uncollected charges if the consignee should happen to go bankrupt.

A package express service, known as XpressPAX, is available through the Greyhound Bus Company. For a nominal fee the bus company provides an appropriate-sized shipping container, packing materials, and assistance in packing shipments. It can frequently provide same-day service to points up to 300 miles.

SUMMARY

Shipping of nursery stock is an operation of considerable importance to nurserymen. Individual nurserymen and nurserymen's organizations have spent and will continue to spend considerable time and energy trying to assure delivery of quality plants to the customer. At the first meeting of the American Association of Nurserymen in 1876, transportation of nursery stock was a topic that received major attention. Delays in shipment and high transportation rates were the primary complaints of the day. However, with positive action on the part of all parties—shipper, carrier, and buyer—directed toward maintaining plant quality during the postharvest preplanting period, it is possible to deliver the product to the ultimate customer in a condition that is a credit to the grower and to the activities of the carrier. "Green survival—it depends on you," the motto of the AAN, is most appropriate when applied to the operation of shipping of nursery stock.

REFERENCES

AMERICAN ASSOCIATION OF NURSERYMEN. 1963. Transportation summary. AAN Newsletter 580:1–19.

HALL, G. C., and C. E. WHITCOMB. 1976. Antitranspirants: an investment or an unnecessary expense? Am. Nurseryman 144(2):14.

OSSIAN, W. 1973. Shipping nursery stock today. Am. Nurseryman 138(1):20; 138(2):14.

U.S. DEPARTMENT OF TRANSPORTATION. 1975. Federal motor carrier safety regulations. Title 49. Transportation, p. 123.

SUGGESTED READING

Guide to Maximizing Recovery of Loss and Damage Claims. 1978. AAN Transportation Consultants-Bohman Industrial Traffic Consultants, 335 East Broadway, Gardner, Mass. 01440.

BARRETT, C. 1983. Practical handbook on private trucking, Traffic Services Corp., Washington, D.C.

PART III   Culture

11 *Soil and Nutrition Management for Field-Grown Plants*

Soil is the field-production nurseryman's number one asset, since it is from the soil that the essential mineral elements and water are obtained for plant growth and development. The soil also provides a medium of support for the plants and is the home for billions of microorganisms that play a vital role in changing the chemical and physical properties of the soil into an ecosystem capable of supporting plant growth. Therefore, it is imperative for a nurseryman to have an appreciation and understanding of this complex system since his livelihood is dependent upon it.

A nurseryman should know (1) the essential mineral elements—how they affect plant growth, their deficiency symptoms, and methods for preventing or correcting deficiencies; (2) the role that soil reaction (pH) plays in the availability of the various mineral elements and ultimately in the growth of plants; (3) the concept of nutrient-element balance and how nutrient-element balance affects the growth of plants; (4) how soils and plants are tested for the various elements; and (5) how to interpret the results of the tests as they relate to the particular situation. To fertilize effectively, a nurseryman should also have a knowledge of cation exchange capacity, fertilizers, soluble salts, the importance of maintaining soil structure, and the organic matter content of soils.

Although there is no unanimity in defining soil, it is commonly thought of as that portion of the earth's surface which has been derived from rock and in some cases organic remains and with which living organisms are usually associated. Rocks that have weathered are broken down by the processes of disintegration and decomposition into smaller particles having a changed physical and chemical state capable of supporting the growth of plants when supplied with water in the proper ambient atmosphere. Soil is the product of the rocks from which it was derived, but is also dependent upon the length of time and the intensity of the chemical, physical, and biological forces that have acted upon it. The soil, in turn, is the source of the essential mineral elements for plant growth.

ESSENTIAL ELEMENTS

The essential mineral elements, often referred to as plant nutrients, may be divided into two groups. The major or *macronutrients* include the elements nitrogen, phosphorus, potassium, calcium, magnesium, and sulfur. Nitrogen or potassium are most commonly deficient in soils of low fertility and commonly need to be added to nursery soils. Under normal conditions, phosphorus, calcium, magnesium, and sulfur are in ample supply in most agricultural soils and therefore seldom limit the growth of woody species.

The second group is called the *micronutrients,* since they are needed in very small quantities. They are also known as the trace or minor elements. They include boron, copper, iron, manganese, molybdenum, zinc, and chlorine. It should be pointed out that although they are needed in only trace or micro quantities, they each perform an essential function in plant growth and development which is not minor.

The function of each of these elements in plant growth and its deficiency symptoms are discussed briefly. For more detailed information, reference should be made to a modern textbook on plant physiology.

Macroelements

Nitrogen (N), as a constituent of protein, is involved in all the physiological processes taking place in plants. A deficiency of nitrogen is expressed in woody plants as a decrease in vigor and a light green to a yellowing of the foliage; the older leaves express the symptoms first. Under a prolonged deficiency, the leaves scorch and drop off. An excess of nitrogen can result in excessive growth and a decreased flowering and fruiting. An excess of nitrogen may also predispose plants to various pathological and physiological disorders, such as fireblight and soft, weak growth.

Phosphorus (P) is needed for root development, flowering, and fruit formation. It is found in large quantities in meristematic tissue and is essential for cell division. A phosphorus deficiency ultimately results in stunted plants. Early indications of inadequate phosphorus within many species of plants are the development of a bronze or purple coloration of the petioles on the underside of the leaves, followed by a yellowing of the leaves, particularly at the time of flowering and fruiting. However, phosphorus deficiency is seldom observed in woody perennial plants growing in a field-production nursery or in the landscape. Apparently, the roots, which penetrate throughout a vast volume of soil, are able to absorb enough phosphorus to supply the plant's need.

Potassium (K), although not an integral part of the plant tissue, is important for plants. It modifies the absorption of other nutrient elements, influences the carbohydrate-nitrogen relationship, and is thought to influence the absorption and utilization of water, which in turn affects the drought and possibly the cold-temperature resistance of plants. A lack of potassium in broad-leaved plants is first expressed by a marginal yellowing of the older leaves, followed by scorching and leaf drop. In needle-leaved plants, an apical brown tip is separated from a green basal portion by a yellow band. There is also a decrease in the number of years that the needles persist on the plants.

   Calcium (Ca) is one of the primary elements in the development of woody plants. It is a constituent of the cell walls; it modifies the permeability of membranes and is important for development of roots. Since calcium is relatively immobile within the plant, deficiency symptoms are exhibited first in the apical portions. Although a deficiency is not too common in woody plants, it is manifested by death of the terminal portions, yellowing and necrosis of the adjacent young leaves, plus severe distortion; margins are ragged and often rolled. This is more commonly associated with seedlings than with mature plants.

   Magnesium (Mg) is an integral part of chlorophyll—the green pigment in plants—making it essential for photosynthesis. Also, certain enzyme systems, and respiration, do not function properly at low magnesium levels. Some form of chlorosis is associated with a magnesium deficiency, but the expression varies considerably with the species. It is reported that dead areas developing suddenly between the veins are an indication of an inadequate supply of magnesium. In advanced stages of magnesium deficiency, shoots defoliate and become devoid of leaves except for a few at the tip.

   Sulfur (S) is a constituent of protein and various volatile compounds. When sulfur is deficient, plants are stunted and the leaves are light green or yellow, starting with the young leaves and progressing to the older leaves. Growth is restricted and stems are thin but remain erect. However, sulfur deficiency has not been a problem in the production of nursery crops. Perhaps this is due to its presence in most complete fertilizers as a contaminant and in various forms of nitrogen, phosphorus, and potassium salts that are used in the production of nursery crops. It is also an air pollutant in industrial areas.

Microelements

   Iron (Fe) is a catalyst in chlorophyll formation and for oxidation-reduction reactions. Its availability in the soil decreases with high pH, high phosphates, or in high concentrations of heavy metals or carbonates. Young leaves exhibit an interveinal chlorosis with the veins remaining green. Woody perennials exhibit dieback of branches if exposed to iron deficiency for extended periods of time.

   Manganese (Mn) is needed for assimilation of carbon dioxide in nitrogen metabolism and for the formation of organic acids and carotene. It may be deficient in soils of high pH or if large quantities of calcareous material have been used as a soil amendment. The deficiency symptoms are similar to those for iron. Manganese deficiency has been reported for red, sugar, and Norway maple, and it probably occurs on other woody species. Manganese toxicity has been observed in some woody species (apple, holly). Early symptoms of Mn toxicity are chlorotic leaves and suppressed growth with smooth, raised pimples (measles) underlain by small dark-brown spots in the young bark of some species. Later the pimples develop sunken areas and the bark begins to crack. In advanced stages, the bark becomes very rough, cracked, and scaly. Manganese toxicity appears to be cultivar-specific and is associated with acid soils, anaerobic conditions, and with some steam-sterilized soils.

Zinc (Zn) functions in cell elongation and in seed development. Zinc deficiency, although not too common in woody ornamentals, is manifested by older leaves having a yellow to bronze color. The leaves are relatively narrow with a wavy margin and rosetted due to reduced internodes. Dieback of shoots can occur where the deficiency is acute.

Boron (B) aids in proper root development, flowering, and fruiting and is necessary for nitrogen and carbohydrate metabolism. The application of excess lime may induce boron deficiency, which is more common in sandy soils than in clays. Death of the growing points, brittleness and dieback of the stems, combined with scorched, curled, and often rosetted leaves are symptoms sometimes associated with boron deficiency in field-production nurseries.

Copper (Cu) is a catalyst in respiration and is needed for carbohydrate and protein metabolism and in seed formation. Although copper deficiency is not too common in woody perennials, it has been reported in young fruit trees and in azalea plants growing for prolonged periods in containers. In fruit trees, the deficiency is expressed by a withering and death of young shoots in the late spring or early summer. In azaleas the new leaves are smaller than normal and soon become scorched; the early symptoms resemble potassium deficiency or frost damage.

Molybdenum (Mo) is needed for protein synthesis, but is needed in such minute quantities that it seldom limits growth of woody plants.

SOIL REACTION

The reaction of a soil (pH) is an indication or a measure of the degree of acidity or alkalinity of a soil. Soil reaction can be stated or measured in a number of ways. It is common to speak of a soil as being slightly acid, moderately acid, or very acid; or in other cases, as being slightly alkaline. A more accurate method of expressing soil reaction is to express it in terms of the hydrogen-ion concentration. Therefore, soil reaction is expressed as the logarithm of the reciprocal of the hydrogen-ion concentration, and a pH scale of 0 to 14 is employed with 7 as the neutral point. The "p" indicates a logarithm and the "H" indicates hydrogen-ion concentration. Each pH unit is divided into tenths. It should be remembered that the scale is logarithmic, and with each increase or decrease of one pH unit the change in hydrogen-ion concentration is 10 times as great. Since the values are logarithms, they do not lend themselves to averages.

The soil reaction (pH) can be determined by the use of a pH meter or by the use of dyes and special pH test papers. Test papers, available in handy dispensers, are color-sensitive and practical for making quick tests. Soils should be mixed with buffers of solutions for maximum accuracy when determining the soil reaction. The operator should be familiar with the limitations of each technique and check his results periodically with known standards. A pH meter should be carefully protected and calibrated prior to use.

The soil reaction has a strong influence upon the availability of the various mineral elements needed for plant growth (Fig. 11–1). Also, plants grow better when grown in soil at the optimum pH range for the particular species. The primary and secondary nutrients are readily available within a pH range of 6.0–8.0. But the availability of these elements declines rapidly as the soil reaction becomes more acid. Iron and manganese are readily available at low pH values, but as the pH of the soil solution increases their availability declines. The lack of iron or manganese, due to high pH of the soil, can become a limiting factor in the production of certain woody species.

The most favorable soil reaction for the growth of most plants is between a pH of 5.5 and 7.5. Within this range, the essential mineral elements are readily available, the microorganisms of the soil carry on their beneficial functions, and fortunately, toxicity due to aluminum is minimized. However, some species of plants grow best under acid conditions (e.g., blueberries and rhododendrons) and others under more alkaline conditions. Nurserymen should be familiar with the optimum pH range for their crops and select sites accordingly for their production. For example, pin oak and red oak grow best in soil with a pH range of 4.5–6.0. They tolerate a pH between 6.0 and 6.8, but in soils with a pH greater than 6.8, they are often chlorotic and grow poorly. The soil reaction (pH) preferences for selected plant species are listed in Table 11–1.

MODIFYING SOIL REACTION

Where the soil reaction is too acid for optimum plant growth, it can be modified by the application of limestone. However, the amount of limestone that needs to be applied will vary with the degree of change that is desired, the soil texture, the content of organic matter, and the form of limestone to be used. Where the soil reaction is too alkaline, it can be acidified by the application of sulfur. The amount to be applied will depend upon the soil type and the number of pH units that the soil reaction is to be modified. The best recommendations for the amount of limestone or sulfur to apply are based on soil tests performed by persons trained in the analysis of soils. Production nurserymen should consult with their county agricultural agents or soils specialist for advice on management practices that are best for their soils and environment.

Effecting a pH change of nursery soils is best done when the land is not in crop production and well in advance of planting the nursery crop. The material should be spread evenly over the soil and thoroughly disked into the soil prior to plowing. In some situations it may be desirable to make split or multiple applications. Tables 11–2, and 11–3 can be used as a guide for the amount of sulfur or limestone to use in affecting a pH change. However, these tables are only estimates

TABLE 11-1 Soil Reaction (pH) Preferences for Selected Plants

Common Name	Botanical Name	4	5	6	7	8
Shade and Flowering Trees						
Almond, flowering	*Prunus triloba*			x	xxxxxxxxxxx	xxxxxxxx
Ash, American mountain	*Sorbus americana*		xxxxxxxx			
Ash, European mountain	*Sorbus aucuparia*			xxxxxxxxx	xxxxxxxx	
Ash, white	*Fraxinus americana*			xxxx	xxxxxx	
Beech, American	*Fagus grandifolia*		xxx	xxxxxxxxxxxxxx		
Birch, American white	*Betula alba*		xxxx	xxxxxxxxx		
Birch, cherry	*Betula lenta*		xxxxxxxxx	xxxxxxxxxx		
Cherry, dwarf flowering	*Prunus glandulosa*			xxxxxxxxx		
Crabapple, plum-leaved	*Malus prunifolia*			xxxxxxxxxx	xxxxxx	
Crabapple, showy	*Malus floribunda*		xxxxxxx	xxxxxxxxx		
Dogwood, flowering	*Cornus florida*		xxxxxxx	xxxxxxxxx		
Elm, American	*Ulmus americana*					
Hawthorn	*Crataegus biltmoreana*			xxxxxxxxx	xxx	
Hawthorn, English	*Crataegus laevigata*			xxxxxxxx	xxxxx	
Hickory, shagbark	*Carya ovata*			xxxxx		
Holly, American	*Ilex opaca*		xxxxxx			
Holly, English	*Ilex aquifolium*			xxxx		
Honey locust	*Gleditsia triacanthos*	xxxxxxxxxxxxx				
Kentucky coffee tree	*Gymnocladus dioica*			xxxxxxxxxx	xxxxxxxxxx	xxxxx
Magnolia, saucer	*Magnolia soulangiana*		xxxxxxxx			
Magnolia, southern	*Magnolia grandiflora*		xxxxxxxx			
Magnolia, star	*Magnolia stellata*		xxxxxxx			
Maidenhair tree	*Ginkgo biloba*		xxxx	xxxxxxxxxxx		
Maple, sugar	*Acer saccharum*			xxxxx	xxxxxxx	
Oak, black	*Quercus velutina*			xxxxxxxxxx	xxxxxx	
Oak, English	*Quercus robur*			xxxxxxxxx		
Oak, pin	*Quercus palustris*		xxxxxxxxxx	xxxxxxxxxx	xxxxxxxxxx	xxxxx

pH Preference

Common name	Scientific name
Oak, red	*Quercus rubra*
Oak, southern live	*Quercus virginiana*
Oak, white	*Quercus alba*
Pecan	*Carya illinoinensis*
Sour gum	*Nyssa sylvatica*
Sourwood	*Oxydendrum arboreum*
Sweet gum	*Liquidambar styraciflua*
Sycamore, American	*Platanus occidentalis*
Tulip tree	*Liriodendron tulipifera*
Willow, weeping	*Salix babylonica*
Witch hazel	*Hammamelis virginiana*

Ornamental Shrubs

Common name	Scientific name
Azalea, hiryu	*Rhododendrum obtusum*
Azalea, pink	*R. periclymenoides*
Barberry, Japanese	*Berberis thunbergii*
Bayberry	*Myrica pennsylvanica*
Beautybush	*Kolkwitzia amabilis*
Boxwood, common	*Buxus sempervirens*
Butterfly bush	*Buddleia davidii*
Buttonbush	*Cephalanthus occidentalis*
Chokeberry, black	*Aronia melanocarpa*
Chokeberry, red	*Aronia arbutifolia*
Cotoneaster	*Cotoneaster tomentosus*
Cotoneaster, rock	*Cotoneaster horizontalis*
Daphne, February	*Daphne mezereum*
Daphne, rose	*Daphne cneorum*
Deutzia	*Deutzia gracilis*
Deutzia, Lemoine	*Deutzia lemoinei*
Dogwood, goldentwig	*C. sericea Flaviramea*
Euonymus, winged	*Euonymus alata*
Fire thorn	*Pyracantha coccinea*

(continued)

TABLE 11-1 Soil Reaction (pH) Preferences for Selected Plants (*continued*)

Common Name	Botanical Name	\<---	pH Preference	---\>		
		4	5	6	7	8
Fringe tree, white	*Chionanthus virginicus*		xxxxx	xxxx		
Hackberry, nettle tree	*Celtis occidentalis*			xxxxxxxxxxxxxxxxxxxxx		
Heather, Scotch	*Calluna vulgaris*		xxxxxxxxxxxxx			
Hibiscus, Chinese	*Hibiscus rose-sinensis*			xxxxxxxxxxxxxxxxxxxxx		
Holly, Japanese	*Ilex crenata*		xxx	xxxx		
Hollygrape, Oregon	*Mahonia aquifolium*			xxxxxxxxxxxxxxxxx		
Honeysuckle, Tatarian	*Lonicera tatarica*				xxxxxxxxxxxxxxxxxxx	
Hydrangea, Peegee	*Hydrangea paniculata* Grandiflora			xxxxxxxxx		
Lilac, common	*Syringa vulgaris*			xxxxxxxxxxx		
Lilac, Persian	*Syringa persica*			xxxxxxxxxxxxxxxx		
Mock orange	*Philadelphus coronarius*			xxxxxxxxxxxxxxxxxx		
Mountain laurel	*Kalmia latifolia*		xxxxxxxxxxxxx			
Oleander	*Nerium oleander*			xxxxxxxxxxxxxxxxxxxxx		
Rhododendron	*R. mucronulatum*		xxxxxxxxxxxx			
Rhododendron, alpine	*R. hirsutum*	xxxxxxxxxxxxxxxxxxxxxxxx				
Rhododendron, Carolina	*R. carolinianum*	xxxxxxxxxxxxxxxxxxxxxxxxxxxxx				
Rose, hybrid tea	*Rose* sp.		xxxx	xxxxx		
Rose, Japanese	*Rosa rugosa*			xxxxxxxxxxxx		
Rose, memorial	*Rosa wichuriana*			xxxxxxxxx		
Rosebay, mountain	*Rhododendron catawbiense*		xxxxxxxx			
Rose of sharon	*Hibiscus syriacus*			xxxxxxxxxxxxxxxxx		
Serviceberry	*Amelanchier canadensis*		xxxxxxxx			
Spirea	*Spirea vanhouttei*			xxxxxxxxx		
Sumac, smooth	*Rhus glabra*		xxxxxxxx			
Sumac, staghorn	*Rhus typhina*		xxxxxxxx			
Viburnum, double-file	*Viburnum plicatum* Tomentosum			xxxxxxxxxxxxxxxx		
Viburnum, maple-leaved	*Viburnum acerifolium*	xxxxxxxxxx				
Wayfaring tree	*Viburnum lantana*			xxxxxxxxxxxxxxxxxxxxx		

Evergreens

Common name	Scientific name				
Arborvitae, American	*Thuja occidentalis*			xxxxxxxxxxxxxxxxxxxxxxxxx	
Fir, balsam	*Abies balsamea*		xxxxxxxx	xxxxxxxxx	
Fir, Douglas	*Pseudotsuga menziesii*	xxxxxxxx			
Fir, Fraser	*Abies fraseri*		xxxxxxxx		
Hemlock, Canada	*Tsuga canadensis*		xxxxxxxx		
Hemlock, Carolina	*Tsuga caroliniana*		xxxxxx		
Juniper, creeping	*Juniperus horizontalis*		xxxxxxxxxxxxx		
Pine, mugho	*Pinus mugo*		xxxxxxxx		
Pine, red	*Pinus resinosa*		xxxxxxxxxxxxx		
Pine, Scots	*Pinus sylvestris*	xxxxxxxxxxxxxxx	xxxxxxxxx		
Pine, white	*Pinus strobus*		xxxxxxxx		
Spruce, Colorado	*Picea pungens*		xxxxxxx	xxxxxxxx	
Spruce, Norway	*Picea abies*				
Spruce, white	*Picea glauca*				
Yew, Japanese	*Taxus cuspidata*				

Vines

Common name	Scientific name			
Bittersweet, American	*Celastrus scandens*	xxxxxxxxxxxxxx		
Clematis, Jackman's	*Clematis jackmanii*		xxxxxxxxxxxxx	
Dutchman's pipe	*Aristolochia durior*		xxxxxxxxxxxxxxxxxxxxxx	
Honeysuckle, trumpet	*Lonicera sempervirens*		xxxxxxxxxxxxxxxxxxxxxxx	
Ivy, Boston	*Parthenocissus tricuspidata*		xxxxxxxxxxxxxxxxxxxxxxx	
Ivy, English	*Hedera helix*		xxxxxxxxxxx	
Virgin's bower	*Clematis paniculata*		xxxxxxxxxxxxxxxxxxxxxxx	
Wisteria, Japanese	*Wisteria floribunda*			

(continued)

193

TABLE 11-1 Soil Reaction (pH) Preferences for Selected Plants (*continued*)

Common Name	Botanical Name	pH Preference				
		4	5	6	7	8
Fruit Plants						
Apple, common	*Malus pumila*			xxxxxxxxxxx		
Apricot	*Prunus armeniaca*				xxxxxxxxx	
Blueberry, high bush	*Vaccinium corymbosum*		xxxxxxxxxxxx			
Cherry, sweet	*Prunus avium*			xxxxxxxxxxxxxx		
Grapefruit	*Citrus paradisi*			xxxxxxxxxxxxxx		
Orange, sweet	*Citrus sinensis*			xxxxxxxxxxxxxx		
Peach	*Prunus persica*			xxxxxxxxxxxxxx		
Pear, common	*Pyrus communis*			xxxxxxxxxxxxx		
Plum, American	*Prunus americana*				xxxxxxxxxxxxxxxxxx	x
Raspberry, black	*Rubus occidentalis*			xxxxxxxxxxxx		
Raspberry, red	*Rubus idaeus*			xxxxxxxxxxxxxx		
Grass						
Bluegrass, annual	*Poa annua*				xxxxxxxxx	
Bluegrass, Canada	*Poa compressa*				xxxxxxxxxxxxxx	x
Bluegrass, Kentucky	*Poa pratensis*			xxxxxxxxxxxxxxxxxx	xxxxx	
Fescue, chewing	*Festuca rubra* var. *commutata*			xxxxxxxxxxx		
Fescue, red	*Festuca rubra*			xxxxxxx		
Ground Covers						
Bearberry, common	*Arctostaphylos uva-ursi*		xxxxxxxxxxxxxxxxx			
Bugleweed, carpet	*Ajuga reptans*				xxxxxxxxxxxxxxxxxxx	x

Source: Spurway (1944).

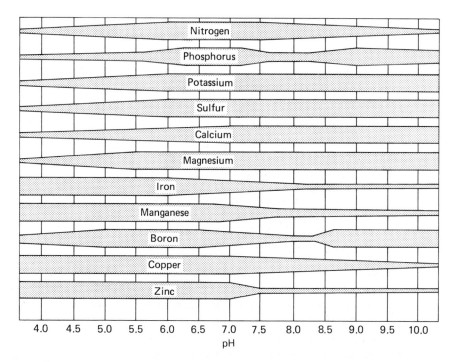

Figure 11–1 Availability of plant nutrients in mineral soil as influenced by pH; the wider the bar, the more available the nutrient is. (Modified from Truog, 1947.)

and do not account for variations in potential acidity, especially exchangeable aluminum. A lime requirement test, known as the SMP or Ohio lime requirement method, is used in a number of states; it measures both the active and the potential acidity. This gives a more precise determination of lime requirement than an estimate from soil pH and soil texture. A comparison of this measurement (Lime Index) and the lime requirement are given in Table 11–4.

The maximum amount of lime that should be applied in any season is 5 tons/ acre. Nursery soils should be retested for additional lime needs prior to preparation of the land for a cover crop.

Various forms of limestone have varying abilities to modify the acidity of soils. This difference in ability is referred to as the "neutralizing value" and is

TABLE 11-2   Materials and Rate to Decrease the Soil pH by 1 Unit below pH 6.0

	Rate (lb/100 ft^2)		
Material	Sandy Loam	Loam	Clay Loam or Peat
Aluminum sulfate	2.5	5	7
Iron sulfate	2.5	5	7
Sulfur	0.5	1	1.5

TABLE 11-3   **Recommended Tons of Limestone per Acre,[a] Estimated from Soil pH and Texture, to Raise the pH of a 6⅔-in. Plow Layer of Different Soils to pH 6.5**

Texture of Plow Layer	pH Range			
	4.5–4.9	5.0–5.4	5.5–5.9	6.0–6.4
Clay and silty clay	6	5	4	2½
Clay loams or loams	5	4	3	2
Sandy loams	4	3	2½	1½[b]
Loamy sands	3	2½	2	1[b]
Sands	2½	2	1½[b]	½[b]

[a]Lime recommendations based on a liming material having 25% passing through a 100-mesh sieve and having a neutralizing value of 90%.

[b]It is preferable to recommend 2 tons/acre so as to obtain uniform application and to justify the expense of application.

Source: Coop. Ext. Serv. Mich. State Univ. Ext. Bull. 471.

equated on the basis of pure calcium carbonate. Pure calcium carbonate has a molecular weight of 100, and soil scientists use it as the basis to equate the neutralizing value of other forms of limestone. For example, the molecular weight of pure calcium hydrate if 74. By dividing 100 by 74, the percent value is 135. This indicates that 1 lb of calcium hydroxide is equal to 1.35 lb of calcium carbonate, or when equated on the basis of 1 ton of pure calcium carbonate, 1480 lb of calcium hydrox-

TABLE 11-4   **Tons of Limestone Needed to Raise Soil pH of Mineral Soils to pH 6.0, 6.5, or 6.8, as Determined by the Lime Index Method**

Lime Index	Tons Lime per Acre (9-in. Plow Depth)[a]		
	To pH 6.0	To pH 6.5	To pH 6.8
7.0	—	—	0.5
6.9	—	0.5	1.0
6.8	1.1	1.5	1.8
6.7	1.9	2.4	2.6
6.6	2.7	3.3	3.6
6.5	3.5	4.3	4.7
6.4	4.3	5.3[b]	5.7[b]
6.3	5.1[b]	6.2	6.7
6.2	5.8	7.2	7.8
6.1	6.6	8.1	8.9
6.0	7.4	9.1	10.0

[a]To convert lime recommendations to depth of plowing other than 9 in., divide above rates by 9 and multiply by the depth of plowing.

[b]The maximum lime recommendation for one season is 5 tons. Retest soil in 2 years for additional lime needs.

Source: Coop. Ext. Serv. Mich. State Univ. Ext. Bull. E-550 (1976).

ide is equally effective. The relative neutralizing value of several liming materials is tabulated in Table 11–5. Most limestone quarries can supply an analysis of the calcium carbonate equivalent of their product. This is required by law in some states.

The lime recommendations given in Table 11–4 are for limestone with a neutralizing value of 90. If the material to be used has a neutralizing value significantly different from 90, the amount should be adjusted. Figure 11–2 can be used for this purpose. For example, a material with a neutralizing value of 135

TABLE 11-5   Neutralizing Value
(Percent Calcium Carbonate Equivalent)
of Various Liming Materials

Material	Neutralizing Value
Calcium carbonate (pure)	100
Magnesium carbonate (pure)	119
Calcium hydrate (pure)	135
Magnesium hydrate (pure)	172
Calcic limestone	<100
Dolomitic limestone	<108
Calcic hydrated lime	<135
Dolomitic hydrated lime	<170

Source: Coop. Ext. Serv. Mich. State Univ. Ext. Bull. 471.

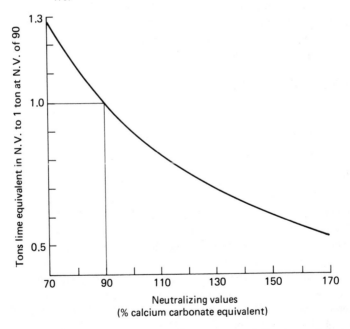

Figure 11–2 Conversion chart to determine amounts of limestone of various neutralizing values (N.V.) that are equivalent to 1 ton of lime with an N.V. of 90. (From Coop. Ext. Serv. Mich. State Univ. Ext. Bull. 471.)

would require 0.65 ton to equal 1 ton of the 90% material. The values in Table 11–4 are multiplied by the factor, in this case 0.65. Liming materials react at different rates because of their chemical composition, coarseness, and hardness. The finer a limestone is ground, the more quickly it will react. Also, the more porous calcite materials will react more quickly than harder dolomitic materials.

CATION EXCHANGE CAPACITY

One of the interesting phenomena of nature is the ability of soil to adsorb various mineral nutrients when applied as fertilizers and then to release them to be absorbed by plants for use in their metabolism. The ability of the soil to hold certain minerals is known as cation exchange capacity (CEC). The exchange capacity of soil developed as a result of the weathering of rocks into small clay particles which possess negatively charged crystal surfaces. The negative charge is due to the dissociation of hydrogen from the exposed hydroxyl (OH^-) radical leaving the attached oxygen with the charge and from charges in the structure of the clay upon weathering. Clay particles adsorb thousands of hydrogen ions (H^+) and other exchangeable cations, such as Ca^{2+}, Mg^{2+}, K^+, and Na^+, upon their surfaces. The force with which these ions are attracted to the clay particles also influences the ease by which they may be exchanged. It is dependent upon the nature of the exchange complex, the size of the ions, the number of valence electrons, the degree of hydration, and the concentration of salts. The smaller the ion and the greater the charge per unit of mass, the tighter it will be held and accordingly the more difficult to replace. On the other hand, ions that are highly hydrated are more easily replaced. The common soil cations Na^+, K^+, Mg^{2+}, Ca^{2+}, and H^+ are listed in order of decreasing hydration. This explains, in part, why hydrogen ions play such an important role in soil, why calcium is the predominant mineral ion in most inorganic soils, and why potassium might be expected to be replaced and leached from a soil by improper fertilizer practices.

Anions, such as $H_2PO_4^-$, NO_3^-, and SO_4^- are absorbed primarily in the organic matter within the soil. They are made available to plants through the decomposition of the organic matter by various microorganisms within the soil. The anions then become part of the soil solution and can be absorbed by the roots of plants.

Cation exchange takes place when a plant makes contact with a clay particle. The root exchanges one or more hydrogen ions for an exchangeable cation which is absorbed by the plant and used in its metabolism (Fig. 11–3). A knowledge of CEC can be of value to a nurseryman planning a soil management program.

Most plants grow best on a specific soil type and under a specific set of environmental conditions. But it is impractical to provide all the ecological conditions required of plants in any one nursery. Therefore, it is desirable to classify the soils of a field production nursery into soil management groups on the basis of their CEC

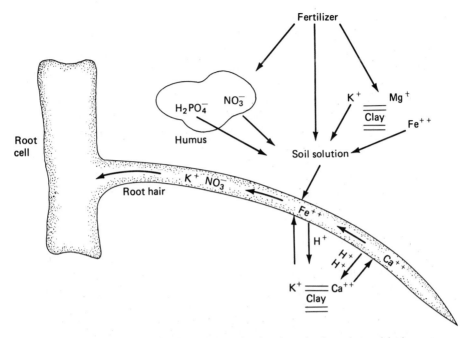

Figure 11–3 Diagrammatic representation of an ion absorption from clay particle, humus particle, and the soil solution.

or pH, to develop a soil management program for each group, and to grow within each group those plants that lend themselves to the program (see Table 11–8).

A knowledge of CEC and levels of fertility are also valuable in developing fertilizer programs for nurseries and landscape plantings. Soils of low CEC should be fertilized more frequently at relatively low rates, since they do not have the physiochemical ability to hold large quantities of nutrient on their exchange complex. Thus, to ensure an adequate supply of nutrients for optimum plant growth, the fertilizer should be applied more often. On sites with a high CEC, the fertilizer may be applied less often and at a higher rate if needed. However, all fertilizer applications should be made on the basis of need, as indicated by a soil test.

NUTRIENT-ELEMENT BALANCE IN PLANTS

Nutrient-element balance is a fundamental concept in plant nutrition. The concept is that plant growth is a function of two variables of nutrition: intensity and balance. The intensity and balance are reflected in the chemical composition of the leaves when the plants are in the same stage of growth or development, all other factors being constant. Maximum growth and yield occur only upon the coincidence of optimum intensity and balance. An imbalance of elements can result in toxicity or deficiency which can limit growth. For example, boron toxicity can be induced by a high ratio of (Ca + K)/Mg or (Ca + Mg)/K but not by a high ratio of (K + Mg)/Ca. A ratio of less than four for (Ca + Mg)/K is desirable for optimum growth of apples and less than three and one-half for alfalfa and corn. Calculations are based on milliequivalents per 100 g. A deficiency of manganese can be induced by a high accumulation of one or all three major bases (Ca, Mg, K) in proportion to manganese. There may be little or no response to increases in nitrogen fertility unless phosphorus levels are in balance with nitrogen. Heavy phosphorus fertilization of soils can induce deficiencies of iron, copper, manganese, and zinc.

LEAF ANALYSIS

The chemical composition of leaves can be determined by chemical analysis. This analysis, made with the aid of a spectrograph and other supporting equipment, provides valuable data on the mineral composition of the plant. But like a financial statement that reflects the financial status of a business as of a particular day, leaf analysis reflects the nutritional status of the plant as of the day the samples were collected.

The nutritional status of plants changes constantly throughout the growing season. For most plants, growing under optimal levels of nutrition, the concentrations of nitrogen and potassium decrease with time: calcium, magnesium, iron, and manganese increase, while phosphorus, boron, and copper remain relatively unchanged. Therefore, to interpret leaf analysis data intelligently, it is necessary to establish a standard method, including when to sample, the part of the plant to sample, and standards to compare the data. Since the nutrition of leaves is fairly well stabilized by the end of the growing season, this is the time that is recommended that samples be collected; with evergreens they may be collected through the end of December. The portion of the plant to be sampled varies with plant type. For deciduous species and evergreens such as pine, the middle foliage from the current year's growth is suggested; for evergreens such as juniper and arborvitae, the current year's growth is sampled. Leaves or shoots should be collected at random and combined into a composite sample for analysis. The data can then be compared with standard values to determine the relative nutritional status. Table 11–6 lists some suggested standards for deciduous and evergreen species; more exact values are available at laboratories that conduct chemical analysis of plants. It may be necessary in some situations to supply the laboratory with healthy foliage for a reference standard since standards have not been established for all woody species. Although exact fertilizer recommendations cannot be made based solely on leaf analysis data, a trained horticulturist with knowledge of the crop and the site where the plants are growing, plus a current soil test, supplemented with information on past fertilizer and cultural practices can usually suggest a cultural program that will improve the quality of growth.

TABLE 11-6 Suggested Foliar, Nutrient-
Element Standards for Deciduous and
Evergreen Plants (Fall Analysis)

Element	Deciduous	Evergreen
	Percent Dry Weight	
Nitrogen	1.50–3.00	2.00–2.35
Phosphorus	0.15–0.26	0.25–0.40
Potassium	0.80–1.60	1.00–1.20
Calcium	1.40–3.00	0.50–1.25
Magnesium	0.30–0.45	0.20–0.35
	Parts per Million	
Iron	150–300	200–300
Copper	25–35	25–40
Manganese	50–200	25–50
Boron	25–50	25–50
Zinc	25–50	25–50
Molybdenum	1–5	1–5

SOIL TESTS

A good soil testing program is desirable to serve as a basis for nurserymen to make sound soil management decisions for maintaining adequate pH levels and a reasonable balance of nutrients to ensure good plant growth. However, it is important to know what testing procedures were used in order to make a meaningful interpretation of the data. Since different extraction techniques are used by soil testing laboratories, it is not always possible to compare test results between laboratories. Soil samples must be taken with care to ensure that the results of the test and the fertilizer recommendations developed from them are meaningful. Soil tests are performed on a very small sample of the greater mass, and if the sample is not representative of the whole, the results are not meaningful. Samples taken from the upper 6–8 in. of soil, which may be satisfactory for annual crops, have only limited value for deep-rooted perennial crops, since they do not reflect the true nutrient status of the soil-root zone from which the plant is absorbing its nutrients. Soil samples (cores 12–18 in. deep) should be taken at a number of locations in each field to be planted to develop fertilized recommendations for long-term nursery crops.

Most soil testing centers provide information on the cation exchange capacity or the soil group, soil reaction (pH), the availability of the macroelements except nitrogen and sulfur, and when requested, the availability of selected microelements, total nitrogen, organic matter content, and soluble salts. For many years phosphorus and potassium were reported as oxides, P_2O_5 and K_2O, respectively, since this is the form that they are found in fertilizer. Currently, most soil testing laboratories report P and K on the elemental basis. P and K are normally in pounds per acre, Ca and Mg are reported either as milliequivalents per 100 grams or in pounds per acre, and the microelements are expressed as parts per million (ppm). To convert P and K to the oxide form, multiply by 2.3 and 1.2, respectively. To convert P_2O_5 and K_2O to the elemental form, multiply by 0.44 and 0.83, respectively.

Very little information is available on soil fertility standards for ornamental plants. The data in Table 11-7 are provided as suggested standards until more definitive data are available.

TABLE 11-7   Suggested Standards of Soil Fertility for Growing Woody Perennials in Field-Production Nurseries

Group	CEC	Available (lb/acre)[a]		Exchangeable (mEq/100 g)[b]	
		P	K	Ca	Mg
Silt loam to loam	12–16	35–70	150–200	5.0–10.0	2
Sandy loam	5–10	25–35	100–150	2.5–4.0	1
Loamy sand to sand	2–4	15–25	60–100	1.5–2.0	0.5

[a]$P \times 2.3 = P_2O_5$; $K \times 1.2 = K_2O$.
[b]1 mEq/100 g Ca = 400 lb/acre; 1 mEq/100 g Mg = 240 lb/acre.

TYPES OF FERTILIZERS

Nurserymen have a vast array of fertilizer materials from which to select in order to meet their individual requirements and preferences. There are many ways to classify fertilizers, but one way is to classify them according to their chemical and physical properties (Table 11–8).

Organic fertilizers are carbonaceous compounds which are either natural (Table 11–9) or synthetic. Most of the natural organic materials are multielement compounds, but the essential elements are present in small quantities, necessitating high application rates to obtain significant amounts of the needed nutrients. They are slowly soluble and can be used with a high degree of safety. The *synthetic organic fertilizers* are manufactured products. Urea, for example, is produced under high pressure from carbon dioxide (CO_2) and ammonia (NH_3), and urea-formaldehyde (UF) is a reaction product of urea and formaldehyde. Urea is highly soluble and must be used with caution, whereas UF is slowly soluble. IBDU is a reaction product between isobutylidene and urea producing a slow-release nitrogenous fertilizer.

Inorganic materials provide the most available source of supply for the essential elements. They are either natural compounds that have been mined and processed into fertilizer, or they are reaction products synthesized for a specific purpose. They are available in dry or liquid formulations and vary greatly in chemical composition and solubility (Table 11–10).

Since the mid-1950s, a number of slow- or controlled-release products have been introduced as fertilizers. Magamp is an improved formulation of magnesium

TABLE 11-8   Chemical and Physical Properties of Fertilizers

Chemical Properties	Physical Properties
I. State	I. State
A. Organic	A. Dry
1. Natural	1. Pulverized
2. Synthetic	2. Granular (prills)
B. Inorganic	3. Tablet
1. Natural	4. Packet
2. Synthetic	5. Encapsulated
II. Element	B. Liquid
A. Single	1. Water-soluble
B. Double	2. Suspension
C. Triple (complete)	II. Release rate
D. Multi	A. Rapid
III. Long-term effect on soil pH	B. Slow (controlled)
A. Acidic (lowers pH)	
B. Neutral	
C. Basic (raises pH)	

ammonium phosphate with the addition of nitrogen and potassium. It is a granular formulation which releases nitrogen slowly due to its solubility in water.

Osmocote is a controlled-release fertilizer. It is a homogenous prill of water-soluble fertilizer covered with a plastic resin. The prills do not dissolve in water, but become hydrated and release the nutrients as a result of osmotic pressure. The process is moisture- and temperature-dependent. Therefore, the nutrients are not readily available when soils are dry or cold.

Slow- or controlled-release fertilizers are best utilized in the production of container-grown plants. They are relatively more expensive, per unit of plant food, than the natural inorganic fertilizers, but because of their release rate, they have a number of advantages. They can be applied at the time of planting and supply the needed nutrients for a full growing season, thus eliminating the need for additional applications of fertilizer. This can result in a considerable saving in labor. They can supply nutrients at a fairly uniform rate; thus plant growth is not limited by excess soluble salts or by leaching. Their use can reduce the loss of soluble materials through leaching and runoff, resulting in a substantial savings, and at the same time minimize contamination of the environment.

When fertilizer is manufactured and packaged for sale, the product label will indicate the chemical analysis. It is industry practice to list fertilizer analysis in the order of the three primary elements, as % elemental N, % P_2O_5, and % K_2O. Fertilizers that contain nitrogen, phosphorus, and potassium are known as complete fertilizers. However, it should be noted that a complete fertilizer does not contain all the essential elements, although some calcium, magnesium, sulfur, and microelements are commonly present in the product as carriers or as contaminants.

Fertilizers may have an acid, alkaline, or neutral reaction, depending upon the materials contained in the product. Compete fertilizers, as blended, are neutral but

TABLE 11-9 Natural Organic Fertilizers

Fertilizer	Approximate Analysis			Rate (lb/100 ft^2)	Comments
	N	P$_2$O$_5$	K$_2$O		
Blood, dried	12	1.5	0.5	3–4	Rapidly available source of nitrogen
Guano					
Bat	6	9	3	3–4	Partially decomposed bat manure from caves in southwest United States
Bird	13	11	2	2–3	Partially decomposed bird manure from islands off coast of South America
Kelp or seaweed	1	0.5	9	5	Good source of K
Manure					
Cattle	0.5	0.3	0.5		Manures are generally low in nutrients, but when used in larger amounts, as a soil conditioner, they do add fertilizer; avoid use of fresh manure or use too soon after steaming; nutrient content variable, particularly with bedding materials used; uncomposted animal manure often contains weed seed
Chicken	1.0	0.5	0.8		
Horse	0.6	0.3	0.6		
Mushroom, spent	1.0	1.0	1.0		
Sheep	0.9	0.5	0.8		
Swine	0.6	0.5	1.0		
Meal					
Bone, raw	4	20	0	5	Phosphorus very slowly soluble
Bone, steamed	2	27	0	5	Phosphorus is soluble, some nitrogen lost by steaming
Cotton seed	6	2.5	2.0	3–4	Acid in reaction, good for azaleas, rhododendrons, blueberries
Hoof and horn	14	0	0	2	Good source of organic nitrogen
Peanut hulls	1	0	1	5	Low in nutrients
Sludge					
Sewage	2.0	1.0	0.5	5	Variable; check source; avoid those possibly contaminated with heavy metals
Activated	6.0	3.0	0.5	3–4	Microorganisms added
Tobacco stems	1.5	1.0	6.0	5	Good source of K$_2$O, alkaline reaction
Wood ashes	0	2.0	6.0	5	Source of K$_2$O, very alkaline

TABLE 11-10 Inorganic and Synthetic Fertilizers, Nutrient Content, Reaction, and Solubility

Sources	N	NO	PO	KO	Ca	S	Reaction	Solubility
Nitrogen								
Ammonium nitrate	33	17					Acid	High
Ammonium sulfate	26					24	Very Acid	Medium
Calcium nitrate	15	15			20		Basic	High
Nitrogen solutions	21–49							High
Sodium nitrate	16	16					Basic	High
Sulfur-coated urea	35					21	Very acid	Variable
Urea	46							Very
Ureaform	38							Variable
Phosphorus								
Monoammonium phosphate	11		48				Acid	Medium
Diammonium phosphate	16–21		48–53				Acid	Medium
Phosphoric acid							Acid	Very
Superphosphoric acid			69–76				Acid	Very
Superphosphate								
Normal			20		20	12		Low
Concentrated			40–50		13			Low
Magnesium								
Magnesium ammonium phosphate	6		29		Mg16		Acid	Low
Magnesium sulfate					Mg10			High
Potassium								
Potassium chloride				48–62				High
Potassium sulfate				48		18		Medium

many will produce an acid reaction upon the soil following chemical breakdown. The reaction of various fertilizers is listed in Table 11–10.

SOLUBLE SALTS

Another characteristic of fertilizers is their solubility. When fertilizer is applied to soil, it comes in contact with water, which causes the material to solubilize. The degree of solubility is a function of the fertilizer carrier (Table 11–10).

Soluble salts when present in the soil solution in excess quantities limits the availability of water to the plant or can reach excessive levels in plant tissue, which restricts growth and can result in death of the plant when the concentration reaches the toxic level for the species. Excess soluble salts are a potential problem to all plantsmen who use highly soluble fertilizers. When a soluble salts problem is suspected, a soil salinity test should be made with the aid of a Solu-bridge. A sample of soil is mixed with distilled water, and the solution is tested for its ability to conduct electricity. Some laboratories use the saturated paste technique, while others use a 2:1 or 5:1 distilled water/soil dilution method. The former has the advantage of being more accurate, especially with sandy soils or with soils to which gypsum or aluminum sulfate has been added. However, the latter is more rapid and less expensive, and if total accuracy is not important, the results can be of practical diagnostic value.

Soluble salts dissociate into ions which have the ability to conduct an electric current. As the concentration of soluble salts increases in the solution, conductance increases. This conductance of electricity can be measured by a Solu-bridge which has been calibrated in units called mhos. The decimal units are converted to whole numbers by employing negative exponents. For example, 0.00300 mho converts to 300×10^{-5} mhos. This is sometimes stated as 3 millimhos or 3000 micromhos. (Most laboratories report conductance in millisiemens/cm (ms/cm).) Table 11–11 provides some guidelines for levels of soluble salts and anticipated plant responses for plants growing in field-production nursery or in a landscape.

Although there is little information available on the tolerance of ornamental plants to soluble salts, there are enough data to indicate that a reading of 3.0 ms/cm (saturated paste extract) or slightly less should be satisfactory for most plants. Some plants, such as arborvitae, juniper, and bottle bush, are very salt-tolerant and can withstand a salt concentration as high as 8–10 ms/cm, while others, such as roses and viburnums, will be killed if the salt level is greater than 3 ms/cm.

FERTILIZER RECOMMENDATIONS

Fertilizer recommendations for woody plants, and for ornamental species in particular, vary considerably. Most recommendations for fertilizing woody species growing in the ground have been developed from a limited number of studies utilizing mature trees. Some of the recommendations come from fertilizer studies

TABLE 11-11   Interpretation of Solu-Bridge Data as Related to Field-Grown Plants

Saturated Paste Extract	Conductivity, millisiemens/cm (ms/cm)[a]		Interpretation
	2:1	5:1	
	<0.15	<0.08–0.30	Satisfactory for seed experimentation, but too low for good plant growth. Soil needs fertilizer
<2.00[a]	0.15–0.50		Satisfactory if soil is high in organic matter
2.0–3.0	0.50–1.80	0.30–0.80	Satisfactory for established plants; upper range too high for seedlings and salt-intolerant species
4.0–8.0	1.80–2.25	0.80–1.00	Toxic levels, reduced growth; do not fertilize
8.0–15.0	2.25–3.40	1.00–1.50	Many species will be stunted; suggest leaching if possible
>16.0	>3.40	>1.50	Too high for most species of plants

[a]ms = millisiemen, replacing millimho (mmho) as the preferred unit for expressing conductivity (soluble salt) measurements. The value remains the same—only the name changes. To convert this value to ppm multiply by 700.

conducted on plants growing in nurseries. Most of the studies were concerned with the three primary elements: nitrogen, phosphorus, and potassium, and with the trace element iron. The studies centered around rates and methods of application. From the results of these fertilizer studies, there is total agreement that the greatest growth response of trees was due to the addition of nitrogen to the soil. Only a few of the studies reported significant increases in growth due to the application of phosphorus or potassium. Chlorosis of oak, plus a few other species, was commonly associated with lack of iron or manganese.

Nitrogen

Current fertilizer recommendations for woody species growing in the ground indicate that surface application is most desirable for nitrogen. Rates of application vary with tree size and with the type of fertilizer. The most common practice is to state the rate in pounds of fertilizer or pounds of nitrogen per 1000 ft^2. A second is to equate the rate of application to the size of the tree: pounds of fertilizer or pounds of nitrogen contained in the fertilizer per inch of trunk diameter. Fertilizer recommendations for trees based on trunk diameter can result in considerable variation in concentration of nitrogen applied per 1000 ft^2 and per plant. Since the greatest growth response in woody species is related to nitrogen, the best recommendation for rate of application is to base the rate on pounds of nitrogen per 1000 ft^2. Then regardless of the size of the tree or the fertilizer analysis, the soil will be enriched with nitrogen at a uniform concentration. The actual rate of application will vary with the amount available in the soil, the soil environment and type of fertilizer, the species to be fertilized, and the objective of the nursery manager.

The amount of nitrogen in the soil available for plant growth is a function of a number of interacting factors. Nitrogen is made available from organic materials by the activity of various microorganisms within the soil, by biological fixation of atmospheric nitrogen, and by decomposition of organic matter. It is removed from the soil by cropping and leaching and is made unavailable to plants by the activities of various soil organisms. The actual level of available nitrogen in the soil is the net result of the positive and negative forces acting at any given moment in time.

Soil microorganisms are most active during periods of warm temperature and least active when the soil is cold or is either very wet or very dry. Leaching takes place during periods of heavy rain and as a result of excessive irrigation. Nitrogen is made unavailable following application of low-N organic matter, such as sawdust. Therefore, tests for available nitrogen must be interpreted with these considerations in mind, since the actual level of available nitrogen is influenced by all these factors.

Since there are many forms of nitrogenous fertilizer available for use by nurserymen, it is important to understand the advantages and disadvantges of the most commonly used nitrogenous fertilizers. Inorganic fertilizers contain either nitrate nitrogen or ammonium nitrogen. Both the ammonium ion (NH_4^+) and the nitrate ion (NO_3^-) can be absorbed and utilized by plants. However, most plants exhibit a preference for the nitrate form.

These two forms of nitrogen react differently in the soil, since NH_4^+ is a cation and the other NO_3^- is an anion. Because nitrate fertilizers are highly soluble and readily absorbed by plant roots, they are the most desirable for use on cold or wet soils. But because of its solubility, it can also be readily leached from soils. On the other hand, the positively charged ammonium ion becomes adsorbed to negatively charged clay or organic colloids, and leaching is retarded. The ammonium ion is converted to nitrate nitrogen by microorganisms under the conditions of warm temperature, available moisture, and good aeration.

Organic forms of nitrogen, with the exception of urea, are generally unavailable for use by plants and must be converted either to ammonium or nitrate nitrogen before they are available for absorption by plants. Urea, however, is water-soluble and can be used directly by plants or can be rapidly converted to NO_3 in warm moist soils. Slow- or controlled-release fertilizers, discussed previously, are also a source of nitrogen for the production of nursery crops.

Although rates of fertilizer application should be set primarily on the basis of a soil test (Table 11–12) or foliage analysis, they should be modified on the basis of plant growth and species response. Plants that have good foliage color and are making good growth may not require additional fertilizer for a year or two, whereas plants that are chlorotic and making poor growth may need an application of fertilizer. In previous studies, deciduous trees have responded with a significant increase in diameter growth when fertilized at a rate of 6 lb nitrogen/1000 ft^2, whereas in another study, field-grown evergreens (yews) produced their best growth at a rate of 3 lb nitrogen/1000 ft^2. Rates in excess of 4 lb nitrogen/1000 ft^2 resulted in a decline in growth.

TABLE 11-12   Nitrogen Fertilizer Guide for
Woody Plants in Field-Production Nurseries
on Mineral Soils

Previous Crop or Manure Application	Nitrogen ^{b}/acre)^a
Legume and manure, 10 tons/acre	25
Legume	50
Manure, 10 tons/acre	60
No legume, no manure	100

^{a}If the season is cool and wet or the field is poorly drained, additional quantities of nitrate nitrogen may be necessary. Plantings on wide spacing may be fertilized by banding nitrogen at lower rates.

Nurserymen wishing to accelerate growth should maintain fairly high levels of available nitrogen in the soil, whereas those desiring to slow down growth should withhold nitrogen. It is possible to deprive the nursery crop of part of its nitrogen source by leaching the soil or by sowing a cover crop. The data in Table 11–12 provide a guide to nitrogen application for the production of woody plants in field-production nurseries on mineral soils.

Phosphorus

The application of phosphate fertilizers is seldom necessary on field-production nursery soils. When it has been determined that phosphorus in the soil is below some "critical" level (Table 11–7), it is best to apply the fertilizer to a sod or green manure crop grown prior to planting of the nursery crop. This practice ensures better distribution of the phosphorus throughout the soil. Either superphosphate (0-20-0) or triple superphosphate (0-46-0) can be used effectively (Table 11–13). In field-production areas where sod or green manure crops are not employed in the

TABLE 11-13   Phosphate-Phosphorus
Fertilizer Guide for Woody Plants in Field-
Production Nurseries on Mineral Soils^a

Available Phosphorus (lb/acre)	Pounds per Acre^b	
	P_2O_5	P
0–19	100	44
20–39	75	33
40–59	50	22
60–79	25	11
80 +	0	0

^{a}Data based on the Bray P_1 (absorbed) method.
^{b}Applied to sod or green manure crop prior to planting nursery crop.

rotation with the nursery crop, phosphate fertilizers can be applied by banding or by the use of a pelletized fertilizer thoroughly incorporated into the soil prior to planting.

Potassium

Potassium ions on the surface of the exchange complex are available for plant growth. Those in the interior of the soil complex, colloidal clay particles, sometimes known as the stored form, are capable of being released slowly to replace the adsorbed ions. Potassium deficiency is not a common problem on most nursery soils, although it can be in sandy soils. Nurserymen who suspect that their soil might be deficient in potassium should have it tested, and if potassium is needed, apply it to the soil prior to planting (Table 11–14). Potassium fertilizers should be worked into the soil to be most effective.

The two common forms of potassium fertilizers are the chloride form, called muriate of potash, and the sulfate form. Muriate of potash contains approximately 60% K_2O, is the least expensive, and is the most commonly used form. The sulfate form contains 48% K_2O and is used on those crops sensitive to chlorides or in places where large quantities of chlorides are present in irrigation water.

Potassium nitrate (KNO_3), which contains 44% K_2O, also contains about 13% nitrates and has a medium salt index (Table 11–10) per unit of plant food. This material is used extensively in fertilizing container-grown plants. It can be used as a foliar spray (5–10 lb/100 gal water), applied with a spreader-sticker as a transitory means of correcting a potassium deficiency on a nursery crop. This should be followed by a good soil development program prior to planting another nursery crop.

TABLE 11-14   Potash-Potassium Fertilizer Guide for
Woody Ornamental Plants in Field-Production
Nurseries on Mineral Soils[a]

Available Soil Potassium (lb/acre)		Pounds per Acre[b]	
Sandy Loams and Loamy Sands	Loams and Clay Loams	K_2O	K
	0–59	200	166
	60–119	150	125
0–59	120–159	100	83
60–119	160–179	75	62
120–169	180–199	50	42
170–209	200–239	25	21
210+	240+	0	0

[a]Data based on 1.0 N neutral ammonium acetate extraction method.

[b]Applied to sod or green manure prior to planting nursery crop.

Calcium

Although most soils contain adequate amounts of calcium to support plant growth, nurserymen should be aware that they are removing relatively large amounts with the sale of their product. Liming and fertilizing of soils to maintain optimum pH and nutrient levels adds large quantities of calcium and may be sufficient to make up for the loss. It should also be noted that calcium plays an important role in the aggregation of soil particles. Soils with adequate calcium are well aggregated, permitting adequate aeration and drainage, which aid in the production of quality plants. Excess calcium in a soil can produce an imbalance of the cations and could induce either a potassium, iron, or manganese deficiency, especially on soils low in these elements.

Magnesium

Magnesium is not commonly deficient in most soils. But a magnesium deficiency can be induced by applying high rates of potassium. The ratio of exchangeable potassium to exchangeable magnesium should not be greater than 3:1 for most crops. Magnesium fertilizer should not be added if the soil magnesium exceeds 3% of the total bases, or when the soil test indicates a level greater than 75 lb/acre.

A quick, temporary source of magnesium for growing plants is to spray the foliage with a solution of magnesium sulfate, Epsom salt (20 lb/100 gal water). Dolomitic limestone applied at the rate of 1 ton/acre where the soil pH is below 5.5 will supply adequate amounts of magnesium for most nursery crops.

Microelements

Iron deficiency is commonly associated with iron-sensitive species (oaks, holly, rhododendron) when they are grown on alkaline soils. It can also occur when plants are growing in compacted or waterlogged soils. Aeration or drainage of the soils will improve air porosity and iron availability. In addition, large amounts of phosphorus or heavy metals can limit the uptake of iron. Amending the soils with organic matter will improve the chelating action on the iron, preventing it from becoming "fixed" or precipitated out of the soil solution. Iron deficiency is relatively difficult to correct in plants growing in the ground. The best corrective measure for woody plants has been soil applications of iron chelate just prior to spring growth, although trunk implants of encapsulated iron are also effective on shade trees. Foliar sprays of iron have only a transitory effect on woody plants.

Manganese deficiency may be corrected by acidification of the soil to pH 6.0. The use of water-soluble manganese sulfate (5 lb/100 gal water) or a chelated manganese foliar spray, with a spreader-sticker, can be used to correct the deficiency. However, they must be applied annually or even twice a year to assure satisfactory results. Trees exhibiting chlorosis should be carefully diagnosed prior to treating, since an application of iron to effect a cure of a manganese deficiency would further upset the Fe-Mn balance in the soil and within the plant. It is desirable to have both a soil test and a foliar analysis to determine the fertilized requirement for manganese.

Boron deficiency can be corrected by borax (1.5 to 2 lb/acre) applied to the soil or as foliar spray of Solubar (0.1–0.3 lb/acre). Excess levels of boron can create serious toxicity conditions for plants. Be sure that boron is deficient and apply at proper concentration to avoid toxicity problems.

Copper deficiency can be corrected readily. Bordeaux mixture applied to the foliage will alleviate the problem. Copper sulfate spray applied at 3–6 oz/100 gal water can also correct the problem.

METHOD OF APPLICATION

Nutrient elements can enter plants through the roots, the foliage, and in some cases through the bark. When fertilizers are applied to the foliage, they must be in liquid form and be applied in dilute solutions. When applied to the soil to be absorbed by the roots, fertilizer can be in either the liquid or dry state and can be a surface application or injected into the root zone. When applied through the bark, they can be in the dry or liquid state, but most often they are encapsulated and implanted into the trunks of trees. When selecting the method to apply fertilizers to nursery crops, nurserymen should consider the nutrients, their ability to be effectively absorbed, the effect of the soil or the environment, equipment availability, the relative cost, and the effects of fertilizer salts on application equipment and the environment.

Surface Application

Band placement along the rows is most commonly used by nurserymen. It is an effective and efficient method for the application of nitrogen, since nitrogenous fertilizers move into the root zone with the downward movement of water. However, direct surface application is not suggested for applying phosphorus, potassium, and other nutrients that become fixed on the exchange complex. These are better applied by incorporation into nursery soils prior to planting.

Fertilizers can be applied to the soil surface with the aid of various types of spreaders. Band application on either side of the row is a satisfactory means, although the fertilizer can be spread evenly over the entire area. Where large acreages are to be fertilized, an airplane can be economically employed.

Fertilizer spreaders should be calibrated to ensure accurate and uniform distribution of the material. Calibration should be done for each fertilizer, field condition, and each individual spreader. Fertilizers vary in their chemical and physical properties; therefore, one calibration of a spreader does not apply to all fertilizers. Also, fields vary from site to site, which has an effect upon rate of travel and distribution rate. The equipment should be recalibrated whenever there is a significant change in surface conditions. Also, rate of application will vary between spreaders and the individual spreader as a result of use. It is a good practice to recalibrate spreaders and to check the rate of distribution periodically to avoid overapplication of fertilizer.

In some situations it may be more economical to contract fertilizer application to a company that specializes in application of fertilizers and pesticides to agricultural crops.

Surface application rates are stated in pounds per acre (lb/acre) or pounds per thousand square feet (lb/1000 ft^2). The two nomographs of Appendixes E and F will accomplish the conversion of lb/acre to lb/1000 ft^2 or lb/1000 ft^2 to lb/acre without calculations.

Subsurface Injection

Incorporation into the soil by subsurface application is the most effective means of applying nutrients that become fixed on the exchange complex or are slow to move into the soil solution. Nurserymen can best incorporate these materials into the soil prior to planting the nursery crop. Also, when affecting a pH change, the lime or sulfur should be thoroughly incorporated into the soil. When a few trees in a block of nursery stock require the addition of potassium or one of the trace elements, these can be injected into the root zone with the aid of a punch bar or soil auger. If anhydrous ammonia is used as a source of nitrogen, this has to be chiseled into the soil.

Foliage Application

Fertilizers can be applied to the leaves of plants, since leaves can effectively absorb the applied nutrients. The actual mechanism of foliar absorption is not fully understood. The nutrient ions apparently penetrate the cuticle either directly or through thin permeable areas associated with guard cells and tricome bases. The process is most active when the leaves are warm, and the leaf surfaces remain wet for fairly long periods. Wetting of the leaf surface is enhanced by the addition of a wetting agent to the spray solution. Nitrogen is absorbed very rapidly, within a few hours, when applied to the foliage. Potassium, calcium, magnesium, manganese, and zinc are absorbed fairly rapidly, in less than 24 hr, whereas it can take days for sulfur, iron, and molybdenum to be absorbed. Urea sprays are a convenient means for correcting nitrogen deficiency in nursery plantings during periods when the soil is cold and wet. It is generally not economical as a regular nursery practice. Calcium, magnesium, manganese, and zinc deficiency can be readily corrected with one or two sprays during the growing season.

Copper, boron, and molybdenum deficiencies can be corrected very easily by adding small amounts of these minor element fertilizers to spray solution. Copper deficiency is uncommon in nurseries that use Bordeaux mixture in the spray program.

The leaves of most plants will respond to foliar sprays of iron, but the new growth that develops after spraying will remain chlorotic. This is due to the lack of translocation of the iron within the plant. Therefore, if foliage sprays are used to correct iron deficiency, repeat applications will be necessary. Problems with iron deficiency in a nursery should be avoided by proper site selection. Correction of a deficiency might better be accomplished through the use of iron chelates injected into the soil or encapsulated iron implanted into the trunk of trees where this is practical.

Bark Application

Applying fertilizer solutions to the bark of trees has not proven to be too effective as a means of fertilizing trees in nurseries.

TIME OF APPLICATION

The question of when is the best time to apply fertilizer has been discussed for years. Various authorities on the topic of nutrition have recommended fall feeding of trees and others have indicated that spring applications of nitrogen are more effective than summer or fall applications. In a 7-year study on the growth of pin oaks, the variation of the individual growing season was reported to be the most important factor affecting tree growth. Also, it is important that ample moisture be available and favorable temperature conditions prevail following the application of fertilizer.

For nursery crops the best time to apply fertilizer, other than nitrogenous materials, is prior to planting, since these materials should be incorporated into the soil. Nitrogenous materials should be applied annually for best results and at a time when growth will be favorably affected. Nitrogenous fertilizer should not be applied when there is a strong possibility of producing growth that will be injured due to either environmental conditions or cultural practices. There are reports in horticultural journals which attribute some forms of winter injury to late application of nitrogenous fertilizer, whereas other reports indicate that plants that receive a fall application of nitrogen survive exposure to cold better than do nonfertilized plants. There are also reports of plants failing to respond with increased growth following fertilizer application, while other reports indicate excellent response.

To explain and justify all these different responses, it is important for nurserymen to understand growth patterns of woody plants and the ecological factors that affect growth. All plants do not respond the same to light, temperature, and moisture. Some plants grow better under long days than others (Table 14–3). Some stop growth and go dormant under short days. Some plants prefer warm temperature, whereas others grow better at lower temperatures. The same is true for moisture.

The plant's growth pattern is a response to many factors, interacting simultaneously.

Woody plants can be classified by growth pattern into two types: (1) heterophyllus (indeterminate growth) types develop two types of leaves during the growing season, those preformed within the bud and those initiated during the current season of growth (e.g., birch, juniper, willow); and (2) homophyllus (determinate growth) types develop one type of leaf during the growing season, preformed within the shoot (e.g., pine, rhododendron, oak).

Heterophyllus plants respond quickly to an application of fertilizer. They continue to grow late into the season as long as the ecological conditions are favorable. However, homophyllus plants do not respond immediately by increased growth, but rather the plant builds up its nutrient reserves and expresses it in a massive growth response the following spring. Under certain artificially produced conditions (long days and warm temperature), these plants can express a growth response during the season shortly after fertilizer application. Therefore, species that are of the heterophyllus type respond best to spring and early summer applications of fertilizer. They might, however, be subject to winter injury if ecological conditions were right and the plants were given a late summer application of fertilizer. Species of the homophyllus type may not exhibit an immediate response to a late spring application of fertilizer, but will build up nutrient reserves from fertilizer applied one year for massive growth response the following year. Plants will absorb and translocate nutrients as long as air and soil temperatures remain favorable. Fall applications of fertilizer to homophyllus species could result in a significant increase in growth the following spring, whereas fall applications of fertilizer to heterophyllus species may be less effective.

ORGANIC MATTER

The maintenance of organic matter in nursery soils is an important soil management consideration for field-production nurserymen committed to a sustained yield program. With the removal of top soil with many nursery products and with the use of clean cultivation practices, particularly the use of herbicides, the organic-matter content in many nurseries is gradually being depleted. This reduction in organic-matter content will ultimately result in soils of poor tilth, leading to poor plant quality and increased production costs.

Organic matter is of value because it directly influences the physical and biological properties of the soil and because some forms of organic matter serve as a source of nutrients. Organic matter that has been converted to humus improves tilth and soil structure. It reduces the tendency of clay soils to become sticky when wet or to "bake and cake" when dry.

Organic matter also improves aeration, water penetration rates in clay soils, and the water- and nutrient-holding capacity in sandy soils, all of which improve root distribution patterns and plant quality. Organic matter serves as a source of energy for microorganisms that are responsible for the conversion of mineral elements into forms available for plant growth. Organic matter may be either grown as a sod or green manure and plowed under, or it may be added by application of either animal manures or various plant products.

Animal Manures

Animal manures have long been used as a source of organic matter and plant nutrients. Although manures contain relatively low concentrations of plant nutrients on a percentage basis, 0.5–1.5% N, 0.1–0.4% P, and 0.35–1.0% K, they supply appreciable quantities when applied at relatively high rates per acre. The actual composition of manure varies considerably (Table 11–15).

Stable manure may be applied at rates as high as 30 tons/acre, although more frequent smaller applications (5–10 tons/acre) are more effective. The manure can best be applied in late winter when the soil is still frozen and cultivated into the soil as soon as it can be worked in the spring. Poultry manure contains two to three times as much nitrogen as other manures and decays rapidly, releasing ammonia, which can cause plant injury. If the poultry manure is thoroughly mixed with soil or sawdust, it is less likely to cause injury. The primary objections to the use of animal manures is the weed problem that follows application and the cost of handling. The weed problem can be minimized either by using manure obtained from confinement feeding operations or by composting the manure prior to use. Handling cost is offset by improved growth. Animal manure is an excellent organic source of slow-release nutrients. They can be used to good advantage on soils that have been subjected to poor management or have been disturbed as a result of some type of landforming operation.

Sod and Green Manure

Sod and green manure crops are grown in rotation with nursery crops to improve soil structure and add organic matter. Grasses in combination with legumes are excellent crops for improving nursery soils. Grasses supply organic matter, especially by their dense root system, while taprooted legumes (e.g., alfalfa) improve the internal drainage. For maximum production of organic matter, sods should be grown for 2 years. In situations where a sod crop cannot be used in rotation with nursery crops, green manure crops can often be used to advantage. They are grown for less than a growing season and are plowed under while in a succulent state and before they set seed. Tall-growing crops are usually chopped to aid incorporation. Some crops that are used as green manure include (1) annual ryegrass, (2) alfalfa, (3) field corn, (4) foxtail millet, (5) soybeans, (6) sorghum, (7) sudan grass, (8) sudan-sorghum hybrids, and (9) in some areas wheat overseeded in the spring with clover.

Sudan grass and suden-sorghum hybrids produce organic matter yields at rates equal to or greater than thickly planted corn. They are more drought-resistant than

TABLE 11-15   Average Nutrient Composition of Manure from Selected Farm Animals

Type of Manure	Percent Water	N	P	K	Ca	Mg	S	Cu	Fe	Mn	Mo
						Pounds per Ton of Manure					
Chicken	55	31.2	8.0	7.0	74.0	5.8	6.2	0.03	0.93	0.18	0.011
Dairy cattle	80	11.2	2.0	10.0	5.6	2.2	1.0	0.01	0.08	0.02	0.002
Hog	75	10.0	2.8	7.6	11.4	1.6	2.7	0.01	0.56	0.04	0.002
Horse	65	13.8	2.0	12.0	15.7	2.8	1.4	0.01	0.27	0.02	0.002
Sheep	65	28.0	4.2	20.0	11.7	3.7	1.8	0.01	0.32	0.02	0.002

corn and can be worked into the soil with greater ease. In the cooler parts of the country (climatic zones 3 and 4), foxtail or pearl millet may be preferred, since they grow better under cooler growing conditions (Fig. 6–1). Sudan grass, sudan-sorghum hybrids, and millet can be mowed when they start to head out, causing them to grow more thickly. Several cycles of growth and mowing can be repeated during the year, greatly increasing yield. Fertilizing green manure and cover crops is an excellent way to improve soil fertility, soil structure, and to reduce weed populations.

Cover Crops

Cover crops are grown to protect the soil against the forces of erosion, and aid in maintaining the organic matter content of the soil. It is a common practice in production nurseries located in the northern part of the country (climatic zones 3, 4, and 5) to sow a crop of oats (*Avena sativa*) or buckwheat (*Fagopyrum esculentum*) between the nursery rows in late August or early September to help harden-off the nursery stock for winter by taking up nitrogen. When the ground freezes, the plants die, but a mulch is left to protect the soil over winter and in the early spring. The light mulch also aids in retaining moisture in the spring, enhancing digging operations. In those areas of the nursery where nursery stock has recently been removed or where it is too late to sow a green manure crop, it may be desirable to sow a winter annual such as winter rye (*Secale cereale*) or ryegrass (*Lolium* spp.) in the late summer or early fall. The crop is plowed under in the spring before it goes to seed. However, where land costs are high, a cash crop such as wheat or field corn may be grown. The grain provides a financial return from the land and at the same time the stubble adds organic matter to the soil, improving the tilth for the next nursery crop. Table 11–16 provides some guidelines for the seeding of green manure or cover crops for nursery plantings.

TABLE 11-16   Suggested Seeding Rates, Planting Depth, and Planting Dates for Selected Green Manures and Cover Crops[a]

Crop	Seeding Rate (lb/acre)	Planting Depth (in.)	Planting Date
Alfalfa	6–10	$\frac{1}{2}$	Spring or summer
Buckwheat	40–60	1–2	Late spring
Corn (field)	1–2 bushels	2	Spring
Kentucky bluegrass	15–30	$\frac{1}{2}$	Late summer, very early spring
Millet	10–15	$\frac{1}{2}$–1	Late spring
Oats	60–80	1–2	Late summer
Ryegrass	10	$\frac{1}{2}$	Fall
Sorghum	5–8	$\frac{1}{2}$	Late spring
Sorghum-sudan hybrids	40	1	Late spring

[a]See county agricultural agent for local recommendations.

Source: After Hildebrand and Copeland (1977).

Companion Plantings

In extensive plantings, where trees are planted on wide spacings, nurserymen should consider using grass aisles as companion or complementary plantings (see Fig. 5–12). Grasses, such as perennial rye grass, fescues, and bluegrass, make an excellent sod cover that can be used as access routes for heavy equipment, especially when the soil is wet. In addition, the sod will control erosion, modify the soil environment, add organic matter when plowed under, reduce the quantity of herbicide application, and reduce time requirements for harvesting the plants and performing various cultural practices related to the growth and development of the trees.

Grass selection will vary between geographic areas of the country, the soil type, and various management practices of the nursery. Advice on species selection, seeding rates, and cultural practices may be obtained from the county agricultural agent or a crop specialist located at a land-grant university.

Mowing of the turf will be necessary during the growing season. This should be done on a regular, periodic basis (7–10 days). However, growth control of sod is also possible with a growth-regulator chemical. Embark, applied according to the manufacturer's instructions, will provide up to 6 weeks of growth suppression.

Organic Amendments

Bark and sawdust have been found to be economical soil amendments in some situations when supplemented with nitrogen. When bark or sawdust or other similar materials are applied to or mixed with soil in which plants are growing, nitrogen deficiency can and often does develop. Microorganisms, which multiply due to the presence of the carbonaceous substrate, require nitrogen for growth. They compete more successfully for available nitrogen than do the economic crops resulting in nitrogen deficiency. However, a supplemental application of approximately 2% available nitrogen per unit weight of sawdust will minimize this problem. A C/N ratio of 20:1 or less is needed to avoid the necessity of adding supplemental nitrogen (Table 11–17). In some soils, low in available P_2O_5, supplemental applications of superphosphate may be needed to avoid phosphorus deficiency. Sawdust has a tendency to lower the pH of soils slightly. Where crops requiring an alkaline soil reaction are to be grown, it may be necessary to apply lime to modify this effect.

Peat moss is used to improve many types of landscape soils, but because of its high cost, it is used only in limited ways in the field production of nursery stock. It is used as a medium in container production of plants, as a propagation medium for some species, and as a packaging material.

In preparing land to be planted with a long-term nursery crop, it is highly desirable to incorporate a liberal quantity of organic matter to replace that removed with the previous crop and ensure a long-range supply, since additional application of organic matter is seldom made while the crop is on the land. The land should be plowed to a depth of 8 in. or more to incorporate and distribute the organic matter

TABLE 11-17   Percent of Dry Weight of Carbon
and Nitrogen and the C/N Ratio of
Selected Organic Materials

Material	% C	% N	C/N
Alfalfa	39	3.0	13:1
Legume-grass hay	40	1.6	80:1
Oat straw	40	0.5	80:1
Sawdust	50	0.2	250:1

into the root zone. Following plowing, the land should be disked and, if necessary, smoothed with a harrow.

SOIL CONSERVATION

Soil conservation is another area in a field-production nursery to which management must direct its attention if the nursery is to remain productive. Soil conservation is managing the soil so that its productivity can be optimized for both current and future plantings. Unfortunately, many nursery practices contribute to loss of soil productivity; these include (1) loss of soil by digging operations and erosion, (2) long periods of clean cultivation, and (3) performing nursery operations when the soil is wet.

The *loss of soil by digging* B&B or balled and potted nursery stock is considerable. Digging an acre of 5-year B&B evergreens removes about 165 tons of soil, representing an average loss of 33 tons per year. Digging shade trees with a 44-in.-diameter ball removes 1.3 tons of soil, or about 470 tons of soil per acre. This is an average of 67 tons per year for a 7-year rotation. In addition to "mining" of soil, with the sale of plants, nurserymen can also lose a substantial amount by erosion. Under conditions of clean tillage, the loss of soil by erosion varies from 19 to 69 tons/acre/year, depending upon slope, soil type, and environmental conditions. When the average annual "mining" loss of soil for shade tree production is combined with the average annual loss of soil by erosion (44 tons/acre), the amount averages 100 tons of soil per year. At this rate, there would be a loss of 4.2 in. of top soil every 7 years.

Clean cultivation of field-grown nursery stock is commonly practiced since growth is usually best; however, it contributes to the loss of soil by erosion and to degradation of soil structure. Allowing the soil surface to remain "naked" following plowing, disking, and cultivating exposes it to erosion. Also, the extensive use of herbicides removes the protective cover of weeds, leaving soil in a prime condition for erosion. The effect of raindrops or sprinkler irrigation water hitting the soil (splash erosion) is the first step in water erosion. Splash erosion breaks down the natural structure of the soil. This breakdown of the soil aggregates results in crusting of the surface and reduced soil porosity. These, in turn, reduce water infiltration, causing more runoff, and increasing the potential for more serious forms of erosion, especially on nonlevel sites.

Performing field operation when the soil is wet is often necessary in field-production nurseries, especially in the spring. This practice will compact the soil and reduce its porosity. The overall effect is to reduce its production potential and add to the cost of production. If the soil can be rolled into a "ball" or a "snake," it is too wet for field operations.

SOIL CONSERVATION PRACTICES

Little can be done to prevent the loss of nursery soil that is sold as part of the product, other than to change to a container-production system or to produce bare-root plants. However, much can be done to minimize the loss of nursery soils by erosion and to maintain or improve soil structure.

Protecting the soil surface with a canopy of vegetation or with mulches will reduce the effect of rain or irrigation water. Anything that can be done to promote the rapid establishment of the nursery crop is likely to reduce the amount of erosion. Planting a sod crop between the rows (Fig. 5–12) is a desirable conservation practice, where it is a viable option. The planting of green manure or cover crops, discussed previously, is also a desirable soil conservation practice as well as a means of increasing organic matter and improving soil structure. The application of mulches, such as bark or animal manure, to the soil or allowing crop residues to remain on the soil following harvest can also protect the soil surface from splash and wind erosion.

The use of heavy equipment on the land, particularly when the soil is wet, should be minimized. Where feasible, "minimum tillage" should be practiced to reduce the frequency that heavy equipment is upon the land. Prior to tilling the soil, consideration should be given to using a chisel plow in place of the standard moldboard plow. The chisel plow leaves crop residue on the surface, which aids in reducing erosion. Also, when possible, fall plowing should be avoided or confined to level fields, since fall plowing leaves soils exposed to erosion for extended periods. *Subsoiling and tilling* can be used to improve the drainage and percolation of water in soils that have become compacted.

Across-the-slope tillage or planting nursery rows on the contour will produce small dams that will slow the flow of water and minimize gully erosion on hilly sites. In areas where the terrain is composed of short, irregular slopes, this type of tillage may not be possible.

Strip-cropping uses the concept of growing clean-cultivated crops in alternate strips with close growing or sod crops. Strip-cropping is most effective in areas where the slopes are too steep to control water erosion by contour tillage alone, but not steep enough to require the construction of terraces. Strip-cropping is useful for nurseries situated on long sloping sites, since it permits a rotation to be developed between nursery crops and sod.

Various water disposal systems can be developed in nurseries to minimize soil losses by erosion, including the construction of terraces, grass waterways, and subsurface drainage systems. Terraces are earth ridges, constructed on the contour, to form a damlike channel for the interception of water, which is then slowly conducted from the field by a grassed waterway or underground drains. The shape, width, and length of waterways will vary with size of the watershed area. The driving of cars and trucks should never be permitted on terraces and waterways if they are to remain functional for the purpose for which they were designed.

The success of conservation practices depends upon good design, construction, proper use, and maintenance. Assistance in design and construction can be obtained from local Soil Conservation District engineers and from the USDA Soil Conservation Service. Proper use and maintenance of soil conservation systems is the responsibility of management.

SUMMARY

Field production is a major method for the production of nursery stock. If fields are to be productive for current and future generations, they must be well managed. By developing and practicing good soil-management methods, it is possible to maintain nursery soil productivity at relatively high levels.

REFERENCES

ALLISON, F. E., and M. S. ANDERSON. 1951. The use of sawdust for mulches and soil improvement. USDA Circ. 891.

AMERICAN ASSOCIATION OF NURSERYMEN. 1948. Your nursery and soil conservation. AAN, Washington, D.C.

BENJAMIN, L. P., L. C. CHADWICK, and K. W. REISCH. 1964. The effectiveness of ureaformaldehyde as a source of nitrogen for container-grown woody ornamental plants. Proc. Am. Soc. Hort. Sci. 84:636-647.

BERG, A., G. CLULO, and C. R. ORTON. 1958. Internal bark necrosis of apple resulting from manganese toxicity. W. Va. Agric. Exp. Sta. Bull. 414T.

BERNSTEIN, L. 1964. Reducing salt injury to ornamental shrubs in the West. USDA Home Garden Bull. 95.

———. 1965. Salt tolerance of fruit crops. USDA Inf. Bull. 292.

BOONSTRA, R., A. L. KENWORTHY, and D. P. WATSON. 1957. Nutritional status of selected plantings of *Taxus media* "Hicksi." Proc. Am. Soc. Hort. Sci. 70:432–436.

BOWER, C. A. 1963. Diagnosing soil salinity. USDA Agric. Inf. Bull. 279.

BRADLEY, G. A., and D. SMITTLE. 1965. Media pH and extractable Fe, Al and Mn in relation to growth of ericaeous plants. Proc. Am. Soc. Hort. Sci. 87:486-493.

CANNON, T. F., L. C. CHADWICK, and K. W. REISCH. 1960. Nitrogen and potassium nutritional studies of *Gleditisia triacanthos Inermis* "Moraine." Proc. Am. Soc. Hort. Sci. 75:693-699.

————, L. C. CHADWICK, and K. W. REISCH. 1960. Nutrient element status of some ornamental trees. Proc. Am. Soc. Hort. Sci. 76:661-666.

CHADWICK, L. C. 1934. The fertilization of shade trees in the nursery. Proc. Am. Soc. Hort. Sci. 32:357-360.

COOK, T., and J. L. GREEN. 1985. Many grasses available for nursery aisles and plant protection. Am. Nurseryman 161(1): 89–96.

DAVIDSON, H. 1960. Nutrient-element composition of leaves from selected species of woody ornamental plants. Proc. Am. Soc. Hort. Sci. 76:667-672.

————, and W. BARRICK. 1975. Fertilizer practices and vegetation control on highway landscape plantings. Agric. Exp. Sta. Mich. State Univ. Res. Rep. 262.

————, and W. MCCALL. 1959. Fertilizer studies on *Taxus*. Quar. Bull. Mich. Agric. Exp. Sta. 42(2):317-322.

DICKEY, R. D. 1968. Identification and correction of copper deficiency. Am. Nurseryman 128(October 15):10.

DUNHAM, C. W., and D. V. TATNALL. 1961. Mineral composition of leaves of three holly species grown in nutrient sand cultures. Proc. Am. Soc. Hort. Sci. 78:564-571.

FENN, P., and R. D. DURBIN. 1974. A nutritional disorder of red oak seedlings. HortScience 9(3):240–241.

FURUTA, T., and W. C. MARTIN. 1961. Effect of fertilizer application rate and method on plant growth. Proc. Am. Soc. Hort. Sci. 77:637-642.

GOOD, G. L., and H. B. TUKEY, JR. 1969. Root growth and nutrient uptake by dormant *Ligustrum ibolium* and *Euonymus atatus* " Compactus." J. Am. Soc. Hort. Sci. 94(3): 324–326.

GOUIN, F. R., and C. B. LINK. 1966. The effects of various levels of nitrogen, phosphorus and potassium on the growth and chemical composition of *Taxus media* "Hatfieldi." Proc. Am. Soc. Hort. Sci. 89:702-705.

HAMILTON, C. L. Terraced outlets and form drainways. USDA Farmers' Bull. 1814, July 1939.

HILDEBRAND, S. C., and L. O. COPELAND. 1977. Coop Ext. Serv. Mich. State Univ. Ext. Bull. E-489.

HIMELICH, E. B., D. NEELY, and W. R. CROWLER, JR. 1965. Experimental field studies on shade tree fertilization. Ill. Nat. Hist. Surv. Biol. Notes 53.

JACOBSON, P., and W. WEISS. Farming terraced land, USDA Soil Conserv. Serv. Leaflet 335, November 1952.

KELLEY, J. D. 1972. Nitrogen and potassium rate effects on growth, leaf nitrogen and winter hardiness of *Pyracantha coccinia* "Lalandi" and *Ilex crenata* "Rotundifolia." J. Am. Soc. Hort. Sci. 97(4):446-448.

————, and R. W. SHIER. 1965. Seasonal changes in the macronutrient composition of the leaves and stems of *Taxus media*. Proc. Am. Soc. Hort. Sci. 86:800–814.

————, and R. W. SHIER. 1965. Seasonal changes in the micronutrient composition of the leaves and stems of *Taxus media*. Proc. Am. Soc. Hort. Sci. 87:545–550.

KIELBASO, J. J., and K. OTTMAN. 1976. Manganese deficiency contributory to maple decline. J. Arboriculture:27-32.

LUNT, H. A., A. M. KOFRANEK, and J. J. OERTLI. 1961. Coated fertilizers: general description and applications. Calif. Agric. 15(12):2-3.

———, and J. J. OERTLI. 1962. Controlled release of fertilizer minerals by incapsulating membranes: II. Efficiency of recovery influence of soil moisture, mode of application and other considerations related to use. Soil Sci. Soc. Am. Proc. 26(6):584-587.

MEYER, M. M., JR. 1969. External and internal nutrition and spring growth of woody ornamental plants. Proc. Int. Plant Propag. Soc. 19:300-305.

———. 1971. Phosphorus utilization from internal and external sources in the growth of woody ornamental plants. J. Am. Soc. Hort. Sci. 96(2):209-212.

———, and H. B. TUKEY, JR. 1965. Nitrogen, phosphorous and potassium plant reserves and spring growth of *Taxus* and *Forsythia*. Proc. Am. Soc. Hort. Sci. 87:537-544.

———, and H. B. TUKEY, JR. 1967. Influence of root temperature and nutrient applications on root growth and mineral content of *Taxus* and *Forsythia* plants during the dormant season. Proc. Am. Soc. Hort. Sci. 90:440-446.

MILLER, R. O., D. C. KIPLINGER, and H. K. TAYAMA. 1967. Soluble salts. Florists Rev., November 2, p. 49.

NEELY, D., E. B. HIMELICK, and W. R. CROWLEY, JR. 1970. Ill. Nat. Hist. Surv. Bull. 30, Art. 4, pp. 235-266.

OERTLI, J., and O. R. LUNT. 1962. Controlled release of fertilizer minerals by incapsulating membranes. 1. Factors influencing the rate of release. Soil Sci. Soc. Am. Proc. 26(6):579-583.

RADER, L. F., L. M. WHITE, and C. W. WHITTAKER. 1943. The salt index—a measure of the effect of fertilizers on the concentration of the soil solution. Soil Sci. 55: 201-218.

ROBERTSON, L. S., D. L. MOKMA, and D. L. QUINSENBERRY. 1977. Soil erosion by water. Coop. Ext. Serv. Mich. State Univ. Ext. Bull. E-1169.

ROGERS, B. L., A. H. THOMPSON, and L. E. SCOTT. 1965. Internal bark necrosis (measles) on Delicious apple trees under field conditions. Proc. Am. Soc. Hort. Sci. 86:46-54.

SCHOENEWEISS, D. F. 1973. Correction of lime-induced chlorosis of pin oak by liquid soil injection. HortScience 8(4):333-334.

SHEAR, C. B., H. L. CRANE, and A. T. MYERS. 1946. Nutrient element balance: a fundamental concept in plant nutrition. Proc. Am. Soc. Hort. Sci. 47:239-248.

———, H. L. CRANE, and A. T. MYERS. 1950. Nutrient element balance: application of the concept to the interpretation of foliar analysis. Proc. Am. Soc. Hort. Sci. 51:319-326.

SMITH, E. M. 1975. Fertilizing field-grown evergreens and shrubs. Am. Nurseryman 142(10):10.

———. 1975. Growth response of fertilized trees. Am. Nurseryman 143(1):11.

SPURWAY, C. H. 1944. Soil reaction (pH) preferences of plants. Mich. State Col., Agric. Exp. Sta. Special Bul. 306.

———, and K. LAWTON. 1949. Soil testing, a practical system of fertility diagnosis. Mich. State Univ. Agric. Exp. Sta. Tech. Bull. 132 (4th revision).

TATNALL, D. V., and C. W. DUNHAM. 1961. Nutrient deficiency symptoms in American, Japanese and Chinese hollies. Proc. Am. Soc. Hort. Sci. 78:560-563.

TRUOG, E. 1947. USDA yearbook of agriculture, 1943–47. Superintendent of Documents, Washington, D.C.

WIKLE, J. 1963. Some comments and questions on soil improvement and fertilization for shade trees. Arborist News:61-69.

WILDE, S. A. 1938. Soil fertility standards for growing northern conifers in forest nurseries. J. Agric. Res. 57:945-952.

_____ . 1946. Soil fertility standards for game food plants. J. Wildl, Manage. 10:77-81.

_____ , and W. E. PATZER. 1940. Soil fertility standards for growing northern hardwoods in forest nurseries. J. Agric. Res. 61:215-221.

WITTWER, S. H. 1963. Foliar application of fertilizer. New Horizons in the Fertilizer World. Tennessee Valley Authority.

YOUNGBERG, C. T., and R. C. AUSTIN. 1954. Fertility standards for raising Douglas fir in forest nurseries. J. For. 52:4-6.

_____ , and R. C. AUSTIN. 1958. The uptake of nutrients by western conifers in forest nurseries. J. For. 56(5):337-340.

ZIMMERMAN, R. H. 1959. Visual symptoms of plant nutrient deficiencies. Proc. Int. Plant Propag. Soc. 9:131-135.

SUGGESTED READING

AMERICAN SOCIETY OF AGRONOMY. 1965. Methods of soil analysis, Parts 1 and 2. Madison, Wisc.

DIRR, M. A. 1975. Plant nutrition and woody ornamental growth and quality. HortScience 10(1):43-45.

DONAHUE, R. L., R. W. MILLER, and J. C. SHICKLUNA. 1977. Soils: an introduction to soils and plant growth. Prentice-Hall, Inc., Englewood Cliffs, NJ.

MENGEL, K., and E. A. KIRKBY. 1978. Principles of plant nutrition. International Potash Institute, Worblaufen-Bern, Switzerland.

U.S. DEPARTMENT OF AGRICULTURE. 1957. Soil, the yearbook of agriculture. Superintendent of Documents, Washington, D.C.

12 *Media and Nutrition Management for Container-Grown Plants*

Producing plants in containers has become a permanent part of the nursery industry and in some parts of the country the practice has replaced field culture as the primary method of production. In contrast to field culture, the volume of medium available per plant is greatly reduced. Also, the root environment is significantly affected by the physical and chemical composition of the medium, the size and shape of the container, the surface upon which it is placed to grow, and the ambient atmosphere surrounding the containers. Therefore, good container-media management is basic to the production of quality container-grown plants. It is necessary to (1) understand the primary functions and establish some basic criteria for container media, (2) be familiar with the physical and chemical properties of some of the more commonly used ingredients and mixes, (3) understand the need for chemical supplements and method of testing and controlling their availability, and (4) understand the need for and methods of media sterilization.

FUNCTIONS AND CRITERIA

In developing a medium for the production of container-grown plants, the functions of the medium in plant growth and development must be understood and criteria determined to produce the most functional medium for the climate and for the nursery objective. The two basic functions of the medium are (1) to serve as a means of anchorage and support for the plant and (2) to serve as a reservoir for water and the mineral nutrients for plant growth and development. In addition, the medium must have a pH conducive to plant growth, a structure that will permit gaseous exchange to provide aeration for the roots and permit water infiltration and movement.

Anchorage and Support

The roots of plants serve to anchor them to the soil, which in turn serves to support the plant. In field production this works, since the roots can grow unrestricted. However, in container culture the roots are restricted to the confines of the container. Therefore, a medium for container production of plants in a nursery must be heavy enough to provide ballast for the species of plant it will support, unless other forms of artificial support are provided, particularly for larger trees and shrubs. Small plants produced in 1- to 5-gal containers and spaced pot to pot can be grown in a medium of low bulk density (BD)—weight per unit volume—whereas larger plants grown on wider spacings require a medium of higher BD. Where the plants are large and the BD of the medium is low, some other form of support is necessary, such as staking or tying to a wire.

Nutrients

Plants produced in containers require the same essential elements as plants produced in field culture. The total supply of minerals available for plant growth is limited by the size of the container. This makes it desirable that the medium used for container production have a relatively high cation exchange capacity (CEC) to serve as a reservoir for mineral elements other than nitrogen or those that will be supplied by other means. Most of the organic ingredients provide this even though at a low level. The CEC for medium mixtures used in container production of plants should be reported on a volume basis, which is expressed as milliequivalents per 100 cubic centimeters (e.g., sand approximately 1 mEq/100 cc, bark approximately 11–13 mEq/100 cc). Maintaining optimum levels of nitrogen during the growing season may be done through the use of slow-release fertilizers (Table 11–9) or by the use of soluble fertilizers applied through the irrigation system (Table 11–10).

Soil (Medium) Reaction (pH)

The optimum pH for organic mixes (Fig. 12–1) tends to be 1–1.5 units lower than those generally considered to be desirable for mineral soils (Fig. 11–1). Liming organic soils with a pH above 5.8 is undesirable because of the reduced availability of P, Mn, B, Cu, and Zn.

Moisture-Holding Capacity and Porosity

Growing plants require large quantities of water for metabolic purposes and to replace that which is lost by transpiration. Therefore, one of the important functions of a good container medium is to store and supply the moisture needed for plant growth. However, for the moisture to be available to the plants requires that the roots must have a supply of oxygen, necessitating that the container medium have

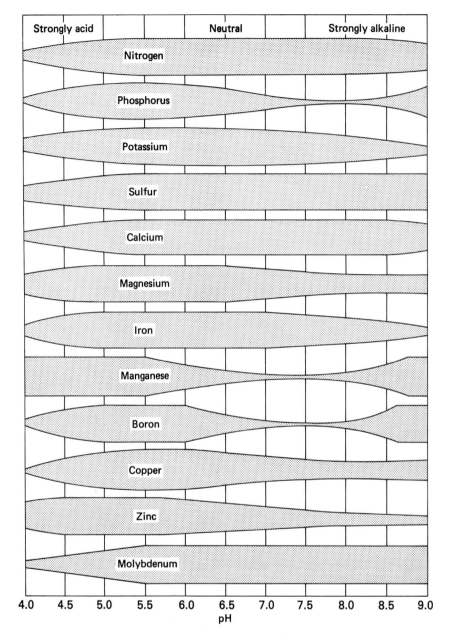

Figure 12–1 Influence of reaction on availability of plant nutrients in organic soils. Widest part of bar indicates maximum availability. (From Lucas and Davis, 1961.)

good aeration porosity so that the roots can carry on respiration and allow for the removal of the carbon dioxide (CO_2) that is generated in the process. This presents somewhat of a problem with containers, since they are relatively shallow and develop a perched water table at the bottom of the container. The shallower the container and the finer the texture, the greater the moisture-holding capacity but the poorer the aeration porosity. On the other hand, deep containers and coarse-textured materials improve the aeration porosity but reduce the moisture-holding capacity.

The effect of shallowness can be partially avoided by incorporating coarse-textured ingredients (sand, bark, perlite) into the container medium. However, sufficient coarse material must be blended into an ingredient of fine texture so that the threshold proportion is exceeded. This is the blend or mix at which pore space is minimized; as the proportion of the coarse texture ingredient is increased beyond the threshold proportion, porosity is increased (Fig. 12–2). Improvement of the porosity of a fine-textured medium requires a substantial addition (80–90% of the total bulk volume) of the coarse-texture ingredient. A medium for the production of container-grown plants should be blended to produce a mix that has good water-holding capacity and also good porosity. This is dependent upon the texture of the various ingredients and the relative proportions within the mix.

Porosity determines the volume of the container, when filled with a medium, that is potentially available for water, air, and for root growth. Pore size determines the actual volume of water and air that remains in a container medium following

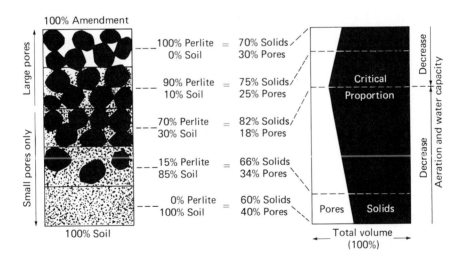

Figure 12–2 Modifying aeration and water-holding capacity of container soil. Starting with 100% soil, additions of perlite up to about 70% (critical proportion) reduce total pore space without increasing the number of larger pores. Starting with 100% perlite, additions of soil up to about 30% reduce total pore space by filling in the larger pores. The critical proportion of amendment to soil varies with the type of amendment and the type of soil. (From Spomer, 1973.)

irrigation and drainage; the small pores function as water-retention pores, whereas large pores function as aeration pores (aeration porosity).

Aeration porosity and water retention of a container medium are also influenced by the depth of the container. A medium in a shallower container will hold a greater volume of water than the same volume of medium in a deeper container. Therefore, when characterizing water retention and aeration porosity of a container medium, it is necessary to consider container depth (see Table 12–1).

TABLE 12-1   Estimation of Porosity

Nurserymen can estimate the total porosity, aeration porosity, and water-retention porosity of a container medium by a simple technique. The only necessary equipment includes the container, a plug for the drainage hole at the bottom of the container, and a graduated cylinder or some other method for measuring water volume.

1. Plug the drain hole and fill the container with water. Measure the volume of water it contains (= container volume).

2. Empty the container and fill it with dry soil mix. Very slowly and very thoroughly saturate the mix in the container by carefully pouring water onto the surface at one edge of the container. Keep track of the volume of water you are adding (= pore volume).

3. Unplug the drain and catch the water that drains out of the container and measure its volume (= aeration pore volume).

4. Porosity is obtained by dividing pore volume (step 2) by container volume (step 1) and multiplying by 100%.

5. Aeration porosity is obtained by dividing aeration pore volume (step 3) by container volume (step 1) and multiplying by 100%.

6. Water retention porosity is obtained by subtracting aeration porosity (step 5) from porosity (step 4).

In summary:

$$\text{Porosity} = \frac{\text{container mix pore volume}}{\text{container volume}} \times 100\%$$

$$\text{Aeration porosity} = \frac{\text{aeration pore volume}}{\text{container volume}} \times 100\%$$

$$\text{Water-retention porosity} = \text{porosity} - \text{aeration porosity}$$

Source: Spomer (1977).

INGREDIENTS

The two most commonly used ingredients in the production of media for container growing of woody plants have been sand and peat moss. However, soil is used in some mixes and various wood-waste products are being used to replace peat moss. Composted hardwood bark is used fairly extensively in the Midwest, pine and

Douglas fir bark is used where it is readily available, and redwood sawdust is used in California.

The following information briefly summarizes some of the properties of the most commonly used ingredients as they pertain to the production of container-grown plants.

Sand consists of weathered mineral particles between 0.05 and 2.0 mm in diameter. But for container-soil mixes, the size range should be between 0.05 and 1.0 mm with less than 10% of the sand in the coarse-sized classification, between 0.5 and 1.0 mm. The mineral composition of the sand is related to the rocks from which it was formed, but for horticultural purposes sand contains few, if any, mineral elements, and has no significant buffering or cation exchange capacity. Sand may or may not be sterile, depending upon the source. The pH of sand varies with source, but most sands have a high pH and may require the addition of an acidifying agent prior to use as a medium for the production of plants.

Peats used in media for the production of container-grown plants are commonly classified into three types: moss peat, reed-sedge peat, and peat humus.

Moss peat is composed principally of sphagnum, hypnum, and other mosses. Sphagnum is the least decomposed of the three types. It is light tan to dark brown in color, lightweight, high in moisture-holding capacity, and high in acidity. Moss peat will hold 10 times its dry weight in moisture, and because of its high acidity it is slow to decompose. Moss peat should not be confused with sphagnum moss, which is the live portion or the young, nondecomposed residue of sphagnum. Sphagnum moss is used by nurserymen in packaging and shipping of tender plants and as a propagation medium.

Reed-sedge peat is formed principally of reeds, sedges, marsh grasses, and other swamp plants. It varies considerably in its degree of decomposition and acidity. The partially decomposed reed-sedge peats are brown to reddish brown in color, whereas the more decomposed types almost black. They have a pH between 4.5 and 7.0 and a medium water-holding capacity.

Peat humus is derived from either reed-sedge or hypnum moss peat in an advanced stage of decomposition. It is dark brown to black in color, has a low water-holding capacity, but is more resistant to decomposition than is moss or reed-sedge peat.

Wood products of various types, including sawdust, wood chips, shredded bark, and wood shavings, are an excellent source of organic material for soil mixtures in the production of container-grown plants. For many years nurserymen declined to use wood products as a soil amendment because it was thought they contained materials that were toxic to plant growth. However, present evidence indicates that sawdust and most other woodwaste products contain relatively few compounds that are toxic to plant growth.

The reason for the "toxic" effect, a stunting and chlorosis of the plant, is related to the carbon-nitrogen ratio of the sawdust and its effect upon the soil-plant nitrogen relationship. When undecomposed wood products, such as sawdust or wood chips, are mixed with soil under favorable conditions of warm temperature and available moisture, they start to decompose. The decomposition is aided by various forms of microflora. These microorganisms require a source of energy carbon, which is supplied by the wood, and a source of nitrogen, which the wood does not supply except in trace quantities. Therefore, the microflora obtain the needed nitrogen from the only other available source, the soil. If there are plants present, the microorganisms compete with them for the available nitrogen, and unless there is enough for both, the plants will exhibit nitrogen deficiency. This problem can be avoided by the addition of nitrogen to the sawdust-soil mixture. If the nitrogen content of the mixture, on a weight basis, is about 1.2–1.5% and optimum conditions for biological activity are present, decomposition will proceed without depleting the supply of available nitrogen to the growing crop. Since sawdust contains about 0.2% nitrogen, the addition of 25–30 lb nitrogen/ton of sawdust is required.

Aged sawdust makes an excellent ingredient for container production of nursery stock. It is lightweight, has good water-holding capacity, and good aeration porosity. It does not require the addition of large quantities of nitrogen to support microbial development, and it is relatively sterile.

Hardwood bark is a lightweight, woodwaste product which when supplemented with nitrogen makes an excellent organic ingredient for the production of container-grown plants. It may be used alone or in combination with sand. It is lightweight, easy to handle, and the CEC exceeds that of peat. Bark contains all the trace elements and significant amounts of the major elements. Some hardwood barks may contain phytotoxic substances that are harmful to plant growth. But by composting for a period of at least 30 days, most of these compounds are eliminated. The material is readily available in many parts of the country and is relatively inexpensive.

Pine and Douglas fir bark is an excellent medium for the production of plants that prefer an acid root environment such as rhododendrons. It is also used either alone or in combination with sand, after the pH has been adjusted, for the production of all types of container-grown plants. Softwood bark has a low bulk density and a fairly good CEC (11–13 mEq/100 cc). It is somewhat difficult to wet, but upon wetting it possesses a good water-holding capacity, together with good aeration. Some barks, such as Douglas fir, contain sharp slivers, which necessitates the use of leather gloves when handling the material.

Perlite is a lightweight, granular material obtained by heat-treating crushed lava. It weighs less than 8 lb/ft^3. It is sterile, has a pH close to neutral, and a water-holding capacity, on the surface of the particles, equal to three to four times its weight. The material is without either buffering or cation exchange capacity. Perlite is a good propagation medium or an amendment to decrease weight and improve aeration of container mixes.

Vermiculite is a very lightweight, platelike material obtained by heat-treating mica. It weighs about the same as perlite, 6–10 lb/ft^3, depending upon the grade; has a good water-holding capacity, equal to three to four times its weight; and a good CEC. Since the material is produced by a heat treatment, it is sterile. Vermiculite makes an excellent propagation medium and a media amendment for producing small container-grown plants. It must be handled with care when wet to avoid compressing the particles. Compressed vermiculite is an undesirable media amendment, since it results in poor drainage and poor aeration porosity.

Turface is a calcined clay that is excellent for improving the aeration porosity of soils or container mixes. Its bulk density is greater than perlite or vermiculite, but it has good internal capacity for holding nutrients and water.

CONTAINER MEDIA

A good container medium must possess the criteria and perform the various functions discussed previously. In addition, it should be: (1) readily available; (2) relatively inexpensive; (3) light enough to be handled conveniently within the nursery and to be transported economically to market; (4) free of pests (weed seeds, disease organisms, insects, nematodes, herbicide residue, etc.) or be capable of being sterilized without the production of toxic substances (e.g., soluble salts, ammonia, biuret, or other phytoxins); (5) economically blended into a uniform, relatively stable medium; and (6) capable of being stored for short periods of time without significant changes in the physical and chemical properties.

Mixes

The early container mixes, prior to 1940, incorporated a loam soil; a clean, sharp sand; and peat in various proportions. This was supplemented with lime, superphosphate, and various fertilizers, which generally included an organic source of nitrogen. But these mixes were not satisfactory because they lacked uniformity and plant performance was highly variable. Soil and sand have a high bulk density (100 lbs/ft^3), making them difficult to handle and costly to transport to market.

John Innes Composts

In 1939 researchers at the John Innes Institute in England published recommendations on the development of two standardized composts that could be used for all kinds of plants. Since that time, they have modified their recommendations only slightly. The basic ingredients of the John Innes composts are a medium loam, containing little or no sand; fibrous or granular, relatively undecomposed peat; and coarse sand. The loam used in the John Innes mixes is the primary ingredient. Its functions are to supply the nutrient-holding capacity for the medium and the actively decomposing humus, which furnishes the microflora needed in a good biologically active soil mixture. The ingredients are blended by volume, according to a strict formula, composted for a period of time, and then sterilized and fortified with various solid amendments to adjust the pH and supplement the nutritive condition of the compost. The basic principles relating to compost development, as stated in the first edition of *Seed and Potting Composts,* are still in use today and have served as the basis for the development of soil mixes and container-culture programs in other countries.

The U.C.-Type Soil Mixes

The U.C. system for producing healthy container-grown plants was developed at the University of California, Los Angeles, in the 1940s and early 1950s. The primary objective of the system was to reduce cost of production by reducing plant losses and by lowering labor costs through mechanization. One part of the system was the development of the U.C.-type soil mixes, which have the qualities of reproducibility and reliability. The physical and chemical properties can be reproduced with a high degree of consistency, and the various mixes will function in a consistent manner under similar production programs.

The basic ingredients for the mixes are fine sand (0.5–0.05 mm) and peat moss of the sphagnum type. However, redwood shavings, sawdust, or rice hulls can substitute for all or part of the peat moss. If rice hulls are used, they should be sterilized to avoid having rice as a weed problem. The ingredients are blended on a percent by volume basis, producing five basic mixes when blended in 25% increments of fine sand to peat moss. The two most commonly used mixes were 75% fine sand plus 25% peat moss, and 50% fine sand plus 50% peat moss.

The U.C. mixes are fortified with various fertilizers to provide an available supply of the major nutrients: N, P, K, Ca, and Mg. The peat moss and fine sand contain a sufficient supply of the microelements to meet the needs of most container-grown plants. However, some acid-requiring plants (e.g., rhododendron, blueberry) and plants grown in containers for long periods of time may require a supplemental application of iron chelate or a minor element fertilizer which contains a mixture of the microelements.

The type of fertilizer to be added varies with the medium, the storage requirement prior to planting, soil salinity problems, and the supplemental fertilizer practices to be followed after planting. Six fertilizer programs are suggested for each of the five mixes, producing a total of 30 container-production media programs.

Prior to mixing the various ingredients, the peat moss should be thoroughly moistened to ensure uniform mixing. The fertilizer materials must be carefully weighed and mixed together, preferably in a small quantity of sand, prior to mixing with the various ingredients of the mix. This will aid in obtaining uniform distribution of the chemical materials throughout the mix and ensure that every cubic yard of mix is the same, both physically and chemically. The U.C. mixes can be sterilized, after blending, with a high degree of assurance that there will be no salinity problems and no detrimental effects upon plants due to soil salinity.

Cornell Peat-Lite Mixes

The Cornell Peat-Lite mixes were developed at Cornell University in the 1960s primarily for seed propagation and production of spring annuals and bedding plants. The basic ingredients of the Peat-Lite mix are sphagnum moss and either vermiculite or perlite, to which is added specific quantities of dolomitic limestone, superphosphate, and a complete fertilizer with a ratio of 1:2:1. To make a cubic yard of these mixes, the ingredients are blended as follows:

Peat-Lite Mix A

11 bushels	Sphagnum peat moss
11 bushels	Horticultural grade 2 or 4 vermiculite
5 lb	Dolomitic lime
1 lb	Single superphosphate (fine)
2-12 lb	5-10-5 fertilizer; 12 lb will supply the nutrient needs of annual plants for about 6 weeks. If less than 12 lb is used, a supplemental fertilizer program is necessary.

Peat-Lite Mix B. Substitute horticulural-grade perlite for the vermiculite.

The Peat-Lite mixes have several advantages for growers of bedding plants: they are light in weight, and the ingredients are uniform, readily available, and sterile. But they have limited use in nursery production, since the medium provides no ballast to support the relatively heavy crowns of woody plants. They are used most successfully for starting seedlings and in the potting of roses and small shrubs for short periods of time (i.e., potting roses in late winter and growing for 1–2 months for spring sale). When they are used for larger plants, it is necessary to provide some artificial means of plant support, such as staking or tying to a wire trellis. Peat-Lite mixes must be thoroughly moistened prior to use and firmly compacted about the roots of plants to assure satisfactory results.

Hardwood Bark

Hardwood bark, a woodwaste by-product from various forest industries throughout the United States, especially in the Midwest and eastern states, is an excellent material, either alone or in combination with sand for use as a medium for the production of container-grown plants. It is desirable to hammermill and essential to compost the bark prior to use as a plant-growth medium. The optimum particle size is between $\frac{1}{8}$ and $\frac{1}{32}$ in. Approximately 35% of the particles should be smaller than $\frac{1}{32}$ in. and approximately 10% should be larger than $\frac{1}{8}$ in. to assure good drainage and aeration.

Hardwood bark has a C/N ratio of 150:1, whereas a ratio of 20:1 is most desirable when it is used as a medium for plant growth. To reduce the C/N ratio, the bark is composted with 2 lb of actual nitrogen (6 lb of ammonium nitrate) per cubic yard. Freshly harvested bark has a pH close to 5.2, but this increases as it ages. To keep the pH in the desirable range for good plant growth, 1 lb each of elemental sulfur and iron sulfate is added per cubic yard of bark at the time of composting. It is not necessary to add calcium or magnesium, since there is an adequate supply of these elements in the bark. Phosphorus (2.5 lb of treble superphosphate per cubic yard) is also added at the time of composting. Potassium (2 lbs/yd^3) should be added at time of composting if it is omitted from the fertilizer program during the production phase. All the chemical supplements must be uniformly mixed with the bark prior to composting.

The compost pile should be constructed on a well-drained site to assure good drainage. After thorough wetting, the ingredients are formed into a pile 6–8 ft high, 6–8 ft wide, but of any convenient length, to assure that heating and composting will take place. During composting the temperature within the pile will reach 140°F, plus or minus a few degrees. After the temperature reaches its peak within 30–60 days and cools by 10–15°F, the pile should be remixed and piled for another period of composting. After the temperature in the pile reaches its second maximum and declines, the material is ready for use as a medium for container-grown plants. The bottom 1 ft of compost should be mixed with some of the upper portions to minimize injury from soluble salts. The postcomposting fertilizer program for plants growing in hardwood bark is dependent upon how the compost is prepared, the amount used in the container mix, and the market objective.

Composted hardwood bark is reported to suppress nematode populations and some parasitic diseases of plants. But it can contain high levels of manganese, which may be toxic to some plants; levels as high as 992–1125 ppm were associated with chlorotic, stunted Japanese holly plants grown in composted hardwood bark.

Softwood Bark

Pine and Douglas fir bark, alone or blended with fine sand, peat moss, and perlite, is used in many parts of the country in the production of container-grown plants. It has a low pH (3.4–4.0) and is an excellent medium for growing plants. It should be hammermilled to pass through a ½-in. mesh screen prior to use as a medium. Bark that has been aged for a couple of years is more desirable than is freshly milled bark. Because of the lack of uniformity of the bark from one geographic area to another, it is desirable to have a chemical and physical analysis made on the material as it is obtained from the mill and to adjust the physical and chemical properties accordingly.

Some recent studies have shown that it may not be necessary to supplement a pine bark medium with limestone and superphosphate. There seem to be adequate supplies of calcium, magnesium, and phosphorus in the bark and in irrigation water to support plant growth for at least one and possibly two growing seasons. However, since bark has a high C/N ratio (about 300:1) it must be supplemented with nitrogen. Also, it is necessary to amend the medium with potassium and the microelements. Suggested levels that should be in the "soil" (container) solution for optimum growth of plants are: nitrogen, 75 ppm; phosphorus, 10 ppm; potassium, 25 ppm; calcium 30 ppm; and magnesium, 15 ppm.

Note that these levels are in the "soil" (container) solution and are not based on a soil-water extract method. They are provided as a guide; the exact levels for any container medium will vary with the actual ingredients, the element content of irrigation water, and the frequency of natural rainfall. Plants that respond best to a higher pH level may need to have the pine bark supplemented with peat moss or fine sand and amended with limestone and superphosphate. Since pine bark dries out fairly rapidly, growers frequently supplement with peat moss or fine sand to reduce frequency of irrigation.

Municipal Compost

Municipal compost has also been used as the organic ingredient in soil mixes for the production of container-grown plants. It consists of garbage or leaf mold that has been ground in a hammermill, sprayed with sewage, and composted in windrows for 12–16 weeks. A mixture of soil-perlite-municipal compost on a 1:1:1 volume basis has produced quality plants when fertilized with a water-soluble, inorganic fertilizer used as either a constant or biweekly liquid feed. If municipal compost or sewage is to be used as a container medium, it should be subjected to a chemical analysis, especially for heavy metals which can produce undesirable effects upon plant growth. Also, in some communities there may be laws that prohibit its use because of various environmental concerns.

Other Materials

A great diversity of other materials, such as stones, ground corncobs, spent hops, Cocobean hulls, rice hulls, and the husks of macadamia nuts have been used as media amendments. However, prior to use they should be checked for their chemical and physical properties and tested on a trial basis prior to extensive use. There are also prepared ready-to-use mixes that can be purchased commercially. These, too, should be tested prior to use and monitored periodically during the growing season to minimize potential problems and assure optimum growth.

CHEMICAL SUPPLEMENTS

Most media manufactured for the production of container-grown plants will require some form of chemical supplement to adjust the pH and to augment the available nutrients. A chemical analysis of the medium and its components should be obtained, unless this information is known.

Peat moss and softwood bark tend to be acidic and may require the addition of limestone to raise the pH if it is below 5.8. However, liming organic soils with a pH above 5.8 is undesirable because of reduced availability of a number of the essential elements. Some sources of peat and hardwood bark are alkaline, and sulfur or iron sulfate should be added to lower the pH. Table 12–2 suggests the pounds of limestone or sulfur needed per cubic yard of peat to affect the desired pH change.

Some of the ingredients used for producing artificial soil mixes are low in available P, Ca, Mg, Fe, and various microelements. Therefore, it is necessary to supplement the medium with an available supply of these nutrients either during composting or just prior to planting. Peat is naturally low in microelements. Manga-

TABLE 12-2   Pounds of Dolomitic Limestone[a] or
Sulfur Needed per Cubic Yard of Peat

Original pH	Desired pH of Peat	
of Peat	pH 4.5–5.2[b]	pH 5.3–6.2[c]
3.4–3.9	8 lb limestone	14 lb limestone
4.0–4.4	4 lb limestone	10 lb limestone
4.5–5.2	None	5 lb limestone
5.3–6.2	2 lb sulfur	None
6.3–7.0	4 lb sulfur	2 lb sulfur

[a]If obtainable, a mixture of equal parts of dolomitic and
calcic limestone is preferred to all-dolomitic limestone.
[b]Desirable pH for rhododendrons, many conifers, and
tropical plants.
[c]Desirable pH for most bedding plants and tree nurseries.
Source: Lucas et al. (1971).

nese may be needed for naturally well-limed reed-sedge peat, whereas copper, molybdenum, and iron are needed for sphagnum moss peat and fibrous acid sedge peat.
If plant deficiency problems appear, the micronutrient mixture in Table 12–3 is suggested for each cubic yard of peat in the mixture. Use only powdered or fine crystal-
line materials and mix gradually as the mix is blended.

Additional amounts of fertilizer may be needed, depending upon the mix and
the length of time that the plants are to be grown in the container. Plants growing in
mixes other than the John Innes and the U.C. mixes will require supplemental nitrogen and potassium shortly after planting. This can be accomplished, most satisfactorily, by the addition of one of the slow- or controlled-release fertilizers at the time
of planting. The rate of application will vary with the mix and the fertility program
of the nursery. If a 1:1 sand/peat medium is used, a rate of application that supplies
nitrogen at 300 ppm is satisfactory to supply the nutrient requirements of the plants
for about 4 months.

Plants that are to be grown for extended periods of time will require further
applications of nitrogen and possibly potassium. This can be applied either as a dry

TABLE 12-3   Suggested Micronutrient Mixtures
for 1 Cubic Yard of Peat

Compound	Weight Needed	
Iron chelate or ferrous sulfate	50	2
Manganese sulfate	30	1
Copper sulfate	10	0.3
Zinc sulfate	6	0.2
Sodium borate (borax)	3	0.1
Sodium molybdate	1	0.03
Total mix	100	3.6

Source: Lucas et al. (1971).

surface application or as a water-soluble fertilizer. The latter can be done most effectively by proportioning a water-soluble fertilizer concentrate solution into the irrigation system (see Chapter 13). A commercial water-soluble fertilizer can be used or a mixture of equal parts of ammonium nitrate and potassium nitrate (23-0-22). An application rate that supplies nitrogen at 100–150 ppm at each watering is used for most media. But a rate of 200–300 ppm N is suggested for hardwood bark, except when the bark has been supplemented with a slow-release fertilizer prior to planting.

TESTING AND MODIFYING

To assure uniformity of production, the media should be tested periodically to assure proper blending prior to planting and that optimum levels of nutrition are maintained during the growing season. Media samples should be tested by a reputable soil testing service for pH, soluble salts, and total available N, P, K, Ca, and Mg. If the blending is being done correctly and the raw materials are uniformly consistent, the values for the various parameters should remain relatively constant. If there is a significant change in any of the values, measures can be taken to correct the situation before it becomes a serious problem.

Soil-testing procedures vary considerably among laboratories. However, efforts are being made to standardize methods, and at some future date one set of standards may apply. Until that time two standards are provided; one as guide to growers who use or subscribe to a service that employs the saturated-soil-extract method (Table 12–4) and the other as a guide to those who use a soil-water ratio method (Table 12–6) of soil testing.

TABLE 12-4   Suggested Nutrient Levels in Saturated Extracts for Container Medium

	Concentration		
	Acceptable[a]	Optimum	High
	ppm in Saturated Extract		
Nitrate-N (NO_3-N)	40–79	80–139	140–199
Phosphorus (P)	3–5	6–10	11–18
Potassium (K)	50–109	110–179	180–256
Calcium (Ca)	70–139	140–219	220–324
Magnesium (Mg)	30–59	60–99	100–149
	-----------------------mS/cm[b]-----------------------		
Soluble salts	.75–1.49	1.50–2.24	2.25–3.49

[a]Acceptable for most plants when optimal growth is not a primary concern.

[b]mS = millisiemen, replacing millimho (mmho) as the preferred unit for expressing conductivity (soluble salt) measurements. The value remains the same—only the name changes. To convert this value to ppm, multiply by 700.

Source: Warncke (1983).

Saturated-Soil-Extract Method

Nitrate-nitrogen levels will vary with the age and species of the crop. Seedlings and newly propagated plants function better at lower levels than do more mature plants. Values above 200 ppm are unnecessarily high, and above 300 ppm may cause nutritional problems. Nitrogen fertilizer should be applied when the level in the saturated extract approaches the lower level. The rates given in Table 12–5 will increase soil nitrate tests about 10 ppm in the soil saturation extract.

Phosphate fertilizers can be applied at liberal rates to a container mix without serious problems from excess soluble salts. Generally, superphosphate (0-20-0) is preferred for container mixes because it contains calcium and sulfur. Two pounds of 0-20-0 fertilizer per cubic yard will raise the saturated soil extract test approximately 5 ppm. For most mixes testing low in phosphorus, 2–3 lb of 0-20-0 per cubic yard will provide an adequate level for the growth of most plants without causing other nutritional problems.

Potassium is commonly deficient in sand, peats, and perlite. It must be added to mixes composed of these materials. Most potassium fertilizers have a high salt index (see Table 11–10); therefore, care must be used in applying them. Carriers such as potassium nitrate, potassium sulfate, or potassium phosphate are preferred for container mixes. The level of potassium in the soil mix, as indexed by the saturated-soil extract test, should be relatively low for young plants and seedlings compared to more mature plants. The levels listed in Table 12–4 are suggested levels until exact levels are established for a specific crop in a specific stage of production. Values in excess of 180 ppm are unnecessarily high and may induce nutritional problems, especially if Ca and/or Mg levels test low. The K level in the soil extract can be increased approximately 50 ppm by mixing 2 oz of 60% K_2O fertilizer into a cubic yard of mix.

Calcium is generally adequate in container mixes with a pH of 5.5 or above. Values above 325 ppm are very high and can result in nutritional problems if Mg and/or K test low. The balance of the cations Ca, K, Mg, and to some degree ammonium and sodium is more important than the actual level. Calcium should represent about 15% of the total salts.

Magnesium in the saturated-soil extract should be less than one-half that for calcium, but should exceed one-half that for potassium. A minimum test regardless

TABLE 12-5   Nitrogen Fertilizer Needed to
Increase Soil Saturation Extract Test
by Approximately 10 ppm

Percent N in Fertilizer	Ounces of Nitrogen Fertilizer Per Cubic Yard of Soil
10	4.0
16	2.4
20	2.0
33	1.2
45	0.8

of the Ca and K levels is about 25 ppm Mg. Finely ground dolomitic limestone is a good source of Mg for container-soil mixes; 2 lb/yd^3 of mix will normally supply ample magnesium. Magnesium sulfate can also be used.

Soil-Water Ratio Method

Nitrate nitrogen will vary considerably, since nitrate availability is a function of temperature and moisture. (See Table 12–6.) Also, nitrates can be readily leached. If the recommended range for nitrates for a specific crop is 20–60 ppm in the soil, nitrogen should be applied when the test drops below 20 ppm. On the other end, as the test approaches 100 ppm, growth may be adversely affected; thus, the medium should be leached.

Phosphorus levels are seldom too low or too high to be dangerous. However, levels below 20 ppm are approaching a deficient level and may limit nitrogen metabolism is some species. And levels in excess of 200 ppm may limit the availability of micronutrients.

Potassium tests over 300 ppm may indicate a soluble-salts problem when chloride carriers are being used. If soluble salts are low, a medium may test up to 1000 ppm K without difficulty, depending upon the crop and soil density. On very sandy or porous media (except those containing vermiculite in the mix), more frequent potassium application is desirable. Where chlorides are a problem, the sulfate form is suggested.

Calcium content is closely associated with the pH of the medium. If the pH is above 5.5, calcium will be adequate in most container mixes. However, if the ratio of Ca/Mg exceeds 5:1 or Ca/K exceeds 20:1 (percent base saturation), magnesium-

TABLE 12-6   Suggested Nutrient Standards for Soil Mixes Having Different Soil Densities and Extracted at Different Ratios

	0.8–1.3 (Mineral Soil)	0.5–0.8	0.2–0.5 (Organic Soil)
Soil density (g/ml):			
Soil extractant ratio:	1:8	1:12	1:24
	Parts per Million in Soil		
Nutrient			
Nitrate-nitrogen (NO$_3$-N)[a]	15–40	20–60	40–120
Phosphorus (P)[b]	20–60	30–90	60–180
Potassium (K)[c]	180–300	270–450	540–900
Calcium (Ca)[c]	>500	>750	>1500
Magnesium (Mg)[c]	>60	>90	>180
	mS/cm		
Soluble salts	<0.8	<1.00	<1.25

[a]Water-soluble extract.

[b]Extracted with 0.018 N acetic acid (Spurway active).

[c]Extracted with neutral, normal ammonium acetate.

or potassium-induced deficiency can result. Additional Mg and K will be needed to correct the imbalance.

Magnesium availability is closely associated with calcium but at a lower magnitude. The ratio of potassium to magnesium should not exceed 3:1 or a magnesium deficiency could be induced.

Micronutrients

Since micronutrients are found in trace amounts, soil tests are not too reliable or are too expensive for routine soil testing. Plant analysis is commonly used to detect deficiency or excess levels. Chlorosis is probably the most common physiological problem related to microelement nutrition and is commonly related to iron deficiency or manganese toxicity. Conditions favoring deficiency include high soil pH, very high phosphorus levels, or excess moisture.

Boron deficiency can be induced by excess applications of lime, nitrogen, or potassium. It has also been associated with acid media that are being leached of boron by overwatering. *Boron toxicity* has been reported in some nurseries producing container-grown plants. The early symptoms of boron toxicity are characterized by leaf-tip yellowing and marginal chlorosis, followed by tip burning and premature leaf drop. In advanced stages terminal growth is rosetted and twig dieback occurs. The toxicity is cause by overfertilizing with fertilizers high in boron.

Copper deficiency, commonly associated with highly organic media, can be prevented by supplementing the media with a micronutrient mixture containing copper (see Table 12–3).

Iron deficiency can be induced in plants by a number of factors other than the lack of iron in the medium. Low iron availability is associated with high pH of the medium, high levels of copper, manganese, or zinc; high phosphates or calcium carbonate, low medium temperature, or excess moisture.

Manganese deficiency is most commonly expressed on plants growing in a highly organic medium with a pH of 6.8 or higher. The condition is aggravated by low temperature and excess moisture.

Zinc deficiency is not too common, but can be caused by cool, wet weather that reduces the availability of zinc.

Soluble Salts

During the growing season the container medium should be tested monthly for soluble salts. The reading should be in the desirable range for the test method (Table 12–7). Readings below optimum indicate low levels of nutrition, which will result in reduced plant growth. A more complete medium test may be needed to determine the proper fertilizer to apply. This can often be determined by checking fertilizer records or by questioning those responsible for the fertilizer program.

TABLE 12-7   Readings and Interpretation of Soluble-Salt Data for Container-Grown Plants

Conductivity,[a] (millisiemens/cm)			
5:1 Organic Soils	2:1 Mineral Soils	Saturated Paste Extract, All Soils	Interpretation
<0.350	<0.5	<2.0	Low nutrient status for growing plants
0.35–.65	0.500–1.0	1.50–2.24	Desirable range for most growing plants; upper range may be high for some species
0.65–0.90	1.0–1.5	2.25–5.00	Higher than desirable for most species
>0.90	>1.5	>5.00	Excess soluble salts, wilting or death of plants

[a]To convert mS/cm to parts per million (approx.), multiply by 700.

Source: Modified slightly from Coop. Ext. Serv. Mich. State Univ. Ext. Bull. 1736 (1983).

MEDIA STERILIZATION

Another important factor in the successful production of container-grown plants is that the medium be free of organisms harmful to plant growth. Newly mined sand is relatively free of harmful organisms and can be used without sterilization. However, most soil and some sand and peat moss that have become contaminated will contain harmful organisms, such as bacteria, fungi, insects, and weed seeds. These organisms can cause serious problems if they are not eliminated from the medium prior to planting.

Various species of fungi, especially *Rhizoctonia* and *Pythium,* have caused the needless loss of thousands of plants in nurseries as a result of root rots. Grubs of insects chewing upon the roots have resulted in many plants being dwarfed, malformed, or destroyed. And weeds competing for available nutrients, moisture, and light reduce growth rates as well as decrease customer acceptance of the product. All of these problems and others can be minimized or eliminated by composting, sterilizing, pasteurizing, or fumigating. Composting was discussed previously under the heading Hardwood Bark.

Heat Treatment

Although plantsmen use the term "sterilization" in reference to heat treatment of soil to rid it of harmful organisms, a more correct term is "pasteurization," since the temperatures used (140–180°F) destroy only certain of the harmful organisms. Various means of heat treatment can be employed, but it is desirable to obtain a soil temperature of 140–150°F and to maintain the temperature for at least 10 min but no more than 30 min to destroy most plant pathogenic fungi and bacteria (Fig.

12–3). This temperature regime will allow certain beneficial organisms to survive, especially nitrifying bacteria, which aid in the nitrification of ammonia. The lower temperature also minimizes the problem of excess ammonia release encountered with temperatures above 160°F. Aerated steam has been used effectively to obtain the 140°F temperature. The necessary equipment can be obtained from agricultural engineering firms specializing in soil sterilization. The heat treatment of nursery soils is thoroughly discussed in the ''U.C. System for Producing Healthy Container-Grown Plants.''

Fumigation

Chemicals can also be used to rid soil of harmful organisms. In general, they are less destructive of the physical properties of the soil, but they are more costly. Also, many chemicals are very specific as to the organisms that they will control. Therefore, chemicals for treating soil must be carefully selected and applied at the proper concentration to a soil mass that is in the proper physical condition.

The optimum media temperature for best results is close to 70°F. When media

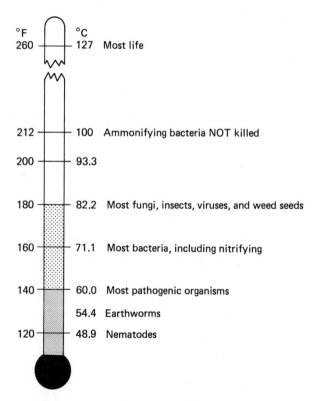

°F

260 — 127 — Most life

212 — 100 — Ammonifying bacteria NOT killed

200 — 93.3

180 — 82.2 — Most fungi, insects, viruses, and weed seeds

160 — 71.1 — Most bacteria, including nitrifying

140 — 60.0 — Most pathogenic organisms

54.4 — Earthworms

120 — 48.9 — Nematodes

°C

Figure 12–3 Temperatures maintained for 15 minutes will destroy most organisms listed.

are cold, wet, and poorly aerated, chemical treatments are ineffective. Following treatment, the media should be aerated for a period of from 2 days to 2 weeks to allow the chemical to dissipate prior to planting. Warm, sandy media need less time to aerate than do damp media. A number of fumigants, available to nurserymen, will effectively sterilize media, including methyl bromide, formaldehyde, vapam, and chloropicrin.

*Methylbromide** is the most commonly used all-purpose nursery soil fumigant. It will destroy most of the common fungi that cause plant disease problems, except verticillium wilt. It is effective against most weed seeds and nematodes. It is easy to use and has a short treatment and post-treatment aeration-time requirement. However, the material is very toxic to people and animals and must be used with caution. If it is handled with reasonable care, it can be a very effective tool for nurserymen in the preplanting control of harmful organisms.

Media and other material to be fumigated must be enclosed in a gasproof chamber, and the methylbromide gas injected into the chamber at a concentration at 2 lb/100 ft^3 for nematode and weed control at 4 lb/100 ft^3 for fungus control. A treatment period of from 24 to 48 hr is desirable followed by an aeration period of 48 hr.

A polyethylene tarp free of holes makes an excellent gasproof enclosure. However, the tarp must cover the material to be fumigated in such a way as to ensure free distribution of the gas within and at the same time prevent the gas from escaping, either through holes or cracks along the edges. A special dispenser is provided for injecting the gas into the chamber.

Formaldehyde is an excellent fungicide that has been used by plantsmen for many years, both as fumigant for inorganic soils and as a surface sterilant for propagation benches and storage facilities. It is very water-soluble and will penetrate a soil mass to the depth of wetting, where it volatilizes and becomes an effective media fumigant. Treated media should be covered for at least 24 hours with a gasproof cover. This must be followed by an aeration period of from 10 to 14 days to permit the gas an opportunity to fully dissipate. Any residual gas can be harmful to young plants. Formaldehyde is very irritating to the eyes and nasal passages and is toxic to plants; it must be used with caution.

Vapam (sodium *N*-methyl dithiocarbamate dihydrate) is also an effective media fumigant. It can be used to control most fungi, insects, nematodes, and weeds. It is water-soluble and can be applied in water either to the medium surface or by injection into the media. The chemical should be sealed into the media with an additional application of water. Vapam is most effective when the medium is at a temperature of 60–70°F. The media should be aerated either by cultivation or turning it in a pile 5–7 days following treatment. The media may be safely planted about 2 weeks following treatment provided that there was adequate aeration to rid the soil of chemical residue.

Chloropicrin, commonly known as tear gas, is another excellent media fumi-

---

*Methylbromide is a restricted-use pesticide.

gant. The medium must be treated in an airtight chamber, as the material is very volatile. It should be slightly damp but well aerated and at a temperature of 65–70°F for best results. The exposure period should last for at least 24 hr, preferably for 48 hr or more if the medium is not well aerated. Plantings may be made when there is no longer any trace of gas, approximately 7 days.

Chloropicrin is a very effective fumigant and herbicide. But it is also a potent tear gas and is corrosive of most metals; therefore, it must be used with caution. Small quantities are added to methyl-bromide as a warning agent. It should not be used in areas where people will be exposed to its irritating property. The treatment area should be free of valuable plants and metal objects. Any metal that is exposed to the gas should be washed with kerosene to prevent corrosion.

POST-TREATMENT

Following treatment, sterilized or pasteurized media should be placed into clean, sterile containers for use or stored in an area that has also been thoroughly sterilized. It is a poor plantsman who would go to considerable effort to rid media of harmful organisms and then expose them immediately to reinoculation by handling it with contaminated equipment or by placing it into contaminated containers or storage bins. Media sterilization is only a part of a total program of good plant culture. All people in the production cycle must be cognizant of maintaining sanitary conditions in plant propagation facilities, growing areas, storage facilities, and in the packaging and shipping areas.

SUMMARY

Producing and marketing of quality plants in containers requires careful planning and constant monitoring of each phase of production to assure attainment of production objectives. Blending of the media mixture and maintaining nutrients at the proper intensity and balance is one part of the total production effort. However, it has been the weakest link in the production cycle at many container-production nurseries. By practicing good sanitation and maintaining suggested nutritional standards, growers can grow quality plants and obtain a good economic return on their investment.

REFERENCES

BODDY, R. M. 1976. Container-grown rhododendrons. Proc. Int. Plant Propag. Soc. 26:87–93.

BOODLEY, J. W., and R. SHELDRAKE, JR. 1972. Cornell Peat-Lite mixes for commercial plant growing. N.Y. State Coll. Agric. Cornell Univ. Inf. Bull. 43.

BOSLEY, R. W. 1967. Ground bark—a container growing medium. Proc. Int. Plant Propag. Soc. 17:366–370.

BROWN, E. F., and F. A. POKORNY. 1975. Physical and chemical properties of media composed of milled pine bark and sand. J. Am. Soc. Hort. Sci. 100(2):119–121.

DAVIDSON, H., and W. McCALL. 1964. Metal ammonium phosphate fertilizers for container-grown plants. Quart. Bull. Mich. Agric. Exp. Sta. 46(3):416–419.

DEWERTH, A. F. 1961. Horticultural Perlite for Texas gardens. Tex. Agric. Prog. 7(6):3–6.

FLINT, H. L., and J. G. McGUIRE. 1961. Effects of different soil levels of nitrogen and potassium on growth of *Forsythia intermedia* and *Viburnum plicatum tomentosum* in containers. Proc. Am. Soc. Hort. Sci. 78:553–559.

————, and J. G. McGUIRE. 1962. Nitrogen range for optimum growth of some woody ornamental species grown in containers. Proc. Am. Soc. Hort. Sci. 80:622–624.

GARTNER, J. B., D. C. SAUPE, J. E. KLETT, and T. R. YOCOM. 1970. Hardwood bark as a medium for container growing. Am. Nurseryman 131(8):11.

————, T. D. HUGHES, and J. E. KLETT. 1972. Using hardwood bark in container grown woody ornamentals to slow-release fertilizers. Am. Nurseryman 135(12):10.

————, S. M. STILL, and J. E. KLETT. 1973. The use of hardwood bark as a growth medium. Proc. Int. Plant Propag. Soc. 23:222–231.

GILLIAN, C. H., and E. M. SMITH. 1980. Sources and symptoms of boron toxicity in container-grown woody ornamentals. J. Arboricult. 6(8):209–212.

GOUIN, F. R., and C. B. LINK. 1973. Growth responses of container-grown woody ornamentals to slow-release fertilizers. HortScience 8(3):208–209.

KELLEY, J. D. 1962. Response of container-grown woody ornamentals to fertilization with urea-formaldehyde and potassium frit. Proc. Am. Soc. Hort. Sci. 81:544–551.

KLETT, J. E., J. B. GARTNER, and T. D. HUGHES. 1972. Utilization of hardwood bark media for growing woody ornamental plants in containers. J. Am. Soc. Hort. Sci. 97(4):448–450.

LUCAS, R. E., and J. K. DAVIS. 1961. Relationships between pH values of organic soils and availabilities of 12 plant nutrients. Soil Sci. 92:177–182.

————, P. E. RIEKE, and R. S. FARNHAM. 1971. Peats for soil improvement and soil mixes. Farm Sci. Ser. Coop. Ext. Serv. Mich. State Univ. Ext. Bull. 516.

MALIEKE, R. B., and J. B. GARTNER. 1975. Hardwood bark as a soil amendment for suppression of plant parasitic nematodes on container-grown plants. HortScience 10(1):33–34.

MATKIN, O. A. 1971. Soil mixes today. Proc. Int. Plant Propag. Soc. 21:162–164.

————, and P. A. CHANDLER. 1957. The U.C. type soil mixes. In U.S. system for producing healthy container-grown plants, Sec. 5, Agric. Exp. Sta., Univ. Calif. Manual 23.

McVEY, G. R. 1977. How soil chemistry can work for you. Proc. Int. Plant Propag. Soc. 27:227–284.

MONTANO, J. M., J. T. FISHER, and D. J. COTTER. 1977. Sawdust for growing containerized forest tree seedlings. Tree Planter's Notes 28(2):6–9.

MORRIS, W. C., and D. C. MILBOCKER. 1972. Repressed growth and leaf chlorosis of Japanese holly grown in hardwood bark. HortScience 7(5):486–487.

RICHARDSON, T. 1976. Rhododendron production. Proc. Int. Plant Propag. Soc. 26:301–303.

RIEKE, P. E., and R. E. LUCAS. 1968. Greenhouse soil notes. Soil Science Dept., Mich. State Univ.

RIGBY, F. A. 1963. Ground bark as a growing medium for container nursery stock. Proc. Int. Plant Propag. Soc. 13:288–291.

SANDERSON, K. C., and W. C. MARTIN, JR. 1974. Performance of woody ornamentals in municipal compost medium under nine fertilizer regimes. HortScience 9(3):242–243.

SPOMER, L. A. 1973. Soils in plant containers: soil amendment, air and water relationships. Ill. Res. 15(3):16–17.

————— . 1975. Principles of nursery container soil amendment. Am. Nurseryman 142(3):12.

————— . 1977. How much total water retention and aeration porosity in my container mix? Ill. State Florists Assoc. Bull. 369:13–15.

STILL, S. M., M. A. DIRR, and J. B. GARTNER. 1976. Phytotoxic effects of several bark extracts on mung bean and cucumber growth. J. Am. Soc. HortSci. 101(1):34–37.

WARNCKE, D. D., and D. M. KRAUSKOPF. 1983. Greenhouse growth media: Testing and Nutrition guidelines, Ext. Bul. E-1736. Coop. Ext. Serv., Michigan State University, East Lansing, Mi.

————— , R. E. LUCAS, P. E. RIEKE, and W. H. CARLSON. 1973. Interpreting saturated paste soil tests for flowers, bedding plants and greenhouse vegetables. Mimeograph, Dept. of Crop and Soil Sciences, Mich. State Univ.

WHITE, J. W., and J. W. MASTALERZ. 1966. Soil moisture as related to "container capacity." Proc. Am. Soc. Hort. Sci. 89:758–765.

WRIGHT, R. D. 1983. Study indicates need for changes in nutrition programs for plants in containers. Am. Nurseryman 157(1):109–111.

YEAGER, T. H., and R. D. WRIGHT. 1983. Phosphorus in pine bark media—what is a suitable level for good plant growth? Am. Nurseryman 157(1):48.

————— , and R. D. WRIGHT. 1983. Phosphorus in pine bark media—is incorporating superphosphate best? Am. Nurseryman 157(1):49.

SUGGESTED READING

BAKER, F., ed. 1957. The U.C. system for producing healthy container-grown plants. Agric. Exp. Sta. Univ. Calif. Manual 23.

BUNT, A. C. 1976. Modern potting composts. The Pennsylvania State University Press, University Park, Pa.

GILLIAM, C. H., and E. M. SMITH. 1980. Fertilization of container-grown nursery stock, Bull. 658, Coop. Ext. Serv., Ohio State Univ.

LAWRENCE, W. J. C., and J. NEWELL. 1962. Seed and potting composts, 5th ed. George Allen & Unwin (Publisher) Ltd., London.

PATTERSON, J. M. 1975. Container growing. American Nurseryman Publishing Company, Chicago.

13 *Irrigation of Nursery Crops*

Nursery crops, like other agricultural crops, require water if they are to develop into healthy, salable plants. Water is an important nutrient required by all plants. It functions in plants as a solvent, a heat regulator, and as a biochemical reagent in photosynthesis. It is a major modifier of growth; its availability or nonavailability during certain phases of growth can seriously affect survival, growth rate, and the ultimate size of the plants. Properly irrigated stock will be larger and more vigorous. Therefore, an understanding of irrigation practices is essential to nurserymen, particularly those who produce plants in containers.

Nurserymen who produce plants by field culture require or use water for two primary reasons: either to assure a higher survival rate following transplanting or to increase growth, whereas nurserymen committed to container culture require water not only to increase survival rates following potting and to increase growth, but they have an absolute requirement for water, almost on a daily basis. Container-grown plants have limited soil-moisture reservoirs, defined by container size and the moisture-holding capacity of the medium, which must be resupplied at short, periodic intervals to assure continued survival. The method of growing is the basis for determining the amount of water, type of equipment, and labor that is needed to meet the irrigation requirements within nurseries.

In addition to providing moisture for survival and growth of the nursery crops, the irrigation system can also be used to apply water-soluble fertilizers, to protect some crops from damage due to late spring frost, to moisten the soil to aid digging and transplanting operations during dry periods, and to seal in volatile soil sterilants and herbicides.

SOURCES OF WATER

A reliable source of clean water is a fundamental requirement for irrigation. Rivers, streams, drainage ditches, lakes, ponds, reservoirs, and wells are the common sources of water. Nurserymen who plan to use water from rivers, streams, drainage ditches, lakes, and ponds that have a multiple or public ownership should be familiar with the state and local riparian (water rights) laws, as they may face possible injunctions prohibiting or limiting their use of public water. States located in arid or semiarid areas of the country have strict laws pertaining to water rights. In other parts of the country, riparian laws are not as well defined. A new irrigator upstream can seriously reduce the amount of water available downstream, as can another irrigator drawing from the same lake or reservoir. Complete ownership of the water rights or purchase of water from a dependable supply is usually preferable. Should it become necessary to sink wells for a source of water, it is suggested that information on underground water be obtained from the state geologist and that a reliable well driller, who is familiar with the area, be employed to do the drilling, develop the well, and conduct a pumping test. Nurserymen producing container-grown nursery stock should have, if possible, an alternative source of water to assure a reserve supply in the event of an emergency.

WATER QUALITY

In addition to sources of supply, water quality should also be investigated. Water high in soluble salts or contaminated with industrial wastes, particularly heavy metals or polluted with herbicides, must be avoided. Most nursery plants will not tolerate saline conditions, and some are injured by high levels of sodium, boron, or chlorides found in some water.

Water quality (levels of salinity) is characterized by electrical conductivity (EC). Since the unit of measurement is very small for most natural water samples, it is commonly expressed as millisiemens/cm (mS/cm). Water for irrigation purposes should have an EC value of less than 0.25 mS/cm (Table 13–1). Water that has an EC in excess of 0.75 mS/cm is high in soluble salts and should be used with caution. Water used on container-grown plants can have levels somewhat higher than average, but it is desirable to apply a sufficient quantity at each irrigation to leach the soil.

TABLE 13-1   Classification of Water for Irrigation

mS/cm[a]	Salinity Level	Irrigation Value
<0.25	Low	Excellent for irrigation on most soils; normal leaching suggested
0.25–0.75	Moderate	Satisfactory for irrigation; moderate leaching suggested
0.75–2.25	High	Avoid use on soil with poor drainage; plant salt-tolerant crops; leaching necessary
>2.26	Very high	Not recommended for irrigation purposes; a few salt-tolerant crops can be grown under special salinity culture

Source: Wilcox (1955).

[a]mS = millisiemen, replacing millimho (mmho) as the preferred unit for expressing conductivity (soluble salt) measurements. The value remains the same—only the name changes. To convert this value to ppm, multiply by 700.

High levels of sodium (Na) in irrigation water can also be detrimental to some plants. However, its relationship to the cations calcium (Ca) and magnesium (Mg) is important in determining its toxic effects. This is known as the sodium-absorption ratio (SAR) and can be calculated from the formula

$$SAR = \frac{Na}{\sqrt{\dfrac{Ca^{2+} + Mg^{2+}}{2}}}$$

The concentration of each element is expressed in milliequivalents per liter. An SAR value of 10 or less is considered safe for most nursery situations. But levels in excess of 10 could present problems on soils with a high cation exchange capacity (fine-textured soils).

Boron, a constituent of all natural waters, is found in toxic concentrations in irrigation water in limited areas of the United States, primarily in the Southwest. Since plants vary in their tolerance to boron in the soil solutions, no exact value can be stated. Nevertheless, relatively low concentrations, in the order of 0.03–0.05 ppm, are needed for normal growth, and relatively high levels (0.5 ppm or greater) should be avoided.

Water containing more than 2.5 mEq/liter of residual sodium carbonate (RSC) is not suitable for irrigation. Water that contains less than 1.25 mEq/liter RSC is probably safe, and those with levels in between are considered marginal.

Appraising water quality for use in irrigation of nursery stock need not be complex. With an understanding of some general chemistry, making a few chemical determinations and some calculations, it is possible to avoid the hazards associated with using poor-quality water. Some states have either private, state, or municipal laboratories where these tests are made for a fee. Details on the analysis of irrigation water are contained in USDA Agricultural Handbook 60.

In areas where high-soluble salts are a problem, it is desirable to construct large, shallow settling ponds to allow the alkali salts to settle out prior to using the water for irrigation or misting. In some situations distilling or even deionizing the water may be desirable prior to using it on sensitive, high-value crops (e.g., azaleas). Sediment and organic debris, harmful to pumps and sprinkler heads, should be screened out. If it is not, the irrigation equipment can be expected to malfunction; nozzle orifices can become plugged or changed in size, but even more serious, the pump may malfunction, which could result in damage to either equipment or to the plant material.

SOIL MOISTURE DETERMINATION

Crops should be irrigated when the soil moisture in the root zone drops to a predetermined level. Soil moisture levels can be determined by feel of the soil, by calculation, or by the use of various types of soil moisture meters. Experienced plantsmen estimate the appropriate time to irrigate nursery stock by knowing the stress symptoms of plants, by the feel of the soil or by the length of time since the last rain or irrigation. To estimate soil moisture by the feel of the soil, samples are collected from various depths in the root zone and the moisture level is estimated by feel (Table 13–2). To calculate soil moisture, a soil sample collected from a depth of 8–12 in. is placed in a tight container, weighed, dried in an oven (12–24 hours at 100°C), and reweighed. Total moisture (TM) in percent is calculated by the formula

$$TM\% = \frac{(\text{original wt of soil}) - (\text{dry wt of soil}) \times 100}{\text{dry wt of soil}}$$

Available moisture is then estimated by subtracting the wilting coefficient of the soil (data available from soils reference manual or county agriculture agent) from the percent TM.

For sandy soils low in organic matter ($<11\%$), a quick technique is to place the soil sample, about 20–25 g, in a screen-bottom metal container set in a metal cap and obtain the weight. Gradually, pour a small quantity (25 cc) of methyl alcohol over the soil and ignite to drive off the moisture. The sample is reweighed and the available moisture calculated by the previous formula.

Various instruments have been developed to provide a measure of soil moisture. The soil moisture meter is well adapted for use in most field-production nurseries. It consists of special plaster of paris blocks that are buried in the soil at the desired depth and location, and then electrical resistance is measured with a moisture meter. The dial of the meter reads in relative soil moisture, 100 representing a fully saturated soil and 50 or less indicating a need for irrigation. A large variety of

TABLE 13-2   Soil Feel Chart

Percentage of Remaining Available Water	Feel or Appearance of Soil		
	Course Textured	Medium Textured	Fine or Very Fine Textured
0% (dry)	Dry, loose, flows through fingers	Powder-dry; sometimes slightly crusted but easily breaks down into powdery condition	Hard, baked, cracked; sometimes has loose crumbs on surface
50% or less (low)	Still appears to be dry; will not form a ball with pressure	Somewhat crumbly, but will hold together with pressure	Somewhat pliable, will ball under pressure
50–100% (good to excellent)	Forms weak ball, breaks easily, will not stick	Forms a ball and is very pliable; sticks readily if relatively high in clay	Easily ribbons out between fingers; has a slick feeling
Above field capacity (over-irrigated)	Free water will be released with kneading	Can squeeze out free water	Puddles and free water forms on surface

Source: Irrigating small acreages. Coop. Ext. Serv. Mich. State Univ. Ext. Bull. 320.

soil moisture tensiometers are available. However, most of these instruments* are too sophisticated for the needs of most nurserymen.

Leaf temperature has been used to a limited extent to determine when to irrigate ornamental plants in the landscape. Since leaf temperature is generally higher for plants exhibiting moisture stress, it is possible to relate leaf temperature to the need to irrigate. Leaf temperatures can be quickly estimated with the aid of a portable infrared radiometer. It could possibly be used to determine irrigation needs in a nursery.

PUMPS AND POWER

After it has been determined that an adequate source of good quality water is available, the next decision is what type of system will be used to distribute the water; this includes pump(s), power source, water distribution system, and sprinkler units. At this point it is advisable to seek the services of an irrigation specialist who can provide the detailed information. But it is desirable for nurserymen to have a basic understanding of the various systems.

Although there are many types of pumps to select from, the horizontal centrifugal and deep-well turbine pumps are fairly standard for irrigation purposes. The horizontal centrifugal pump is easy to operate, is highly efficient, but is limited to a suction lift of about 22 ft or less and must be primed. Turbine pumps, although more costly than centrifugal pumps and generally more difficult to inspect and repair, are not limited to the 22 ft depth and do not require priming.

The actual selection will depend upon (1) the volume of water to be pumped during the peak use period and (2) the total head in feet† (dynamic pumping head), which is the sum of:

1. The total rise in feet from the pumping level to the elevation of the highest point in the irrigation system
2. The friction head in feet for the main line plus the longest lateral (information available from manufacturer)
3. The average sprinkler operating pressure, expressed as friction head in feet (information available from manufacturer)
4. Various miscellaneous friction losses (valves, fittings, etc.) estimated to be 10% of the total head in feet

Power to operate the pump is generally supplied by gasoline, propane, or diesel engines, or by electric motors. If an electric motor is to be employed as a power

*See McDonald and Running (1979).

†The total head in feet may be converted to pounds per square inch (psi) by dividing by 2.31, which is the height in feet of a column of water 1 square inch in area that weights 1 pound.

source, the power company should be contacted prior to purchase to determine availability and cost of electric power and to coordinate installation activities.

Energy is expressed in horsepower; 1 horsepower is equivalent to 33,000 foot-pounds per minute, or 0.746 kilowatt. The horsepower rating of an engine or motor is the amount of power that the engine or motor will develop when operated at full load for short periods of time. Brake horsepower is the effective horsepower that the machine is capable of producing over extended periods at the power shaft. The brake horsepower (BHP) requirement can be calculated by the formula (1 gal water = 8.35 lb):

$$BHP = \frac{GPM \times 8.35 \times \text{total head (in feet)}}{33,000 \times \text{pump efficiency}}$$

For example, the brake horsepower needed for a pump required to deliver 300 GPM against a total head of 200 ft with a pump efficiency of 75% would be 20:

$$BHP = \frac{300 \times 8.35 \times 200}{33,000 \times 0.75} = 20$$

For most portable irrigation systems, a gasoline engine may be the best choice. An electric motor or diesel engine is more desirable for permanent systems. When using gasoline or diesel engines, it is desirable to increase the BHP requirement by 25–30%, since the engine is not as efficient over extended periods of use as it is for brief periods of operation under ideal conditions. Also, if the engine were designed to operate on a moving vehicle, the cooling system might have to be modified (e.g., larger radiator and possibly a shroud around the fan) or irrigation water can be run through the radiator. The pump and power sources used in portable systems can be mounted as a unit on a skid, a wheeled trailer, or a truck-bed. An estimate of fuel consumption may be made if one assumes that a well-tuned gasoline engine used for pumping consumes 0.1 gal (U.S.)/hp/hr and for a diesel engine 0.07–0.08 gal (U.S.)/hp/hr.

Tractor power can be used to provide the necessary horsepower to drive power-take-off-driven pumps. But when tractors are used for this purpose, nurserymen should check with the farm equipment dealer as to the maximum continuous dependable power that the tractor engine should deliver at the PTO shaft to drive the pump. In addition, when such units are employed, care must be taken to properly connect and align the PTO shaft. Improper connection or alignment results in excessive wearing of parts and could result in breakage.

Stationary units should be located close to the water source and mounted on a level, solid foundation. Since engines used to power irrigation pumps are often left running unattended for long periods, it is desirable to provide certain safety devices to shut off the engine in the event of a mechanical failure and to prevent bodily injury. Three common failures are: (1) the pump overheats, (2) it loses oil pressure, and (3) it loses prime. If possible, the power unit should be enclosed in a locked building or a fenced area. In addition, container-production nurseries should have both an auxiliary source of power and a pump to substitute in the event the primary source fails.

A few points to consider that may aid in the proper functioning of the pump are: (1) the pipe or hose on the suction side of the pump should be one size larger than the discharge side in order to reduce friction and improve efficiency of the pump; (2) the intake should be placed low enough into the water to assure that an air swirl does not develop over the intake screen, allowing air to be drawn into the system causing a loss of suction; (3) it should also be placed a few inches above the bottom to reduce the intake of sediment; and (4) where a surface source of water is used, a strainer should be used to prevent various forms of debris from being drawn into the pump and causing trouble. In some water sources, a debris barrier may need to be constructed in addition to the strainer to prevent plugging of the intake.

Centrifugal pumps must be primed. There are a number of devices that can be connected to the pump to accomplish this, but a simple method is to keep a barrel or tank of water close by, which is used to fill the suction pipe and pump chamber.

DISTRIBUTION SYSTEMS

Distribution systems for irrigation may be classified by the method of conveying water or by the degree of permanence of the system. Surface irrigation methods are adapted to relatively flat areas with medium- to heavy-textured soils. Subsurface irrigation is best adapted to peat, muck, and sandy soils, whereas overhead irrigation is adaptable to a wide variety of areas. It is especially well adapted for use in most nurseries. Water can be applied fairly uniformly over uneven topography, and the system is highly adaptable to the many variable situations found in nurseries.

In a permanent installation, the pump, the power source, the main lines and laterals, and in some cases the sprinkler heads, are in fixed positions. The pump and power source are enclosed in a building. The pipes used in the permanent system may be reinforced concrete, asbestos cement, or poly(vinyl chloride) (PVC). All are satisfactory and will withstand the operating pressure of the system if the proper pressure-rated pipe has been selected. The lines should be of a diameter large enough to permit delivery of water without excessive friction loss. Since most of the pipes in a stationary system are below ground, they must be set deep enough to permit cultivation, and in cold climates deep enough to prevent freezing or be installed on a slight gradient to permit draining prior to the onset of freezing temperatures. The permanent system, although relatively more expensive, requires less labor to operate. They are used primarily in high-value, intensive-production areas (e.g., propagation, seed beds, liner, and container production).

In a semiportable system, the pump, power source, and main distribution lines are permanent, but the lateral lines and application equipment are portable. In a fully portable system, everything can be moved from place to place. The pipe used in portable systems is mostly manufactured from either lightweight aluminum or PVC and is equipped with various types of quick-coupling devices. For efficiency it is suggested that all irrigation pipe and couplers in a system be of the same brand.

The portable system, although the least expensive to install, requires considerable labor to operate. It is used most commonly in field-production areas.

Sprinkler heads are available in a wide selection of types. Nurserymen should select the type best adapted to their needs and to the soil's ability to absorb water. Water should be applied at a rate equal to but no faster than the soil's absorptive capacity or water is lost to evaporation and soil erosion occurs, especially on hilly terrain. Rotating sprinklers used in nurseries are commonly spaced 50–60 ft apart, operate at a pressure of 50–60 psi, and deliver 5–20 GPM. The spacing between heads and lateral lines, on an average, should not exceed 65–70% of the diameter of the spray pattern of the sprinkler head.

Some nurserymen use traveling, gun-type sprinklers (Fig. 13–1) that discharge about 500 GPM at 80–90 psi pressure. They cover large areas and save labor but require more power to operate and may deliver water too fast for the soil's absorptive capacity.

Figure 13–1 Traveling gun-type irrigation sprinkler in a field-production nursery.

WATERING FIELD-GROWN CROPS

Since field-grown nursery crops are watered to increase survival rate following transplanting or to increase growth, and since they may be produced on either close or wide spacing, depending upon the type of plant material and the market objective, it is desirable to discuss irrigation of these crops accordingly.

To Increase Survival Rates

Following transplanting, the plants must be watered immediately. This can be accomplished with some type of irrigation system or with the aid of a water wagon. In intensive areas, a permanent overhead system may be most appropriate, but as the spacing is increased, a semiportable system may be the most economical approach. In areas where the density of plants per unit area is low, the most economical approach may be the use of a water wagon. However, in situations where the crop is of high value (e.g., large-caliper shade trees), it may be more desirable to use trickle irrigation.

To Increase Growth

Most field-production nurseries are located in areas where the natural rainfall throughout the growing season is sufficient, at least in most years, to supply the water necessary for growth. Therefore, they seldom install irrigation systems to increase growth. However, production nurseries located in drier climates and nurseries that produce high-value crops find it financially advantageous to invest in some form of supplemental irrigation to increase growth rates. In some situations, the system may be used only once every 5–6 years, whereas in other situations it may be used yearly. In nurseries where the stock is grown fairly intensively, a semiportable system can be most effective and efficient. But in nurseries where the plants are grown on fairly wide spacing, the use of trickle irrigation may be more efficient.

Trickle irrigation is gaining in acceptance by nurserymen for the production of large shade trees (Fig. 13–2). It is based on the concept that best plant performance is obtained by maintaining a favorable soil moisture condition in the root zone. With trickle irrigation it is possible to produce a salable tree more rapidly and with a more compact root system. Water is applied under low pressure (less than 15 psi) and at a slow rate (1–2 GPH) for a time period sufficient to maintain the soil in which the roots are developing at or close to field capacity. Since only a portion of the soil area (10–20%) is irrigated, less water is used (Fig. 13–3). A time clock and solenoid valve can be installed into the line to activate the system for a predetermined time period each day when in use.

Water is delivered to each tree by means of either a microtube or a pressure-compensating emitter. When microtubes are used, it is necessary to control the water delivery rate. This is best accomplished by inserting a flow regulating valve in each lateral and adjusting the number and size or length of the microtubes so that the system is balanced. For example, using a 1.0-GPM flow valve will require using either 30 microtubes at 2.0 GPH, or 60 microtubes at 1.0 GPH, or 120 microtubes at 0.5 GPH. The use of pressure-compensating emitters, although more expensive, negates the needs for balancing of the system. Emitters are available in various flow rates, permitting flexibility in designing a system to meet the production plan of the nursery.

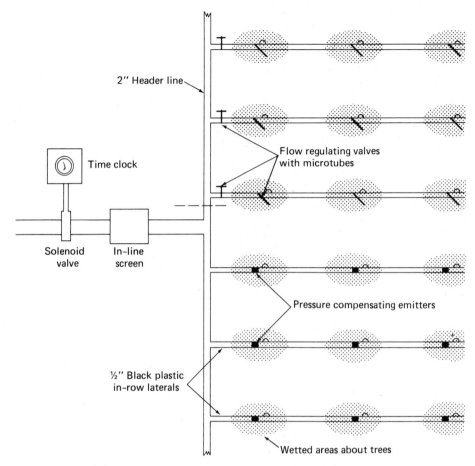

Figure 13–2   Trickle irrigation in a nursery. Upper half of the diagram illustrates the use of flow regulating valves and microtubes; lower half of the diagram illustrates use of pressure-compensating emitters.

Estimating Water Requirements

Irrigating field-grown nursery crops is based primarily upon experience, but it does vary with the size of the area to be irrigated, the size of the plant material, and the level of moisture in the soil. Since acreages vary, it is desirable to discuss water requirements on an acre basis and adjust total requirements accordingly. To apply 1 acre-in. of water requires 27,154 gal of water. It is a common practice in many nurseries to apply ½ in., 1 in., or 2 in. of water at a time. This would require between 13,600 and 54,300 gal of water, whereas in other nurseries water for growth is applied when the soil moisture drops to some predetermined level. For example, a soil with a 30% moisture-holding capacity is to be irrigated when the soil moisture in the upper 9 in. has dropped to 50% of field capacity. Since only 30% of the 9-in.

Figure 13–3 Trickle irrigation.

depth is moisture, it may be estimated that this equals 2.7 in. of water. Fifty percent of this value equals 1.35 in. or a requirement of 37,000 gal of water to restore the soil to field capacity. If the irrigation system is 75% effective (allowing for evaporation and drift), it would require approximately 50,000 gal of water or 1.85 acre-in.

The water should be applied at a rate not to exceed the infiltration and percolation rates of the soil, and under some conditions the rate of application may be further limited by work schedules. At a percolation rate of ½ acre-in./hr, it would take 3 hr and 40 min to apply the needed water, in the previous example. If applied at a faster rate, the net result would be either a puddling of the soil or erosion of the soil, plus the extra expense of pumping more water than necessary.

A source of supply and a pump with a capacity of 13,600 gal/hr (230 gal/min) per acre would be needed. Nurserymen can, by making similar calculations, estimate their water needs on a per acre basis and then with a knowledge of water availability, work schedules, and costs involved, estimate the size of the irrigation system that will be required for a specific situation.

WATERING CONTAINER-GROWN PLANTS

Container-grown plants are watered with the aid of an irrigation system modified to meet the needs of the situation. In parts of the country where water is costly or availability is limited, the system should be both effective and efficient. In areas where water is inexpensive, readily available, and where runoff is not a problem, the system need only be effective. To be effective, water must be applied to the containers when it is needed and in an amount necessary to maintain quality growth. To be efficient, the water must be applied to the interior of the containers.

Enough water must be applied to each container to replace that which is lost by evapotranspiration, to provide for growth, and to assure control of salinity within the medium. The daily loss due to evapotranspiration is a function of environment (temperature, humidity, wind, etc.) and the size and species of the plants. Experienced plantsmen estimate this loss on a daily basis by the appearance of their plants. Also, a correlation can be developed with the loss of water, by evaporation, from a pan of water located in close proximity to the plants.

Salinity control in container-grown plants requires that the entire soil mass become wetted and that some water leach through the container and drain away from the root zone. In some studies, as little as 0.14 quart of water per day was needed to irrigate plants growing in 1-gal containers, whereas 2 gal water/day were needed to water larger plants growing in 15-gal containers. The actual water regimen for a nursery growing container-grown plants will have to be developed by experience. There are a number of systems available to supply water to container-grown plants; each has its advantages and limitations. A system or systems that will accomplish the job most effectively with minimum degradation of the environment should be employed.

Overhead sprinkler irrigation is the most common system used to water small container-grown plants. It applies the water over the tops of the plants at a fairly rapid rate. It is relatively inexpensive to install and operate. But it can be relatively inefficient in the use of water, depending upon placement and size of containers; as much as 80% of the water can be lost between the containers. It is most efficient when watering 1- to 5-gal containers, spaced close together. It is least efficient when watering containers on wide spacing. However, where water is inexpensive and where no damage results to the environment, it may be the most economical system to use.

The actual design of a permanent system for a large container nursery will vary with the size of the area and the capacity of the pump. But the input and output should be in balance, and the design must provide for overlap of distribution patterns to assure fairly even distribution of water. A modular design adapted to meet the needs of various situations is effective for many container-production areas. The output of water is balanced with the input and the area modified accordingly. For example, using a pump that delivers 1600 gallons per minute (GPM) would permit the use of 100 sprinkler heads with a discharge of 16 GPM or the use of 200 heads with discharge of 8 GPM. Since it is desirable to have as even a water distribution pattern as possible, it is more advantageous to use the larger number of heads at low GPM but at the higher suggested operating pressure.

If a container area is designed as shown in Fig. 13–4, it is possible to develop a modular design for the irrigation system. One approach would be to arrange the water distribution by beds, using full-circle (360°) sprinkler heads in the center,

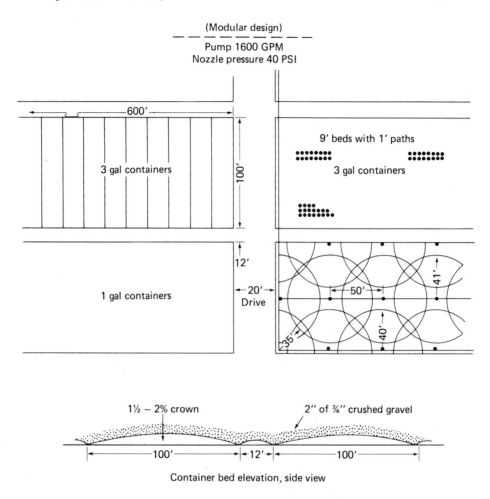

Figure 13–4 Container production area overhead irrigation system.

half-circle (180°) heads on the sides, and quarter-circle (90°) heads on the corners. If the beds are designed to be 100 ft wide and the sprinkler heads were distributed on a GPM equivalent basis over eight beds, it would require 11 full-circle heads at 8.35 GPM with a radius of 41 ft, 24 half-circle heads at 4.40 GPM with a radius of 40 ft, and 4 quarter-circles at 2.86 GPM with a radius of 35 ft per bed, and the beds would be 600 ft long. The eight beds, totaling 480,000 ft^2, a little over 11 acres, would require approximately 3 hr to irrigate with 1 in. of water. This would amount to approximately 0.7 in. of water falling on the container-bed area if 30% was lost to evaporation and drift. Total water efficiency would depend upon spacing of the containers. When spaced pot to pot in the equilateral triangle design, the water efficiency would be close to 63%.

Small to medium-sized areas can be watered effectively by using self-propelled rotating sprinklers. Each container, within the radius of discharge, receives an equal volume of water as the sprinklers propel themselves forward. The advantages of this system are: (1) uniform water distribution, (2) highly portable, and (3) relatively inexpensive. However, it does require more labor to operate.

Subsurface irrigation, also known as capillary irrigation, is used to water plants in greenhouses and by nurserymen in Europe, but it has not been widely used by nurserymen in the United States. It requires a level area for construction of a capillary reservoir and soils with good capillary conductivity. It works best for small containers placed close together. The water level in the bed can be controlled effectively with a float valve and a microswitch (Fig. 13–5).

Surface irrigation applies water to the surface of the medium within the container and is a most efficient means for watering large containers. It requires an extensive system of pipes and tubes, which gives rise to its more commonly used name, "spaghetti" system. This system must be designed to meet the water requirements of the plants and the cultural operations of the nursery. In general, the system utilizes 1-in. plastic pipe as a secondary supply line to which are attached a number of 3- to 5-ft distribution tubes to which are attached a number of small diameter tubes to carry the water to each container (Fig. 13–6). Depending upon the texture of the soil and the size of the container, it may be necessary to spread the water in some way so that the entire surface is wetted rather than just a small area beneath the emitter.

A few problem areas that have been encountered with the use of plastic tubing are: (1) plugging with dirt and mineral deposits; (2) displacement of the tubes by workers or animals; (3) rodents biting the tubes, causing them to leak; (4) algae developing in clear tubing; and (5) water freezing in the tubes, causing splitting. The rodent problem can be minimized by the use of rodenticides, and the algae problem can be minimized by using black tubing. To avoid having water freeze in the tubes, the system is drained or blown out prior to freezing temperatures. Blowing out the system with an air compressor is the most effective way to assure that it is free of water.

Poly(vinyl chloride) (PVC) pipes can be used to overcome many of the problems associated with the more flexible tubing. By using nozzles of the same material and with the aid of solvents, it is possible to put together a system that is extremely functional. The main lines and laterals can be buried below ground, eliminating the problem of exposed laterals; and not being exposed to the sun also increases the useful life of the system. Many types of nozzles, emitters, and spitters are available to apply water directly to the containers at controlled flow rates which increase the effective and economic use of water and soluble fertilizers. Sand traps or filters should be installed to prevent plugging of the nozzles. Also, with the addition of electronic control units it is possible to regulate irrigation periods for time intervals of a few seconds to many minutes. Electronic controls provide a high degree of flexibility to the system. It can be expanded very easily by the simple addition of a few extra subunit controls and low-voltage solenoid valves.

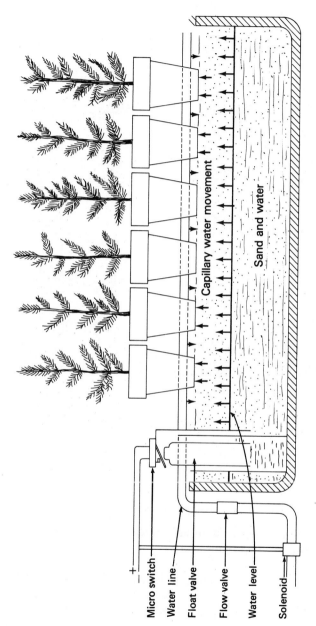

Micro switch

Water line

Float valve

Flow valve

Water level

Solenoid

Capillary water movement

Sand and water

Figure 13–5 Capillary irrigation bed.

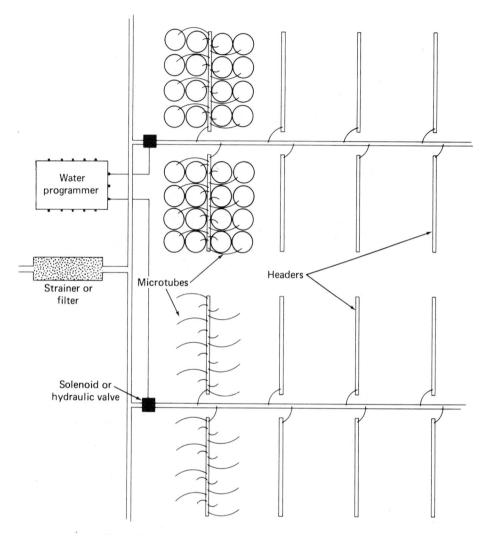

Figure 13–6 Container irrigation automated microtube system.

Estimating Water Requirements for Container-Grown Plants

The amount of water required to water container-grown plants varies with a number of factors, including the type and size of the plant material, the container capacity for holding water, climatic conditions (temperature, humidity, wind), and the type of irrigation system. Some species of plants transpire moisture at a faster rate than do others. Also, large plants, contained in a pot of similar size and conformation, use water at a more rapid rate than do smaller plants of the same species.

The *capacity of the containers* to hold moisture varies with each type of medium and with the depth and conformation of the container. Materials such as peat moss and composted bark have a much higher moisture-holding capacity than does material such as sand or milled bark. Therefore, plants growing in a medium with a low container capacity for moisture must be watered more frequently than those growing in a medium with a high container capacity. However, this varies with the volume of the medium in the container and with the height/diameter ratio of the container. Plants growing in wide, shallow or tall, narrow containers require watering more frequently than do plants growing in containers that have a height/diameter ratio that is close to 1.0. Wide, shallow containers lose substantial amounts of water by evaporation; whereas tall, narrow containers do not hold as much available water, owing to the downward force of the longer water column.

Climatic conditions strongly influence the need for water. Transpiration rates are rapid during periods of warm temperature and low relative humidity, as are evaporation rates from soil surfaces, requiring more frequent watering of container-grown plants. Transpiration loss is greatest during periods of bright sunshine, when leaf temperatures can be 20–30°F higher than air temperature. During such periods a high vapor-pressure deficit develops between the plant and the ambient air (see Chapter 17), resulting in a rapid loss of moisture from the plants.

The water requirement of container-grown plants is influenced by each of these factors and must be considered when planning the irrigation program. When small containers are placed close together in beds, the most effective way to water the plants is by overhead irrigation, even though some of the water will fall between the containers and upon paths and roadways. The actual amount will vary with the size of the container and the watering practice of the nursery. However, 1-gal containers, which have an actual volume of close to 100 fluid ounces (3 liters) would have a water requirement of 7.6 fluid ounces when the upper half of the medium reached 50% water-holding capacity (assuming that the medium has a moisture-holding capacity of 30%). This would require 0.7 acre-in. of water or approximately 20,000 gal/acre per irrigation. It is fairly common practice to apply ½–1 in. of water at each irrigation and to vary the frequency of application as influenced by the need for water. During periods of cool, cloudy weather the plants may need to be irrigated only once in 3–6 days, whereas during hot, dry periods they may require water every day and for some species even twice a day. Overhead irrigation is best accomplished in the late afternoon or early evening, to minimize loss of moisture due to evaporation. However, for plants that are subject to diseases (e.g., botrytis and mildew) it is best to apply the water early in the morning or to use surface irrigation.

When using overhead or surface irrigation, the plants should be grouped according to the size of the container and a large enough volume of water should be applied so that some flows out the drainage holes. The actual water requirement will vary with the factors previously discussed, but about 2 gal of water is needed per irrigation for containers described as the 15-gal size.

Excess Water

In some parts of the country disposing of the excess water following the irrigation of container-grown plants can be a problem. Prior to 1975, excess water that did not percolate into the soil was channeled into drainage ditches and discharged either into county drainage systems or municipal storm sewers. Since the mid-1970s, many municipalities have enacted laws prohibiting the discharge of water high in soluble salts into storm sewers. Therefore, this excess water must be disposed of by other means.

One step in solving the problem is to use irrigation water more efficiently, reducing the volume of wastewater that is generated by container production. The wastewater can be disposed of in some manner or it can be impounded or reused for irrigation. If the site conditions and local laws permit, the wastewater can be disposed of through a leach-field system. The runoff from the beds can be channeled into a series of settling tanks (e.g., 30-in. cement culverts placed on end), where the particulate matter is allowed to settle out before the water flows into the leach field. The county drain commissioner or appropriate water management authority should be consulted prior to constructing the system. A permit may be required, and the authority may be in a position to offer constructive suggestions relative to the construction and operation of the system. If the wastewater cannot be disposed of via a leach field or if it is desired to reuse the water, it will be necessary to construct a collecting pond. Information pertaining to the construction of collecting ponds can be obtained from the U.S. Soil Conservation Service.

Waste irrigation water impounded in a collecting pond is generally high in soluble salts (Table 13–1) and could be polluted with herbicides or disease organisms. Therefore, it should not be reused for watering of nursery stock without proper testing. If the water is free of pollutants and the soluble salt level is low, it can be used to irrigate container-grown plants. Where the level of soluble salts is too high for use on nursery stock, it might be possible to use the water to irrigate a salt-tolerant agricultural crop. If this is not a feasible option, the wastewater will either have to be desalted to remove part or all of the soluble salts prior to reuse or be diluted with water low in soluble salts. This can be accomplished with the aid of a proportioner. The resulting mixture has a salt concentration acceptable for irrigating container-grown plants.

By developing a fully integrated system of production that (1) makes use of slow-release fertilizers to maintain optimum nutrient levels, especially for nitrogen and potassium; (2) minimizes the use of soluble fertilizers; and (3) maximizes efficient use of water, it is possible to solve the excess water problem in a manner that it becomes an asset rather than a liability to the nursery.

Fertilizing by Means of an Irrigation System

Sprinkler irrigation can be used to apply fertilizers. Most water-soluble fertilizers can be applied through the irrigation system, but because of economic considerations and various chemical and biological reactions that take place within the soil, it is generally not practical to apply all these materials through the irrigation system. Application should be restricted to those that can be economically applied through the irrigation system and which do not form complex chemical compounds in the soil that render them unavailable for plant growth.

Fertilizing through the irrigation system saves labor and permits greater control over levels of nutrition. Many growers apply small quantities of fertilizer (especially nitrogen) at each watering. When a constant fertilizer program is employed, it is necessary to soil-test on a regular basis, keep accurate, meaningful records, and adjust the fertilizer program to the condition of the crop and the environment. Various agencies, including the Cooperative Extension Service, fertilizer companies, and private horticultural consulting firms, are available to develop fertilizer programs for the crops to be grown in a given environment. Some agencies also publish bulletins that are helpful in developing and understanding fertilizer programs for crop production.

Nitrogen. Most forms of nitrogen, except those that contain free ammonia, can be applied successfully through the irrigation system. Sources containing free ammonia can damage the leaves of plants, and much of the ammonia would be lost by volatilization. Three common nitrogen salts—ammonium nitrate, ammonium sulfate, and potassium nitrate—can be used when applied at recommended rates.

Potassium. The common potassium salts—potassium chloride, potassium sulfate, potassium nitrate, and potassium carbonate—are all soluble in water and can be applied through the irrigation system if necessary, particularly with container-grown plants.

Phosphorus. Most of the common fertilizer salts of phosphorus are relatively insoluble and if introduced into the irrigation system may clog the smaller sprinkler heads. The soluble form may be economically used for container production, but it is not suggested for field culture because of its high cost.

Other nutrient elements. Most of the other nutrient elements can be applied through the irrigation system if necessary. However, most agricultural soils have a sufficient supply for field-grown nursery stock, and for container-grown plants they should be added to the medium at the time of soil preparation.

Fertilizer amendments can be easily introduced into the irrigation system by a number of means. One simple method is to pour the dissolved fertilizer into the water source and to allow the pump to draw the solution into the system. However, this is not a very accurate method. Most accurate and dependable methods require that the nutrient solutions be injected or proportioned into the distribution system.

For centrifugal pumping systems, the suction pipe can be tapped close to the pump and fitted with the necessary pipe or hoses to connect the nutrient supply to the irrigation system. The pump will draw the solution into the system when the valve is opened. With turbine pumps the nutrient solution must be injected into the system under a pressure greater than that of the irrigation system.

Soluble fertilizers can be injected into the irrigation system by means of various types of proportioners or injectors. These mechanical devices are designed and constructed to combine specific amounts of concentrated stock solution and water in various predetermined ratios. When 1 unit of stock solution is combined with 99 units of water, forming a total of 100 units, the proportioner is listed as having a dilution ratio of 1:100, whereas when the combination is 1 unit to 11 units, making a total of 12, the proportion is listed as 1:12.

Proportioners, currently available, utilize either Bernoulli's principle or positive displacement. In the first type, a venturi is constructed in the water main, and the line supplying the liquid concentrate is connected at the low pressure point in the venturi. This system is subject to variation in dilution ratios as a result of differences in flow rate or in line pressure. However, these limitations can be modified with the aid of pressure regulators and adjustable valves.

Positive displacement units inject a measured quantity of stock solution into a measured volume of water with the aid of pistons of varied stroke length and cylinders of known diameters and lengths. Such units are designed to give relatively consistent dilution ratios over rather wide variations in water pressure. When selecting a proportioner (injector) for a container-production nursery, consideration should be given to the capacity of the system, the dilution ratios available, desired mobility, and maintenance of the unit.

The major advantages to be gained by nurserymen utilizing proportioners are: (1) fertilizer can be applied uniformly at a known concentration, (2) the fertilizer may be applied at the optimum concentration for the species and for the prevailing climatic condition, (3) the fertilizer is applied at the same time that the plants are watered thus saving labor, and (4) the loss of plants due to excess soluble salts is minimized.

Fertilizer concentration may be stated by any one of a number of methods, but one of the best for constant feeding is to state the concentration in parts per million (ppm). The most common concentrations used for fertilizing container-grown plants are 50, 100, or 200 ppm. To obtain a specific concentration with the aid of a proportioner, it is necessary to formulate a concentrated stock solution of known concentration. To accomplish this, it is necessary to know the dilution ratio of the proportioner and the percentage availability of the nutrient element to be applied. If, for example, it is desired to apply nitrogen at a concentration of 100 ppm with the aid of a 1:100 proportioner and the fertilizer analysis is 33-0-0, the stock solution should contain 4.05 oz/gal.

$$\text{wt/gal of water} = \frac{\text{ppm} \times \text{weight of water} \times \text{proportioner ratio}}{\% \text{ nutrient in fertilizer}}$$

$$\text{oz/gal of water} = \frac{\dfrac{100}{1{,}000{,}000} \times 8.34 \text{ lb/gal} \times 16 \text{ oz/lb} \times 100}{0.33}$$

$$= \frac{1 \times 10^{-4} \times 1.33 \times 10^2 \text{ oz/gal} \times 1 \times 10^2}{0.33} = \frac{1.33}{0.33} = 4.05$$

This information for various types of proportioners and fertilizers is tabulated in tables available from many suppliers of water-soluble fertilizers, or it can be readily estimated from the fertilizer proportioner nomograph (Appendix G).

Hydraulic displacement of fertilizer solutions from a tank is an efficient, inexpensive, nonelectrical injection system adaptable to trickle irrigation systems. The tank(s) must be air- and watertight. The flow through the tank can be controlled by placing a pressure regulator in the line.

The prevailing climatic condition will influence the metabolism of plants and their need for moisture and fertilizer. During periods of high temperature and high light intensities, most plants grow faster requiring more water and nutrients. During periods of low temperature and low light intensities, plants grow at a slower rate and utilize less water and nutrients. Constant feeding automatically adjusts to these conditions, since fertilizer is applied simultaneously.

Acidifying Water

At times it may be advantageous to acidify irrigation water. This is particularly true for nurseries that grow their crops in containers or benches and use water that has an alkaline reaction. Water used to irrigate nursery and greenhouse crops nearly always contains calcium and magnesium carbonate. The concentrations will vary with geographic areas and the depth of water supply, but carbonates cause the water to have an alkaline reaction. The constant use of alkaline water tends to increase the alkalinity of the soil. Since many species of plants do not grow well in alkaline soils, it is desirable, in some situations, to acidify the water. This can be accomplished by neutralizing the alkalinity of the water with the aid of acid.

A high grade of phosphoric acid has been used to neutralize the alkalinity of greenhouse water for many years, and more recently the process has been used in the production of container-grown plants in nurseries. The advantages of acidification are:

1. Avoids a gradual increase in the soil reaction (pH) from carbonate accumulation
2. Permits injection of one or more of the anions essential for plant growth with minimum modification of salt concentration
3. Minimizes plugging of small-diameter irrigation equipment
4. Reduces sodium uptake by foliage in areas where sodium is a problem salt

When acid is mixed with concentrated fertilizer solutions, the resulting mixture will contain acids of the salts present in the fertilizer. These mixtures have a high corrosive potential to the irrigation equipment that is exposed to the concentrated solutions prior to dilution. Thus, separate injectors are advisable when employing both acid treatment of irrigation water and concentrated fertilizer solutions.

TABLE 13-3   Percent Grade or Degree Baumé, Acid Factor, and Comments on
Three Acids Used to Acidify Irrigation Water in Nurseries and Greenhouses

Acid	Percent Grade or Degree Baumé	Acid Factor (oz/1000 gal)	Notes
Phosphoric	75%	7.0	Most commonly used; contains 52% P_2O_5; use food grade; avoid by-product acids—contain harmful heavy metals
Sulfuric	66°Be (98%)	3.2	Dangerous to handle; an explosion can occur if water is added to the acid
Nitric	42°Be (67%)	10.5	Contains 15% N; avoid mixing with organic materials; dangerous to handle

Source: Adapted from Matkin and Petersen (1971).

Acidified water used in irrigation of nursery stock should have a pH between 5.8 to 6.5, which is considered optimum for use on most plants. To estimate the quantity of acid required, determine the milliequivalents per liter of carbonates in the water and multiply by the acid factor (Table 13–3). For example, water analysis reports 2.5 mEq/liter of carbonates. The acid injector has a ratio of 1:200 and a 50-gal acid stock solution tank is available. Two hundred × 50 equals 10,000 gal of water to be neutralized (ten 1000-gal units). To neutralize with 75% phosphoric acid requires 175 fluid ounces (10 × 7.0 × 2.5) be mixed with the 50 gal of water for acid injection. The treated water as it is delivered from the nozzle should be tested and the acid solution adjusted accordingly to obtain the desired pH. The solution should be monitored on a regular basis to assure uniformity of water quality.

Acids can be very dangerous materials and should be used with great caution. They are available in various strengths and degrees of purity. Sulfuric acid is commonly available at 66° Baumé grade, which is highly concentrated. When added to water, considerable heat is generated. Therefore, it should be added slowly in small quantities, preferably with rapid stirring. Water should not be added to the acid, as an explosion can occur.

Frost Protection

Sprinkler irrigation can also be used to protect certain nursery crops from cold-temperature injury. Southern nurseries are exposed periodically to temperatures below freezing during the winter months, and northern nurseries are exposed periodically to cold injury due to radiation frosts in the spring following dehardening of plant tissue. Also, the roots of plants growing in containers may not benefit from the latent heat and could suffer cold-temperature injury even though their branches and foliage survive. Such plants, if continuously sprayed with water during the danger period, can be protected against this form of injury. This is due to the liberation of latent heat upon the freezing of water. Part of the liberated heat is absorbed by the plants, which is enough to protect the foliage from freeze injury down to a temperature approaching 10°F, depending upon the volume of water applied. But to accomplish this, water must be applied continuously or in frequent repeat intervals if applied with the aid of rotating sprinklers. This amounts to approximately ⅛ in. of water/hr, which is equivalent to 60 GPM/acre. Sprinklers should rotate at least once every 20–30 sec to provide frost rotection. To assure protection, the irrigation system must be in good working condition and be activated when the temperature approaches 34°F and continue until the temperature warms to above 32°F and the ice has melted from the plants. A reliable temperature alarm system should be installed at plant level in the area to be protected to warn that the frost protection system should be activated. Close communication with the local weather station is desirable during frost-sensitive periods.

Certain types of plants, unfortunately, are much too brittle to withstand the ice load that builds up during such a situation and should not be treated, as the damage due to breakage could be far greater than the protection offered against a radiation frost. Freezing of water to liberate the latent heat is not too effective in protecting plants against windborne freezes, since the wind removes the liberated heat too rapidly to be effective. This also creates an evaporative cooling situation, which reduces plant temperatures below air temperature.

Excess Soil Moisture

Although plants require water for growth, too much water about their roots for too long a period of time can cause problems. The problem results from oxygen restriction to the growing roots. The roots have a continual need for oxygen to carry on the process of respiration, which in turn produces energy needed for growth. When plants suffer from excess moisture, they often exhibit one or more of the following symptoms: wilting of the foliage and succulent shoots, chlorosis of the foliage, reduced vigor, necrosis of the foliage and tender shoots, and death. The degree of expression of the symptoms is dependent upon the plant species and the duration of the flooded condition.

Plants that have been growing well, as a result of good culture, will often exhibit a sudden wilting of new leaves and shoots when their roots are inundated with water, especially if the water remains for more than a few hours. Plants that have been exposed to flood conditions for a number of days may completely dehydrate some weeks after the flood. This is due to injury that was done to the roots during the flood period. Plants that are classified as drought-tolerant have a greater tendency to exhibit this type of injury. However, most plants will dehydrate if the excess water remains in the soil long enough to damage their root hairs.

Excess moisture in a propagation bench or liner bed will often result in wilting and death of new shoots. Examination of the cuttings will reveal dead bark on the basal portion of the cutting and a discoloration of the pith. In advanced stages the basal area of the cutting will exhibit rot. However, similar symptoms can be produced by an application of root-inducing hormone at too high a concentration.

Trees and shrubs planted into areas with poor drainage will soon exhibit chlorosis of the foliage and lack of vigor. Where the poor drainage situation is compounded by excessive water, the plants may fail to leaf out in the spring and will die.

The reasons for excess water in the root zone of plants are many and varied. However, they can be reduced to two primary causes: poor drainage and excessive or too frequent applications of water. Poor drainage may be due to soils of medium to low porosity or to artificially created situations that impede drainage. If plants must be planted in poorly drained sites, some thought should be given to selecting species that are adapted to such a site, or to artificially draining the areas.

When planting in pots, containers, benches, or in disturbed-soil areas, attention must be given to providing for adequate drainage. All too often pots and containers have no drainage holes or the holes have become plugged, and disturbed sites have had the soil structure destroyed so that the planting site functions as a sealed basin. The practice of mulching to reduce weed growth and evaporation from the soil surface can sometimes accentuate an excess-moisture problem in the soil. This is particularly true on clay sites during periods of abundant rainfall.

For a plant to grow it must have water, but too much water can be detrimental. Good drainage is one of the cardinal points in growing healthy plants. Never plant into containers without drainage holes, and check the percolation rate of clay and disturbed soils prior to planting. If it is found to be lacking, some type of artificial drainage should be installed prior to planting.

SUMMARY

Water is a biochemical reagent for photosynthesis and as such is a major modifier of plant growth. It is used as a carrier or a distribution agent for water-soluble fertilizers and for various pesticides and growth regulations. It can also be used to protect tender nursery crops from damage due to late spring frosts and to moisten the soil to aid digging and transplanting operations. Various types of irrigation systems are available for use in a nursery. The specific type should be selected based upon objectives and economic considerations. Intensive production areas such as container-production and propagation facilities warrant an investment in a permanent, labor-efficient system, whereas extensive field-production areas may warrant only an investment in a semiportable system or a trickle-irrigation system for shade trees.

Other considerations in selecting and developing an irrigation system for a nursery are daily water needs, availability of quality water, power for operation of the equipment, and the disposition of excess waste water from container-production areas, at least in some states. The effective and efficient use of an irrigation system can increase the productive potential of many nurseries and improve their profitability where this is a major management objective.

REFERENCES

BOODLEY, J. W., C. F. GORTZIG, R. W. LANGHANS, and J. W. LAYER. 1966. Fertilizer proportioners for floriculture and nursery crop production management. N. Y. State Coll. Agric. Cornell Ext. Bull. 1175.

BOOKER, L. J. 1967. Irrigating container-plants. Am. Nurseryman 126(7):71.

_____ , and N. W. STICE. 1964. Mechanized irrigation for nurseries. Proc. Int. Plant Propag. Soc. 14:336.

BOSLEY, R. W. 1966. A fertilizer injection system. Proc. Int. Plant Propag. Soc. 16:311–314.

BOUYOUCUS, G. J. 1937. Evaporating the water with burning alcohol as a rapid means of determining moisture content of soils. Soil Sci. 44:337-383.

_____ . 1950. A practical soil moisture meter as a scientific guide to irrigation practices. Agron. J. 42:104–107.

COSTELLO, L., and J. L. PAUL. 1975. Moisture relations in transplanted container-plants. HortScience 10(4):371–372.

DAVIS, J. R., and R. L. COOK. 1954. Fertilizing through irrigation water. Mich. State Univ. Ext. Bull. 324.

_____ , and R. L. COOK. 1955. Frost protection with sprinkler irrigation. Mich. State Univ. Ext. Bull. 327.

FURUTA, T. 1973. Studies of plant subsystems in container production. Am. Nurseryman 138(12):8.

_____ . 1974. Irrigation of ornamentals. Proc. Int. Plant Propag. Soc. 24:99–104.

KENWORTHY, A. L. 1974. Trickle irrigation, simplified guidelines for orchard installation and use. Farm Sci. Mich. State Univ. Agric. Exp. Sta. Res Rep. 248.

KIDDER, E. H., and R. Z. WHEATON. 1958. Supplemental irrigation. Mich. State Univ. Ext. Bull. 309.

MATKIN, O. A., and F. H. PETERSEN. 1971. Why and how to acidify irrigation water. Am. Nurseryman 133(12):14.

MONK, R. 1962. Tolerance of some trees and shrubs to saline conditions. Proc. Am. Soc. Hort. Sci. 81:556–561.

OKI, G. 1964. B–1–F fertilizer metering system proceedings. Proc. Int. Plant Propag. Soc. 14:335.

PATEL, S. I., and H. H. TINGA. 1973. Growth of subirrigated Japanese holly as affected by soil type and depth. HortScience 8(1):27–28.

PONDER, H. G., and A. L. KENWORTHY. 1975. Hydraulic displacement of tank fertilizer solution(s) into a trickle irrigation system. HortScience 10(3):261–262.

_____ , and A. L. KENWORTHY. 1976. Trickle irrigation of shade trees growing in the nursery. I. Influence on growth. J. Am. Soc. Hort. Sci. 101(2):100–103.

RICHARDS, L. A. 1954. Saline and alkali soils. USDA Agric. Handb. 60.

ROBERTS, B. 1972. The role of water in shade tree growth. Am. Nurseryman 135(3):12.

ROHWER, C., and M. R. LEWIS. 1940. Small irrigation pumping plants. USDA Farmer's Bull. 1857.

SACHS, R. M., T. KRETCHUM, and T. MOCH. 1975. Minimum irrigation requirements for landscape plants. J. Am. Soc. Hort. Sci. 100(5):499–502.

SPURWAY, C. H., and C. E. WILDON. 1938. Water conditioning for greenhouses. Mich. Agric. Exp. Sta. Circ. Bul. 166:3–10.

STAEBNER, F. E. 1940. Supplemental irrigation. USDA Farmer's Bull. 1846.

STOECKELER, J. H., and E. AAMODT. 1940. Use of tensiometers in regulating watering in forest nurseries. Plant Physiol. 15:589–607.

TOMLINSON, W. M. 1964. Automatic one-gallon container irrigation. Proc. Int. Plant Propag. Soc. 14:308–312.

WALLIS, M. T. 1971. Capillary watering. Proceedings of the Refresher Course for Nurserymen, Pershore College of Horticulture, Pershore, England, pp. 32–33.

WHITE, R. G., and E. H. KIDDER. Tractor power take-off driver pumps. Mich. State Univ. Coop. Ext. Serv. Misc. Ser. Circ. E–23.

WILCOX, L. V. 1955. Classification and use of irrigation waters. USDA Circ. 969.

SUGGESTED READING

JOHNSON, M. 1972. Irrigation, nursery container production. Coop. Ext. Serv. Univ. Mass. Publ. 73, pp. 23–25.

McDONALD, S. E. and S. W. RUNNINH. 1979. Monitoring irrigation in western forest tree nurseries. USDA, Forest Service, Rocky Mtn. Forest and Range Exp. Sta., Gen Tech. Rpt. Rm–61.

PAIN, C. H., W. W. HINZ, C. RIED, and K. R. FROST. 1975. Sprinkler irrigation. Sprinkler Irrigation Association, Silver Springs, Md.

RUBEY, H. 1954. Supplemental irrigation for eastern United States. The Interstate Printers and Publishers, Inc., Danville, Ill.

14 *Modifying Plant Growth and Development in the Nursery*

Plants, like any other biological organism, are the product of heredity and environment. Trees growing in a natural environment develop a form and structure related to the multiplicity of stresses to which they are exposed over a period of time. A tree that develops in a dense stand within a forest will have a narrow crown and a tall, lean stem due to crowding and limited light within the stand, whereas a tree that develops in an open area will have a broader, fuller crown with a stem of greater caliper and more taper. Trees growing in a nursery also develop a form and structure related to the stresses imposed upon them by nature and by the nurserymen who produce them. In addition to the major environmental modifiers—climate, moisture, soil, nutrients, and light—plants in a nursery can also be modified in their development by various cultural modifiers, such as spacing, staking, pruning, spraying of chemicals, planting, digging, and by a host of biological modifiers, such as diseases, insects, vertebrates, weeds, and human beings (Table 14–1). Unfortunately, too little attention has been given to the effects of the various cultural modifiers (practices) on the development of plants in nurseries, whereas considerable information is available on the major environmental and biological modifiers.

SHOOT MODIFICATION

Spacing was discussed in Chapter 5 from the point of view of organization of the nursery for land utilization and various management practices. However, spacing also has an effect upon the growth and development of plants in the nursery. Plants, either in the field or in containers, that are to be sold as specimens must be spaced far enough apart so that they can grow in an unrestricted manner. If they are spaced too closely, or allowed to remain too long in high-density plantings, their branches

TABLE 14-1 Summary of Primary and Cultural Modifiers of Various Plant Characteristics or Plant Qualities

Plant Part	Quality or Characteristic	Primary Modifiers	Cultural Modifiers
Stem (trunk)	Diameter (caliper)	Site, moisture, light, wind	Spacing, shoot pruning, fertilizing, spacing, shoot pruning, staking
	Taper	Same as for diameter	Fertilizing, pruning, space, day length, root pruning, cultivation, chemicals
	Height	Light, moisture	Same as for stem height
Branches	Length and compactness	Species selection, moisture, light	Pruning, branch spreading, cytokinin
	Branch angle	Species or cultivar selection	Fertilizing, root pruning, irrigation
Foilage	Color and size	Light, moisture, species selection	Dormant oil on some species
	Sheen of needles	Cultivar selection	Chemical defoliants, root pruning
	Defoliation	Cold temperature, short days	
Roots	Depth	Site, species selection, soil aeration	Root pruning, copper screening
	Branching	Species or cultivar selection	Root pruning
	Compactness	Drainage	Trickle irrigation, fertilizer placement, organic matter
	Malformation (Curl and kink) (J or bilateral)	Container	Improper planting Method of planting
Flowers	Induction	Maturity	Photoperiod, chemicals, C/N ratio, pruning, root pruning, ringing, bending
	Inhibition	Juvenility	Chemicals, C/N ratio, pruning
Fruit	Set	Pistillate (female) flowers	Pollinizers, hormone sprays, fertilizer (N)
	Prevention	Male plants of dioecious species, double-flowered forms	Hormone sprays, removing flower buds
Plant	Cold acclimation	Low-temperature, short-photoperiods, ecotype	Root pruning, withholding water

touch, they become malformed, and their sales appeal decreases. With sapling trees, whether grown in the field or in containers, there is a tendency to overlook the importance of spacing and to grow them too close. At close spacing, saplings tend to grow taller, but the lower foliage is shaded and tends to drop off. At wider spacing, which allows a greater volume of space per plant, they develop more caliper, better taper, and better appearance. Where possible, nursery rows for saplings should be oriented in a north-south direction to maximize exposure of the lower branches of young trees to sunlight.

The density of seeding also affects the growth and development of seedlings. Most buyers prefer seedlings of good caliper (³⁄₁₆–¼ in. or ¼ in. and up) with appropriate height and appearance, plus a well-developed root system. However, too low a density in the seedbed results in fewer seedlings that are too large for profitable management. The optimum density should be determined for each species to be grown. Information on seeds and seedling culture is contained in USDA Agricultural Handbook 450, *Seeds of Woody Plants in the United States,* and in *Plant Propagation Principles and Practices* (see Appendix A).

Staking and Pruning

Staking and pruning are strong modifiers of plant form and structure. Since they are closely related and interact with wind, they will be discussed together. Pruning the stem (trunk, bole) of young trees induces a preferential distribution of the photosynthates toward the upper portion of the stems, whereas the action of wind induces a preferential distribution of the photosynthates toward the lower portion of the stem. Staking young trees has a tendency to promote growth of the upper portion of the stem to the detriment of the basal portion. In experiments where the stems of young trees were staked for a number of years, it was found that the stems became unstable and could not support their crowns when the stakes were removed and subjected to the stress of crown weight and wind action. Unstaked trees exposed to the stress of moderate, multidirectional wind produced stems that supported their crowns under the stress of normal wind conditions. Staked trees grew taller but produced stems of less caliper and less taper. Unstaked trees, exposed to moderate multidirectional winds, produced stem growth that was uniformly distributed around the circumference of the stem and was of normal cell structure, whereas trees exposed to a unilateral wind force tended to increase the growth of the stem in the area of maximum stress. This can be seen on trees along an ocean front and on trees improperly staked (Fig. 14–1). Removing the lower branches from the stem contributed to a decrease in caliper and taper of some but not all species of trees.

The development of stems of trees is related to the amount of photosynthate available and its distribution within the tree. There is a strong tendency for the photosynthate (carbohydrates) to accumulate and be utilized in growth processes in the upper portions of a tree. But, owing to physical stresses that are produced in free-swaying stems, there may be an increase in the level of auxin which causes the

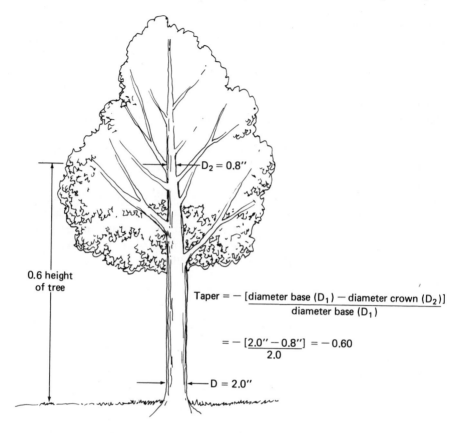

$D_2 = 0.8''$

0.6 height of tree

Taper $= - \dfrac{[\text{diameter base } (D_1) - \text{diameter crown } (D_2)]}{\text{diameter base } (D_1)}$

$= - \dfrac{[2.0'' - 0.8'']}{2.0} = -0.60$

$D = 2.0''$

Figure 14-1 Determination of taper for a young tree.

food materials to be distributed to the stress areas, resulting in greater caliper and improved taper of the stem.

Taper is the gradual decrease in diameter of the trunk in an apical direction. Taper can be calculated between two points on the stem by dividing the diameter difference between the two points by the diameter of the basal point (Fig. 14-1). Since diameter of the apical measurement is usually smaller, the taper value is negative. It has been determined experimentally that the taper parameter for sapling trees, where the wind load occurs at a point about 0.6 of the height of the tree, should be close to −0.60. A taper of this magnitude produces a tree in which stress is distributed uniformly in the region of the trunk where wood development is most advanced and decreases rapidly in the region toward the top, where the wood is least developed.

One objective in producing shade trees in a nursery is to develop a straight, strong leader. For most species, this can be accomplished by allowing the saplings to sway in the wind. But with some species and with budded clones, especially when growing on sites where the wind is strong or primarily from one direction, it may be necessary to support the sapling temporarily by staking. If staking is done, it should be confined to the lower portion of the stem, allowing the upper portion to sway in the wind. The support should be removed as soon as the tree has developed sufficient caliper to support the crown.

Pruning practices vary with cultivar, market objective, and the personal preference of nurserymen. All pruning in the nursery should be done to enhance the natural form and beauty of the plants. The market objective will also influence the type and amount of pruning that can be done. A market objective that calls for small plants at low price does not permit much pruning, whereas a market objective that is to supply specimen shade trees requires considerable pruning.

Pruning is both an art and a science. It is a practice often abused by the uneducated. Good pruning practices and proper timing can enhance the beauty of nursery plants. Poor pruning and improper timing can seriously reduce their value.

A good nursery pruning program commences with the planting of the liners. Spreading evergreens and some shrubs should be cut back to induce branching and compactness of growth. Trees that normally grow with a central leader should have multiple leaders reduced to one—the straightest. Trunk pruning of shade trees may or may not be done, depending upon the market objective and preference of the nurseryman. Some nurserymen prefer to retain lateral branches and branchlets as long as possible to aid in the development of the trunk, whereas others prefer to strip the buds and branchlets from the trunk to aid in developing smooth bark. Small branchlets can easily be removed by running a gloved hand along the trunk. If branchlets are left on, they can be headed back to permit cultural operations within the blocks. When the desired caliper and taper are established, the lower laterals can be removed to produce a tree with the desired form.

In addition to developing good stem structure for trees, pruning young plants in the nursery is done to improve the crown structure. Thinning the crown will reduce the weight and wind resistance during the early life of young trees, thus aiding in stem development. Excurrent tree species should be limited to a single leader. Double or multiple leaders often are subtended by narrow branch angles which are generally weak and tend to break during storms in later life. Also, branches that join the stem at acute angles should be removed if they are not absolutely necessary for the overall form of the tree. They, too, are weak structurally and can be easily damaged as they grow larger. Branches selected for the main scaffolds should form wide angles (30–60°) to assure that they will withstand stress when they are older. As the tree grows and matures in the nursery, branches that grow inward or that cross and rub other more desirable branches should be removed. In more vigorous species, it may be necessary to headback branches that grow more rapidly than others to keep the crown in balance. Should it become necessary to headback a leader, owing to excessive growth, the cut should be made directly above a bud. If the tree has two or more buds per node, a desirable practice is to remove all but one of these buds. This encourages the development of a single leader and avoids the problem of multiple leaders. To minimize the development of a crook at the point where the new leader develops, support the bud with a small piece of masking tape wrapped about the bud's stem. This practice aids in the development of straight, upright growth of the new developing leader.

Evergreens are pruned or sheared either to enhance their natural form or to correct malformations in growth. Most large evergreens require little pruning; a double or multiple leader may need to be removed periodically. Rapidly growing pines are best pruned during a flush of growth (candle stage) to ensure the development of terminal buds; to delay until the flush of growth has terminated results in poorly shaped trees. Evergreen shrubs (e.g., junipers and yews) will often benefit by two shearings during the growing season, developing into dense plants.

Time of pruning.   Deciduous shade trees growing in nurseries are best pruned in winter. Priority should be given to those species that have a propensity for copious sap flow in the spring. Beech, birch, maples, and yellow wood should be pruned in December or early January to permit time for the wounds to dry and thereby reduce the amount of sap flow in the spring. Species such as ginkgo and oak can be delayed until late winter, as they produce little or no sap flow from pruning wounds.

Spring pruning of plants in nurseries should be kept to a minimum since this is the time of most active growth for most plants. It is also the time of maximum spore release, with the greatest potential for infection of plants through wounds. Pruning of shade trees in spring should be limited to new plantings and those trees that may require some corrective maintenance. Other activities in the nursery often have a greater priority in the spring, including harvesting, shipping, and planting.

Late spring or early summer, depending on the season, is the time to prune evergreens, such as pines, spruce, and Douglas fir: just before their spring flush of growth.

Summer pruning in nurseries is confined primarily to vigorously growing shrubs and to those indeterminate types of trees, such as ash, honey locust, pin oak, and zelkova, that grow too rapidly in relationship to trunk development. Pruning is needed to keep the crown of the tree in balance with taper development of the trunk and to improve branching. Avoid pruning determinate types of trees in late spring or early summer, to avoid stimulating a second flush of growth that could be subject to attack by borers or leafhoppers that otherwise could have been avoided.

Late summer and fall is another peak season for digging and shipping for many nurseries; therefore, pruning is delayed until late fall or early winter. It is also a poor time to prune plants in most parts of the country since the new growth that results may not harden in time for the onset of winter.

Clean tools must be used when pruning in the nursery. It is a good practice to clean and sterilize pruning equipment at the end of each row and especially after pruning a tree or shrub that was or is suspected of being infected with a disease. All open wounds are potential sites for disease infection. Closure of pruning wounds can be hastened by keeping the plants in a healthy, vigorous condition by maintaining adequate levels of moisture and nutrition. The application of tree paint to wounds is of minimal value and is seldom used in nurseries.

Water Modifiers

The growth of plants in the nursery is greatly influenced by the availability of water. Trees suffering from moisture stress produce significantly less growth than trees growing under optimum levels of soil moisture. Trickle-irrigated trees growing in nursery rows exhibited greater trunk diameter increase than do nonirrigated trees. Plants growing in containers can also be modified by availability of water. Maximum growth of forsythia plants was achieved when the media were irrigated after 0.1 atm but before 1.0 atm of moisture stress was attained (Table 14–2). Significant growth reduction resulted when soils were allowed to dry to a point where 5 or more atmospheres of moisture stress had developed. Maintaining medium soil moisture at high levels is unnecessary after growth has stopped due to limitations by other climatic modifiers, such as low temperature or short day lengths.

TABLE 14-2 Influence of Five Moisture Regimes on Growth of
Forsythia intermedia Grown in Containers

	Oven Dry Weight (g)	
Moisture Regime	Mean Shoot Growth	Mean Root Growth
Irregular below 0.1-atm stress	3.69	5.06
Irregular at 0.1-atm stress	5.28	6.65
Irregular at 1-atm stress	5.26	5.81
Irregular at 5-atm stress	3.99	4.81
Irregular at 15-atm stress	2.19	3.26
L.S.D.		
0.05	1.37	0.31
0.01	1.86	0.42

Source: Wikle et al. (1961).

Chemical Modifiers

Shoot growth of some species can be modified by chemical means. Various chemicals are effective in reducing growth of shoots, while others are effective in accelerating shoot growth. Still other materials can be used as chemical pruning agents and for control of sprouting.

Maleic hydrazide (MH-40), succinic acid (commonly known as aminozide), abscissic acid (ABA), ancymidol, and other chemical growth regulators have been used to restrict the growth of woody plants. Gibberellic acid accelerates the growth of some species of woody plants. Selected fatty acids (e.g., Off-Shoot-O) can be used as chemical pruning agents, whereas the ethyl ester of napthaleneacetic acid has been used to inhibit sprouting following pruning, and from the base of some grafted or budded plants (e.g., crabapples). However, most of the chemical modifiers are still in the developmental stage and should be used with caution. Only products that are registered for a specific use should be used, and they should be applied according to the product label.

The effectiveness of chemical growth regulators varies with species, stage of growth, climatic conditions, and method of application. As a general rule, plants that have hairy leaves and distinct internodes respond better to foliar sprays than do plants that have waxy leaves or enclosed growing points. Also, plants in the early stages of vegetative growth respond better than those that are dormant, in flower, or in a late stage of growth. Foliar applications should be made when the temperature is between 60 and 80°F and the relative humidity is high (50% or greater). At low temperatures the chemical fails to penetrate, and at high temperature with low relative humidities the materials evaporate prior to penetration. The chemicals should remain on the foliage for at least 1 hr to assure effective penetration. The effectiveness of treatment is also influenced by formulation of the chemical. Some materials are emulsions and must be carefully mixed with water to produce a stable mixture. Emulsions should be applied as a fine mist uniformly over the entire plant. Excessive applications should be avoided, since large accumulations of the emulsion can girdle stems of tender plants. Chemical pruning agents selectively kill the meristematic growing point of a shoot without affecting the subsequent growth of lateral buds; therefore, timing and method of application are extremely important. The best response on woody species has been when the chemical was applied as a fine mist when the plants were in the early stages of a flush of growth and the new shoots were 2–4 in. in length. Sprays applied prior to bud break, in the spring, have not been effective, and later applications have resulted in phytotoxicity.

Sprouting, which commonly develops at the base of grafts, can be successfully inhibited in nursery stock by a single spray application of naphthaleneacetic acid ethyl ester (NAA-ethyl ester), when applied at a concentration of either 0.25 or 0.50% to the base of the trees just prior to bud swell in the spring.

Chemical growth regulators have also been used to modify the angle of branching on young trees. Although the technique has not been tested extensively, applying cytokinins at a concentration of 0.02% on the lateral buds of young apple trees resulted in crotch angles of 60° versus 36° for nontreated buds.

Modification by Light

The growth of stems can be influenced by light. The juvenile growth and development of seedlings of many woody species can be modified by light intensity and photoperiod. Long photoperiods, produced by extending the natural day length to approximately 16 hr by supplementary low-intensity light (100 foot-candles [ft-c]) or by breaking the night period with a short period of light (Fig. 14–2), will cause many species of plants to remain vegetative (Table 14–3). Species such as rhododendron and white oak grow in flushes. By control of light intensity or photoperiod, where possible, growth of many species of plants can be accelerated. However, all other modifiers (temperature, moisture, nutrition) must be maintained at optimal levels. The plants must also be conditioned for low-temperature survival

Figure 14–2   Lights used to break the night period; photoperiodic responsive plants remain vegetative. (Courtesy Conard-Pyle Co.)

prior to planting outdoors if the plants are to be grown in areas exposed to low temperature.

Blue spruce seedlings grown in a greenhouse for 20 weeks under continuous light at 900 ft-c made six times the growth of similar seedlings grown under short days. They also made twice the growth of seedlings grown under a light regime that provided 12 hr of light at 900 ft-c or a 2-hr light break (50 ft-c) in the middle of the dark period. Seedlings of hardwood species responded in a similar manner.

In another experiment, 1-year-old nursery-grown seedlings of 20 hardwood species were grown for 20 weeks with supplemental light at night. VHO fluorescent lamps supplied 700–800 ft-c of light to the seedlings. Control plants were grown both in a greenhouse without light and in a nursery adjacent to the greenhouse. At the end of the experiment, 18 of the 20 species had responded to supplemental light

**TABLE 14-3   Partial List of Woody Species Vegetatively
Responsive to Long Days**

Botanical Name	Common Name
Acer negundo	Boxelder
Acer palmatum	Japanese maple
Acer rubrum	Red maple
Acer saccharum[a]	Sugar maple
Aesculus hippocastanum[a]	Common horsechestnut
Betula pendula	European white birch
Betula platyphylla	Asian white birch
Catalpa bigononiodies	Common catalpa
Catalpa speciosa	Western catalpa
Cercis canadensis	American redbud
Cornus florida	Flowering dogwood
Cornus kousa	Japanese dogwood
Cornus nutallii	Mountain dogwood
Fagus grandifolia	American beech
Fagus sylvatica[a]	European beech
Hibiscus syricus	Rose-of-sharon
Juniperus horizontalis	Creeping juniper
Kolkwitzia amabilis	Beautybush
Larix decidua	European larch
Larix sibirica	Siberian larch
Liquidambar styraciflua[a]	American sweet gum
Liriodendron tulipifera[a]	Tulip tree
Magnolia soulageana	Saucer magnolia
Paulownia tomentosa[a]	Princess tree
Phellodendrom amurense	Cork tree
Picea abies[a]	Norway spruce
Pinus banksiana[a]	Jack pine
Pinus caribaea	Cuban pine
Pinus echinata	Shortleaf pine
Pinus resinosa	Red pine
Pinus sylvestris	Scots pine
Pinus taeda	Loblolly pine
Platanus occidentalis	Eastern sycamore
Populus alba	White poplar
Populus balsamifera	Balsam poplar
Populus deltoides	Eastern cottonwood
Quercus alba[a]	White oak
Quercus robur	English oak
Quercus rubra[a]	Red oak
Rhododendron catawbiense[a]	Mountain rosebay
Robina pseudoacacia	Black locust
Salix babylonica	Weeping willow
Tsuga canadensis	Canada hemlock
Ulmus americana	American elm
Viburnum carlesii	Korean spice viburnum
Viburnum opulus	Cranberry bush
Weigela florida	European flowering weigela

[a]Growth in flushes.

by increased height growth. Smoke trees under supplemental light made nine times more growth than similar seedlings grown in the nursery. Most hardwood species doubled or quadrupled their growth rates when given supplemental light at night. It is highly probable that most species of woody plants, in their juvenile state, are amenable to increased growth by the use of extended photoperiods.

It is also possible to increase growth of some species by shading. For example, it is reported that Red-Osier dogwood made their best growth when grown under 75% natural light. Also, *Viburnum opulus* 'Nanum' grew best when placed under 30–47% shade than those placed in 65% shade or in full sun. Similar findings have been observed for other species. Apparently, light saturation for some species is less than full natural light; growing these species in partial shade results in improved growth. The majority of species responding to shade are those found naturally growing as understory plants in forests.

ROOT MODIFICATION

Root pruning as practiced in nurseries is done to reduce vegetative growth, develop more compact root systems, aid in the hardening of plants for digging prior to placing them in storage or shipping to market, modify the root system to fit a given container, and encourage a radial root distribution. Root modification in the nursery is generally accomplished by various methods of root pruning. But roots can also be modified by planting method, fertilizer placement, trickle irrigation, the use of barriers, such as: air, water, and copper screens, and with container-grown plants by the container.

Plants that are becoming too large for the space available in a field nursery or are growing too rapidly can be modified in growth by root pruning, which will reduce the rate of vegetative growth and help control size. To ensure greater success in transplanting, nurserymen root prune plants that develop sparse root systems or taproots (e.g., *Sophora japonica, Pinus sylvestris*). Root pruning for these purposes is best done when the plants are young, either before planting in the field or 1–2 years after planting. Root pruning in the field should be done after the plants have completed a flush of growth and when there is an adequate supply of soil moisture. Root pruning should not be done during a flush of growth, during drought periods, or just prior to an anticipated drought. Immediately following root pruning, the area should be watered to settle the soil about the roots, to establish soil to root contact, and to assure a supply of water for the plants' metabolic requirements. If no irrigation is available, delay root pruning until there is a high probability of rain.

Root pruning in the field is generally accomplished with a "U-blade." The blade is attached to a high-powered tractor (Fig. 1–3) and either pushed or pulled at the appropriate soil depth to prune the roots.

The method of planting can materially modify the root system of nursery-grown trees. At the time of planting, it is essential that the roots of bare root plants be carefully positioned to assure uniform, radial distribution. When bare root trees and shrubs are hand-planted, the roots are generally well distributed. But with mechanical planters there is a great chance of roots being poorly distributed. Some machines open a narrow trench into which the roots are inserted. This often results in a bilateral root system, especially in heavy soils. In other situations, if the roots are dragged in planting, the plants develop a unilateral root system (Fig. 14–3). Plants with either a uni- or bilateral root system do not develop good anchorage in the soil and blow over fairly easily in wind storms. They are restricted to a limited moisture supply and are prone to dehydrate more rapidly during the periods of drought than plants with well-distributed, radial root systems.

Aeration

Root systems can be modified by aeration and the addition of various soil amendments. Aerating compacted soils will often result in improved root growth. Incorporating organic matter and slow-release fertilizers into the soil about the roots can greatly influence their development. This technique can be used when preparing large trees for transplanting. A trench is dug around the tree in the area where maximum root growth is desired. It is then backfilled with a loam soil enriched with organic matter and a slow-release form of fertilizer. In a few months the trench will be filled with a mass of fibrous roots that aid in successful transplanting.

Figure 14–3   Unilateral root system, the results of roots that were dragged when planted as a liner.

Trickle Irrigation

Trickle irrigation is effective in modifying the root system of plants growing in field-production nurseries. An examination of the roots of a number of species of trees grown under trickle irrigation showed that sugar maples produced more fibrous roots, whereas honey locust produced larger roots than did nonirrigated trees. Pin oaks produced both more fibrous roots and larger roots. Trickle irrigation did not affect the depth of root penetration but did increase the mass of the root system contained within the root ball.

Container Effects

Root systems of container-grown plants can be modified by the size, depth, and shape of the container, as well as by various root pruning techniques. Root development of container-grown plants is proportional to the volume of medium in the container in which the plant is growing, which in turn is a function of the diameter and the depth of the container. The shape of the container is also a significant root modifier. In round containers with smooth interior surfaces, plants that remain for too long a period of time develop root curl, whereas in square containers or in round containers with vertical ridges on the sides, the roots have a tendency to grow to the corner or to the ridge and then grow down rather than develop in a circular manner. Nurserymen producing seedlings in containers to be used as field liners which in turn will be harvested as B&B plants should avoid small-volume containers, especially those with a low diameter-to-depth ratio. Square containers with a depth of 4–6 in. have been found to be most satisfactory in producing plants with a well-developed root system. Liners produced in deeper containers fail to develop good fibrous roots in the upper portion of the containers, and when grown in narrow pots tend to develop a spiral root system. The roots of container-grown plants can also be effectively root-pruned by growing the plants either on a wire bench or on a copper screen. When grown on the wire bench, the roots are air-pruned, whereas when grown on a copper screen, they are pruned by the toxic effect of the copper.

Temperature Response

The temperature of the root medium can also modify the growth of roots. For most plants, the optimum temperature range for root growth is 60–80°F. Both low and high temperatures can result in injury to or death of roots. Plants growing in metal or high-density polyethylene containers exposed to direct solar radiation will often have media temperatures in the range of 100–120°F. These high-temperature effects can be reduced by shading the sides of exposed containers or by using fiber or papier-mâché-type containers, which are poor conductors of heat. The use of light-colored containers (white, yellow, or silver), which reflect the sun's heat, will significantly reduce the medium temperature as compared to the use of black or dark green containers, which absorb more of the heat and transfer it to the soil medium. (See Chapter 17 for low-temperature effects.)

FLOWERING AND FRUITING

Modifying flowering and fruiting varies with the objective of nurserymen. Nursery-men often want plants to produce flowers or fruits, because they are more marketa-ble. At other times they may want to prevent flowering or fruiting, since fruiting usually causes a reduction in growth.

They may also desire to keep plants in a juvenile condition, since cuttings from juvenile plants initiate roots more readily than do cuttings from mature plants. Flowering plants that are heavily set with flower buds or are in flower will not only sell much more readily than similar-sized plants without buds or flowers, but the plants will command a higher price in the marketplace. There is also a sales advan-tage to having fruit on plants such as English and American holly, fire thorn, moun-tain ash, and others, since this is what the customers desire.

The physiology of flowering and fruiting is very complex and is thoroughly discussed in other books and scientific reviews (see Suggested Readings). But the basic information developed by plant scientists can be used by nurserymen to mod-ify the flowering and fruiting of plants in the nursery. For years nurserymen have attempted to induce the plants to flower by stem pruning, root pruning, ringing of stems, bending of branches, bark inversion, and withholding water and nitrogen. They have maintained plants in a juvenile condition by heavy pruning and by ap-plying high levels of nitrogen. Since the mid-1950s, plant scientists have learned to control the growth and flowering of a number of woody plants by modifying the photoperiod, and since the 1960s they have been able to modify, to a certain degree, the flowering response of woody species with the aid of chemical growth regulators.

Early spring pruning of young vigorous apple trees helps to stimulate growth but discourages the formation of flower buds, whereas pruning similar trees at the time of flower bud differentiation can stimulate flower bud formation but retard veg-etative growth. The same response has been reported for the application of nitrogen fertilizer to young apple trees. For many years it was thought that applying nitrogen to plants would keep them in a vegetative condition, while withholding nitrogen would cause them to differentiate flower buds. It has been demonstrated, on young apple trees, that applying nitrogen in the late fall or early spring prior to growth will, in fact, induce more vegetative growth. But once extension growth has ceased, an application of nitrogen can stimulate floral differentiation in those buds still undifferentiated. Timing is the important factor.

Root pruning or digging plants such as flowering dogwood a year in advance of sale is done by some nurserymen to stimulate the initiation and development of floral primordia. Root pruning is basically a growth-retarding process, but if per-formed at the right time in the growth cycle it can be effective in stimulating flower bud development on some species (e.g., wisteria). The pruning should be done when the foliage is fully developed and just prior to bud initiation for the species.

The *practice of ringing* (girdling) or scoring and bark inversion are used by orchardists to induce a "tardy" fruit tree into bearing, and it has been and is used, to a limited degree, to promote flowering. Ringing is the practice of removing a strip of bark from a branch or the trunk of a tree, whereas scoring is cutting through the bark of a tree into the wood without removing any bark. Bark inversion involves removing a ring of bark from the trunk of the tree and replacing it in an inverted position. The operation is best performed in the spring of the year when the bark is slipping; this will leave the cambium in place to heal the wound. It is recommended that the exposed area be protected from the sun to prevent drying. The injury disrupts the downward movement of elaborated carbohydrates and organic substances, thus reducing root growth. The net effect is to decrease vegetative growth and to induce flower bud initiation. Ringing should not be practiced on stone fruits, since it usually results in death of the tree.

The *effect of photoperiod* on the flowering of plants has been known since 1920 when the length of the day was found to be the controlling factor in the flowering of tobacco. Since that time photoperiodism has been thoroughly researched and is known to control many other responses in plants, including germination of some seeds, shoot elongation, rhizome formation, sex expression, winter hardening, and others. Commercial flower growers soon took advantage of the knowledge that chrysanthemums and poinsettias could be induced to flower by short days. They used long days to keep plants vegetative and induced them into bloom by putting them under short days. This is commonly done by pulling black cloth over the plants in the late afternoon or by interrupting the night period by a half-hour of low-intensity light. Unfortunately, there are only a few reports relating the influence of photoperiod to flower initiation and expression in woody plants (Table 14–4).

Flower bud formation in *Rhododendron catawbiense* is enhanced by growing the plants on long days (16 hours) until the flush of growth is about one-half complete (10–14 days), at which time they should be transferred to short days. Maintaining the plants under long days results in malformed flower buds with leaflike bracts and petal-like stamens.

Flower development and expression in *Abelia grandiflora* and *Hibiscus syriacus* occur under long days on the current season's growth. However, flowering in weigela is more typical of other wood species in which initiation of flower buds occurs one season and flowering the next season after certain physiological requirements are satisfied. Weigela can be induced to flower the same season by growing the plants on long days for a period of 6–8 weeks, exposing the plants to short days for 6–8 weeks, followed by defoliation and a return to long days. Within 7–8 weeks following return to long days, the plants will be in full bloom. There are some cultivars of weigela that produce flower buds and bloom on current season's wood when exposed to long days. Weigela fails to bloom when exposed to short days.

Chemical growth regulators can also be used to modify the flowering response in some woody ornamental plants. In weigela, spraying plants growing under long days with maleic hydrazide (MH) 2500 ppm is as effective as subjecting the plants to short days for 6–8 weeks. Plants sprayed with MH will bloom about 7–8 weeks following treatment.

Flower bud development in rhododendron can be enhanced by soil or foliage

TABLE 14-4   Classification of Woody Species with
Respect to Day-Length Requirement for Flowering

Botanical Name	Common Name
Long-Day Species	
Abelia grandiflora	Glossy abelia
Caryopteris incana	Blue spiraea
Hibiscus syriacus	Rose-of-sharon
Ribes rubrum	Red currant
Short-Day Species	
Bougainvillea glabra	Paper flower
Coffea arabica	Coffee
Long-Day/Short-Day Species	
Cestrum nocturnum	Night jessamine
Rhododendron catawbiense	Mountain rosebay
Day-Neutral Species	
Buddleia davidii	Summer lilac
Calluna vulgaris	Scotch heather
Cornus florida	Flowering dogwood
Hydrangea macrophylla	French hydrangea
Malvaviscus arboreus mexicanus	Turk's cap
Pinus sp.	Pine
Salix repens	Creeping willow
Syringa vulgaris	Common lilac
Viburnum sp.	Viburnum

Source: Davidson and Hamner (1957).

application of growth regulators. Soil applications of Phosfon (2,4-dichlorobenzyl-tributal phosphonium chloride) 0.4 g/gal container or foliar applications of succinic acid (0.25–1.0%) enhanced the development of flower buds on young plants. Azalea plants can also be induced by short days or by the use of growth retardants. The growth regulator should be applied to elongating shoots at the time that shoot elongation is about one-third to one-half complete, since this is the time that the meristem is most precocious. Flowering and fruiting of holly can be enhanced by the use of growth retardants. Phosfon applied as a soil drench to young holly plants in a vegetative condition resulted in flowering and an abundance of fruit.

Fruiting of trees for use in orchard plantings is an essential requirement and is generally considered to be a desirable attribute in most ornamental trees, but not in all. Under some situations the development of fruit on plants can be less than desirable. Most people like to see fruit on holly, yews, mountain ash, and crabapples, but wish to avoid fruit set on ginkgo, mulberry, maple, and elm. Others would like to prevent the fruiting of crabapples, apples, cherries, and so on. Thus, nurserymen must be able to meet the demands of all groups relative to fruiting. To assure fruiting, it is necessary to plant those that have the ability to produce fruit, that is plant species that have perfect or monoecious flowers or female plants of dioecious species.

Perfect flowers are those that have both anthers and pistils in the same flower. In most species they will produce fruit by self-pollination, but others species may require cross pollination to set fruit. It is important to know if cross pollination is required for fruit production in fruit tree species. Most of the following fruit trees are self-fruitful: apricots, citrus, European-type plums (fruitfulness aided by planting two varieties), figs (except Smyrna types), peaches (except J. H. Hale and a few other varieties), quince, and sour cherries. A number of apples, pears, sweet cherries, and American-Japanese-type plums are self-unfruitful. To ensure fruit set, plant at least two and sometimes three varieties near each other. Some fruit tree varieties produce little or no pollen, or their pollen fails to fertilize the ovules. Therefore, at least two varieties should be planted in the same vicinity: *apples:* Baldwin, Gravenstein, Turley, Rhode Island Greening, Stamen, and Winesap; *pears:* Bartlett and Seckel; *sweet cherry:* Bing, Lambert, Napoleon. When planning an orchard, it is advisable to check the planting plan with a fruit specialist to assure proper plant selections and fruitfulness of all trees.

In *monoecious species* the reproductive structures are in separate flowers but on the same plant (e.g., pine, spruce), but only the female flowers or strobile produces fruit. In dioecious species the reproductive structures are on separate plants. The word "dioecious" is derived from the Greek words *di* (two) and *oikos* (house): thus, two households. The fruit is borne by the female plants, but a pollinizer (a male plant) must be located in the vicinity to ensure fertilization. A number of valuable fruit and ornamental plants are dioecious (Table 14–5).

Over the years plants have been selected and grown either for their outstanding fruiting characteristics (e.g., holly, pyracantha, yew) or for the lack of fruiting (e.g., ginkgo, mulberry, yew). When propagated by vegetative means, theses selections become established as either male or female clones. For example, in *Taxus* the clones 'Densiformis,' 'Nigra,' and 'Wellsley' are male, whereas 'Kelsey,' 'Vermeulen,' and 'Jeffrey' are female. But 'Brown,' 'Hatfield,' and 'Hicks' have both male and female plants being sold within the clone. In the case of 'Hicks,' there were apparently two selections made, one male and the other female. They should have separate clonal names. Brown was introduced as a male clone, but at some point there was a mixup in propagation, or sex reversion took place and went unnoticed. In order to conform to standards of nomenclature, a clone must maintain the characteristics for which it was selected. Thus, considerable care must be exercised in propagation and production to assure trueness to name.

Fruiting can be avoided, at lease in some species, by planting either the male form of dioecious species or by planting double-flowered forms (e.g., horsechestnut, cherries, Paul's scarlet hawthorn). Many of the double-flowering forms are unfruitful because of the morphology of their floral structures.

Fruit set can be influenced by temperature and to some degree by day length. Fruit set in Burford holly, for example, was enhanced by growing the plants under short days (9-hr day length) and low-temperature regimes (18°/14°C day/night tem-

TABLE 14-5   Partial List of Genera with One or More Dioecious Species

Genera	Common Name
Acer	Maple
Actinidia	Actinidia
Ailanthus	Tree of heaven
Aucuba	Aucuba
Baccharis	Saltbush
Celastrus	Bittersweet
Cephalotaxus	Plum-yew
Chionanthus	Fringe tree
Cotinus	Smoke tree
Diospyros	Persimmon
Fraxinus	Ash
Ginkgo	Maidenhair tree
Glymnocladus	Kentucky coffee tree
Helwingia	Helwingia
Hippophae	Sea buckthorn
Ilex	Holly
Juniperus	Juniper
Lindera	Spice bush
Maclura	Osage orange
Morus	Mulberry
Myrica	Bog myrtle
Nemopanthus	Mountain holly
Orixa	Orixa
Phellodendron	Cork tree
Populus	Poplar
Rhus	Sumac
Ribes	Currant
Salix	Willow
Schisandra	Magnolia vine
Shepherdia	Buffalo berry
Skimmia	Skimmia
Smilax	Greenbrier
Taxus	Yew
Vitis	Grape
Zanthoxylum	Prickly ash

perature). Plants grown under long days and higher day/night temperature made more vegetative growth but set less fruit.

Fruiting can also be prevented, at least in some species, by the use of chemical sprays (e.g., naphthyleneacetic acid [NAA], maleic hydrazide [MH-30], caustic agents, and emulsifiable polyethylene films). Various caustic agents such as dinitro compounds can be used to prevent fruiting, but some foliage burn can be expected. Sprays of emulsifiable polyethylene applied to *Thuja* at full bloom completely prevented cone formation, but the material was of little value in preventing fruiting on other species. NAA has been the most versatile hormone spray for preventing fruiting of trees.

Before applying chemical sprays to prevent fruit set or to remove unwanted fruit, nurserymen should be familiar with a number of limitations in their use.

1. All chemicals have registered uses. By law, a chemical must be registered with the Environmental Protection Agency (EPA) before it can be used. Unfortunately, many of the chemicals have been cleared for use only on fruit crops.

2. Concentration is critical. At low concentration, hormone sprays cause the set of fruit; at high concentrations they can cause phytotoxic effects on the flowers and growing shoots.

3. The time of application and weather conditions can modify the response. If applied at the wrong stage of flower or fruit development, the response can be different from that which was anticipated. If applied prior to a rain or a cold period, the results may be negative. If hormone sprays are to be used to prevent the development of fruit, they should be applied at the proper time for a given species and at the recommended concentration. If a dinitro is used, it should be applied in such a manner as to avoid contact with the foliage of evergreens, since it may cause them to drop their needles.

WINTER SURVIVAL

The winter survival of plants is important to nurserymen everywhere, but especially to those located in the colder climates. Nurserymen have a sizable investment in plant material, which if injured, could result in a serious economic loss. They are, therefore, concerned with the causes of winter injury and measures that can be taken to prevent or minimize the extent of damage. Winter injury to plants can be caused by desiccation, low temperature, or by various physical and biological agents.

Winter desiccation injury is most commonly associated with evergreens, both narrow- and broad-leaved, and semievergreens. During the late winter months when the soil in the root zone is frozen and the foliage is exposed to radiation from the sun, the leaves lose moisture which the plant cannot replace. This results in desiccation of the leaves and sometimes of the stems of sensitive species. The response varies with species and even with cultivars within the species. For example, *Pinus strobus* is more sensitive to windburn injury than is *Pinus nigra*. This is also true for *Taxus baccata* compared to *Taxus cuspidata* or *Taxus media*. Within *T. cuspidata* the cultivars most sensitive to desiccation in the Midwest are 'Aurescens' and 'Thayesae.' In the *T. media* group the most sensitive are 'Brownii' and 'Green Mountain.' This may be due to the degree of water deficiency that the plants can endure. It can be prevented by shielding tender species from the direct rays of the sun and from wind during the winter months. The application of antidesiccants (transpiration inhibitors) to minimize desiccation injury has not been fully successful. Some success has been reported when the antidesiccant is applied in two applications during the winter, especially covering the lower surface of the leaves.

Low-temperature injury can be classified into three areas: (1) early fall or late spring frosts, (2) extremely cold temperature, and (3) rapid change from warm to cold. Early fall or late spring frosts, at temperatures slightly below freezing, will often injure plants that would normally withstand temperatures some 30–40° lower if the plants had been fully acclimated for winter. These frosts are the unseasonably low temperatures that occur every 5–10 years. When it occurs in the fall of the year, the injury is manifested by the splitting of stems in plants like azaleas, holly, and rhododendrons. The same type of injury can take place in the late winter if there is a period (3–5 days) of warm temperature (40–50°F) followed by a rapid drop in temperature across the freezing point. A condition like this occurred in the Midwest in 1973 and in 1984, causing extensive injury to young evergreen transplants. However, when the frost takes place in late spring, the drop in temperature may not be as great, and the injury is primarily the freezing of the tender new shoots. Although the injury may appear to be rather extensive, the plant will soon recover and in 3 months to a year the aesthetic damage will be remedied, but the nursery may have sustained an economic loss. Extremely low temperatures, which normally occur in midwinter, can result in injury to flower buds, roots, shoot buds, branches, or stems, and at times if the temperature is low enough in death of the plant.

Plants that survive cold periods have the unique ability to acclimate themselves prior to the onset of cold temperatures. The actual mechanism of cold acclimation is not fully understood.* But it appears that decreasing day length and/or gradually decreasing temperatures in the fall of the year aids in increasing cold acclimation of woody plants in northern latitudes. Exposing weigela, rhododendron, and hibiscus to short days prior to the onset of low temperatures was effective in inducing cold hardiness, whereas exposing the plants to long days prior to the onset of low temperature resulted in considerable winter injury.

Exposure to short days and low temperatures prior to the onset of freezing temperatures aided in developing cold hardiness in yews and Red-Osier dogwood, whereas only declining air temperature was associated with increased cold acclimation of 'Hetzi' juniper and other conifers. Woody plants respond to the short days and/or low temperature by a significant reduction in the water content of their stems. In Red-Osier dogwood, it was noted that there was a decrease in water permeability of root cells which acted as a barrier to water uptake. Thus, it appears that cold acclimation is related in part to moisture relationships and tenderness of growth. High soil moisture and high levels of fertility do not appear to bear a direct relationship on winter hardiness. However, species that do not harden in response to short days may be predisposed to low-temperature injury by maintaining high levels of moisture and nutrition during a warm fall.

To aid in hardening plant material for winter, avoid cultural practices that predispose the plants to injury.

1. Do not expose plants to long days or high temperatures prior to the onset of winter. Plants that were growing under lights or in warm places (greenhouse)

*Readers wishing to study this area in detail are referred to the articles listed under Suggested Reading.

should be gradually conditioned for winter either by 2–3 weeks' exposure to low temperature or short days.

2. Avoid late (time varies with area of the country) pruning, cultivating, fertilizing, and field irrigation of plants susceptible to winter injury.

3. Dig tender plants (e.g., althea, buddleia, deutzia) prior to onset of low temperature and place them into winter storage, where temperature control is possible.

4. Avoid growing plants that are not cold-hardy.

Various physical and biological agents, including frost, ice and snow, snowmobiles, rabbits, mice, and deer, can also be the cause of winter injury to plants in the nursery. Frost heaving is primarily associated with young plants transplanted into clay or clay loam soils in the fall. As the ground freezes and thaws, the young plants which have not established firm root contact with the soil are heaved out of the ground and eventually dehydrate and die unless they are replanted prior to dehydration. This type of injury can be avoided by planting fall transplants onto well-drained sites or by delaying the planting onto clay sites until spring.

Damage due to ice and snow is a physical injury sustained by plants due to the weight of the materials. In most cases the injury is immediately visible, but with some plants (e.g., boxwood) the injury may not be apparent for a year or two following the ice or snow storm. The plant appears to recover from the physical crushing of the snow or ice, grows well the following summer, but begins to die the following year. The delayed appearance of damage is because only the lower bark was injured. The plant is able to obtain water and nutrients from the soil for about a year, but eventually the roots die as a result of the injury to the bark, which in effect girdled the stem. This type of injury can be avoided by providing support to the plants prior to the onset of winter. This may be a wire or wire fencing stretched along both sides of a row of boxwood or similar plants.

With the advent of the recreational use of snowmobiles, some nurserymen, in northern areas of the country, have experienced injury to plants due to snowmobiles. This injury has been confined mostly to the loss of leaders from young evergreens, such as pine, spruce, and fir. The leaders are broken by the vehicle as the driver speeds across the snow-covered landscape unaware of the damage being done to the plants below. The only protection from this type of injury is to fence or post the property against trespass, which may or may not be effective.

Rabbits, mice, and deer can do considerable damage to nursery stock during the winter months. Rabbits will either chew the bark off the stems and larger branches of deciduous trees or they will bite off the tops and side branches of smaller transplants. All types of young fruit trees, crabapples, flowering dogwood, and sweetgum are subject to their depredation. Rabbits can be kept out of limited areas of the nursery by various types of exclosures. But the most satisfactory method in extensive plantings is to reduce their population by shooting (permit may be necessary). The use of repellents to keep them away from valuable plants is of limited value.

Mice depredate nursery stock mostly by girdling plants at the ground line (Fig. 14–4). Occasionally, when the snow level is high, their activity is extended up onto the trunk and lateral branches. Mice have a special fondness for crabapples, arborvitae, junipers, and yews but will also work on pines and deciduous trees, if their preferred food source is not available, although they seldom chew on any trees within the stone fruit classification (e.g., peach, cherry). Removal of their natural shelter, such as weeds and sod, will aid in minimizing their depredations, but it is not a guarantee. Various types of poison baits can be used to reduce mice populations, but nurserymen must be cautious in their use, since they are toxic to fish, birds, and warm-blooded animals. Where possible, encouraging or stocking an area with natural predators may be one of the best methods of reducing rodent populations in nurseries located in rural areas.

Deer can cause extensive damage to nursery stock by chewing buds and tender branches (i.e., arborvitae, birch, yew), rubbing the trunks of young trees when developing their antlers, and trampling small plants when they are in large herds. Injury due to deer activity can be minimized by the use of repellents and fences but shooting (by permit) may be necessary if the herd is large and known to have its winter feeding area in the vicinity of the nursery.

Nurserymen must take steps to minimize the depredations of deer and rodents prior to critical damage periods. Baits should be in place before snow covers the

Figure 14–4   Girdling of trees by mice in a nursery.

ground, and repellents must be applied while it is still warm. Inspection of the nursery should be made weekly during the winter months to check for deer or rodent activity. If deer or rodents are found to be active, appropriate action can be taken to reduce their population and minimize damage to valuable plants. Table 14–6 is a partial list of animal repellents. They should be used according to label instructions. Tabasco sauce (also Louisiana hot sauce) 1 tablespoonful/gal has been used fairly successfully as a repellent to protect plants from injury due to the activities of deer, mice, and rabbits. Plants to be protected should be sprayed biweekly. A small amount of spreader-sticker (tablespoon/gal) added to the mixture will improve its effectiveness. Additional information on repellents and bait for the control of birds, deer, mice, and rabbits in the nursery may be obtained from the local county agricultural agent or the U.S. Fisheries and Wildlife Service. In many states it is unlawful to gas, poison, shoot, trap, or otherwise harm wild animals or wild birds without special permits. Nurserymen should check with the law enforcement divisions of their Department of Natural Resources and obtain the necessary permits prior to instituting a vertebrate control program that invokes harming wildlife.

TABLE 14-6   Partial List of Animal Repellents

Material	Repellent for:
Alkylpyridines	Dogs
Aluminum powder	Seed deterrent for birds
Bloodmeal	Rabbits
Bone tar oils	Deer, dogs, and rabbits
Copper naphthenate	Porcupine and squirrels
Lemon grass, oil of	Dogs
Mustard, oil of	Dogs, rats, and raccoons
Nicotine sulfate	Many animals
Rosin	Deer and rabbits
Sodium pentachlorophonate	Mice and rats
Sulfur	Rodents
Tabasco sauce	Deer and rabbits
Thiram (tetramethylthiuramdisulfide)	Animals and birds
TNB-A (trinitrobenzene-aniline complex)	Rabbits
ZAC (zinc dimethyldithiocarbamatecyclohexylamine)	Deer and rodents

SUMMARY

Plants growing in a nursery can be modified in their growth by various environmental, cultural, and biological modifiers. These modifiers may have either a positive or negative effect upon the plants. By good ecological management, it is possible for nurserymen to produce high-quality plants while reducing the negative effects of pests.

REFERENCES

ADAMS, D. G., and A. N. ROBERTS. 1968. Time of flower initiation in *Rhododendron* 'Roseum Elegans' as related to shoot and leaf elongation. HortScience 3(4)278–279.

BEATTIE, D. J., and H. L. FLINT. 1973. Effect of K level on frost hardiness of stems of *Forsythia intermedia* Zab. 'Lynwood'. J. Am. Soc. Hort. Sci. 98(6):539–541.

CATHEY, H. M. 1965. Initiation and flowering of rhododendron on following regulation by light and growth retardants. Proc. Am. Soc. Hort. Sci. 86: 753–760.

————. 1968. Response of some ornamental plants to synthetic abscissic acid. Proc. Am. Soc. Hort. Sci. 93:693–698.

————. 1970. Chemical pruning of plants. Am. Nurseryman 131(9):8.

CHADWICK, L. C. 1962. Use of growth regulators to prevent fruiting. Am. Nurseryman 115(6):96.

CHEN P., P. H. LI, and C. J. WEISER. 1975. Induction of frost hardiness in red-osier dogwood stems by water stress. HortScience 10(4):372–374.

COLLINS, W. C. 1962. Hardening plant materials for winter. Proc. Int. Plant Propag. Soc. 12:86–88.

CRILEY, R. A. 1969. Effect of short photoperiods, cyocel and gibberellic acid upon flower bud initiation and development in azalea 'Hexe'. J. Am. Soc. Hort. Sci. 94(4):392–396.

DAVIDSON, H., M. J. BUKOVAC, and D. C. MACLEAN. 1963. Photoperiodic and chemical control of vegetative growth and flowering in weigela. Proc. Am. Soc. Hort. Sci. 82:589–595.

————, and C. L. HAMNER. 1957. Photoperiodic responses of selected woody ornamental shrubs. Quart. Bull. Mich. Agric. Exp. Sta. Mich. State Univ. 40(2):327–343.

————, and A. OLNEY. 1964. Clonal and sexual differences in the propagation of Taxus. Proc. Int. Plant Propag. Soc. 17:156–161.

————, and D. P. WATSON. 1959. Teratological effects of photoperiod on *Rhododendron catawbiense* Mich. Proc. Am. Soc. Hort. Sci. 73:490–494.

DAVIS, R. E., and C. E. WHITCOMB. 1977. Effects of propagation container size on development of high quality seedlings. Proc. Int. Plant Propag. Soc. 25:448–453.

DEWILDE, R. 1962. Hardening of plant materials for winter. Proc. Int. Plant Propag. Soc. 12:84–85.

DRINKARD, A. W., JR. 1915. Some effects of pruning, rootpruning, ringing and stripping on the formation of fruit buds on dwarf apple trees. Va. Agric. Exp. Sta. Tech. Bull. 5:96–120.

FLEMER, W., III. 1981. How and when to prune nursery stock. Am. Nurseryman 153(8):11, 126–132.

FLETZ, T. A. 1973. Soil temperature influences. Am. Nurseryman 137(1):16.

FUCHIGAMI, L. H., C. J. WEISER, and D. R. RICHARDSON. 1973. The influence of sugars on growth and cold acclimation of excised stems of red-osier dogwood. J. Am. Soc. Hort. Sci 98(5):444–447.

FURUTA, T., W. C. STONE, W. HUMPHREY, and T. MOCK. 1973. Chemical control of root growth in containers. Am. Nurseryman 137(8):9.

GARNER, W. W., and H. A. ALLARD. 1920. Effect of the relative length of day and night and other factors of the environment on growth and reproduction in plants. J. Agric. Res. 18:553–606.

GOUIN, F. R. 1977. Hot news for rodents and deer. HortScience 12(1):10.

GOURLEY, J. H., and F. S. HOWLETT. 1972. Ringing applied to the commercial orchard. Ohio Agric. Exp. Sta. Bull. 410.

HANOVER, J. W., and D. A. REICOSKY. 1972. Accelerated growth for early testing of spruce seedlings. For. Sci. 181(1):92–94.

————— , E. YOUNG, W. A. LEMMIEN, and M. VAN SLOOTEN. 1976. Accelerated-optimal-growth: a new concept in tree production. Mich. State Univ. Agric. Exp. Sta. Res. Rep. 317.

HARRIS, R. W. 1969. Staking and pruning young *Myoporum laetum* trees. J. Am. Soc. Hort. Sci. 94(1):359–361.

————— , W. B. DAVIS, N. W. STICE, and D. LONG. 1971. Root pruning improves nursery tree quality. J. Am. Soc. Hort. Sci. 96(1):105–108.

————— , W. B. DAVIS, N. W. STICE, and D. LONG. 1971. Influence of transplanting time in nursery production. J. Am. Soc. Hort. Sci. 96(1):109–111.

————— , et al. 1972. Spacing of container-grown trees in the nursery. J. Am. Soc. Hort. Sci. 97(4):503–506.

HASKELL, T. 1953. Practical blossom control for the arborist. Proc. Nat. Shade Tree Conf. 29:4–17.

HAVIS, J. R. 1964. Freezing of rhododendron leaves. Proc. Am. Soc. Hort. Sci. 84:570–574.

————— . 1965. Desiccation as a factor in winter injury of rhododendron. Proc. Am. Soc. Hort. Sci. 86:764–769.

————— . 1973. High summer temperatures of containers in New England. Am. Nursery-man 137(2):7.

————— , R. D. FITZGERALD, and D. N. MAYNARD. 1972. Cold-hardness response of *Ilex crenata* Thumb. 'Hetzi' roots to nitrogen source and potassium. HortScience 7(2)|fj195–196.

HENINGER, R. L., and D. P. WHITE. 1974. Tree seedling growth at different soil tempera-tures. For. Sci. 20:363–367.

HOWE, G. H. 1914. Ringing fruit trees. N.Y. (Geneva) Agric. Exp. Sta. Bull. 391.

KELLEY, J. D. 1972. Nitrogen and potassium rate effect on growth, leaf nitrogen and winter hardiness of *Pyracantha coccinea* 'Lalandi' and *Ilex crenata* 'Rotundifolia'. J. Am. Soc. Hort. Sci. 97(4):446–448.

KLINGAMAN, L., and J. H. KING, 1983. What size and shape of container are best for growing seedlings? Am. Nurseryman 157(1):87–93.

KOZEL, P. C., and K. W. REISCH. 1972. Guidelines for chemical pruning. Am. Nurseryman 135(2):13.

KRIZEK, D. T., and R. H. ZIMMERMAN. 1973. Comparative growth of birch seedlings grown in the greenhouse and growth chambers. J. Am. Soc. Hort. Sci. 98(4):370–373.

KUHNS, L. J., and T. D. SNYDER. 1975. Phytotoxicity of copper-treated burlap on balled and burlapped *Cotoneaster divaricata*. HortScience 10(6):613–614.

LARSON, P. R. 1965. Stem form of young *Larix* as influenced by wind and pruning. For. Sci. 11(4):412–424.

LEISER, A. T., and J. D. KEMPER. 1968. A theoretical analysis of a critical height of staking landscape trees. Proc. Am. Soc. Hort. Sci. 92:713–720.

————, and J. D. KEMPER. 1973. Analysis of stress distribution in the sapling tree trunk. J. Am. Soc. Hort. Sci. 98(2):164–170.

————, et al. 1972. Staking and pruning influence trunk development of young trees. J. Am. Soc. Hort. Sci. 97(4):498–502.

LUMIS, G. P., and H. DAVIDSON. 1967. Preventing fruit formation on landscape trees. HortScience 2(2):61–62.

————, R. A. MECKLENBURG, and K. C. SINK. 1972. Factors influencing winter hardiness of flower buds and stems of evergreen azaleas. J. Am. Soc. Hort. Sci. 97(1):124–127.

MARTH, P. C. 1963. Effect of growth retardants on flowering fruiting and vegetative growth of holly (*Ilex*). Proc. Am. Soc. Hort. Sci. 83:777–781.

McGUIRE, J. J., and H. L. FLINT. 1962. Effects of temperature and light on frost hardiness of conifers. Proc. Am. Soc. Hort. Sci. 80:630–635.

————, J. T. KITCHIN, and R. DAVIDSON. 1965. The effect of different growth retardants on growth and flowering of *Rhododendron obtusum* 'Hinodegri'. Proc. Am. Soc. Hort. Sci. 86:761–763.

McKENZIE, J. S., C. J. WEISER, and P. H. LI. 1974. Changes in water relations of *Cornus stolonifera* during cold acclimation. J. Am. Soc. Hort. Sci. 99(3):223–228.

MEIER, K. 1972. Pruning: the key to salable plants. Am. Nurseryman 136(6):112.

MITYGA, H. G., and F. O. LANPHEAR. 1971. Factors influencing the cold hardiness of *Taxus cuspidata* roots. J. Am. Soc. Hort. Sci. 96(1):83–86.

MYERS, S. P., and P. C. KOZEL. 1972. Practical procedures for increasing flower bud initiation of rhododendron. Am. Nurseryman 135(3):13.

ROBINSON, J. T., and D. HAMILTON. 1983. Effects of light levels on Viburnum growth, nutrient uptake and hardiness. Am. Nurseryman 157(3):93–95.

VAARTAJA, O. 1954. Photoperiodic ecotype of trees. Can. J. Bot. 32:392–399.

WEIGLE, J. L., and A. R. BECK. 1971. Flowering characteristics of weigela and their relationship to progeny age at first bloom. J. Am. Soc. Hort. Sci. 96:685–686.

WHITCOMB, C. E. 1981. Growing tree seedlings in containers. Bull. 755, Agric. Exp. Sta. Okla. State Univ.

WHITE, W. C., and C. J. WEISER. 1964. The relations of tissue desiccation, extreme cold and rapid temperature fluctuations to winter injury of American arborvitae. Proc. Am. Soc. Hort. Sci. 85:554–563.

WIKLE, J. S., H. DAVIDSON, and E. A. ERICKSON. 1961. Soil moisture studies with container-grown plants. Quart. Bull. Mich. Agric. Exp. Sta., Mich. State Univ. 44(1)|fj125–128.

WILLIAMS, D. J., and B. C. MOSER. 1974. Response of woody ornamentals to a fatty acid pinching agent. HortScience 9(4):349–350.

WILLIAMS, M. W., and H. D. BILLINGSLEY. 1970. Increasing the number and crotch angles of primary branches of apple trees with cytokinins and gibberellic acid. J. Am. Soc. Hort. Sci. 95(5):649–651.

WILLIAMS, R. R., and R. W. RENNISON. 1963. Summer nitrogen: a new method of bringing apple trees into bearing. Exp. Hort. 9:34–38.

WONG, T. L., R. W. HARRIS, and R. E. FISSELL. 1971. Influence of high soil temperatures on fine woody plant species. J. Am. Hort. Sci. 96(1):80–82.

WRIGHT, R. D. 1976. Influorescence development and fruit set in *Ilex cornuta* Lindl. et Paxt. cv. "Burfordii" as influenced by temperature and photoperiod. J. Am. Soc. Hort. Sci. 101(2):182–184.

ZEHNDER, L. R., and F. O. LANPHEAR. 1966. The influence of temperature and light on the cold hardiness of *Taxus cuspidata*. Proc. Am. Soc. Hort. Sci. 89:706–713.

SUGGESTED READING

CATHEY, H. M. 1975. Comparative plant growth retarding activities of ancymidal with ACPC, Phosfan, Chlormequat and SADH on ornamental plant species. HortScience 10(3):204–216.

GEISLER, D., and D. C. FERREE. 1984. Responses of plants to root pruning. Horticult. Rev. (6):155–188.

LEVITT, J. 1956. The hardiness of plants. Academic Press, Inc., New York.

PERRY, T. O. 1981. Trees roots—where they grow: implications and practical significance. New Horizons. Horticultural Research Institute, Washington, D.C.

SACHS, R. M., and W. P. HACKET. 1972. Chemical inhibition of plant height. HortScience 7(5):440–447.

WEISER, C. J. 1970. Cold resistance and acclimation in woody plants. HortScience 5(5):403–410.

————. 1970. Cold resistance and injury in woody plants. Science 169:1269–1278.

ZIMMERMAN, R. H. 1972. Juvenility and flowering in woody plants. HortScience 7(5): 447–455.

15 *Controlling Weeds, Insects, and Diseases*

Weeds, insects, and diseases are the three most noxious, negative modifiers of plant growth in nurseries. They are common to all nurseries and cause a significant loss in either quantity of production or in plant quality, which, in turn, can result in a significant economic loss to a nursery. The negative aspects of these and other pests can best be minimized by an integrated crop production program that is directed toward quality plant production, which is the overall objective of the nursery. The program should be oriented primarily toward preventing pest problems from developing in the nursery. When they do develop, the program should be oriented to rapid eradication of the pest to minimize damage to valuable plants.

Pest problems can best be prevented by following cultural practices designed to produce healthy, vigorous plants. Plants that are properly spaced, correctly pruned, fertilized, and watered are much less prone to pest problems than are plants that are exposed to undesirable environmental conditions. Improper irrigation management, especially overwatering in the propagation or container-production areas, predisposes plants to attacks by insects and to infection by disease organisms that are either spread by water or require warm, humid environments in which to develop.

WEED CONTROL

The goal of a weed control program is to provide optimum growth for nursery stock, while suppressing or eliminating weed competition for light, moisture, and nutrients. Weeds can restrict the growth of trees and shrubs. They also provide a habitat for rodents, and they act as host to many destructive insects and diseases. Effective weed control in nurseries requires timely and efficient use of biological, cultural, environmental, and chemical means. Since the development of selective herbicides in the late 1940s, many growers have depended solely on chemicals. This may be a mistake. Selective herbicides should be used with caution. Repeated use of one technique or chemical leads to development of tolerant weed growth or invasion and establishment of resistant weed species. Integration of several strategies can prevent these problems. Before starting a weed control program, analyze your situation and then determine the best course of action.

Analyze the Situation

How vulnerable is the nursery crop to injury from various control methods? Vulnerability is highest at the seedling stage for the crop and weeds. Therefore, at that stage, avoid any activity that would injure the nursery crop. On the other hand, follow practices that could destroy weeds at the time of seed germination or kill them in the seedling stage. It is important to know at which stages of growth your crop is vulnerable to various weed control measures. Some plants, such as yew and arborvitae, are very sensitive to stem injury when young. They will often die if the stem is injured by hoeing or cultivating. Young plants with green stems are very susceptible to stem injury from contact herbicides, but are not affected by herbicides if the bark is brown and well developed.

What type of nursery site do you have? Weed control measures in nurseries are influenced by the production method. Plants in a broadcast seedbed cannot be cultivated. Fumigation is the best way to rid the soil of weed seeds prior to sowing seeds of trees and shrubs. In the production of liners, where space is greater than in seedbeds but not as great as in production blocks, it is generally economically feasible to incorporate a pre-emergence herbicide prior to planting. However, on a relatively weed-free site, this process can be skipped and the plants cultivated, hand hoed, or treated with herbicide. In extensive plantings on wide spacing, the best weed control is to apply a pre-emergence herbicide to weed-free soil and cultivate, or a combination of the two (herbicide in the rows and cultivate between the rows). If weeds are present, apply a post-emergence herbicide. Another control method is to grow sod between the rows and apply an herbicide in the rows. The sod allows access to the crops during wet periods, returns organic matter to the soil, and provides erosion control. The sod should not be highly aggressive. Container production requires weed control both in the containers and in the container area. Weeds in containers can be minimized by using a weed-free growing medium and by fumigating or pasteurizing the medium prior to planting. Control weeds in the container area by setting the containers on a soil-free surface such as crushed stone or black plastic. Be sure to provide good drainage for this surface. If herbicides are applied by topical methods to container-grown plants, use granular formulations followed by irrigation to ensure effective weed control. It is necessary to control weeds in the areas surrounding nursery production sites. All too often these areas are neglected and weed seeds are blown into crop rows and containers.

What are your problem weeds? The third consideration includes identification of the weed species, its vulnerability to control measures, and the source of the weed problem. Too often, weed control measures, especially herbicides, result in little or no weed control or disaster to the nursery crop. It is necessary to know the weed species to be controlled and the best means of controlling it without damaging the crop. Annual weeds are easily controlled at or soon after germination. Therefore, you should start the control early; a delay of a few days can negate the control. Selective herbicides are very specific as to the weeds they will or will not kill; pre-emergence herbicides are of little value if applied as a post-emergence treatment. Cultivation is most effective when weed plants are small, and more difficult and often less effective on larger plants. Many perennial weeds, such as quackgrass and bermuda grass, are impossible to control by cultivation; in fact, they are propagated vegetatively and spread by cultivation. If you know the source of a weed problem, you can take measures to eliminate weeds from the source. Most weeds spread to the nursery site from nearby areas or through irrigation from ponds. By controlling them in these sites, you can avoid many weed problems. Some weeds spread within a nursery area by equipment contaminated with seeds. Other weeds can be introduced in soil, peatmoss, or plants from other sources. This problem, which is often overlooked, can become serious.

What are the conditions of your production environment? The fourth factor to consider is the effect of the environment—soil type, moisture, temperature, and wind—on a weed control program. Many granular herbicides are most effective if they are cultivated into the soil or water-sealed into the soil or medium immediately following application. Sandy soils require less active ingredient per unit area than clay or organic soils. Do not cultivate when the ground is wet. Seldom, if ever, apply herbicides when it is windy. Herbicide effectiveness is often reduced if the temperature is below 50°F or above 85°F. Liquid applications are best applied on a calm day when the temperature is between 65 and 75°F and when the humidity is moderate to high.

Biological, Cultural, Environmental, and Chemical Controls

Which controls will work best for you? The advantages and limitations of various weed control measures are the final consideration. Controls are biological, cultural, environmental, and chemical. Sometimes one control measure is adequate, while certain situations may require a combination of several controls to provide the best results.

Biological measures require the use of plants, people, or animals. Complementary grass aisle plantings between the rows can be advantageous, but if improperly managed, could directly compete with and inhibit the nursery crops. The integration of grass aisles and nursery plant rows can achieve effective weed control through competition and limited, selective application of herbicides. Hand weeding is very effective but is generally limited to small, intensive, or high-value plantings, since it is very costly. Geese are effective weed controllers, at least in nurseries, but they require proper management for optimum results and they are messy.

Cultural or mechanical weed control has been successful for centuries. Hoeing is effective but expensive and is generally limited to intensive nursery plantings. Mechanical means are used on extensive plantings but are also costly since they require power equipment and an operator. They can be cost effective if they are properly timed. Cultivation is best when weeds are small and the soil is not too wet. Mechanical methods should not be used on weed species that grow by rhizomes, such as quackgrass or bermuda grass, since sectioning the rhizome is a means of propagating and spreading the weed over wide areas. Mechanical cultivation can injure stems of trees and shrubs if the operator is careless in using the hoe or operating certain types of equipment.

Weeds can be controlled environmentally by manipulating light and temperature. A weed barrier such as sheets of black plastic placed over the soil surface restricts light and imposes a physical barrier to the germinating weed seedlings. High temperature obtained by controlled burning from various burning devices can be used to kill weeds and destroy weed seeds. It can be used effectively within and around the perimeter of nurseries, especially container-production nurseries. Pasteurization of soil and potting media can also effectively reduce weed problems. Soil or media heated to 160°F for about 30 minutes will destroy most weed seeds. Pasteurized media are used primarily in the production of container-grown plants.

If used properly, herbicides can effectively control weeds in nurseries. If improperly used (the wrong chemical, repeated use of one chemical, errors in calculation or application, improper timing, drift, and carelessness), herbicides can produce devastating and costly results. Always read the label and follow label instructions. Many herbicide disasters could have been avoided if label instructions had been followed. Remember, it is the manufacturer who warrants the product. If the material is used contrary to label instructions, the warranty is null and void. As the name implies, herbicides are plant killers (*herb* means "plant" and *cide* means "killer"). Used properly, they are an excellent tool. Used improperly, they can seriously injure or kill economic plants as well as weeds. Some herbicides, such as Paraquat, are toxic to animals and people, so they are available only for restricted use. In all cases, the objective of the weed control program will determine which chemical is best for effective, efficient control of weeds with minimum damage to the economic plants.

Although herbicides can be classified in many ways, three of the most practical are emergence, selectivity, and movement within the plant. Pre-emergence herbicides control weeds by destroying seedlings as they germinate. Most effective weed control with pre-emergence herbicides is obtained when the soil has been tilled and all weeds eliminated. Most pre-emergence chemicals will not kill seedlings or established weeds. Tilled soil allows for better herbicide penetration and distribution. When ½ in. of rainfall or irrigation follows within a few days after application of pre-emergence herbicides, most effective weed control is obtained. Application to moist soils is usually preferred to that of dry soils. Excessive moisture may reduce effectiveness of certain herbicides such as Treflan. Certain pre-emergence chemicals are affected by soil temperature. Products such as Casoron, Eptam, and Treflan must be soil incorporated at higher temperatures or volatilization can occur and effectiveness lost. Studies have shown that a considerable variation exists in the effectiveness of pre-emergence herbicides with different soil types. Casoron, for example, is more effective in heavy clay soils than in light sandy soils, while Treflan controls weeds more efficiently in light or sandy soils. Organic matter in soil or in container mixes reacts with and absorbs herbicides. In general, the more organic matter, the higher the herbicide rates required to control weeds. Furloe Chloro-IPC and Dacthal are reduced in effectiveness by cultivation following treatment. Soil treated with Casoron, Devrinol, Dual, Kerb, Princep, Ronstar, Surflan, and Treflan can be disturbed with shallow (1 to 1½ in.) cultivation without reducing weed control. Cultivating deeper than 2 in. will reduce the effectiveness of all the herbicides. Table 15–1 lists pre-emergence herbicides used in nursery operations. Post-emergence herbicides destroy weed growth after emergence. Post-emergence chemicals are used for general weed cleanup around buildings, waterways, fence rows, and so on. Used with extreme caution, these materials may be used in tree and shrub plantings. Avoid herbicide contact with foliage, trunks, or stems with green tissue of desired crops, as damage will result from each of these materials. Table 15–2 lists post-emergence herbicides used in nursery operations. Selective herbicides kill only selected species of plants, not others. Nonselective herbicides are used to kill all species. Translocated or systemic herbicides move within the plant. Some are translocated following foliar application, such as Round-up, while others are translocated following soil application, such as Princep. Nonsystemic or contact herbicides, such as Paraquat, kill on contact and do not translocate.

The effectiveness of a chemical weed control is only as successful as the person responsible for selection, calculation, calibration, and application of herbicides. All herbicides will control weeds as specified on the label; therefore, it is up to the grower to follow the proper conditions necessary to achieve the desired results. Acceptable weed control can be achieved in field-grown nursery crops throughout the year with two or three applications of the appropriate herbicides. A late fall or winter pre-emergence herbicide treatment should be followed by a late spring or early summer application following the initial cultivation. The combination of autumn and spring treatments usually results in the most effective weed control program. Depending on the herbicide applied in summer, more than one application may be needed. If cover crops are to be grown in autumn, use a short residual herbicide such as Dacthal, Lasso, or Dual rather than Princep combinations, which may inhibit seed germination. Supplemental post-emergence treatments may be necessary to control perennial weeds and those annuals not controlled with the pre-emergence herbicides. Table 15–3 gives suggested chemical weed control programs for nurseries.

A combination of Ronstar plus Devrinol may be used safely on many types of woody plants in containers. With widely spaced larger containers or small numbers

TABLE 15-1   **Pre-emergence Herbicides Used in Nursery Operations**

Product	Uses, Cautions, and Limitations[a]
Casoron (Dichlobenil)	Controls most annual and perennial grasses and broad-leaved weeds; good control of bindweed, thistle, and quackgrass; soil-incorporate in spring or fall; avoid on sensitive species: fir, hemlock, spruce (Thompson-Hayward)
Dacthal (DCPA)	Can be used in plantings of most woody perennials, including ground cover plants; provides weed control for about 6–8 weeks; does not control ragweed, smartweed, velvet leaf, and wild mustard (S.D.S. Bio Tech Corp)
Devrinol (Napropamide)	Controls annual grasses and broad-leaved weeds, including chickweed and groundsel; soil-incorporate or water seal for best results (Stauffer)
Dual 8E (Metolachlor)	Selective pre-emergence herbicide that controls a number of broad-leaved weeds; can be used as preplant treatment; chemical must be soil-incorporated for best results (Ciba-Geigy)
Enide 90W (Diphenamid)	Selective pre-emergence herbicide that controls most annual grasses and many broad-leaved weeds; soil-incorporate by water in cultivation for best results (Upjohn)
Furloe Chloro-IPC (Chlorpropham)	Control chickweed and other winter annual weeds; apply when economic plants are dormant (PPG Industries)
Kerb (Pronamide)	Controls perennial grasses and winter weeds, including chickweed; best applied in the fall; *do not* use on organic soils, boxwood, and myrtle or near turfgrass (Rohm & Haas)
Goal 2E (Oxyfluorfen)	Selective pre- and post-emergence herbicide that gives a wide spectrum control of broad-leaved weeds and grasses; cleared for use on conifer seedbeds prior to seed germination (Rohm & Haas)
Ornamental Herbicide 2	Granular herbicide; combination of oxyfluorfen and pendimethalin which gives broad-spectrum control of many weeds, both container and field-grown; do not use in closed structures (polyhouses, etc.) (Scott)
Lasso (Alchlor)	Controls annual grasses and a number of broad-leaved weeds, including purslane; wash foliage of economic crops immediately following topical application to avoid injury (Monsanto)
Princep (Simazine)	Broad-spectrum weed control in nurseries; euonymus and lilac are sensitive; *not* effective against bindweed; controls oxalis (Ciba-Geigy)
Surflan (Oryzalin)	Good control of grasses, chickweed, lambsquarters, pigweed, and purslane; does not require soil incorporation but water is necessary to trigger herbicide activity (Elanco)
Ronstar (Oxadiazon)	Broad-spectrum weed control in a wide range of trees, shrubs, and ground covers in the field or in containers; for best results, seal-in with water following application (Rhône-Poulene)
Treflan (Trifluralin)	Best used as a pre-plant treatment, incorporate into the soil; one of the safest materials for use in nursery (Elanco)

[a]Company names in parentheses.

Source: Adapted from Davidson (1984).

TABLE 15-2 Post-emergence Herbicides Used in Nursery Operations[a]

Product	Uses, Cautions, and Limitations[b]
Amitrol (Amitrol-T)	An excellent translocated herbicide that inhibits chlorophyll formation; kills most perennial weeds, including poison ivy (Union Carbide)
Amizine	Combination of amitrol and simazine used to gain both post-emergence and pre-emergence weed control (Union Carbide)
Dalapon (Dowpon)	Translocated herbicide effective in control of quackgrass, cattails, and weeds in noncrop areas; apply to actively growing weeds; avoid applying just prior (6–8 hr) to irrigation or predicted rain, since the product needs time to be absorbed by the leaves of the weeds (Dow Chemical Co.)
Glyphosate (Roundup)	Translocated herbicide useful in woody perennials; direct spray to weed foliage, but avoid contact with stems of green or thin-barked economic plants; apply proper concentration to avoid rapid killing of weed stem, since transport to the roots is via phloem (bark) tissue; leaves no soil residue; avoid multiple applications to the same crop to avoid possible injury; accumulation in economic plants can cause chlorosis, dieback, witches-broom, and death (Monsanto)
Poast (Sethoxydim)	Selective, broad-spectrum herbicide for control of annual and perennial grasses in a number of deciduous and evergreen nursery-grown species; must be supplemented with an oil concentrate; follow label instructions for concentrations, time, and method of applications and species (BASF Wyandotte)
Paraquat (restricted use material)	Contact (nontranslocated) herbicide; good for killing young, actively growing weeds; mature weeds are less likely to be killed since the chemical is not translocated; handle with caution; avoid contact with skin, eyes, or clothing; avoid inhaling spray drift (Chevron)

[a]These materials must be used with considerable caution around valuable plant materials. Avoid chemical contact with green tissue, including the trunk of young trees and shrubs, basal shoots, and small branchlets on the trunk, since these are absorption sites for translocated herbicides.
[b]Company names in parentheses.
Source: Adapted from Davidson (1984).

of containers a broadcast treatment wastes a lot of herbicide that falls between the containers. One way to prevent this waste is to dilute the granular herbicides with sand and spread a measured amount evenly around the surface of each container. The granules can be thoroughly mixed with sand in a cement mixer in 5-gal batches, for example, and then used as a pre-emergence treatment that will prevent most weed growth for 10 to 12 weeks.

Application Equipment

Many types of sprayers are available for applying herbicides. You do not need expensive, high-gallonage, high-pressure spray equipment. A weed-control sprayer should have the following features:

TABLE 15-3   Suggested Chemical Weed Control Programs for Nurseries

A. Field Production

Weeds	Suggested Control
Summer annual weeds: barnyard grass, crabgrass, fall panicum, foxtails, lambsquarters, pigweed, and purslane.	*Pre-emergence herbicides:* Dacthal, Enide, Lasso, Princep, Ronstar, and Surflan
Perennial weeds: bindweed, dandelion, dock, quackgrass, mugwort, and nutsedge	*Fall application:* Casoron or Kerb
Winter annual weeds: annual bluegrass, chickweed, and pennycress	*Directed spray:* Roundup, Amitrol *Herbicides:* Betasan, Casoron, Chloro-IPC (Furloe), Devrinol, or Princep

B. Container Production

Preplant
   Pasteurization: 160–180°F for 30 minutes
   Fumigation: methyl bromide
   Herbicide: Treflan
Postplant
   Spring and summer: Dacthal, Devrinol, Enide, Lasso II, Princep, or Ronstar
   Fall: Chloro-IPC, Devrinol, and Princep
Slow-release formulations: Herbicides in granular or tablet formulation are easier to apply to container-grown nursery stock than are liquid formulations. For best results, use pre-emergence herbicides applied to a weed-free container medium and irrigate immediately following application.

Source: Adapted from Davidson (1984).

1. It should be a low-pressure pump that is easily replaced, not subject to damage by wettable powders, and has a minimum capacity of 9 gal/minute.

2. It should have solution agitation (stirring) with either mechanical or a bypass from the pump. If a power-takeoff sprayer does not provide agitation, add a bypass to a galvanized tee between the pump and pressure gauge. To increase agitation in the tank, place an agitator nozzle on the end of the overflow hose. In this case, a separate valve on the bypass line will regulate pressure. If the pump does not have enough capacity for agitation under specific spraying conditions, provide it by using both the next-lower tractor gear and nozzle tips with a smaller orifice.

3. Wettable powders will not go through the 100-mesh screens which are sometimes provided, so use 50-mesh screens for suction line and nozzles.

4. The spray boom should have nozzles adjustable for distance between nozzles on the boom and for height above the ground. This is especially important for band spraying.

5. The pressure gauge should measure pressure accurately up to 100 psi.

6. The best nozzle size for general use is equivalent to an 8004 Teejet. For most work, a wide-angle (73 or 80°), flat fan nozzle is best because the boom can be held close to the ground to reduce drift. This is most important when it is windy.

One of the most important factors in effective weed spraying is accurate calibration in determining the amount of spray material applied per acre. A range of 20 to 60 gal/acre, at a pressure of 20 to 60 psi is satisfactory. Adjust the boom height so that the spray overlaps about a third of the spray pattern. For overall spraying, using 80° nozzles, this places the nozzles about 18 to 20 in. apart on the boom and 18 to 20 in. from the spray surface. The following is a good way to calibrate a sprayer:

1. First check equipment for proper mounting and functioning of pump and nozzles.
2. Replace worn or defective equipment.
3. Use only bristle brushes and wooden matchsticks or toothpicks to clean out plugged nozzles.
4. Check the discharge of each nozzle for uniform pattern and quantity of discharge.
5. Thoroughly rinse and test equipment prior to calibrating the sprayer.
6. Fill the spray tank with water only.
7. Spray a measured area, in a field if possible, at a fixed tractor speed and pressure gauge setting. Be sure to allow for partial coverage if bands are used.
8. Measure the amount of water needed to refill the tank. Divide this amount by the fraction of an acre sprayed to get the gallons applied per acre.
9. Mix the amount of chemical desired per acre with water to give this much spray material. For example: if 10 gal were applied on ¼ acre, the volume of spray material applied would be 40 gal/acre. If you change the tractor speed or gear, pressure setting, nozzle size, or number of nozzles, the amount of liquid applied per acre will be different, and recalibration will be necessary.

Band Application in Row Crops

Since weeds in the crop row are usually the hardest to control, it may cost only 50% as much to spray herbicides in a band over the row rather than to cover the whole area. For band applications, adjust for the area actually sprayed, not for the total acres in the field. For example, suppose that the recommendation for a chemical is 4 lb/acre, and 12-in. strips are sprayed over 36-in. rows. Only one-third of the ground area will be covered with spray material, so only 1⅓ lb of chemical (one-third of 4 lb) will be required per acre. Four pounds of chemical will then cover 3 acres of the crop. To adjust the sprayer for band application, place the boom so that there is one nozzle over each row, and plug the nozzles between rows. This is not always easy with standard booms, but you can buy adjustable booms, adapters, or use an offset 45° nozzle for use with taller plant materials.

Cleaning Herbicide Sprayers

Keep weed control sprayers clean, especially if you use them to spray more than one crop or to apply fungicides and insecticides. Many nurseries will label a sprayer "for herbicide use only" to prevent plant injury from any herbicide residue. Do not use a sprayer to apply insecticides or fungicides if the sprayer has contained a 2,4-D type of herbicide.

When cleaning, thoroughly rinse the entire sprayer with water, inside and out, including boom, hoses, and nozzles, both before and after cleaning. Partially fill the sprayer with water before you add the cleaning agent. Keep the pump running so that the cleaning solution will circulate throughout the sprayer. Do not leave corrosive cleaning agents in the tank or spray system more than 2 hours. When you are using only pre-emergence sprays, a good rinsing with water is enough. For other spraying purposes, remove weed killers from sprayers by adding 1 gal of household ammonia or 5 lb of sal soda to 100 gal of water. Allow this solution to stand in the sprayer for at least 2 hours. Drain it out through the boom and nozzles, and rinse the sprayer with water. Do not let spray solutions stand in the tank overnight. Do not allow solutions to run into streams or other water sources.

Granular Spreaders

Granular herbicides are applied with some form of spreader, which must be calibrated for accurate application of herbicides. Some spreaders are adjustable for rate of delivery, others are not; it is best to utilize adjustable spreaders. After setting the delivery mode, fill the bin with a known weight of the herbicide and apply the material to a measured area, for example, 440 ft^2 (one-hundredth of an acre). Reweigh the remaining herbicide; the difference in weight times 100 will equal the rate being applied per acre. Adjust the delivery mode as needed to increase or decrease the rate, and recalibrate. Repeat as necessary until the proper rate of application is attained. For example, you wish to apply Devrinol 2G at a rate of 5 lb/1000 ft^2 (220 lb/acre) to a group of 1-gal container-grown junipers that occupy an area of 20,000 ft^2. You need to apply 100 lb of the product to the area. If the bin of spreader has a capacity of 25 lb, you will need to apply that amount to 5000 ft^2 or 2½ lb to a 500-ft^2 test application area. If the spreader is not delivering close to this rate, you will have to adjust the delivery mode.

INSECT CONTROL

Control of pests in the nursery is unique in the business of agriculture. Because the product sold is a living plant (usually with accompanying soil), the chances of spreading parasites with plants are greater. Consequently, it becomes necessary for the nursery grower to keep nursery crops free of noxious insects, diseases, and weeds as much as possible. Many pest problems in the landscape encountered by homeowners and professional landscape managers are directly related to pests that accompanied nursery stock from a commercial nursery.

Another unique aspect of pest control in the nursery industry is the aid provided by the state department of agriculture in the identification of pests during the annual nursery inspection. Department of agriculture inspectors often diagnose pests and suggest control measures. The grower is informed of the problem and its solution so that control measures can be taken immediately. Should the grower not comply with suitable control measures, the inspector, as a last resort, can stop sales of the infested nursery stock (see Chapter 6).

Many growers recognize the gravity of pests infesting nursery stock and often apply insecticides and acaricides on a preventative schedule. Usually, a mixture of insecticide/acaricide is applied on a 2-week or monthly basis during the growing season. Thus the nursery grower is relatively assured of complete insect and mite control. Some growers depend on their own inspection of their nursery stock. This method saves time and money over the preventative method, but it is more risky if plants are not inspected on a regular schedule. Pest problems may escape notice until economic damage has occurred and the stock must be discarded or held until new foliage hides pest damage.

Nursery growers are constantly searching for ways to cut costs. Many grow varieties that are hardy and relatively pest free. This may seem like an easy way out, but the benefits for the consumer are more than imaginary. If the grower must constantly struggle to control a pest such as southern red mites on a variety such as Heller holly, think what a problem that plant will be in the landscape for a homeowner or landscape manager. Unless they are given constant scrutiny for mites, chances are that these plants will always have a chlorotic appearance and uneven growth. If the nursery grower grows varieties that the operation can manage with ease, the consumer will start with a vigorous plant and will probably encounter few problems with its care.

When pest problems are encountered, the grower may call the county extension agent or the nursery plant inspector for control information. A grower may also consult with state extension service recommendations, which give information on insect, mite, and disease control; plant growth regulations; and weed control. Suggestions for pest control are also found in nursery association publications, which are available to members. Furthermore, nursery trade journals occasionally carry articles on pest control in the commercial nursery.

An often-overlooked area in planning and operation of a nursery is development of an information center. This area should contain a library of standard reference books and other publications on nursery management, plant materials, fertilizers, equipment, and other subjects related to ornamental plants and nursery operations. A file should be developed of cooperative extension service bulletins that give information concerning nursery management in your growing area. Many nurseries are using computers for storage of up-to-date information on pest control chemicals which have EPA approval and rates to be used as well as for cultural, operational, and daily business uses. A catalog and operational files should be kept of the equipment and materials used in the operation of a nursery. This will facilitate daily operations, servicing, and parts replacement of equipment as well as increase ease of obtaining frequently used materials such as pesticides, herbicides, fertilizers, containers, and potting media ingredients.

Types of Insecticides

Information concerning the type of pest, its feeding habits, and its life cycle remains essential in determining the appropriate insecticide to use as well as the rate and method of application that will achieve satisfactory control. Since not all insects and mites are a threat to plants, a suspected pest will occasionally be recognized as a harmless or even a beneficial species. Consequently, the nursery information center should be geared to proper pest identification and responsible control measures.

Insect feeding habits determine, to some extent, the type of chemical control to be used. Pesticides can be classified as stomach poisons, contact residuals, or fumigants; only the first two groups will be discussed. Fumigants must be used in enclosed areas and have very little application to the typical commercial nursery conditions.

Chewing insects, such as caterpillars, beetles, and grasshoppers, are the targets of stomach poisons. A diverse array of organic and inorganic chemicals make up this group. Stomach poisons must be ingested to kill pests. Since piercing-sucking pests (aphids, mites, leafhoppers, etc.) feed below leaf surfaces, they often avoid contact with stomach poisons. However, contact-residual chemicals, such as malathion, kill a wider range of pests. Such chemicals poison insects or mites that crawl on treated surfaces, eat treated leaves, or are sprayed directly.

The length of time a pesticide lasts depends to some extent on the chemical group to which it belongs. Materials like the plant-derived pesticide pyrethrin may last less than 1 hour, although similar synthetic pesticides are now being made that linger considerably longer. In general, an insecticide classified as a chlorinated hydrocarbon is long lasting. A good example is chlordane, which is applied to the soil for termite control. Such a treatment may be effective for several decades. The majority of pesticides recommended for insect and mite control on trees and shrubs belong to the related organophosphate and carbamate groups. Less persistent than chlorinated hydrocarbons, most organophosphates and carbamates do not remain effective for more than 1–4 weeks. Many of the organophosphates and carbamates are systemic and may give 6 or more weeks of residual activity in treated plants.

Information on toxicity to man, formulations, chemical groups, and mode of action for most insecticides labeled for insect control on nursery crops is given in Table 15–4. This listing is not to be used as recommendations for control but as an aid to better understand the use and classification of pesticides. All pesticides must be used in accordance with the directions for use on the label. *When treating a specific plant or pest, refer to the label!* The pesticide trade names are listed in the first column in alphabetical order, with the common name listed in parentheses. In the second column, the LD-50 listed refers to the acute oral LD-50 of a rat. LD-50 indicates the amount of toxicant necessary to effect a 50% kill of the rats being treated. It is expressed in weight of the chemical per unit of body weight (mg/kg). The lower the LD-50, the more poisonous the chemical. The LD-50 is based on the pure active ingredient and not on the various formulations that contain that ingredient. The third column indicates the formulations available for use. Certain formula-

TABLE 15-4 Some Pesticides Labeled for Use on Insects and Related Pests of Shrubs

Pesticide	LD_{50} of Pure Active Ingredient	Formulations[a]	Classification	Mode of Action	Targets and Remarks
Acaraben (chlorobenzilate)	960	25% WP, 45.5% EC	Chlorinated hydrocarbon	Contact	Mites
Azodrin (monocrotophos)	8–23	55% EC	Organophosphate	Contact, systemic	Aphids, bugs, caterpillars, leafminers, mites, leafhoppers, sawflies, thrips
Cygon, De-Fend, Rebelate (dimethoate)	320–380	23.4% EC	Organophosphate	Systemic	Aphids, lace bugs, thrips; will cause defoliation or deformation of Chinese hollies (*Ilex cornuta*); may damage 'President Clay' and 'Modesty' azaleas
(diazinon)	300–400	50% WP, 48% EC, 14.3% G	Organophosphate	Contact	Aphids, caterpillars, leafminers, thrips, whiteflies; may be effective as a soil drench to control certain pests
Dibrom (naled)	430	58% EC	Chlorinated hydrocarbon	Contact	Spider mites
Dimecron (phosphamidon)	20–22.4	75.5% EC	Organophosphate	Contact, systemic	Eastern tent caterpillars, webworms, mites, scales on deciduous fruit crops
Dipel, Biotrol (*Bacillus thuringiensis*)	>4000	1.5–3.2% WP	Bacterial	Stomach	Caterpillars
Di-Syston (disulfoton)	2.6–12.5	15% G	Organophosphate	Systemic	Lace bugs, leafhoppers, scales, thrips, whiteflies; control may persist for 6 to 8 weeks from treatment

Name		Formulation	Chemical class	Action	Pests controlled
Dithione (sulfotepp)	7–10	Fumigant	Organophosphate	Contact	Aphids, mites, thrips, whiteflies
Dursban (chlorpyrifos)	97–276	15% G, 41.2% EC	Organophosphate	Systemic	Borers, caterpillars, leafhoppers, mealybugs, mites, scales, spittlebugs, thrips, whiteflies
Dylox, Proxol (trichlorfon)	450–630	41.2% EC, 80% WP	Organophosphate	Contact	Bugs, caterpillars, leafminers, webworms
NIA 1240, Vegfru-Rosmite (ethion)	280	25% WP, 5% D, 46% EC + 82% EC, 5% G	Organophosphate	Contact	Scales, lace bugs, mites
Guthion (azinphos-methyl)	13–16.4	50% WP, 22% EC	Organophosphate	Systemic	Aphids, lace bugs, leafhoppers, scales, thrips
Isotox (mixture)	88–125	EC (mixture)	Carbamate, chlorinated hydrocarbon, organophosphate	Systemic	Isotox is usually a mixture of Kelthane, Sevin, and Metasystox R, although the mixture may vary
Karathane (dinocap)	980	25% WP, 48% EC	Nitro-phenoxy	Contact	Mites; will also control powdery mildew
Kelthane (dicofol)	809	35% WP, 18.6% EC	Chlorinated hydrocarbon	Contact	Mites
(lindane)	18–125	20% EC	Chlorinated hydrocarbon	Contact	Bark beetles, borers
(malathion)	1375	57% EC	Organophosphate	Contact	Aphids, lace bugs, mealybugs, scales, thrips
Marlate (methoxychlor)	6000	24.8% EC	Chlorinated hydrocarbon	Contact	Bark beetles, caterpillars, leafhoppers; long residual action
Metasystox R (oxydemeton-methyl)	56–180	25% EC	Organophosphate	Contact, systemic	Aphids, lace bugs, leafhoppers, mites, thrips

(continued)

TABLE 15-4 *(continued)*

Pesticide	LD$_{50}$ of Pure Active Ingredient	Formulations[a]	Classification	Mode of Action	Targets and Remarks
Morestan (oxythioquinox)	2500–3000	25% WP	Miscellaneous quinoxaline	Contact	Mites; used as a prebloom spray on most deciduous fruits and in both prebloom and postbloom sprays on apples and pears
Omite (propargite)	2200	70% EC, 30% WP, 4% D	Phenoxysulfite	Systemic	Mites; widely used on fruit trees; does not affect bees and is less harmful than many other acaricides to predatory mites; has residual killing action
Orthene (acephate)	945	15.6% EC, 75% WP	Organophosphate	Contact, systemic	Aphids, caterpillars, lace bugs, leafhoppers, thrips, webworms; may be phytotoxic to young tender growth; moderate persistence with residual systemic activity of approximately 10–15 days
Pentac (dienochlor)	3160	50% WP	Chlorinated hydrocarbon	Contact	Mites; has long residual action, although slow in action initially; most effective during cold weather
Plictran (cyhexatin)	540	50% WP	Metallo-organic (tin base)	Systemic	Mites
Sevin (carbaryl)	500	50% WP	Carbamate	Stomach, contact	Chewing pests, thrips
Summer Oil (petroleum oils)	>4000	95% EC	Petroleum	Contact	Aphids, lace bugs, scales, mites

Name		Formulation	Chemical class	Mode of action	Pests/remarks
Systox (demeton)	2.5–12.0	25% EC, 66% EC	Organophosphate	Systemic	Aphids, lace bugs, mealybugs, mites, whiteflies; rapidly penetrates plant tissues and is translocated in the plant and detoxicated
Tedion (tetradifon)	14,700	Fumigant, 25% WP	Sulfonate	Contact	Effective in killing larval stages of mites
Temik (aldicarb)	0.93	10% G	Carbamate	Systemic	Aphids; do not use with lime or other highly alkaline materials; Temik should not be mixed with other pesticides or fertilizers prior to use
Thiodan (endosulfan)	30–110	24.2% EC, 50% WP	Chlorinated hydrocarbon	Contact	Aphids, borers, mites, weevils, whiteflies
(toxaphene)	69	20% D	Chlorinated hydrocarbon	Contact	Bagworms, fall armyworms, lace bugs, leafhoppers, earwigs
Trithion (carbophenothion)	32.2	25% WP, 45% EC	Organophosphate	Contact, systemic	Aphids, mealybugs, mites, bagworms, potato leafhoppers, scales; long residual action
Vapona, DDVP (dichlorvos)	56–80	23% EC, smoke generator	Organophosphate	Contact, stomach, fumigant	Aphids, mites, whiteflies
Vendex (fenbutatin-oxide)	2000	50% WP	Metallo-organic (tin base)	Contact	Mites
Vydate L (oxamyl)	5.4	24% EC	Carbamate	Systemic	Flea beetles, mites, nematodes
Zectran (mexacarbate)	19	25% WP	Carbamate	Contact	Aphids, caterpillars, mites, scales; product discontinued by manufacturer

[a]EC, Emulsifiable concentrate; WP, wettable powder; D, dust; G, granular.

Source: Adapted from Baker (1984).

tions are safer than others or more convenient to use, and these factors should be considered when selecting one of these products. The fourth column refers to the basic chemical structure of the active ingredient. If a certain pesticide is not giving effective control, a pesticide in a different class may give better results. Many growers continue using the same class of pesticide until it no longer seems effective, and then switch to a different class. Others alternate classes with each application. Either method is acceptable as long as applications are thorough. The method used is usually a matter of the grower's preference. The mode of action in the next column refers to how a pesticide actually kills a pest. Contact insecticides require contact with the insect to be effective. Direct spray on the pest or on the area frequented by the pest is necessary for the pesticide to be effective. Systemic pesticides are absorbed by the plants through the roots and leaf tissue and then ingested by the pest during feeding. Most systemic insecticides that are applied as sprays are also contact pesticides. Granular formulations such as Di-Syston are systemics designed to be applied to the soil surface but are not contact insecticides. Pertinent information about the pesticide is listed in the last column.

Factors Affecting Results of Sprays

A grower may take the time and trouble to spray plants, only to be disappointed with the results. Although the chemical is usually blamed, this conclusion is rarely well founded. As a matter of fact, errors in pesticide application, such as improper storage, improper timing, and wrong concentration, most often account for apparent pesticide failure. The best and most expensive insecticide will produce poor results unless it applied thoroughly and at the proper time. To be most effective, the pesticide must be applied when pests are present and vulnerable, and at the proper rate in sufficient gallonage to permit thorough coverages of upper and lower surfaces of leaves and branches. However, even a well-timed and thorough application is likely to be a failure if the correct pesticide is not used. Since few insecticides control all insects and mites, carefully check the label to make sure the chemical in hand is registered to control the problem pest.

Environmental conditions also affect the efficacy of a pesticide application. At temperatures below 50°F or above 95°F, insecticides may lose some of their activity. Therefore, applications other than dormant oils are usually not recommended in winter. Warm weather applications are best made in early morning or late evening when the wind is still and the temperature cool.

Nursery crops may be reinfested by a resurgence of the original pest population or by other flying insects. Even if a large percentage of pests in an infestation is killed, those remaining may rebuild the population to damaging levels. Such an occurrence is not unusual, since most insecticides applied to nursery crops last only 1 to 7 days. Therefore, recommendations often emphasize repeated applications at specific intervals to eliminate the pests.

Resistance is a general term which, in the broad sense, means insects that were previously killed by an insecticide have produced offspring that are no longer killed by it. To illustrate, let us suppose that an insecticide is applied and it kills 95% of the insects in a population, but there are 5% of the insects which received the same dosage but survived the treatment. This 5% is considered resistant to the insecticide. They live to produce another generation, and this generation, having had resistant parents, passes on to its offspring the resistance factors. Most likely there will be a greater number of new individuals carrying resistance to the insecticide compared to the first-treated population. As repeated insecticide applications are made and more generations produced, it is only a matter of time before the majority of the insects in question will survive the insecticidal application. A possible explanation is that the insecticide has acted as a selecting agent, killing those members of the population which are susceptible to the chemical and leaving those which are resistant. Survivors breed and produce subsequent resistant generations. Resistance develops fastest in insects which have high rates of reproduction.

Last of all, improper pesticide storage is a possible contributor to pesticide inefficacy. Insecticides and miticides tend to degrade over a period of time once they have been opened. This problem may be common for the grower who purchases more pesticide than can be used in a single year or season. Moisture, air, light, and temperature extremes all adversely affect stored chemicals. Generally, pesticides should be stored in a dry, dark place where the temperature never falls below freezing or exceeds 100°F.

DISEASE PREVENTION, MONITORING, AND CONTROL

A nursery grower should use an ''umbrella''-type concept that gathers all existing information on potential or existing disease problems to organize a coordinated effort against pathogens in all phases of the nursery operation. Usually, this concept includes the following three courses of action: prevention activities that occur prior to disease incidence; monitoring early detection of diseases during the plant production phase; and control activities selected to reduce disease damage. Since most nurseries have distinct areas for stock plants, propagation, and production, the practices of prevention, monitoring, and control will be discussed for each area.

Disease Prevention

Stock plant area. Land for stock plant establishment should be cleared. All roots of hardwood species, especially native oaks, should be removed. Residual root debris in soil often serve as a food source for the shoestring and mushroom root rot fungi. If soilborne diseases have been a problem in the past, such as bacterial crown gall and root knot nematode injury, apply a broad-spectrum, preplant soil fumigant or nematicide. Field-grown stock blocks must allow adequate spacing between plants. This spacing will allow rapid drying of foliage, impede the spread of pathogens and other pests among plants, and facilitate better spray coverage of pesticides. Application of irrigation water should be so timed to consider the amount of natural rainfall. This will avoid saturated soils or droughty conditions that can stress root systems. Plant stress is one predisposing factor to root diseases. For woody ornamental species with persistent foliar disease problems, irrigation should occur between midmorning to early afternoon; always avoid wetting foliage prior to night hours. Daytime watering has been shown to aid in reducing foliar disease severity for certain species.

Certain safeguards must be taken to assure that those stock plants from which cuttings are taken remain healthy. Isolate all new stock plants to determine their health status prior to introduction into the existing nursery. Stock plants should be isolated from all possible sources of infection. Weedy and known disease areas should be avoided. Establish an independence between the production and merchandising part of the nursery and the maintenance of the stock blocks of plants. Stock blocks have been effective because of the ease and the low cost necessary to maintain such a small area. Practice regular spray schedules to control foliage, stem, or flower diseases. Drenching with soil fungicides is added insurance. Check with your state Cooperative Extension Service for specific chemical recommendations in your area.

Propagation area. Propagation cycles of a particular species should be timed to maximize the most rapid rooting for that species (additional information on plant propagation may be consulted in texts listed in Appendix A). This would limit exposure of cuttings to potential cutting or root-rotting organisms. Water sources should always be checked for contamination by root-rotting fungi. This should be the case when a root-rot problem has been a persistent problem in a particular area for several years. Shallow water systems, such as ponds, rivers, creeks, canals, or shallow wells, should not be used for irrigation in propagation. In coastal areas where saltwater intrusion is a problem, growers should not utilize a water source that is high or variable in soluble salts for propagation. High salts can stress root systems, thereby predisposing cuttings or young liners to root disease.

Success in propagation is often realized by observing reasonable sanitary procedures when collecting cuttings. Collect cuttings from tops of healthy plants. Top cuttings are usually free of soilborne pathogens. Plants grown on aboveground level supports or trellises are generally free of soil pathogens. Avoid taking cuttings from plants at or near the soil level. Never use root divisions unless absolutely necessary. It is better to break rather than cut cuttings from stock plants. If knives or pruning shears are used to collect cuttings, have each worker use two separate pairs—one left soaking in disinfectant while the other is being used. A household bleach (e.g., Clorox) solution (1 part bleach to 9 parts water) or 70% alcohol is effective. Bleach solutions should be changed every 30 minutes since the disinfecting qualities diminish rapidly. Keep in mind that the bleach solution will cause rusting of ferrous metals. Therefore, thoroughly clean cutting blades twice daily. Frequent sharpening is also a must. Place cuttings on chemically disinfected surfaces of benches, flats, and baskets. A chlorine bleach solution is a good surface disinfectant. Mix up new solutions approximately every 30 minutes. Occasional use of copper naphthenate (2%)

will disinfect wooden surfaces. Some growers spread unused newspaper or wrapping paper on disinfected work surfaces for added insurances. Never place cuttings on the ground. Never dip cuttings in water unless the water is pathogen free. This is a disadvantage of the liquid rooting hormone formulations. Some growers dip or soak cuttings in a fungicide suspension prior to sticking. Change the solution as often as is economically possible to maintain disinfecting concentrations.

Flats should be disinfected either after propagation or before reuse. Thoroughly remove rooting media adhering to the surfaces of flats or other containers with a brush before placing in a disinfectant (chlorine bleach or 2% copper naphthenate). Galvanized metal trays are preferred over wood because they are easier to clean and disinfect.

Never reuse propagating media. Media should be loose, porous, and well aerated. If propagation mixes contain soil, or if ground beds are used, pretreat before use with methyl bromide or heat. Media must be stored so that they do not become contaminated with disease-causing organisms. Propagation media should be mixed on a clean concrete slab so that runoff water, such as rain or irrigation, will not introduce pathogens. Remember that a clean medium can become contaminated if handled carelessly or subject to foot traffic.

Propagation areas should be kept clean. All benches must be free of infested media, leaves, and other refuse. Use a household bleach or commercial disinfectant on all surfaces. Use wooden benches treated with copper napthenate. A waiting period is necessary after treatment. Benches treated with most other disinfectants do not require a waiting period before use. All infested plant debris should be removed from the entire propagation area. Although this is sometimes tedious, it is very effective in reducing disease problems. Some growers provide their workers with carpenter aprons in which to place this debris during daily activities, and this discourages dropping the plant debris on the ground. A covered garbage can should be placed at the end of each greenhouse for plant debris. Cans without lids have little value in a sanitation program. Apply regular fungicide spray schedules to aid in the control of diseases that occur above ground. As added insurance against contamination, root media may be drenched immediately before or after sticking and at 4-week intervals with a fungicide combination developed to control the water molds, such as *Rhizoctonia* spp. and other fungi. Avoid unnecessary handling of clean media in the propagating containers or beds. Avoid dipping hands into media while conversing or checking moisture content. Use low water pressure when irrigating to avoid splashing. Prohibit anyone from walking over treated areas. Hose nozzles should be hung on conveniently located hooks, not thrown carelessly on the ground. Workers' hands should be washed after working with raw contaminated media, soil, or unclean plants to avoid introduction of pathogens. Space cuttings properly when sticking. Poor air circulation contributes to an environment that favors diseases caused by *Rhizoctonia* spp. Avoid excessive overhead irrigation. Growers should regulate their misting schedule to allow no mist on plants 2 hours before sunset. On rainy, humid days, misting is terminated earlier in the day. Wet foliage and high moisture regimes in rooting mixes provide a favorable environment for certain serious diseases. Remove any cuttings from containers or even whole flats of cuttings from the propagation area that exhibit disease symptoms; then treat the propagation area with a fungicide or disinfectant. Have a pathologist diagnose the problem so that appropriate action can be taken.

Production area.   Woody species that are commonly affected by certain diseases can be grouped in adjacent areas within the nursery. This will allow for greater ease in scouting and more rapid detection of diseases. Better pesticide control of diseases is usually the result. Examples of pathogens attacking several crops include *Entomosporium* leaf spots, *Cylindrocladium* aerial blights, and powdery mildews. Consider blocking disease-prone plants together for day watering. Mid-morning to early afternoon irrigation will minimize the actual hours the foliage remains wet. This practice reduces the potential for foliar diseases. Restrict nursery beds or block sizes to allow for more efficient pesticide application with existing spray equipment. Block sizes should be based on the spread of the mature plants, not newly planted liners. Spacing between plants on beds allows for better spray penetration of plants. This is not practical for 3- and 4-gal containers.

The basic concepts described previously in the propagation program are applicable in liner production. Liners should be grown above ground level to prevent contamination by soilborne pathogens. Special attention should be given to irrigation frequencies and splashing. Keep hose nozzles off the ground and clean and disinfect benches prior to use. If you must purchase liners, it is important that you obtain high-quality, disease-free plants. Many growers in the past have purchased diseased liners, and unfortunately, this is a losing proposition because the disease probably cannot be cured. In addition, the diseased liners introduce pathogens into the nursery.

When developing a sanitation program for plants after potting, you should consider the following suggestions. In the preparation of a growing mix, use a cement slab of the proper elevation to prevent contamination by surface water runoff from surrounding areas. Mixing on the ground often leads to plant failure because of contamination by pathogens, insects, and weeds. Equipment should be assigned to this area. Ideally, it should not be moved off the slab. Avoid unnecessary foot traffic on the area. Consideration of slab size should also be made, because many slabs are too small. Determine components of the medium to be used: This determines drainage, aeration, and water-holding capacities. These factors influence root growth (good or bad). Too much or too little of the foregoing media characteristics can provide those necessary environmental conditions within the mix for disease development. A well-aerated and well-drained mix is the most ideal. Plant no deeper in containers than the liners originally grew. You should store containers and media on a clean, nonsoil surface that is not subject to splashing water or runoff water. A large concrete pad is excellent for media preparation and storage. It is very important to prevent introduction of pathogens during storage and handling.

All sanitation program efforts made previously are wasted if plants are placed directly on the ground. Contaminated soil is often splashed into containers, and this often leads to disease development. Growers should place containers on black plastic sheeting; prevent low spots by constructing beds as smooth as possible, so that beds should be crowned by elevating centers of the beds higher than the edges (see Fig. 13–4); provide drainage ditches at bed edges; and compact the soil prior to spreading plastic sheeting to prevent settling of soil. Some growers are using gravel on top of the plastic sheeting. Beds constructed in this manner have been shown to reduce contamination by runoff water and to reduce splattering of soil. This approach aids in disease suppression; therefore, there is a corresponding reduction in plant disease losses. Increased cost initially is the main drawback for gravel beds. However, this is offset by increases in the number of salable plants. There is also an increase in longevity of the container area which reduces the annual labor and material expenditure.

A good grower frequently knocks plants out of the container to observe moisture and root condition. Diseases detected early can be controlled more easily. This practice can also reduce pathogen movement to large numbers of plants. Diseased plants should be removed from the growing area as soon as possible. The disposal area should be located well away from the growing area, storage area, potting area, and water source.

Disease Monitoring

A systematic monitoring system by nursery personnel (disease scouts) aids in forecasting certain seasonal disease problems. The recognition of a particular production situation or practice that predisposes plants to disease would be recognized by the scouting activities, and thus these problems could be corrected before disease becomes a serious problem. The scouting system is effective only when followed by rapid deployment of control practices. Therefore, a weak link between detection and disease control negates the usefulness of an entire disease control concept.

The production characteristics of an ornamental nursery are conducive to a disease epidemic if early stages of disease development are not detected. Therefore, more efficient and systematic disease monitoring practices should be incorporated into current growing activities by expanding the labor force or utilizing the existing one. The obvious gains from early disease detection include reduction in plant loss, improvement in plant quality, reduction in production costs and few production delays, and increased profits.

Stock plant area.   This area should be routinely inspected every 2 to 4 weeks throughout the growing season. Two months prior to taking cuttings, this routine inspection should occur weekly. Inspect a minimum of 5% of the total plants in a block of one species and choose different plants each time. Begin inspection of plants from the windward side of a block and the side bordering an uncultivated area. Inspect the plants in a random fashion; check new and old growth, but concentrate predominantly on the new, more susceptible growth. Examine both leaf surfaces for disease symptoms. Observe leaves for a decrease in size, change in color, or general loss in vigor. These symptoms could indicate lower stem or root problems. When common diseases are detected in a nursery, all susceptible plant species should be carefully monitored on a regular schedule. The incidences of diseases that are common to a number of woody ornamentals will depend on a specific nursery's geographical location in the United States. Record where diseases occur and their precise location in stock blocks. This could help in the planning of future monitoring and control activities. Disease symptoms alone are often unreliable in a diagnosis; therefore, seek professional diagnostic services. Contact your local Cooperative Extension Service for instructions on the proper collection and submission of disease samples to a plant disease diagnostic laboratory.

Propagation area.   Propagation beds should be routinely inspected on a 1- to 2-day interval while plants remain in this cycle. Be sure that misting systems function properly; examine rooting media for water saturation. A too-wet condition has been shown to predispose seedlings or cuttings to diseases. Examine seedlings or cuttings for damping-off disease. Damp-off appears as a small number of plants within a small area that have wilted or collapsed at the medium line. Propagation beds should be inspected for localized spots of root or cutting-end rot diseases. Foliage of cuttings will darken and drop from plants exhibiting obvious cutting-end discoloration or rot. Be aware of leaf diseases which often occur on foliage of cuttings. The propagation environment is ideal for disease spread. Collect and submit appropriate samples to the nearest diagnostic facility for an accurate diagnosis of any questionable disease problem.

Production area.   Plants purchased from outside the nursery should be placed in a holding or quarantine area for at least 3 weeks. Make weekly inspections for insects and diseases so that problems can be either corrected or discarded. Production areas should be inspected every 10 to 14 days; this should involve a minimum of 5% of the total plants per bed. Select different plants for each subsequent inspection. Inspect both the windward side and any side bordering an uncultivated area; foliar pathogens can be expected to enter a production site from either area. Monitor randomly in blocks. Check both old and new growth for obvious disease symptoms. Be alert for root-rot symptoms during monitoring. Roots of plants exhibiting decreased vigor, off-color, smaller leaf size, or wilt should be examined. Remove the container and examine the root system. Peripheral roots that are dark, discolored, and sluff easily to the touch indicate root problems. Lack of root penetration in the lower one-third of the growing media is another indication of root problems. A zone or band of off-color plants across a block may or may not be exhibiting wilt or dieback symptoms. The cause of such problems has been associated with overlapping irrigation patterns or two irrigation zones that fail to meet. The practice of resetting rooted cuttings or liners into containers located in the field where plants have failed to grow could be detrimental to the plant. Soil pathogens, if not responsible for the first plant's death, may exist in the plant residue in increased populations. When a particular disease is detected on several plant species, all other known susceptible species should be carefully examined. Record all disease observations and associated production problems for future monitoring and control activities. When specific diseases cannot be accurately diagnosed on-site, collect and submit appropriate samples to a plant disease diagnostic laboratory in your state.

Disease Control

Nurseries that have used disease control programs indicate that the difficulty lies in the control phase rather than in the disease detection components. Nurseries that use scouts obtain adequate disease detection, but translation into disease control activities is often lost or ignored. Growers understand the need for active control measures, but these actions are often given a low priority within the nursery as compared to the propagation, potting, irrigation, and sales. Developing specialization within existing nursery labor forces to control potential diseases can be beneficial in making management decisions. Individuals within the nursery could be given the responsibility for receiving disease monitoring reports on which disease control decisions are made. A group within the nursery could be responsible for all disease control activities, including pesticide application. The departmentalization of a pest control group would help to develop a greater expertise in the selection and application of pesticides. Increased consistency in technology and safety as they relate to pesticide application would also result.

After the execution of certain control decisions and actions, an evaluation of such decisions would be beneficial. This would include success of disease control and the practicality of the precise actions taken as they relate to the accuracy of the monitoring system. Such evaluations should be based on visual observations, past records, and effects of those control measures used previously. This type of assessment allows for a more positive approach to the preventive phase of disease control and may indicate the need for additional monitoring efforts.

Stock plant area.   Stock plants with localized disease problems can often be controlled easily and rapidly by selective pruning or handpicking of disease foliage. A thorough cleanup of all infected plants and uninfected plant debris should be included. Certain stock plants with severe disease problems, such as crown gall or mushroom root rot, should be rogued from the stock plant area. Control measures for foliar diseases should be initiated rapidly to ensure that cuttings used in propagation are apparently free from disease. As stated previously, the propagation cycle creates a perfect environment for disease epidemics if pathogens are present in plant tissue. Obtain the most current and effective chemical control measures from the nearest Cooperative Extension Service office after making accurate diagnoses.

Propagation area.   Areas of declining or dead plants with root diseases within propagation beds should be carefully removed, including rooting medium. Certain root-rotting fungi, such as *Sclerotium rolfsii* or *Rhizoctonia solani*, will produce an asexual, reproductive structure called a sclerotium. These structures are quite small and can be moved by various means from one site in the propagation bed to another. Extreme care should be taken when roguing individually infected plants. Where a root rot is the problem, apply an appropriate drench fungicide in the propagation bed. Drench the entire bed, not just the obvious diseased spots. Since some soil fungicides are specific for a particular organism, an accurate diagnosis is imperative. Root-rot incidences should always be recorded and rooting media should never be reused. Severe root-rot diseases of plants in propagation beds do not affect all plants; some will survive. It is always tempting to use these surviving plants, which should be discarded. Since most growers will pot survivors, be sure to treat the potting mix with an appropriate fungicide as a protective measure. Monitor plants, and repeat fungicide application at intervals described on the label. Rooting liners exhibiting foliar disease symptoms should be sprayed with an appropriate fungicide before introduction into the production area and spraying should be continued on a regular basis. Consult your local county extension agent for specific recommendations.

Production area.   All fungicide selection and application must be based on the latest and most accurate recommendations. Some diseases occurring on aerial portions of plants can be controlled by selective shearing or pruning of infected plant parts. Removal of severely blighted leaves will improve the efficacy of subsequent fungicide applications. Severely diseased plants should be rogued from the production site and appropriately discarded. Plants that must be rogued specifically are those with root rot, crown gall, and blight. This is especially important since chemical control for these diseases is unsatisfactory.

Disease control decisions directed toward root rot should consider several factors. If root-rot diseases caused by *Phytophthora* and *Pythium* spp. are prevalent, disease development is favored by saturated soil moisture levels. Frequent and excessive irrigation will favor the continued reproduction and spread of these fungal pathogens. Therefore, proper water management must be recognized as an important facet of disease control. When root diseases exist, avoid water or fertility extremes. Both will place additional stress on an already weakened plant. Systemic fungicides are more effective than protectant fungicides. These compounds affect the target fungus in plant tissue. Drench fungicides applied to soil to control root-rotting fungi should be deposited on and in the growing medium and not applied to foliage. If these products are applied through overhead irrigation, they should be washed off by additional water. The moisture content of the growing medium should be near or at the container capacity when a fungicide drench is applied. Avoid applications to very dry mixes, because this can cause severe root damage.

For foliar situations, certain facets of the disease cycle should be reviewed prior to control activities. Most foliar fungal pathogens require long periods of leaf wetness if infection is to take place. This is one reason that late afternoon rainfall or irrigation is not good. When foliar disease severity is high, minimize the irrigation cycle. Application of fungicides or bactericides should not be expected to control a disease immediately. The variable length of time between penetration by a spore or bacterium and the appearance of the first recognizable symptom of disease, such as leaf spot, is the incubation period. This time may span days or weeks and will continue despite the application of a protectant fungicide with no kickback action onto the plant surface. This means that the disease can be expected to increase in incidence and severity until all incubation periods that began before pesticide applications become recognizable symptoms. Do not give up on the pesticide prematurely. To be effective, many diseases necessitate pesticide coverage on both leaf surfaces. Leaf-underside coverage is particularly important with certain fungal pathogens, such as the *Cercospora* spp. on ligustrum and pittosporum, that reproduce from the lower leaf surface. Irrigate plants prior to spraying to allow the longest contact of pesticide and foliage prior to the next watering.

Types of fungicides. Chemical control of most fungal diseases depends on the application of fungicides before the pathogen arrives. Fungicides used in this way are referred to as protectants (see Table 15–5). Most broad-spectrum fungicides are of this type. Protectants prevent fungal spores from germinating or kill them as they germinate, prior to penetrating the plant surface. These fungicides are ineffective after infection occurs except to reduce new infections. A few fungicides destroy pathogenic fungi after infection has occurred. These fungicides are called eradicants or theraputants. Their effectiveness is limited to a period of a few hours or days following infection. This post-infection control is referred to as kickback action. An exception is the eradication of powdery mildew with sulfur.

Most protectant fungicides are not absorbed by the plant and are not translocated within the plant. They form a protective barrier over the surface of the plant to prevent infection. Some redistribution of these fungicides may occur during rainy periods, but the effectiveness of the fungicide is dependent on thorough coverage during application. They must be applied and dry on the plant before they are exposed to rain or overhead irrigation and they must be present on the plant surface when the pathogen arrives. Captan, mancozeb, Daconil 2787, and thiram are examples of nonsystemic protectant fungicides.

Recent technology has produced several fungicides that are absorbed and translocated within the plants. This type of fungicide is called a systemic. Even though systemics are translocated to new growth, they are essentially protectant fungicides. Most systemics cannot kill fungi that have established themselves inside a plant. Benlate, which is effective against a number of the Ascomycetes and Deuteromycetes, and Subdue, which is effective against members of the Phycomycetes, are examples of systemic fungicides. A number of the systemic fungicides also have kickback action. Bayleton, for example, is effective against the apple powdery mildew pathogen for up to 48 hours after infection.

Protective fungicides are washed from the sprayed plant surfaces over a period of several days by rain and overhead irrigation and new unsprayed growth may emerge from buds. Protective fungicides therefore need to be applied several times at appropriate intervals during the period when the pathogen is active and the host is

TABLE 15-5 Fungicide Disease Applications on Nursery Plants

Common Name[a]	Trade Name[b]	Anthracnose	Botrytis Blight	Damping-off and Root Rot (by Phycomycetes)	Damping-off and Rot (not by Phycomycetes)	Downy Mildew	Leaf and Twig Blight	Leaf Spot and Needlecast	Petal Blight	Powdery Mildew	Rust	Scab	Action[c]
Benomyl	Benlate	X	X		X		X	X	X	X		X	S
	Terson 1991												
Captafol	Difolatan 4F	X					X	X	X			X	P, E
Captan	Captan	X	X		X		X	X	X			X	P, E
	Merpan												
	Orthocide												
CGA 38140	Fongarid			X									S, P
Chlorothalonil	Bravo	X	X		X	X	X	X	X	X	X	X	P
	Daconil 2787												
	Exotherm Termil												
Copper	Copper	X	X			X	X	X	X			X	P
Copper Sulfate + Lime	Bordeaux Mix	X	X			X	X	X	X			X	P
Cycloheximide	Acti-dione PM								X	X	X		P
	Antispray												
Dichlone	Phygon											X	P
	Quintar												
Dichloran, DCNA, Ditranil	Allisan		X		X		X		X				P
	Botran												
	Resisan												
Dinocap + Mancozeb	Dikar									X	X	X	P
Dodemorph	Karathane									X			P
	Milban												
Etridiazole (ethazol)	Terrazole			X									P
	Truban												

Common name	Trade name[a]	Type[b,c]
Fenaminosulf	Lesan (Dexon)	P
Ferbam	Carbamate	P
	Ferbam	
	Trifungol	
Folpet	Folpan	P
	Phaltan	P
Iprodione	Chipco 26019	P
Mancozeb	Dithane M-45	P
	Fore	
	Manzate 200	
Maneb	Dithane M-22	P
Metalaxyl	Subdue	S
PCNB	Fungiclor	P
	Terraclor	
Piperalin	Pipron	P
Sulfur	Sulfur	P
Thiophanate	Banrot	S
	Topsin M	
Thiram	AAtack	P
	Arasan	
	Tersan 75	
	Thiram 75	
Triadimefon	Bayleton	S
Triforine	Funginex	S, P, E
	Saprol	
Vinclozolin	Ornalin	P
	Ronilan	
Zineb	Dithane Z-78	P
	Zineb 75	

[a]These are trade names of fungicides used in the nursery industry. Not all of these fungicides are labeled or recommended in all states. This list is not intended to be a complete list of all fungicides used in nurseries. There are numerous products which are combinations of two or more compounds; these are not included in this list.

[b]This list is for reference only and does not represent an endorsement or imply criticism of the products.

[c]S = systemic, P = protectant, E = eradicant.

Source: Adapted from Jones (1982).

susceptible. To use it most effectively, the grower should understand the action of a fungicide that is being applied. Protectant fungicides are normally applied on 7- to 14-day intervals, but more frequent applications may be necessary in periods of heavy rains or frequent overhead irrigation. Systemic fungicides, on the other hand, are effective during wet or dry periods since they are translocated within the plant. Table 15–5 shows the action of some fungicides.

Portions of this chapter were adapted from extension publications listed in the references section. These references as well as the others contain much more additional information on controlling weeds, insects, and diseases in nursery operations. Since pesticide recommendations are fairly specific and their use regulated by law, it is suggested that nursery growers should regularly obtain current pesticide recommendations from their local county agricultural extension agent or from the state pesticide specialist, generally listed at the various land-grant universities.

SUMMARY

Weeds, insects, and diseases are the three most noxious, negative modifiers of plant growth in nurseries. The negative aspects of these pests can be minimized by an integrated pest control program with a crop production system that is directed toward following optimum cultural practices to produce healthy, vigorous plants. Plants that are properly spaced, correctly pruned, fertilized, and watered are much less prone to pest problems than are plants that are exposed to undesirable environmental conditions.

REFERENCES

AKERS, M. S., P. L. CARPENTER, and S. C. WELLER. 1984. Herbicide systems for nursery plantings. HortScience 19(4):502–504.

BAKER, J. R., ed. 1984. Insect and related pests of shrubs. N.C. Agric. Ext. Serv. Ag-189.

DAVIDSON, H. 1984. Weed control in nurseries and landscape areas. Mich. Coop. Ext. Ser. Bull. E-1677.

DICKEY, R. D., E. W. MCELWEE, C. A. CONOVER, and J. N. JOINER. 1978. Container growing of woody ornamental nursery plants in Florida. Florida Agric. Exp. Sta. Bull. 793.

JONES, R. K., and R. C. LAMBE, EDS. 1982. Diseases of woody ornamental plants and their control in nurseries. N.C. Agric. Ext. Serv. Ag-286.

KUHNS, L. J. 1982. How to control weeds—the basics and the herbicides. Am. Nurseryman 155(5):29–49.

————. 1982. How to control weeds—herbicide recommendations. Am. Nurseryman 155(5):50–61.

MILLER, R. L., and D. G. NIELSEN. 1985. Insect and mite control on wood ornamentals and selected perennials. Ohio Coop. Ext. Ser. Bull. 504.

MOORMAN, G. W. 1984. How nurserymen can plan effective disease-control programs. Am. Nurseryman 160(4):66–71.

PETERSON, C., R. HEATLEY, G. ADAMS, D. SMITLEY, and D. ROBERTS. 1987. Diagnosing problems of ornamental landscape plants. Mich. Coop. Ext. Serv. Bull. E-2024.

SKROCH, W. A. 1985. Basic principles of weed growth influence effective herbicide use. Am. Nurseryman 162(5):112–115.

SMITH, E. M. 1985. Chemical weed control in commercial nursery and landscape plantings. Ohio Coop. Ext. Serv. Bull. MM297.

URBANO, C. C. 1985. Some recommended herbicides and rates. Am. Nurseryman 161(8): 87–88.

SUGGESTED READING

BESTE, C. E. Committee Chairman. 1983. Herbicide handbook of Weed Science Society of America, 5th ed. WSSA, Champaign, Ill.

BOHMONT, B. L. 1983. The new pesticide user's guide. Reston Publishing Co., Inc., Reston, Va.

BUCHHOLTZ, K. P. Committee Chairman. 1981. Weeds of the north central States. 'North Central Regional Technical Committee NC-121. Bulletin No. 772.

KLINGMAN, G. C., F. M. ASHTON, and L. J. NOORDHOFF. 1982. Weed science: principles and practices, 2nd ed. Wiley-Interscience, New York.

MANION, P. D. 1981. Tree disease concepts. Prentice-Hall, Inc., Englewood Cliffs, N.J.

McGRATH, H., J. FELDMESSER, and L. D. YOUNG, eds. 1986. Guidelines for the control of plant diseases and nematodes. USDA Agric. Hand. 656.

MEISTER, R. T. 1987. Farm chemicals handbook. Meister Publishing Company, Willoughby, Ohio.

_____ . 1987. Weed control manual 1987 and herbicide guide. Meister Publishing Company, Willoughby, Ohio.

MILLER, D. M. 1986. Crop protection chemicals reference, 2nd. ed. Chemical Publishing Co., Inc., New York.

MILLER, J. F. Committee Chairman. Weeds of the southern United States. Ga. Coop. Ext. Serv.

RIFFLE, J. W., and G. W. PETERSON. 1986. Diseases of trees in the Great Plains. USDA Forest Service, General Technical Report RM-129.

SCHUBERT, O. E. 1986. A compendium of chemical weed control research in ornamentals in the United States (1944–1985). Supplement to HortScience 21(2).

SCHWARTZ, P. H., and D. R. HAMEL, eds. 1980. Guidelines for the control of insect and mite pests of foods, fibers, feeds, ornamentals, livestock, households, forests, and forest products. USDA Agric. Hand. 571.

TATTAR, T. A. 1978. Diseases of shade trees. Academic Press, New York.

16 *Nursery Crop Production*

In this chapter we trace the basic information needed for starting and operating a field- or container-production nursery. A nursery business can be a profitable enterprise, but it requires a sizable investment of money for labor and equipment, plus a considerable amount of management time. The part-time nursery owner often becomes dissatisfied with the unforeseen and exacting conditions under which a successful nursery must be operated. Therefore, it is not usually managed part-time, and is not considered an easy money-maker or income supplement.

The purpose of this chapter is to provide a schedule of operations from plant selection to harvest for field or container production (Fig. 16–1). Portions of this chapter were adapted from extension publications listed in the reference section. These references as well as the others contain much more additional information on nursery practices. Many cultural recommendations and methods of production will be given as examples; however, the authors realize that local conditions and specific technologies may not be applicable to your situation. To satisfy your special needs, you should consult with Cooperative Extension Specialists at your state university.

PLANNING THE OPERATION

Deciding on what trees and shrubs to grow is an important first step and a most perplexing question for the grower. Consider growing those trees and shrubs for which there is a potential market, that are well suited to your site, and that fit your expertise. Of course, there are many trees and shrub species that satisfy these criteria. Nursery catalogs and standard textbooks may be consulted for detailed information. Observing what is popularly grown in the market area and consulting with other growers will also give valuable clues to help you decide on species and quanti-

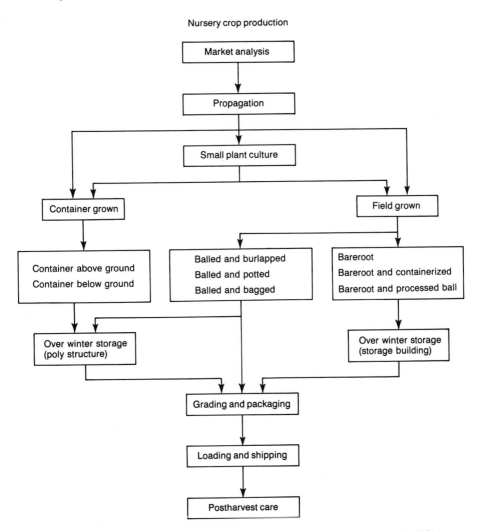

Figure 16–1 Flowchart of nursery crop production. (Adapted from Stinson et al., 1971.)

ties. A conservative approach might be to choose a few of the good sellers that are easy to grow, and gradually increase inventories to meet market demand.

There are several genera of trees and shrubs that are common to many ornamental landscapes and will probably remain so for many future years. The tree genera are *Acer, Cornus, Gleditsia, Magnolia, Malus, Abies, Picea, Pinus, Prunus,* and *Quercus,* while the shrub genera include *Berberis,* Cotoneaster, *Buxus,* Forsythia, *Ilex, Juniperus, Rhododendron, Rosa, Taxus,* and *Viburnum.* Selected and improved cultivars are available for most of these commonly accepted plants. Avoid plants that are losing their popularity or seem to be going out of style. Many older crabapple (*Malus*) cultivars that are susceptible to disease are being replaced by resistant selections. A grower should always determine the preferred sizes, foliage and flower colors, textures, densities, or formal and informal plant forms to meet market demands successfully.

How will the plants be harvested? This management decision influences production practices as well as handling procedures. For example, plants may be marketed bareroot, bareroot and containerized, bareroot with processed balls, balled and burlapped, balled and potted, or container grown. Some of the harvesting and marketing characteristics are given in Table 16–1.

Should a grower produce or buy liners? A beginning nursery grower may find it more convenient and profitable to purchase plants for lining-out than to produce

TABLE 16-1   Marketing Alternatives for Field-Production or Container-Production Systems

Methods	Characteristics	Marketing Period	Plant Types
Bareroot	Dormant digging; soil removed from roots; storage facilities needed; less shipping weight	Dormant season	Deciduous
Bareroot and containerized	Same as bareroot, except roots reestablished in container growing mix	Dormant season	Deciduous
Bareroot and processed ball	Same as bareroot, except roots enclosed in burlap and pack in growing mix	Dormant season	Deciduous
Balled and burlapped	Ball of soil remains; expanded digging season; improved postharvest life	Spring or fall season with proper conditions	Evergreens, deciduous
Balled and potted	Same as balled and burlapped, except less precision on digging; roots protected in sturdy containers	Same as balled and burlapped	Evergreens, deciduous
Balled and bagged	Same as balled and burlapped, except less time and effort in digging; more roots retained; sandy soils may be used	Spring, summer, or fall seasons	Evergreens, deciduous
Container above ground	Less handling damage; extends market season; more uniformity; reduces shipping weight	Spring, summer, or fall seasons	Evergreens, deciduous
Container below ground	Same as container above ground, except protection of roots in winter; plant stability in wind; no circling roots in bottom of container	Spring, summer, or fall seasons	Evergreens, deciduous

Source: Adapted from Ponder et al. (1983).

them. Liner production requires expert attention to many details, as well as special propagation facilities and small plant culture production areas. If liners are purchased for the first few years, a new grower can concentrate on growing quality plants at a profit and avoid the risks involved in propagation. After concentrating on growing practices and establishing the business, the new grower might consider improving profits by producing lining-out stock.

LINER PRODUCTION FROM SEED

Desirable and quality tree and shrub seedlings are much more likely to be obtained when the seed source or parentage is known. Seed should be from sources that are well adapted to the nursery's market area. Local seed collection is best because it provides for identification of parentage and allows harvest at the correct maturity. However, there may be just a few species in a range and a limited amount of seed present in the local area. Also, local seed collection involves labor costs and handling knowledge.

If possible, a nursery should have its own seed orchard from which the propagator can collect from known and acceptable plants. Many of our ornamental landscape plants, such as red maple, redbud, dogwood, sugar maple, and oaks, have broad geographic distribution. These native species usually adapt and grow much better than do introduced ornamentals. Research with redbuds and dogwoods has shown that plants produced from southern seed will winter kill in the north, while plants from northern seed sources grow slower in the south than plants from southern seed sources. Regardless of whether seed is collected locally or purchased, growers should be aware of prior collection and handling conditions. Commercial firms will usually cooperate in defining seed origin and identifying parentage if this information is known.

Some seed may be sown shortly after collection. Seeds of some trees and shrub species will germinate and grow immediately, while others will require an overwintering process to satisfy dormancy requirements. Seed from some species will require special treatments to meet germination requirements. This specific information and more can be found in several standard texts. *USDA Handbook 450* and *Plant Propagation—Principles and Practices* by Hartmann and Kester (see Appendix A) are considered by many horticulturalists to be valuable information resources for plant propagators and growers of ornamental landscape plants.

LINER PRODUCTION FROM VEGETATIVE METHODS

Vegetative or asexual propagation has become an established means of producing plants by using roots, stems, or leaves of stock plants that have the desired ornamental landscape traits. Asexual propagation is popular because it produces an identical clone with the same genetic makeup as the original stock plant. Asexual propagation is accomplished by several methods, such as cuttage, graftage, layerage, division, and tissue culture. Specific techniques on each of these methods for ornamentals is thoroughly covered in other publications (see Appendix A).

SMALL PLANT CULTURE

Seedlings or rooted cuttings may be transplanted from the propagation beds or flats into well-prepared ground beds, small containers, or directly into field-production rows. When plants are kept in small plant culture the objective is to provide protection and optimum conditions for rapid vigorous growth by allowing sufficient space between plants, by giving adequate water and fertilizer, and by eliminating competition from weeds and pests.

Certain types of nursery plants, such as narrow-leaved and broad-leaved evergreens, are usually transplanted into liner beds or coldframes for growing 1 or 2 years rather than directly into fields. Table 16–2 gives recommended spacing in transplant beds, coldframes, and fields for different types of plants. Vigorously growing seedlings, well-rooted cuttings, or properly knitted grafts should be transplanted, while unhealthy and poorly developed plants from propagation should be rogued out and discarded. Only those plants of the best quality should be allowed to occupy valuable production space. For additional information on production quota estimates, space requirements, planting designs, labeling blocks or rows, programming, and record keeping, review Chapter 5.

TABLE 16-2   Suggested Spacing for Young Nursery Stock in Small-Plant Culture When Transplanted into Transplant Beds, Cold Frames, or Fields

Type of Plant	Propagated by:	Being Transplanted into:	Recommended Spacing	
			Between Rows	In the Row
Narrow-leaved evergreens	Seed	Beds	6–10 in.	3–6 in.
		Fields	3½–4 ft	4–5 ft
	Cuttings	Frames	6 in.	3 in.
		Fields	3½–4 ft	2–3 ft
	Grafts	Frames	8 in.	4–6 in.
		Fields	3½–4 ft	2–3 ft
Deciduous	Seed	Beds	8–12 in.	4–6 in.
		Fields	3½–4 ft	2–3 ft
	Cuttings and grafts	Fields	3½–4 ft	2–3 ft
Broad-leaved evergreens	Seed	Beds	4–10 in.	4–10 in.
	Cuttings and grafts	Frames	4–10 in.	4–10 in.
	Seed, cuttings, and grafts	Fields	3½–4 ft	2½–3 ft

Source: Adapted from Stinson et al. (1971).

Fertilization Programs for Liners

Suggested fertilizer programs for nitrogen in small plant culture include selecting from 1 or 2 below:

1. *Ground beds.* Apply annually to deciduous trees and shrubs, 5–6 lb; narrow-leaved evergreens, 4–5 lb; and broad-leaved evergreens, 2–3 lb of nitrogen/1000 ft^2. A well-drained, medium-textured loam soil with a pH of 6.0 to 6.5 is preferred for most nursery plants.

2. *Containers (pots or flats).* Supplemental fertilizer during the growing season is necessary for optimum growth of most container-grown crops. Limited volume and nutrient reserve of containers, low cation-exchange capacities of most commonly used soil-less media, and rapid leaching of nutrients from frequent irrigations all contribute to the need for supplemental fertilization. A choice of three fertilizer programs includes a complete slow-release fertilizer at the manufacturer's recommended rate; or a slow-release fertilizer applied in combination with soluble fertilizer at 150 ppm N (weekly); or when no other form of nitrogen is applied in slow-release or granular form, soluble N at 250–300 ppm N (weekly) is suggested. The key to proper management of micronutrients and container media is to have the pH between 5.0 and 6.0. Once the pH rises above 7.0, most micronutrients become tied up in the medium and are unavailable.

These recommendations may vary with species, stages of plant growth, environmental conditions, and the concentration of other essential elements. These recommendations are intended to be general guidelines only. Although it is difficult to determine the exact nutrient levels to apply for each species, broad ranges of plants can be grown under similar fertility levels. For example, if growers will group their plants (*Taxus* together, *Ilex* together, and so on), fertilization within a genus usually varies less than between genera. Satisfactory growth can be obtained by fertilizing at a specific concentration within a genus. Further groupings according to plant size within a species enhances more efficient fertilization, watering, pruning, and other cultural practices. For further information on nutrition management, refer to Chapter 11 for field-grown plants and to Chapter 12 for container-grown plants.

Handling Softwood Cuttings

Softwood cuttings that are well rooted in flats have traditionally been moved from the propagation area to outdoor frames, where they are usually shaded for several days before exposure to full sunlight. Many progressive growers have started using the same structure for propagation and small plant culture to eliminate the need for moving at this stage. The structure conforms to the hardening-off needs of the tender young plants, the growing-on requirements, and overwintering protection. Some growers prefer ground beds instead of flats; however, the fact that the flats can be moved directly to the place where the plants will be planted is a great convenience. If adequate space and cutting material is available, many growers in warmer climates (U.S.D.A. hardiness zones 9 and 10) direct-stick three cuttings in

1- or 2-gal containers placed outdoors with a pot-to-pot arrangement for mist propagation. This is a more efficient procedure that saves time, materials, and labor but requires more land. Traditionally, many tree species have been propagated by budding. In recent years, graft incompatibility problems have developed on 5- to 10-year-old plants, such as red maple. Softwood cuttings have started to replace budded trees and provide improvements in production.

Handling Hardwood Cuttings

Hardwood cuttings of narrow-leaved evergreens and dormant deciduous plants, which root and develop shoots at the same time, are usually carried over in the propagation greenhouse at reduced temperatures. If slower-growing narrow-leaved evergreens require shaded beds for several years before being lined out in the field, they are moved to beds or frames in early spring after rooting. Hardwood cuttings of vigorous deciduous plants, such as forsythia and privet, may be collected in early winter, held in cold storage to form callus, and then lined out in early spring. These cuttings should form roots in a few weeks, followed by shoot growth. If shoots elongate before these stored cuttings are planted, death occurs in the field. Grafted stock of dormant deciduous trees are often handled in the same way as dormant callused and unrooted cuttings. If plants are grafted dormant and placed in storage for knitting (callusing), they are usually lined out in early spring. Grafting understock for evergreens is usually started in pots and managed in the greenhouse until the scion is fully callused and growing well.

Handling Seedlings

Many types of fast-growing seedlings are direct-seeded in field rows or ground beds and grown to a marketable size. Some of these plants are used as understock for budding. Budding is nearly always performed on well-established field-grown plants. Seedlings of broad-leaved and narrow-leaved evergreens and deciduous plants may be started and grown in seed beds for 1 or 2 years under shade if needed, before being lined out in the field. Seeds may be sown in early spring to prevent overwintering losses from birds, rodents, erosion, and so on. Narrow-leaved evergreen seedlings to be dug and potted to serve as grafting understock, to be lined out in the field, or to be handled as container-grown plants, are usually transplanted in early spring.

FIELD-GROWN CROPS

Producing nursery plants in the field for garden centers or landscape contractors may take from 2 to 7 years from the date of propagation, depending on the type of plant grown, until the plants are sold. Determining the most efficient field design, crop rotation schedule, soil management, transplanting, fertilization, irrigation, pruning, pest control, winter protection, and harvesting are important to the success of a field nursery operation. The main goal for a nursery business is to produce good-quality plants at a profit.

Field Planting Design

Spacing plants in the field should make efficient use of land and facilitate traffic flow and ease of access. Distance between rows should depend on final market size and on the width of equipment to perform field operations, such as planting, maintaining, and harvesting crops. Table 16–3 gives the recommended spacing and the numbers of years to reach marketable size for different types of nursery plants. When large equipment will be used in a field and the between-row spacing is greater than the in-row spacing, there should be two tree rows and multiple shrub rows for every aisle row. This wide row design provides for better space utilization. Stock marketed bareroot is normally planted closer in-row, with less between-row space. Selective harvesting of young plants may be used to obtain desired spacing in-row and to improve cash flow.

Whichever field design is chosen (see Chapter 5), it is important to be able to get into the field throughout the year. Grass sod established in aisles with a weed-free strip in rows allows for maximum accessibility to the field (Fig. 5–12). Established sod aisles will support heavy-equipment movement when the soil is wet, reduce soil compaction and erosion, and decrease considerably the area to be kept weedfree. Maintenance mowing or growth-retardant applications will be required on sod aisles.

TABLE 16-3 Spacing and Average Production Time Required for Different Types of Field-Grown Nursery Crops in Hardiness Zones 9 or 8 and 7 or 6

	Spacing		Production Time in Years by Hardiness Zone	
Type of Plant	Between Rows	In Rows	9 or 8	7 or 6
Large deciduous trees	3½–5 ft	18 in.	1	2
	3½–5 ft	36–48 in.	4	5
	8–14 ft	3½–6 ft	6	7
Small deciduous trees	3½–4 ft	18 in.	2	2–3
	3½–4 ft	36–48 in.	3–5	4–6
Evergreen trees	4 ft	2–2½ ft	4	6
Deciduous shrubs	3½–4 ft	12–24 in.	2–3	3–4
Evergreen shrubs	3½–4 ft	2–3 ft	3	5

Source: Adapted from Stinson et al. (1971).

Crop Rotation Plans and Soil Management

The rotation of field-grown nursery crops requires more planning than rotations for farm crops because some nursery crops require 2 years to reach marketable size, while other types require 7 or more years. If a nursery wishes to have an annual supply of standard deciduous trees, a crop, such as red maple, must be planted each year so that red maples will be ready for marketing 7 years later. For example, if the nursery is to market 1000 red maples each year, it must plant 1000 trees each year. Actually, 1053 might need to be planted to allow for 5% losses in the field from numerous causes (see Table 5–2). In any one year, an established nursery could be growing 7371 red maples. In addition, extra fields will be planted to a green-manure crop for 1 or 2 years for soil improvement. Similar crop rotation plantings must be done for each type of plant grown in the nursery. Some nurseries will review past sales trends for each species and use an adjustment factor (i.e., 10%) to increase or decrease future plantings to meet market demands.

Good soil conservation procedures denotes correct soil management and certain supporting practices, such as contouring, terracing, and diversion ditching. In some nurseries these supporting practices are essential, but in all nurseries, good soil management is paramount. Important soil management practices include attention to crop rotation, which aids in the maintenance of organic matter, thus improving soil structure and tilth, drainage, and fertility.

Organic matter is confined largely to the surface soil. The removal of a block of balled evergreens removes a large amount of the surface soil, leaving the subsoil, which is low in organic matter. The percentage of topsoil removed depends on planting distances and size of ball dug. Figuring spacing at 42-in. rows and 36 in. in the row and the balls dug at 15-in. depths, the following approximate percentages of soil to the 15-in. depth are removed: 15-in. balls remove 10%; 18-in. balls remove 15%; 24-in. balls remove 25%; and 30-in. balls remove 40%. This is a heavy loss of topsoil each time a block of evergreens is removed with a ball of soil, and this condition must be corrected before the soil is again in good condition to produce crops.

The problems of good soil management within the field nursery are much the same as those existing in general farm crop production. Crop rotation has long been considered an essential practice in the successful production of farm crops. A well-developed crop rotation plan for a nursery includes the use of sod, green manure, fall cover, winter cover, and companion crops alternated with or accompanying the nursery crops. It is difficult to build up organic matter in a depleted soil. One of the best methods is the use of sod crops. Experimental evidence would seem to indicate that even with extensive use of green-manure crops, it is barely possible to maintain the organic contents of the soil.

Although there is little precedent to follow, nurseries may be able to obtain the desired results by having the land in sod or green-manure crops 30–40% of the time. The length of time that it takes to produce a salable crop of nursery stock and the method followed in digging the crop are factors influencing the rotation adopted.

The objective of effective soil-building practices is to maintain a favorable productivity balance. The following rotations are suggested; however, they can be modified to fit the practices followed in individual nurseries. NC with 1–6 represents nursery crop and 1–6 years in field. SG means small grain seeded to grass and legumes. GMWC represents green manure and winter cover crops and S means sod crop.

1. Perennials or liners to mature in 1 year and dug from the field bareroot.
   Rotation plan: Repeat 4 or 5 years with nursery crop followed by sod crop (grass and legumes) for 2 years.

   NC-1, NC-1, (NC-1), SG, S

2. Shrubs to mature in 2 years and dug bareroot.
   Rotation plan: Repeat at 4 years with nursery crop for 2 years and sod crop (grass and legumes) for 2 years.

   NC-1, NC-2, SG, S-1

   Rotation plan: Repeat at 7 years with nursery crop for 2 years, green manure and winter cover crops for 1 year, with nursery crop for 2 years, and sod crop (grass and legumes) for 2 years.

   NC-1, NC-2, GMWC, NC-1, NC-2, SG, S-1

3. Shrubs or small trees in 3 years and dug bareroot.
   Rotation plan: Repeat at 5 years with nursery crop for 3 years and sod crop (grass and legumes) for 2 years.

   NC-1, NC-2, NC-3, SG, S-1

4. Small trees, large shrubs, or small evergreens in 4 years and dug bareroot or with a ball.
   Rotation plan: Repeat at 6 or 7 years with nursery crop for 4 years and sod crop (grass and legumes) for 2 or 3 years.

   NC-1, NC-2, NC-3, NC-4, SG, S-1, (S-2)

5. Evergreens or trees in 5 years and dug with a ball.
   Rotation plan: Repeat at 8 years with nursery crop for 5 years and sod crop (grass and legumes) for 3 years.

   NC-1, NC-2, NC-3, NC-4, NC-5, SG, S-1, S-2

6. Evergreens or trees in 6 years and dug with a ball.
   Rotation plan: Repeat at 9 years with nursery crop for 6 years and sod crop (grass and legumes) for 3 years.

   NC-1, NC-2, NC-3, NC-4, NC-5, NC-6, SG, S-1, S-2

With the use of sod in the traveled aisles, it may be possible to keep a field in production for longer periods of time with consecutive nursery crops. After a crop has been harvested, the sod aisle would be plowed and planted and the old crop row would become the aisle planted to sod. This plan could be continued for an extended period. The idea might not work if very heavy equipment were moved down the aisle rows too often. The heavy equipment could cause soil compaction and subsequently reduce crop growth. At this time, it is not known whether enough soil compaction would occur for this to be a real concern.

For some field operations, fall plowing may be more of an advantage than winter cover crop. With fall plowing the physical condition of the soil is improved with alternative freezing and thawing of the soil and allows for exposure of pests, earlier spring planting, and a lighter spring work load. Although many nurseries use the moldboard plow, some have found that the chisel plow gives better results. A chisel plow mixes the field debris or green-manure crops all through the soil instead of depositing it in a layer at the bottom of the plowed layer. It is not recommended if the cover crop has long branches, because they may become tangled in the plow blades. For best results the plow should be pulled across the field a second time with the furrows at right angles to those of the first pass. A crawler tractor is recommended to avoid soil compaction. Final soil preparation should consist of disking or harrowing twice before planting. For additional information on soil management, see Chapter 11.

Fertilization

It is more convenient to apply fertilizer to planting sites well ahead of planting crops. Ideally, the needed mineral elements should be applied to cover crops either 1 or 2 years before planting crops. The result is a more uniform and desirable soil fertility at planting time. Any needed lime should be applied at least 6 months before planting crops. Fertilizer and lime needs for phosphorus, potassium, magnesium, and calcium should be determined through soil test recommendations. Representative samples for each field should be collected and sent to a soil testing lab before planting and at least every other year. Regular soil testing and foliar analysis often detects nutritional problems before they become serious.

Unless requested, soil test procedures do not routinely analyze for nitrogen, which is generally the most critical nutrient. Nitrogen fertilizers must be applied each year due to leaching and crop use. Generally, annual nitrogen rates per acre for field-grown crops should be 200–250 lb for deciduous trees and shrubs, 150–200 lb for narrow-leaved evergreens, and 100–150 lb for broad-leaved evergreens. Higher rates are for lighter soils and lower rates used on heavier soils. The total amount of nitrogen applied should be divided into two or three applications annually. With two applications, spring and fall are recommended times of treatment, with approximately half the nitrogen per acre applied on each date. If three nitrogen applications are made, the third application would best be applied in early summer, with approximately one-third the total nitrogen per acre applied on each date. Weather conditions may modify timing and amounts of applications each year. Higher rates of nitrogen fertilization on newly planted crops may cause damage to plants during periods of drought stress.

To compute how much fertilizer to apply per acre, divide the pounds of nitrogen per acre needed by the percent analysis of the desired nutrient. For example, if you want to apply 100 lb of nitrogen per acre and you use ammonium nitrate, a 33-0-0 fertilizer formulation, divide 100 by 0.33, which gives you an application rate of about 300 lb. To adjust levels of phosphorus and potassium for woody ornamentals, the suggested rates in Tables 11–13 and 11–14 should be satisfactory.

Most field-production nurseries broadcast inorganic, granular fertilizers using hopper drop or rotary-type spreaders. However, in-row banded-fertilizer treatments are becoming more popular because of the increasing cost of fertilizer and the advantage of directing root growth. When band placement is utilized, application rates may be reduced to two-thirds with narrow row spacing and to half with wider rows. Banding of fertilizer is more practical during the first 2 years of growth for many nursery crops. Some growers employ the combination of fertilizer bands, in-row weed control, trickle irrigation, and sod aisles since it encourages more root development in the soil mass close to the plant's main stem that will be moved when the plant is dug.

Transplanting Liners

The objective for field-grown crops is to provide optimum conditions for rapid vigorous growth by allowing sufficient space between plants, by providing adequate water and nutrition, and by preventing excessive competition from pests and weeds. Information on pest control strategies in propagation, small plant culture, and production is discussed in Chapter 15. After the small-plant culture stage, liners are ready to be moved into production fields in either fall or spring. Fall planting is preferred by many growers because some root growth will take place before ground temperatures drop below 45°F and because there is usually ample soil moisture for the liners to become established before spring shoot growth. A minimum of 6 weeks should be allowed for root development before the ground freezes. Fall transplants are better able to withstand the stresses of the hot and sunny summer days. For spring planting, liners should be transplanted after the ground thaws and as soon as the soil is workable. Be sure that young liners are well established before the first critical summer; this cannot be overemphasized. If the transplant survives the first summer with a good root system, the chances of the plant living to salable size are excellent. Only the best liners should be transplanted for field production. Field irrigation, if location permits, should be considered insurance against drought stress and poor growth instead of an added production expense.

Planting when the ground is too wet causes soil compaction and undesirable clods to form in clay soils, with subsequent poor root growth and development. A good way to get an indication of soil moisture is to pick up a handful and roll the soil out into a ribbon with your thumb and index finger. If the ribbon breaks into sections about an ⅛ to ¼ in. in length, the soil is suitable for working. Loose, gritty, or sandy soils can often be worked satisfactorily when slightly wet with no harmful effects (see Chapter 13).

Most nursery transplanters (Fig. 3–3) are modifications of the tobacco or potato transplanters and use the same basic principle of operation. Transplanters are designed to be pulled by a tractor to plant one or more rows at a time. The basic components are a plow that opens up the furrow, seats mounted behind and on either side of the plow, a tabletop mounted in front of the seats to hold the liners, and V-shaped blades behind the plow to close the soil around the liner. To set a uniform distance between the liners, some planters use dripping water as gauge. The drip rate of the water is controlled by an adjustable valve on the water tank. By adjusting the drip rate, the distance between the plants can be changed.

Puddling liners before transplanting them into the field prevents the roots of bareroot liners from drying out before they are planted. The procedure is as follows:

1. Dig a hole 3 ft across and 2 ft deep.
2. Fill the hole half full with water.
3. Add clay soil to the water until a slurry is formed, about the consistency of buttermilk. Disease-control chemicals may be added to the bath to protect the roots.
4. Quick dip the root systems of the liners in the slurry.
5. Protect the roots with moist packing material, such as sphagnum moss and wrap with burlap.

Liners should be puddled just before they are to be transported to the field. Container-grown (flats or pots) liners should have the growing medium removed by dipping in water before puddling. This procedure allows the roots to be placed in direct contact with the field soil. If the growing medium is not removed, it will dry out faster than the surrounding soil. Water is not able to move by capillary pressure from the field soil into the growing medium, because of differences in texture and pore space. During planting it is important not to drag the liner on the bottom of the furrow, or an undesirable J-shaped root system will develop (Fig. 14–3). If a heavy soil is too wet during planting, the sides of the furrow may become glazed by the plow blade and inhibit root growth away from the furrow.

Irrigation

Portable irrigation systems were once popular, but are rarely used any more because of the labor involved in moving the pipes from field to field. These overhead systems require high-capacity pumps to apply large volumes of water. Based on available evidence, trickle irrigation appears to be the system of the future for field production. There are many advantages; for example, it is less expensive to install, it is a durable product that does not require constant movement, and it re quires less water than an overhead system. A major advantage of trickle is that plants can be dug during dry spells simply by running the system before digging. Trickle irrigation prevents drought stress rather than correcting it, by daily application of small amounts of water directly to the root zone in the row, and not wasting water between rows. Crops can also be fertilized through a trickle system by injecting fertilizer into the main line near the pump. The injection can be done either with a positive pressure injector or by using a bypass method. This allows the grower to fertilize as needed by the crop with less labor.

Trickle irrigation is a simple system to install and can easily be performed by the grower. The water source can be a pond, stream, or well; however, a well is preferable since it usually provides a cleaner supply of water. A 2-in. well with a 2-hp pump is adequate; whereas for conventional irrigation systems water flow is measured in gallons per minute, trickle irrigation is measured in gallons per hour. The main line that comes from the pump to the field is usually 2-in. black polyethylene or PVC pipe (Fig. 13–2). A time clock connected to a solenoid valve allows the system to run a specified length of time each day. To strain out any particles that might plug the irrigation system, a 100-mesh in-line screen filter should be connected on the pump side of the solenoid valve. The interval of irrigation time may be adjusted to satisfy the needs of different crops during the growing season. For large acreages, several solenoid valves attached to a zonal time clock will allow several fields to be run from the same pump in sequential order. For example, if there are six fields to run off one pump, the system could be run for 2 hours in the first field, the zonal time clock would switch off the water on the first field and turn on the water to the second field for 2 hours, and so on. The 2-in. main line runs underground from the pump to the field and then runs along perpendicular to the crop rows. Risers are attached to the main line at each crop row and a ½-in. black polyethylene pipe runs from the riser down each row. One emitter or water outlet is placed by each plant.

There are several types of emitters that may be used. The least expensive is the microtube (Fig. 13–3), which is a very small piece of polyethylene pipe (0.025-, 0.035-, or 0.045-in. I.D.) that is inserted into the ½-in. line. The flow rate of the water is determined by the inside diameter of the microtube and by its length. Either 1 or 2 gal/hour is desirable. With the microtube system, the length of tube must be varied as the ½-in. line changes grade (shortened uphill and lengthened downhill) to provide a uniform flow rate. Pressure-compensating emitters are also available at a slightly higher cost, but their installation eliminates the labor required in adjusting microtube lengths. These emitters automatically adjust to changes in line pressure caused by grade changes and give a uniform flow rate throughout the field.

Root Pruning

The root systems of most tree and shrub crops may spread 3 to 9 ft from the base of the plant. Since most bareroot or soil balls are dug from 12 to 24 in. in diameter, unless something is done to confine the root system, a considerable portion of the roots will be lost when the plant is dug. If root growth is not modified, the loss of the roots can have a severe shock on the plants, which may even be fatal. Root pruning as practiced in nurseries is the cutting off of the distal parts of roots to stimulate lateral root formation closer to the main stem of the plant. It is not practical to root prune each plant in a nursery row individually. Therefore, growers will effect the same results by disking or plowing in the aisle row close to the plants. Root pruning is done in some nurseries with a U-shaped blade that is drawn under the plants in the row by a tractor (Fig. 1–3). This prunes basal roots and those that extend into the aisle, but not those in the row. Root pruning should be done in late summer or fall, at a time when top growth has ceased or is declining. The roots will continue to grow actively until the soil temperature drops below 45°F. Therefore, the root system can be pruned and new roots formed without the plant being stressed by top growth. New spring top growth can then adjust to the slightly restricted water intake capability of the pruned root system. Root pruning is often done during the second year for rapidly growing shrubs, every 2–3 years for trees, and sometimes in late summer before stock is to be dug.

There are two other methods being used to restrict root growth. Some growers are using a combination of fertilizer bands, in-row weed control, trickle irrigation, and sod aisles to encourage more in-row root growth. Another approach being tested is the use of a root-control bag that is placed in the transplant hole and backfilled with field soil to plant the liner. There are advantages and disadvantages of this root-control bag, with a final verdict still to be made. The advantages include: less time and labor in digging; higher proportion of roots retained in the ball; forms a ball in sandy soils; and a longer postharvest life on retail lots without rewrapping. A few disadvantages are: the cost of the bag plus poly sheet for the bottom of the hole; more time required with planting; trickle irrigation may be needed in dry summers, because of limited soil volume for roots; and the bag must be removed when planted in the landscape.

Culture for Specific Types of Crops

Although all nursery crops require regular attention as far as moisture, nutrition, and pest control are concerned, each type has slightly different cultural requirements from the others. Transplanting requirements, spacing, appropriate pruning, soil type and pH needs, and length of time to reach marketable size are matters that must be managed for optimum growth.

Deciduous shade trees are usually lined out in the field as 1- or 2-year-old plants (seedlings, grafts, or cuttings) at an 18-in. spacing. About the third year the trees are dug bareroot for market or replanted for growing on at a wider spacing. For those that will be grown on, final tree size and intermediate harvest are the primary considerations for in-row spacing. A general rule is to plant the trees 3 ft apart for each inch of anticipated trunk diameter. For example, trees to be sold at 2-in. diameter should be planted 6 ft apart in-row with about a 10-ft row spacing, depending on harvesting equipment. Generally, for 2-in. caliper trees sold balled and burlapped, in-row spacing is 5–6 ft, with 9–12 ft between rows. Trees to be harvested as bareroot stock are normally planted closer together, with less between-row space. After the first year, the leader should add about 18–24 in. or more of new growth each year for the faster-growing deciduous shade trees, while slow growers will average 12–18 in. of new growth annually.

Some growers cut back tree liners in late winter to a 2-in. stub in order to force a straight trunk from vigorous sprout growth that flushes out. If some cutbacks produce an excess of sucker growth, the dominant sprout should be kept for training and the excess suckers removed in late spring. This is a useful practice on species where it is difficult to obtain a straight trunk, such as oaks. Grafted or budded cultivars with stems that have a tendency to bend over from excessive top growth are tied to individual stakes to protect the bud sprout, to prevent wind breakage, and to assure straight trunks. Stakes should be confined to the lower portion of the stem, allowing the upper portion to sway in the wind. The stakes are driven into the soil on the prevailing-wind side of the small trees so that the wind will not rub the tree against the stake and damage the bark. The support should be removed as soon as the tree has developed sufficient caliper to support the crown (Fig. 14–1). The supports are usually removed at the end of the second growing season.

The first dormant (late winter) pruning should include tying up crooked leaders, trimming very bent leaders back to upright buds, and shortening long side branches back to 10 to 12 in. The second winter pruning should induce symmetry in the plants by heading back long side branches to about 12 to 15 in. to produce a narrow, pyramidal crown with a central leader. Two-year transplants should not be too severely pruned in winter or the new flush can result in the production of excessively long and soft tender shoots that will be susceptible to wind breakage and drought stress in summer. Two-year trees should also be limbed up about 12–18 in. above the ground. In late spring after bud break, soft trunk sprouts can be rubbed off easily in seconds. Low sprouts on the trunks provide two useful purposes and should not be removed too high on young trees. The low sprouts shade the tree to reduce the chance of summer sunscald and the leaves manufacture food to increase trunk diameter.

Nursery pruning to direct the growth of young trees and to correct any structural weakness is very important if mature trees are to function as expected in the landscape. As the trees develop, excess side branches are removed so that those that are left are spaced about 12–18 in. apart. Branches selected for permanent scaffolds must have wide angles of attachment with the trunk for greatest strength. Radial branch distribution should allow 5–7 main scaffolds to fill the circle of space around the trunk. With radial spacing, branches radiate from the trunk like spokes on a wheel. Because no limb is directly over another, they do not compete for light.

Dormant (late winter) pruning produces a more natural growth pattern, in contrast to summer pruning. Trees pruned in late winter make vigorous flushes of growth in spring that harden off before the insects that damage terminals have built up to summer population levels. A basic rule to follow in pruning young trees is to concentrate heavy removal in winter and as light as possible in summer. Summer pruning may have a dwarfing effect by removing leaves that manufacture necessary food for growth in height and trunk caliper. Therefore, except for light shaping to shorten any disproportionately long branches, and of course to remove broken, injured, or diseased wood, summer pruning should not be practiced. Deciduous shade trees, such as birch, maples, and elms, have a tendency to lose sap profusely if they are pruned in late winter. Pruning bleeders earlier in winter permits the fresh cuts to dry out and the ends of the sap ducts to shrivel before sap movement in spring.

The culture of deciduous flowering trees (cherry, crabapple, hawthorns, dogwood, redbud, magnolia, etc.) is similar to that of deciduous shade trees. Liners are field planted as 1- or 2-year-old seedlings, cuttings, or grafts. They are usually grown to marketable sizes at a spacing of 18 in. in the row and dug bareroot. Most upright (excurrent) types are pruned to a single leader, while spreading (decurrent) trees are allowed to develop as multistem specimens with several leaders. Branches within 3–4 ft of the ground on marketable-size plants are removed early in the summer to allow wound healing before spring sale. Deciduous flowering trees are usually ready to market in 6 years or sooner.

Deciduous shrubs are lined out at 12- to 24-in. spacings as 1- or 2-year-old seedlings or cuttings. Many deciduous shrubs will produce much bushier growth with more canes and branching from the base if they are spaced adequately and pruned several times during field culture. Plants used for hedging, especially, need to be well branched at the base with a dense form. Shrub liners should be headed back about half their height during the first winter pruning. Fall transplants should be allowed to develop a root system before forcing vigorous spring growth. Further dormant trimming of laterals during the second and third year will benefit the appearance of many shrub types. The roots are pruned in either the second or third year, depending on plant type. Slow- to medium-growing cultivars are usually ready to be harvested after 3 years in the field, while large growing cultivars are ready after 4 years. Most deciduous shrubs are dug bareroot.

Narrow-leaved evergreen shrubs that are started as rooted cuttings, such as juniper, arborvitae, *Taxus,* and *Chamaecyparis,* are usually lined out on 2- or 3-ft spacings. Upright types may be pruned to maintain one leader, and laterals are often sheared several times to give dense, symmetrical growth. Crops are root pruned in the second and fourth years, and are dug either balled and burlapped or balled and potted after 5 years in the field. Spreaders are handled in a similar manner as upright narrow-leaved evergreen shrubs, except that they are not pruned to one leader. The pruning procedure for spreaders is to cut back some each year to produce a tight shape and to prevent spindly growth. To maintain healthy growth of lower branches, cut back the longer branches that develop on the top so that the lower branches will be exposed to light. Spreaders are root pruned in the third year and are dug either balled and burlapped or balled and potted after 4 or 5 years in the field.

Narrow-leaved evergreen trees, such as pine, spruce, and fir, are usually lined out at 2- to 3-ft spacing as 2- or 3-year-old seedlings or grafts. Many species make only one rapid flush of growth in late spring. The first pruning occurs when new growth or elongated candles have almost reached their maximum length and the needles are still short, the tip of all candles (including the central leader) should be removed. This technique causes many new buds to form in the axils of the needles. The following spring's growth will be much more densely branched, bushy, and symmetrical. If you shorten the candles by more than one-fourth, it merely reduces the tree size without producing any more lateral branching. Tip pruning is usually done until the plants reach 5 to 6 ft in height, then fertilizer rates are reduced to prevent excessively long internodes and unreachable branches. Narrow-leaved evergreens are grown in an area protected from winter winds, which could cause browning of foliage. Evergreens also require a well-drained soil for optimum growth, as well as a loam that contains sufficient clay to hold a soil ball at the time of harvest.

Broad-leaved evergreen shrubs (azalea, *Rhododendron*, holly, boxwood, *Pieris*, etc.) are usually lined out at 18–24 in. in the row as 1- or 2-year-old cuttings, depending on species. Many broad-leaved evergreen shrubs develop shallow, dense root systems and prefer moisture-retaining organic soils or mulching. These shrubs are grown in the same manner as narrow-leaved evergreen shrubs, except for the species that require an acid soil (see Table 11–1). This plant type is particularly susceptible to winter injury and must be grown with good windbreak protection. Shrubs are spaced and pruned to encourage dense growth; thus a careful shaping in late winter is usually sufficient. If flower buds remain on young plants and flowers are allowed to set seed, this will reduce vegetative growth. Therefore, pruning flowering species should include cutting off the flower buds on small plants to be reserved for future growth. If thinning of the crop is planned, with some plants to be sold and other to be grown on, pruning the reserve shrubs will direct digging to the salable plants. Broad-leaved evergreen shrubs are balled and usually marketed after 4–5 years in the field.

CONTAINER-GROWN CROPS

In the nursery trade there is a distinction made between potted stock, container-grown stock, and containerized stock. Potted stock refers to seedlings, rooted cuttings, or recently grafted plants that are grown for a period of time in small pots before they are planted in containers or lined out in the field. Container-grown stock is grown in the container from a seedling, rooted cutting, or graft to salable size in a relatively small volume of growth medium. Containerized stock is a field-grown plant that is dug and put in a container to be sold.

Plant Types for Container Culture

Many woody species of plants are successfully grown in nurseries, in containers, and possibly in the future nearly all woody species will be container-grown. Today it is estimated that 80–90% of the woody ornamental plants produced in warmer climates, such as Florida, are grown in containers, and this trend keeps increasing. The reasons for this success include: extension of sales and planting seasons; development of more attractive sales packages; easier transportability for the producer and consumer; greater control of environmental and cultural production factors; and more efficient use of production and sales areas. Other advantages, as well as challenges, are listed in Table 2–2.

Ideal plants for container culture are those with poorly developed root systems, which can easily be handled in containers, those that do not require expensive and extensive winter protection, and those that can be produced to salable size in a minimum length of time. Generally, any shallow-rooted plant, whether deciduous or evergreen, is best grown in containers. Many plants that can be grown in one part of the country cannot be grown in other places because they grow poorly in some environments. Plants should also be selected with the modified environment of the container in mind. Good-quality yews are very difficult to produce as container-grown stock, so they are seldom attempted. Deciduous plants have not been found to be a problem. Growth forms are similar to field-grown plants if the containers are adequately spaced to allow for rapid growth. However, from a business point of view, it is not practical to grow deciduous plants in containers since they can be grown much more cheaply in the field. Certain types of plants respond well to container culture, and they are more profitable to produce when grown in containers: broad-leaved evergreen shrubs, such as azalea, many *Rhododendron* cultivars, holly, boxwood, *Euonymus*, *Pyracantha*, and many tropical foliage species; and narrow-leaved evergreen shrubs, such as spreading and dwarf forms of juniper, pine, *Chamaecyparis*, spruce, fir, and hemlock.

Production Schedule for Container-Grown Plants

The primary objective of a production schedule for container-grown plants is to grow high-quality plants for the most profit. A grower may lose sight of the profit motive in attempting to produce the best-quality plants. Since container-grown plants represent a greater capital investment to produce than field-grown plants, it becomes essential to reduce costs by producing the plant in as short a time period as possible. A grower should start with good-sized vigorous plants. Although it is not good practice to stuff extra-large field-grown plants into containers, it is also not wise to put a 2-in. seedling or cutting into a 5-gal container. Nursery crops should be programmed so that the plants are of appropriate size and are vigorous when they are transplanted to the container. Stock to be container-grown is usually planted in early spring, although recently some retail nurseries have begun planting large liners in early fall to guarantee a supply for early spring sales.

Generally, most types of nursery stock in 1-gal containers are grown for a period of 2 years, although some stock reaches marketable size in 1 year, depending on environmental influences. A few slow-growing dwarf types may be grown for 3 or 4 years. Table 16–4 indicates the approximate years for production of different types of container-grown nursery crops in several container sizes.

The rule for proper spacing of container-grown plants is that the leaf tips of adjacent plants should just be touching. This spacing procedure results in compact growth of good quality as well as an efficient use of production space. Spacing too

TABLE 16-4   Average Production time and Sizes of Container-Grown Nursery Crops for Different Plant Types Growing in Hardiness Zones 9 or 8 and 7 or 6

Type of Plant	Plant Size	Container Size (gal)[a]	Production Time in Years by Hardiness Zone	
			9 or 8	7 or 6
Shade and flowering trees	Height: 12–15 in.	1	1	1
	15–18 in.	1	1	1
	18–24 in.	1	1	1
	2–3 ft	2	1.5	2
	3–4 ft	2	2	3
	4–5 ft	5	2.5	3
	5–6 ft	5	3	4
Small-growing deciduous shrubs	Height: 9–12 in.	1	1	1
	12–15 in.	1	1	2
	15–18 in.	1	1	2
	18–24 in.	2	2	3
Medium-growing deciduous shrubs	Height: 12–15 in.	2	1	2
	15–18 in.	2	1	2
	18–24 in.	2	1.5	2
	24–30 in.	5	2	3
Spreading narrow-leaved evergreen shrubs	Width: 6–9 in.	1	0.5	1
	9–12 in.	1	1	1
	12–15 in.	2	1	2
	15–18 in.	2	1.5	2
	18–24 in.	5	2	3
Dwarf or globe narrow-leaved evergreen shrubs	Height: 6–9 in.	1		1
	9–12 in.	1	1	1
	12–15 in.	2	1.5	2
	15–18 in.	2	2	3
	18–24 in.	5	3	4
Narrow-leaved evergreen trees	Height: 12–15 in.	1	1	2
	15–18 in.	2	1	2
	1824 in.	2	1.5	3
	24–30 in.	5	2	4
	30–36	5	2	4

(continued)

TABLE 16-4 (*continued*)

Type of Plant	Plant Size	Container Size (gal)[a]	Production Time in Years by Hardiness Zone	
			9 or 8	7 or 6
Spreading broad-leaved evergreen shrubs	Width: 9–12 in.	1	1	1
	12–15 in.	2	1.5	2
	15–18 in.	2	2	3
	18–24 in.	5	2.5	3
Dwarf or Globe broad-leaved evergreen shrubs	Height: 9–12 in.	1	1	1
	12–15 in.	2	1	2
	15–18	2	1.5	3
	18–24 in.	5	2	3
Large-growing broad-leaved evergreen shrubs or small trees	Height: 12–15 in.	1	1	1
	15–18 in.	2	1	2
	18–24 in.	2	1.5	3
	24–30 in.	5	2	3
	30–36	5	2	4

[a]American Association of Nurserymen trade designations and container specifications are as follows: 1 gal equals minimum of 5.5 in. across top and height of 6 in. or equivalent volume; 2 gal equals minimum of 7 in across top and height of 7.5 in or equivalent volume; 5 gal equals minimum of 9 in. across top and height of 10 in. or equivalent volume.

Source: Adapted from Stinson et al. (1971).

closely results in spindly growth and loss of the lower foliage. If you apply this spacing rule, most spring transplants can be placed pot tight or rim to rim for the first year of growth. This production technique shades and protects newly establishing roots in pots from hot summer rays of the sun until the top growth develops a canopy over the pot rim. At the beginning of the second year they are usually spaced as far apart as the crown diameter of the plants. This spacing requires three times the original space at the start of the second year. Many growers in cold climates provide for this expansion space by having extra-wide aisles between the overwintering structures.

In planning the production of container-grown crops, the following should be considered: a planting schedule, including types of plants, numbers needed, container sizes, and planting dates; total area required for each crop and all-weather surfaces for access to the plants; types and quantity of growing media and fertilizer program (see Chapter 12); building space, equipment, tools, irrigation system (see Chapter 13), and winter protection structures required (see Chapter 17); and labor for planting, moving, and cultural practices. The crop succession is fairly simple for 1-year crops, because each year one crop replaces another. Crops requiring 2 years will need about three times as much growing space the second year as they did the first year. Crops requiring 3 or 4 years usually remain at the second-year spacing. A crop-succession plan, with the space requirements drawn to scale, should be worked out in advance of planting so that costly errors (under- or overestimates) will not be made.

Site Preparation and Growing Surfaces

Site preparation should include provisions for adequate drainage, an efficient layout, freedom from weeds, year-round use, and a suitable base. A good site for growing nursery crops in containers should be well drained in order to carry off large amounts of water in a short time during rainstorms or by overhead summer irrigation. Careful site planning can reduce costs. It should include an efficient layout of growing areas and roadways for maximum use of machinery. Roadways should be constructed to carry heavily loaded trailer trucks with sufficient area allowed at all turns for the trucks to be maneuvered easily. Where container stock is being handled in large quantities with pallets and forklifts or wagons and tractors, it has been found worthwhile to pave those high-traffic areas with asphalt.

The base or growing surface should be relatively inexpensive to install and maintain. The site should be free of weeds and should be one that permits working year-round. Several types of materials have been used for bases for container plants in different parts of the country. The type that is best for a particular location usually depends on cost and availability. Those most commonly used include black plastic, fabric weed barrier, crushed stone, or asphalt. The least expensive solution is to spread black polyethylene sheets over a well-drained surface. Before plastic is laid down in the nursery, the area should be carefully graded, smoothed, and firmed so that the center of the bed is raised with a 2% crown above the edges for beds 100 ft wide (see Fig. 13–4). This grading will prevent puddling of water around containers and aid in rapid movement of water from the container bed. Loss of plants may result from water standing in low places on the plastic if the bed is not graded properly for good drainage. Some containers are manufactured with drainage holes in the bottom or very close to the bottom. These smooth bottom pots may cause problems on a plastic surface or gravel base. This is particularly true for plants susceptible to root rot. A herbicide, such as dichlobenil (Casoron), may be applied to the soil before the film is put in place. When the containers are placed on the film, weeds will not grow under the plastic, roots stay in the pots, and mud is eliminated. Black plastic will disintegrate and must be replaced after each crop. Another, but more expensive solution is to put down 6 in. of crushed stone ($\frac{1}{2}$ to $\frac{3}{4}$ in. diameter) over the black plastic and place the containers on the stone. This scheme has all the advantages of film, plus the additional benefit of being more permanent. Some growers are experimenting with a fabric weed barrier. The material is more expensive than sheets of black plastic, but it is more durable and allows for better drainage.

Containerizing Nursery Crops

Nursery stock can be planted in 1- to 5-gal containers by labor and machines using rooted cuttings, 1-year-old seedlings, dormant unrooted cuttings, dormant grafts, or plants previously grown in smaller pots. Some nurseries propagate their own plants, while others prefer to purchase liners. Planting is usually done in the late winter or spring as soon as shipments begin to open up areas for the newly potted plants. The plants should be placed in the center of the container, at the depth at which they originally grew (usually the root collar), with growing medium placed around the roots to assure good contact. The container is filled to within ½ to 1 in. (depending on pot size) of the rim to leave a space for water accumulation during irrigation. Most nurseries (small or large) devise an assembly line system with machines and labor so that the planting operation can be done efficiently. Usually, there are separate crews or individuals responsible for supplying plants and pots, filling pots, placing plants in pots, loading the planted plants, and moving them to the growing area, where they are set in place. A crew of five workers is usually able to plant, place, and hand water at the rate of 7000–12,000 per day provided that the procedure is well planned by management. The same crew can do up to 20,000 per day with a semiautomatic potting machine once they become familiar with the procedures. A plan that works well in small nursery operations is to place the filled containers on a flatbed truck or wagon, with two workers punching holes, two workers planting and placing the plants into the beds, and one worker watering. The worker that is watering will need to stop periodically and move the truck or wagon down the aisle between two beds. A modification of this procedure would be to have the containers already filled, properly spaced, and irrigated before planting in the growing area. This procedure is used for larger container sizes. Each worker performing physically demanding jobs should be rotated frequently for the comfort of the worker and maximum efficiency of the operation.

Pruning Container-Grown Plants

Pruning and shearing practices are the same for both a finished plant in a container and field-grown crops. Because of their usually faster growth rate when container grown, all the various types of plants should be sheared and formed more frequently in container culture. It is normally necessary to cut back leaders three or four times each growing season. If prostrate forms are not spaced adequately and pruned regularly, they will have a tendency to grow with a more upright habit and detract from the salable form.

There are several objectives of pruning container-grown nursery stock. One objective is to get as large a plant as possible, as quickly as possible, and at the same time, obtain a healthy plant with a form or shape that will be marketable. Usually, this means a plant that is dense, compact, symmetrical, healthy, and vigorous, a plant that is produced and sold at a profit. Another important objective of pruning is to produce a plant that transplants successfully, whether planted by a landscape contractor or homeowner. A good balance between root and shoot growth in container culture is vital to the successful establishment of a plant when it is planted in the landscape.

Definite rules for pruning ornamental plants in a nursery are difficult to give because plants vary widely in habit of growth. Pruning is both a dwarfing and an invigorating cultural practice, depending on how and when the heading-back or thinning-out pruning is done. Usually, a larger plant can be produced faster with minimum pruning, as severe pruning produces a smaller but more dense plant. The natural growth habit of a plant indicates the pruning needed to shape the plant. Rounding off (pruning sides and tops without regard to natural form) is a poor method of pruning. Because pruning is both a dwarfing (in summer) and invigorating (in winter) process, the commercial grower should use a combination system of pruning, which includes both heading-back terminals and thinning-out branches. This consists of heading back to increase density of thin plants, thinning areas of an otherwise dense plant, and thinning of dense growth to produce a plant that is taller and wider than it should be for its container size. Thinning may be used to increase the size of flowers and fruit by reducing the number of flowering branches after buds have developed. This is accomplished by increasing the amount of water and nutrients available for flower buds left on the plant. Heading-back plants before flower buds are set increases the number of branches and flowers but will usually reduce flower and fruit size.

Effective pruning of nursery plants begins with selection of the cuttings as well as pruning practiced early in the life of plants propagated from cuttings or seedlings. A compact container-grown plant can be produced more easily from large 4- to 6-in. cuttings than from smaller 2- to 3-in. cuttings. Smaller cuttings sometimes root faster, but take longer to produce plants to the size where heading back is done to increase the density of the potted plants. However, a 4- to 6-in. cutting usually has enough leaves to produce good rooting, and because of this will reach the stage sooner where pruning is begun to produce well-branched plants. When transplanting rooted cuttings, excessively long roots should be cut back. This will encourage branching and growth of new roots, and reduce development of kinked, circling, and girdling roots. In small-plant culture, cuttings and seedlings of species trained as shrubs should be pruned early and frequently to produce many breaks (lateral branches) low on the main stem to encourage good production and distribution of canes for scaffold branches.

The grower should carefully manage the pruning procedures because they are labor intensive and expensive. Much less time is required to prune small plants than larger ones. The main scaffold branches should be formed early so that later growth will be well distributed over the plant and more easily controlled. Young plants should be pruned as often as needed to produce the branching necessary for the best-quality plant. The number of times that pruning will be required from first potting until plants are sold will vary depending on several factors: natural habit of plant species or cultivar; adequate spacing; fertilization level; time in nursery production; size of container in balance with top growth; local conditions as it affects length of growing season; and time of the year that plants are potted. A combination of heading back and thinning should be practiced on older plants to produce compact growth in the natural shape of the plant rather than to shear plants indiscriminately, regardless of growth habit, density, or size.

HARVESTING METHODS

Usually, nursery crop schedules are planned to produce marketable-size plants for late winter shipments to meet the demand for early spring sales. Traditionally, the selling of nursery stock in the fall has been minimal. However, in recent years, fall nursery stock sales have increased due in part to the efforts of the National Planting Council, with their "Fall is for planting" theme, and the landscape industry's desire to improve fall sales. If more nursery stock could be sold in the fall season, fewer plants would need to be held in winter storage.

Bareroot Digging and Handling

Deciduous trees and shrubs are dug in the fall when top growth slows and leaves drop, indicating the first signs of dormancy. If deciduous plants are dug before reaching this dormant stage, they may grow very poorly when replanted the same fall or the following spring. A tractor-drawn U-blade is used for undercutting and lifting the plants from the row. Some nurseries use a modified potato digger for digging smaller sizes, such as rose bushes. Once the plants are dug they may be trimmed, graded, and bunched in the field or stacked in covered wagons with roots protected from drying out and transported to cold or common storage facilities. More often, the plants are quickly moved to storage to prevent drying; and the trimming, grading, labeling, and packaging to fill orders are done during the winter months when little outdoor work can be done. Trimming is done to remove dead, diseased, and broken roots and branches. Also, those trees and shrubs to be marketed as containerized stock can be potted using a container-growing medium.

Cold or common storage of bareroot nursery stock has several advantages for the nursery operation. Fall digging helps to spread the work load of preparing stock for sale over the winter months. It is more convenient for labor to label, grade, and bundle plants for rapid handling in the busy spring shipping season. Cold storage extends the period in the spring when nursery stock can safely be kept bareroot, thus extending the sales period. In the northern and midwestern United States, the spring season is short and it is important that nurseries shipping into those regions have dormant plant material to ship when planting time arrives. Cold storage also results in minimum losses from winter weather and animals, plus less digging in the wet early spring conditions.

Several types of storage are used for overwintering of bareroot nursery stock (see Chapter 17). The preferred modern method of storing bareroot stock is refrigerated storage with temperatures maintained between 32 and 38°F. An advantage of this system is that the low temperatures enable a grower to better control growth of parasitic and saprophytic fungi. Many of the damaging fungi will grow well at temperatures below those at which woody plants break dormancy. Treating plants with fungicides will also help to control fungi. A constant concern with overwinter storage is drying out of the root system. Buildings should be moisture-tight, with the roots packed in a moist packing material. Shingletow is a commonly used packing material for roots. Artificial humidification devices designed to maintain humidity near 95% within the entire storage area provide automated environmental control.

Once a building is filled with nursery stock, the mass of the plants affects the distribution of the air, so that some areas are colder or damper than others. These variations can be checked by placing high/low thermometers at several levels and locations in the building. Sensitive plants should be placed in the best spots (more constant temperature and humidity), and those which are easily stored can be placed in the poorer locations. In any case, walkways must be arranged to allow both for easy access to the stock and for good air circulation. Plants with very dense and fibrous root systems are especially susceptible to decay in storage. These types should be put in spots with better airflow and semi-evergreen types should be located where they can be easily and routinely inspected. When bareroot plants are sold, moist packing material should be provided around the roots and then the roots should be wrapped with a moist-retaining material, such as plastic. Those trees and shrubs to be marketed as bareroot and processed ball have the roots packed with an organic planting medium and secured firmly with burlap, just before delivery.

Digging and Handling Balled Stock

Generally, the larger sizes of deciduous types and all evergreen types of field-grown nursery stock are dug as a balled and burlapped, balled and potted, or balled and bagged. Many people assume that all trees are now dug with mechanical diggers, which is not true. It is still often more efficient and desirable to dig large orders of small trees bareroot or small quantities balled and burlapped by hand. Large shade trees of 3-in. caliper and above are dug mechanically.

Use of mechanical diggers increases the number of plants that can be dug in a day. Some growers use wire baskets with a burlap lining to drop the root balls in once the plants are dug. The wire baskets can be ordered in many sizes and can be tightened around the ball with hooks. There are, of course, many other types of containers available that can be used in conjunction with mechanical diggers, such as the balled and bagged system mentioned previously. It is important to dig the proper-size ball for a particular size plant. The American Association of Nurserymen (AAN) has designated certain minimum specifications (see Chapter 6).

A relatively new method of handling field-grown nursery stock that has become popular in the last few years is balled and potted digging. This means digging plants with a ball of earth and then potting the plants immediately into a container. This technique allows plants to be dug practically year round, giving the flexibility of root balls without the precise digging and wrapping involved with balling and burlapping. These plants are usually dug in early spring, potted and sold as soon as the roots become established in the container; or they may be dug in August and September after the top growth has ceased but while the roots are still actively growing (soil temperature above 45°F). Balled and potted plants usually adjust to their container in 4–6 weeks and are ready to be sold, or held over in polyethylene structures for an early spring market. Field potting is also feasible during the hot summer months after plants have made their initial flush of growth. These plants should be dug early in the morning, potted, and moved to a holding area quickly so that the root system does not dry out. The holding area should be shady and have an overhead sprinkler irrigation system. The plants should be held in this area until sufficient root regeneration occurs and leaves remain in a turgid condition.

Handling Container-Grown Stock

Container-grown nursery stock is ready to be sold when it has reached an appropriate size for the container. Table 16–4 indicates the usual time it takes to grow different types of stock to salable size. Sorting the stock into groups by grade is a time-consuming operation. Each plant must be examined and labeled. A limitation on container-grown stock is that it cannot be carried through an additional year in the same container. If plants are held too long in the same container, the root system will become pot bound (will have developed into a heavy, tight spiral around the inside wall and bottom of the container). When the plants are finally sold and planted, the root growth into the soil surrounding that spiral mass will be very slow to develop, if at all.

The Minnesota in-ground container-production system was developed in 1981 to overcome three serious problems associated with traditional container-growing methods: root circling in the container, plant stability in the wind, and winter injury of roots. The system was designed for tree production and has some unique features. A sturdy plastic container is buried in the ground to its top. Drainage holes 2 in. from the bottom create a reservoir for water pruning the roots by lack of oxygen. A 3-in. layer of gravel is placed in the bottom of the container to support the growing medium above the standing water. A fiber mat is placed on top of the gravel to prevent the growing medium from settling into the water-saturated gravel bed. An open-bottom liner is placed inside the buried container to hold the growing medium and to plant the tree liner. Trickle irrigation may be used to supply and manage the water needs of the tree. Field test results are limited, but the potential merits of this in-ground container system continue to be encouraging.

Most container-grown nursery plants are sold in early spring. Actually, both container-grown and balled stock can be successfully planted from early spring to late fall, but most customers prefer to plant in the spring. This planting tradition came about because deciduous field stock is usually transplanted at these times.

Postharvest Care of Nursery Plants

Considerable effort by nursery operations is given in production, as previously mentioned, and in the postharvest storage and shipping practices (see Chapters 10 and 17) to provide the best possible care for nursery stock. Often, this special handling is negated by insufficient care in the garden center or improper planting in the landscape. Growers should inform retailers and customers about proper care and landscape management practices. Many growers are using care tags on every plant species offered for sale. Cooperative Extension Service bulletins are available for retailers to provide their customers with instructions on planting, watering, fertilizing, pruning, and pest control. This service costs little, and the potential benefits are great for our industry.

SUMMARY

Nursery crop schedules begin with a market analysis to determine production quotas for different types of ornamental landscape plants. Once a production quota has been established to meet market demands, propagation by seed, cuttage, and/or graftage starts the systematic production practices for liners in small-plant culture that will be planted either as field-grown crops or container-grown crops in order to meet production quotas. Nursery growers must satisfy the cultural requirements of each crop for optimum growth of quality plants, which is the overall objective of the nursery.

REFERENCES

CHADWICK, L. C. 1953. Soils, sod, green manure, winter cover, and companion crops, and fertilizers for nursery stock production. Ohio Nursery Notes 22(5 and 6).

CHAPMAN, D. J. 1983. Cutting propagation for shade tree cultivars encourages development of regional plants. Am. Nurseryman 158(4):39–44.

COOK, T., and J. L. GREEN. 1985. Many grasses available for nursery aisles and plant protection. Am. Nurseryman 161(1):89–96.

DICKEY, R. D., E. W. McELWEE, C. A. CONOVER, and J. N. JOINER. 1978. Container growing of woody ornamental nursery plants in Florida. Florida Agric. Exp. Sta. Bull. 793.

FLEMER, W. F., III. 1981. How and when to prune nursery stock. Am. Nurseryman, CL III(8):11–132.

GILLIAM, C. H., and E. M. SMITH. 1980. Fertilization of container-grown nursery stock. Ohio Coop. Ext. Serv. Bull. 658.

KENNEDY, L. W., and E. M. SMITH. 1981. Care of nursery stock in retail outlets. Ohio Coop. Ext. Serv. Bull. 562.

MARTIN, C. W., and D. J. CHAPMAN. 1985. Softwood cuttage can be an easy and useful propagation method. Am. Nurseryman 161(11):37–39.

McGUIRE, J. J. 1972. Growing ornamental plants in containers: a handbook for the nurseryman. Rhode Island Coop. Ext. Bull. 197.

MOLLER, G. M. 1985. How one Oregon grower produces trees from softwood cuttings. Am. Nurseryman 162(5):68–69.

PELLETT, H. 1983. An update on the Minnesota System of container production. Am. Nurseryman 157(1):95–101.

PETERSON, C., and R. HEATLEY. 1986. Planting and care of ornamental landscape plants. Mich. Coop. Ext. Serv. Bull. E-1947.

———, and R. HEATLEY. 1986. Selecting ornamental plants. Mich. Coop. Ext. Serv. Bull. E-1936.

———, R. HEATLEY, G. ADAMS, D. SMITLEY, and D. ROBERTS. 1987. Diagnosing problems of ornamental landscape plants. Mich. Coop. Ext. Serv. Bull. E-2024.

PONDER, H., C. GILLIAM, and R. L. SHUMACK. 1983. Starting and operating a field shade tree nursery. Ala. Coop. Ext. Serv. Circular ANR-235.

REIGER, R., and C. E. WHITCOMB. 1983. Growers can now confine roots to in-field containers. Am. Nurseryman 158(8):31–34.

SMEAL, P. L., and J. S. COARTNEY. 1985. Starting a nursery business in Virginia. Va. Coop. Ext. Serv. Publ. 430-015.

SMITH, E. M., and C. H. GILLIAM. 1981. Fertilizing landscape and field grown nursery crops. Ohio Coop. Ext. Serv. Bull. 650.

STINSON, R. F., D. R. McCLAY, and G. Z. STEVENS. 1971. Nursery production—a teacher's manual. Pa. Agric. Exp. Sta. Teacher Education Series, 12(45).

YAWNEY, H. W. 1984. How to root and overwinter sugar maple cuttings. Am. Nurseryman 160(8):95–102.

SUGGESTED READING

BLUHN, W. L., and J. L. GREEN. 1979. Growing nursery stock—is it for me? Oregon State Univ. Ext. Serv. Manual 5.

DURYEA, M. L., and T. D. LANDIS. 1984. Forest nursery manual: production of bareroot seedlings. Martinus Nijhoff/Dr. W. Junk Publishers, Hingham, Mass.

INGRAM, D. L., J. T. MIDCAP, and D. L. GUNTER. 1980. Starting a wholesale nursery business. Fla. Coop. Ext. Serv. Circular 409A.

STANLEY, J., and A. TOOGOOD. 1981. The modern nurseryman. Faber & Faber Ltd., London.

WELCH, W. C. 1974. Entering the nursery or greenhouse business. Texas Agric. Ext. Serv. Bull. L-1221.

17 *Nursery Storage Facilities*

Storage facilities are employed by nurserymen for many reasons, including temporary and winter storage of plants, seeds, equipment, and supplies. The greatest need is for the storage of plants.

The oldest and most basic reason for the storage of plants in controlled environments is to maintain viability and quality during the period after removal from their production sites until they are replanted either in the nursery or in the landscape. Once plants are dug in the field or taken from the container-growing area, they are removed from their primary source of water. If they are not properly cared for, they will dehydrate and die.

Controlled-environment storage is also used for the protection of tender or semitender plants that would be injured or killed if left exposed to the rigors of the winter climate. This is especially true for container-grown plants, which may be vulnerable to root injury if the temperature falls below the critical minimum for the species. Also, when the soil is frozen, many species are very vulnerable to desiccation, particularly during periods of high sunlight, wind, or both.

Storage facilities can also be used to precondition plants for flowering and transplanting. Many bulbs and plants, such as azaleas and hydrangeas, that are forced for special holidays, require a period of exposure to cold temperature before they will bloom; this can best be accomplished in controlled-temperature rooms. Cool temperatures obtained in storage buildings can be used to delay bud break and to hold back the growth of plants in early spring so that the spring planting season can be extended. Also, they can be used to condition the tender growth on landscape plants that are dug in full leaf during the growing season, assuring a greater success following transplanting. In addition to modifying the environment to affect a plant response, storage facilities are used to aid in the processing and marketing of plants. In many parts of the nation the spring digging season starts late, because of climatic conditions. It is often much too short to allow sufficient time to dig, process, and deliver plant material for spring sales. On the other hand, the fall season is generally mild, and there is sufficient time to dig and store plants. Many nurseries have constructed plant storage facilities so that plants can be dug in the fall, then placed into winter storage, where they are processed (graded, packaged into wholesale units, labeled) and maintained in good condition for many months until they are shipped in later winter or early spring.

Plant propagators use cold-temperature storage facilities to store seeds, cuttings, budwood, and scions. Since seed production is affected by a multitude of environmental, biological, and physiological factors, it is necessary to collect seed when it is available and to store it for use in years when there is little or no seed produced. For example, shortleaf pine (*Pinus echinata*), which is an important conifer for reforestation in the south, produces a good crop of seed about once in 10 years. Therefore, it is necessary to collect and store the seed for a decade or longer to ensure an adequate annual supply. Fortunately, seeds from most woody plants can be stored successfully for long periods of time. This topic is thoroughly discussed in USDA Agriculture Handbook 450, *Seeds of Woody Plants in the United States* (see Appendix A). Storing rooted cuttings in polyethylene bags under controlled low temperature allows the propagator to use high-cost greenhouse space more efficiently. It is possible to obtain two or three crops of cuttings from the same bench space that would normally be used to propagate and hold one batch of cuttings until the time of planting.

Plant storage is another tool by which the nursery manager can gain a degree of control over both the plants and various marketing problems. There are a number of different types of facilities in which plants can be stored; each has its advantages and disadvantages. The nurseryman should consider these carefully and then construct those that best fit his or her and the plants' needs.

STORAGE FACILITIES

Use of *heeling-in grounds* is the oldest and simplest method of plant storage. It was used in ancient times and is still used extensively today. It is a method of temporary storage, providing minimal control of the environment, although sometimes plants are stored for many months. The plants are placed either on top of the ground or into a trench and the roots or rootballs are covered with a loose, damp medium. A mixture of peat and sawdust is often used to protect the roots of bare-root plants, since it is lightweight, retains moisture, and is easily worked about the roots. Year-old wood chips are used also for temporary storage of B&B plants where they are available. This method is used fairly extensively in nurseries, garden centers, and at landscape sites prior to planting (Fig. 17–1).

Dormant, bare-root, deciduous plants should be heeled-in with their stems oriented parallel to the nooontime rays of the sun. This helps to minimize desiccation of the stems during storage. When plants are received in a dehydrated state, they will benefit by soaking in water for 2–3 hr prior to heeling-in or planting. The

Figure 17–1　Nursery stock in temporary heeling-in storage. (Courtesy Kluck Nursery.)

roots of plants should not be exposed to long periods of freezing temperatures, especially below 25°F, since roots are very vulnerable to low-temperature injury (Table 17–1). They should be mulched prior to the onset of freezing temperatures. Balled and burlapped (B&B) or containerized plants that are mulched after the soil balls have frozen are very prone to desiccation injury.

Cold frames, of all types of construction, have been used for hundreds of years to modify the environment about young tender plants. In addition to their use as propagation structures, they can be used to overwinter plants. Although both shallow and deep-pit frames can be used as an overwintering structure, the deep pit provides the best protection. The environment is modified by the warmth of the soil and by the shadow cast by the south wall of the pit during the winter storage period. Therefore, the best orientation of the cold frames used for winter storage is in an east-west direction. To ensure successful storage, the plants must be fully dormant prior to sealing of the frame for the winter storage period. To ensure maintaining low storage temperature conditions within the cold frame, the sash may need to be shaded, and the structure or the plants within may need to be insulated. Bales of straw, a straw mulch, microfoam, or other appropriate materials can be used for this purpose.

Microfoam tunnels are the modern version of the cold frame and the heeling-in grounds. They are used to overwinter small container-grown plants, in situ. The dormant plants are laid on their sides, close together, in long narrow rows. The

TABLE 17-1   Average **Killing Temperatures**[a] for Roots of Selected Species of
Woody Ornamental Plants

		Killing Temperature	
Botanical Name	Common Name	°C	°F
Magnolia soulangiana	Saucer magnolia	−5.0	23
Magnolia stellata	Star magnolia	−5.0	23
Cornus florida	Flowering dogwood	−6.7	20
Daphne cneorum	Garland flower	−6.7	20
Ilex crenata 'Convexa'	Convex Japanese holly	−6.7	20
Ilex crenata 'Hetzi'	Hetz Japanese holly	−6.7	20
Ilex opaca	American holly	−6.7	20
Ilex crenata 'Stokesii'	Stokes Japanese holly	−6.7	20
Pyracantha coccinea	Fire thorn	−7.8	18
Cryptomeria japonica	Japanese cedar	−8.9	16
Cotoneaster horizontalis	Rock cotoneaster	−9.4	15
Viburnum carlesii	Korean spice viburnum	−9.4	15
Cytisus praecox	Warminster broom	−9.4	15
Buxus sempervirens	Common boxwood	−9.4	15
Ilex glabra	Inkberry	−9.4	15
Euonymus fortunei 'Carrierei'	Carrier euonymus	−9.4	15
Euonymus fortunei 'Argenteo-marginata'	Variegated euonymus	−9.4	15
Hederia helix 'Baltica'	Baltic ivy	−9.4	15
Pachysandra terminalis	Japanese pachysandra	−9.4	15
Vinca minor	Common periwinkle	−9.4	15
Pieris japonica 'Compacta'	Compact lily-of-the-valley bush	−9.4	15
Acer palmatum 'Atropurpureum'	Bloodleaf Japanese maple	−10.0	14
Cotoneaster adpressa praecox	Nan-Shan cotoneaster	−12.2	10
Taxus media 'Nigra'	Black Anglojap yew	−12.2	10
Rhododendron 'Gibraltar'	Gibraltar azalea	−12.2	10
Rhododendron 'Hinodegiri'	Azalea hybrid	−12.2	10
Pieris japonica	Lily-of-the-valley bush	−12.2	10
Leucothoe fontanesiana	Drooping leucothoe	−15.0	5.0
Pieris floribunda	Fetterbush	−15.0	5.0
Euonymus fortunei 'Colorata'	Purple leaf wintercreeper	−15.0	5.0
Juniperus horizontalis	Creeping juniper	−17.8	0.0
Juniperus horizontalis 'Douglasii'	Waukegan juniper	−17.8	0.0
Rhododendron carolinianum	Carolina rhododendron	−17.8	0.0
Rhododendron catawbiense	Mountain rosebay	−17.8	0.0
Rhododendron P. J. M. hybrids	P. J. M. rhododendron	−23.3	−10
Potentilla fruticosa	Shrubby cinquefoil	−23.3	−10
Picea glauca	White spruce	−23.3	−10
Picea omorika	Serbian spruce	−23.3	−10

[a]Highest temperature that killed more than 50% of root system and reduced top growth.
Source: Adapted from Havis (1976).

length and width of the rows are determined by the nurseryman, as are the size of the microfoam and white poly sheets used to cover the plants. (A width of 48 ft is common since the poly comes in a 50-ft width.) The plants are then covered with microfoam, which in turn is covered with sheets of white polyethylene. The edges of the poly are then covered with soil to seal the tunnels.

A suggested guideline as to when to cover in the fall and to uncover in spring is to use the F-dates (date of first frost in the fall and last frost in the spring). A time to cover in the fall might be F + 30 or F + 45, and to uncover in the spring might be F − 30 or F − 45. The exact dates will vary with the latitude of the nursery and with seasonal variation. When uncovering in the spring, be prepared to recover a time or two due to the return of freezing temperatures.

This method utilizes the moderating affects of soil heat to protect the covered plant from cold-temperature injury. In addition, the polyethylene cover protects the plants against desiccation injury. The ground temperature within the microfoam tunnel remains considerably warmer than the outside air temperature; some nurseries have reported ground temperature remaining in the low to mid-50s (°F) throughout the storage period.

A few precautions are necessary to ensure the success of this method: (1) All plants must be dormant prior to being covered; (2) the ground area must be well drained and free of organic debris; and (3) plants that are wet due to rain, snow, dew, or frost should not be covered, although the container medium should be well watered a day or two prior to covering.

The *shade house*, more commonly known as the lathhouse when lath construction is employed, modifies temperature, light intensity, and relative humidity. These, in turn, reduce the amount of transpiration that takes place from the plants stored within. Large groves of trees can serve the same purpose. The shade house is commonly utilized for the temporary storage of plant material during the shipping season and is often used in conjunction with the heeling-in grounds. Some nurseries utilize the shade house in the production of shade-tolerant species such as *Pachysandra* and *Vinca* and in the production of young evergreen transplants (e.g., *Taxus*).

When building lathhouses or constructing seed or transplant beds that will be protected with lath covers, it is best to construct them so that the lath strips are oriented in a vertical position on the south and west sides and in a north-south direction on the top. This orientation of the lath provides for a moving sun-shade pattern on a daily basis. During hot, dry periods this small difference can be critical, especially for young seedlings or recently transplanted plants. Structure orientation is less important when it is covered with shade cloth rather than with lath.

Plastic houses, although originally designed as a temporary structure for growing plants, are now used extensively for the winter storage of plants, especially for evergreens in northern areas. The houses are primarily of a quonset-type construction (Fig. 17–2) and covered with one or two layers of polyethylene. The double-layer, air-separated structure provides greater insulation due to the dead air

Figure 17–2 Plastic storage house for overwintering evergreens. (Courtesy Conard-Pyle Co.)

space between the two layers of polyethylene. A small electric air blower positioned to blow air between the layers provides enough air pressure to keep the plastic layers separated, even on very large structures. The film used as the cover for plastic houses should be 4- to 6-mil polyethylene, to withstand the stress caused by winter storms. The film may be either clear or milky, depending upon the storage objective. The house should be constructed and the plastic installed in such a way as to form a relatively vaportight chamber to aid in maintaining a high relative humidity within the structure. Where clear plastic is utilized or where there is not a vapor seal, it will be necessary to shade or irrigate the plants occasionally in the late winter or early spring. It may also be necessary to ventilate to keep the temperature low to avoid rapid dehydration of plant tissue and prevent early breaking of dormancy. However, when houses are vented, they must be irrigated more frequently to replace the moisture lost during venting.

Polyhouses, constructed primarily for overwintering of evergreens in the most northern regions of the country, are best when they are designed with a low profile to reduce the heat-transfer area and to aid in retaining snow for insulation; oriented in a north-south direction to reduce solar heating; and covered with milky plastic to minimize penetration of the sun's rays. The combination of low profile, north-south orientation, and milky plastic aids in maintaining the desired environment for keeping stored evergreens in good condition through the winter period. However, plants stored in plastic houses can be induced into early growth by constructing them with a higher profile, orientating in an east-west direction, and covering with clear plastic. The plants must be irrigated periodically, since they will transpire more moisture under the warmer, low-humidity conditions. It will be necessary to ventilate the house on sunny days to minimize high interior temperatures, but venting should be avoided when soil balls are frozen.

The *common storage* is a building designed to take advantage of changes in air density and the insulating properties of soil. When air cools, it becomes heavy and flows like a fluid into areas of lower elevation forcing the lighter, warmer air up into the higher elevations. Early common storage buildings were constructed either below ground or in hillsides to gain these advantages. However, since the development of high-quality insulation materials, most common storage facilities are constructed totally above ground. By timely control of vents in the lower part of the walls and in the roof of the buildings, or by opening the drive-through doors at both ends of the building in the evening when the outside air temperature is lower than the interior temperature and closing them at sun-up, low temperatures can be maintained fairly successfully within the building during winter and early spring. However, common storage is not too effective in maintaining dormancy of plants in the late spring because of loss of cold-temperature control.

Refrigerated storage is an advanced model of insulated common storage. It is used to gain a greater degree of control over temperature and humidity to extend the storage period. The construction of a refrigerated storage is similar to that of an insulated common storage except that (1) the insulation is generally thicker, (2) the floor is of concrete and may be insulated, (3) refrigeration equipment is installed to control the temperature, and (4) humidification devices are used to control humidity.

There are many types of excellent insulating materials available, and since most of them have relatively low thermal conductivity, the choice of an insulator to use in the construction of a refrigerated storage will depend more on the total cost of construction and the cost of upkeep. The semirigid plastic or polystyrene foam types are easy to install and are relatively inexpensive. The thickness of insulation that is needed varies with the temperature differential between the outside and the interior of the storage and the relative cost of insulation versus the cost of refrigeration equipment and operating energy. For most nurseries in the northern part of the United States, the insulation equivalent of 4 in. of corkboard on the walls and 6 in. on the ceiling appears to be adequate. This is equal to a total resistance (R_t) value* of 20 for vermiculite-filled cinderblock walls and about 23 for the ceiling.

Whenever there are temperature differences on two sides of a wall, such as the walls of a storage facility, there will be movement of water vapor from the warm side to the cold side. When this takes place, the insulation becomes damp, thus reducing its effectiveness. A vapor barrier of material such as aluminum foil, polyethylene film, or asphalt-covered or impregnated materials should be installed to impede the flow of moisture into the insulation.

---

*Calculated from values obtained from Heating, Ventilating, and Air Conditioning Guide, Amer. Assoc. Heat., Ref., and Air Conditioning Eng., N.Y., 1959.

It is not advisable to place a vapor barrier on both sides of the insulation, since the moisture can become trapped within the insulation. The cool side should always remain unsealed to allow the insulation an opportunity to dry if it should become damp. The barrier should be placed on the high-vapor-pressure side, which is the interior side of the insulation for most nursery storage buildings during the winter months. Nursery storage buildings can be insulated with a moisture-resistant, rodent-proof insulation material that can be sprayed onto the interior walls and ceiling, thus avoiding the need to install a vapor barrier. A polyurethane, low-flame foam can be used for insulation, but it is flammable and when burned produces a gas that is very toxic to human beings and animals. It should be used only when suitable thermal barriers are provided.

Details on the construction and operation of nursery storages are contained in *Storage of Nursery Stock*, available from the American Association of Nurserymen, and USDA Agricultural Handbook 66, *The Commercial Storage of Fruits, Vegetables and Florist and Nursery Stocks*.

ADDITIONAL FACILITIES

In addition to the previously discussed facilities used for the storage of plant material, the following facilities are used to prolong the storage life of various high-value horticultural products. They may at some time in the future be used more extensively for the storage of high-value nursery products. Therefore, a brief description of each is warranted.

The *jacketed system* of storage, originally designed for the storage of frozen foods, has been adapted for the storage of fresh fruit, vegetables, and nursery products. It is used fairly extensively by European nurserymen to provide better storage conditions and control pathogens such as botrytis. Bare-root nursery stock has been stored successfully up to 8 months with a good rate of survival following planting in the field. The system is designed to maintain a suitable low temperature (0°C/32°F), high relative humidity (95–98%), with a minimum amount of air movement. The jacket-cooled storage is a standard insulated refrigerated storage room with a built-in inner storage chamber constructed to asbestos plates which have high heat transmission. The inner storage room air is cooled by circulating cold air in the air space between the inner storage chamber (called the jacket) and the outer insulated storage room. This system prevents the plant material from being in direct contact with the cold, dry air from the evaporator. Also, the relative humidity within the storage room is not directly affected by the refrigeration equipment. The jacketed system prevents the condensation of water vapor in the insulation of the room and reduces frost formation on the refrigeration coils.

To assure high relative humidity within the jacketed chamber, the floor is wetted prior to loading, damp sphagnum moss is used on the roots of the plants, and the floor is dampened periodically, as needed, during the storage period.

Since the inner jacketed storage room temperature is dependent upon the air flowing outside the jacket, it is important that the outer chamber be controlled to within a half degree of the desired temperature with the aid of electronic thermostats. It is desirable that a number of sensors be employed and that they be aspirated.

A design that has proven practical and maintains a uniform temperature throughout the jacketed storage is one in which the rate of cool air flow in the side wall spaces between the jacket and outer storage wall is uniform all around the room. The air is blown into the ceiling space with fans and then flows by gravity down through the wall spaces and returns under the floor to the cooling coils. The volume of air flowing over the jacket should be sufficient to limit the temperature differential to 3°F (1.5°C) between the air entering and that leaving the jacket wall spaces. A vapor barrier is required to prevent the movement of moisture from the storage chamber into the jacket atmosphere. Details of design to meet the individual requirements can be obtained from the extension specialist in postharvest physiology, located at a land grant university, or from engineering firms familiar with the construction and operation of storage facilities.

The *filacell* is another method for maintaining a high relative humidity within a storage chamber at low temperature. A filacell is an efficient air washer that provides a high humidity at low temperatures with a high rate of air circulation. The filacell provides a massive wet-surface area within a small volume (2000 linear feet of nonfilament polypropylene per cubic foot of cell). It functions by chilled water moving down through the cell after being evenly sprayed, at low pressure (3–5 psi), over the upper surface as air moves upward through the cell. The temperature of the water controls the air temperature to within a variation of $\frac{1}{2}$°C.

In practice, a bank of filacell units is supported over a large tank of water. The water temperature in the tank is controlled with refrigeration or heating units. The water is pumped to a spray nozzle located above the filacell. As the water moves downward in the cells, air is forced upward at a high velocity (600 ft^3/min) producing a moisture-ladened air that both cools and humidifies the storage.

Controlled atmospher (CA) *storage*, designed for the long-term storage of apples and pears, is not used for the storage of nursery stock, since the economic gain does not, at present, justify the investment in the construction of a gastight building. It decreases the rate of respiration, which is accomplished by increasing the level of carbon dioxide while decreasing the level of oxygen in the atmosphere. High concentrations of CO_2, 40% and greater, have been used to retard bud break and growth of dormant rose plants and herbaceous perennials. Use of this technique has been limited to small size containers. But it could be a useful technique to control bud break of dormant nursery stock.

Hypobaric storage or low-pressure storage (LPS) is a relatively new concept for the storage of perishable commodities. The idea originated in the late 1960s with S. P. Burg of Miami, Florida. The commodity to be stored is maintained in a refrigerated, vacuum chamber at a constant subatmospheric pressure. The chamber is ventilated with fresh, humid air by continuously evacuating the storage chamber with a vacuum pump. The optimum temperature, absolute pressure, and rate of air change vary with the commodity. LPS has been used successfully for the storage of a number of high-value flowers, fruits, and vegetables. Its economic feasibility for the storage of nursery products depends on the cost versus gain considerations compared to standard storage methods.

The selection and development of a plant storage facility must be related to the storage requirements and value of the plants to be stored, but must also meet the needs of management in attaining production and market objectives. It must be adjusted to the climate of the area where it is to be built and operated. Because construction of storage facilities represents a large capital investment, they should be carefully planned, constructed, and maintained. If properly managed, they are another tool that management can use to gain control over the environment, to provide quality plant material at the time the customer desires delivery, and to better program utilization of the labor force.

FACTORS INVOLVED IN STORAGE OF NURSERY CROPS

Five important factors for the successful winter storage of nursery crops are physiological condition of the plants placed into storage, effective control of storage temperature, maintenance of a high relative humidity, air quality, and sanitation.

Physiological Condition of Plants

Nursery stock intended for winter storage should be fully mature and dormant, free of insects, diseases, and mechanical injury. Deciduous species should be defoliated. Changing climatic conditions in the fall of the year, including short days and cold temperatures, initiate maturation of plant tissue to withstand the rigors of winter. These same conditions also aid in conditioning plants for winter storage. Mature plant tissue is less prone to injury due to cold temperature and desiccation than is immature tissue. Determinate species and plants that respond to short days appear to develop cold-temperature hardiness sooner than indeterminate species or plants that are not responsive to day length. Shoots and vegetative buds develop a greater tolerance to cold temperature than do roots or flower buds. Some species stored above ground in containers are more subject to root injury than are their shoots. Flower buds are often killed by exposure to specific low temperature, while the shoot buds remain fully viable.

Bare-root conifers, to be lifted in the fall for overwinter storage, should have completed their growth phase. The end of the root-growth period coincides with the time that soil temperature in the root zone declines to 50°F (10°C) and the white root tips are ½ in. or less in length. An examination of the root system can be a subjective guide to time of digging. Root systems of Norway spruce seedlings become inactive early in the fall and are sequentially followed by balsam fir, Douglas fir, white pine, and then red, Scots, and Austrian pine.

In addition to hardening of the roots of plants prior to harvesting, care must also be taken relative to handling of the plants during the digging and gathering operations prior to placing the plants in storage. To assure the best possible chance of having good plant survival during storage, the plants should be carefully lifted from the growing area with a minimum of injury to the plants. All too often, serious injuries are inflicted on plants during the harvesting operations. The five most common types of injuries associated with plant harvesting operations in nurseries, include abrasion of stems, breakage of branches, girdling of stems—especially at the root collar—breakage of roots, and worst of all, serious reduction of the functional root system. All of these injuries can be avoided by proper handling of the plants during the harvesting operation.

Dormant, mature plants should be placed in storage prior to onset of the adverse environmental conditions that prevail during winter. Nurserymen can speed up the process of maturation so that plant material programmed for winter storage can be begun earlier and the workload spread out over a longer time period. This can be accomplished to some degree by (1) withholding water in late summer, (2) withholding ammonium-nitrogen fertilizers in late summer, (3) root pruning in early fall, and (4) avoidance of top pruning after midsummer. Although it is not possible to control natural rainfall, irrigation practices can be terminated to aid in maturing plants. Plants in a healthy, vigorous condition will store better than unhealthy plants in a weaker condition. Therefore, plants should be maintained on a fertilizer program that results in good vigor. However, some plants appear to be less hardy when fertilized late in the growing season, with ammonium-nitrogen fertilizer.

Deciduous plants that fail to defoliate naturally, prior to digging for storage, can be aided in the process by employing one or more of the following practices: (1) hand stripping, (2) use of rubber-fingered mechanical beaters, (3) grazing activities of sheep, (4) sweating, and (5) by the use of chemical defoliants. Hand stripping, although used, is too expensive to employ when labor costs are high. Mechanical beaters or sheep can do considerable damage to the plants and should be used with care. However, all three methods have been or are used to defoliate nursery stock. The process of sweating is still used to remove remaining leaves prior to storing deciduous plants. It is time-consuming and, if not carefully done, can cause considerable injury to plants due to overheating.

Chemically induced defoliation, prior to digging for storage, is a potentially promising method of defoliation. Unfortunately, no single chemical has been found to be effective on a wide variety of plants. Research has demonstrated certain chemicals to be effective defoliants on some crops. Potassium iodide at a concentration of 0.2–0.3% was effective in causing defoliation (75–100%) in most cultivars of apple, cherry, peach, and apricots, although seedling fruit trees responded poorly. Bromodine was effective on a number of species. When applied at a concentration of 0.25% (200–300 gal/acre-in.), in two or three applications, at weekly intervals, leaf abscission (90–100%) was effected in cherry, pear, and peach. A 0.50% concentration was needed for similar results on apple and prune, and a 1% spray has effectively defoliated roses. Nacconol NR (0.5–4.0%) has been used to defoliate nursery stock in some nurseries. Ethrel (2-chloroethylphosphonic acid) applied at 2000 ppm in two or three weekly applications was effective in defoliating apples and Italian prune, whereas only 500–1000 ppm was needed to defoliate Mazzard cherry and Bartlett pear. However, a combination of ethephon (200–400 ppm) with a surfactant has caused injury to shoots of some cultivars of apple when used as a defoliant.

Nurserymen planning to use chemical defoliants should test the chemicals on a limited basis prior to extensive field application, since plant response is variable with species, cultivar, environment, and condition of the plant at time of treatment. Best response has been in late season, to hasten the natural abscission process. Legally, only chemicals registered as a chemical defoliant for nursery stock may be used.

After the plants have been dug, they must be transported to the storage building, graded, and placed into storage. Some plants, for example, roses, may be graded and bundled in the field and then transported to storage. However, most plants are dug and transported to a temporary storage until most of the digging has been completed. Following the rush of the digging season, the material is graded, pruned, tagged, bound, or packaged into wholesale units and placed in storage.

In most common storages, the plants are placed into ricks, whereas in refrigerated storages the practice is to use bins, pallets, or polylined boxes and stack them with the aid of forklift trucks. Snap-on frames, made of tubular steel, can be attached to pallets for storing container-sized material or B&B plants. Portable metal racks are used by some nurseries to good advantage. These freestanding, portable storage racks are available in a number of sizes and allow the storage manager greater flexibility in the utilization of the storage area than is permitted with stationary wooden structures. Also, the metal construction has a longer functional life than does wood. When possible, species that respond in a similar fashion should be stored together. Experience and good plant sense can be used as a guide in choosing the species that store well together. Superior storage life of nursery plants requires that only mature, quality plants be placed in storage.

Temperature Control

Temperature has been defined as the degree of hotness or coldness measured on a definite scale and its degree determines the flow of heat. When a warm object is brought in contact with a cold object, the former is cooled while the latter is warmed. Thus, heat flows from the warm object to the cool object. If a layer of felt, rockwool, styrofoam, or a vacuum is placed between the two objects, the rate of change in temperature is much slower. It is this principle which is employed in the construction and operation of common and refrigerated storages.

Temperature plays an important part in all metabolic functions of plants. At high temperatures, photosynthesis, respiration, transpiration, and so on, go on at a rapid rate, whereas at a lower temperature the rate is much slower. The storage life of plants is prolonged by reducing respiration and transpiration to a low level by maintaining the plants at as low a temperature as possible without injury to the plants. Low ambient temperatures also reduce the incidence of infection by fungi.

In general, most deciduous, bare-root, plant material, when maintained at a temperature of 32–35°F, will remain dormant and free of mold. However, some will not and must be maintained at a colder temperature. It has been found, for example, that cherries, peaches, and lilac do best if maintained at a temperature of 33–35°F, whereas roses, herbaceous perennials, strawberry plants, and conifer seedlings do best if kept at a temperature below freezing in the vicinity of 28–30°F. Rooted cuttings store successfully at temperatures between 33 and 39°F.

Plant material in containers and B&B plants overwintered in plastic houses, which afford minimum control of temperature, are highly susceptible to root injury at temperatures below 24°F (Table 17–1). Therefore, measures must be taken to protect the roots of sensitive species from cold-temperature injury; this normally involves mulching.

The actual killing temperature will vary with the degree of plant dormancy at the time of exposure to the low-temperature stress. When plants are preconditioned for low-temperature storage and the temperature remains uniformly low prior to exposure to cold-temperature stress, the roots will generally survive provided that the temperature does not go below the average killing temperature for the species. However, if the low-temperature stress follows a period of fluctuating temperatures, especially temperatures that are conducive to growth, the roots could be injured at temperatures significantly higher than the average killing temperature. Also, the roots of newly rooted cuttings have a tendency to be less tolerant of cold-temperature stress than plants with a year or more of growth. To minimize root injury, plants should be stored at a temperature at least 3–5°F above the average killing temperature.

Best results in the storage of bare-root nursery stock are obtained if the temperature of the storage room is held fairly constant. Fluctuations of more than 3°F above or below the desired temperature are undesirable. An increase in temperature can result in decreasing storage life of the nursery stock, development of sprouts, and increased incidence of decay. A decrease in temperature by a few degrees can result in the formation of dew, and a large drop in temperature, below the critical temperature minimum, can result in freezing injury to the roots.

Large variations in storage room temperature can be avoided if the building is properly constructed, insulated, and provided with sufficient refrigeration equipment. Under these conditions, the temperature difference between the refrigerant and the ambient air of the storage room is kept relatively small (2–3°F). Temperature control is generally maintained better in large rooms than in small ones when both are filled to capacity. This is because the larger mass functions as a cold temperature "sink," moderating temperature changes.

Good-quality thermometers should be used to check temperatures of the storage room on a regular basis and to obtain data for the maintenance of continuous-temperature records. In many nursery storage rooms, thermometers are placed on a pole near a door at a height of 5½ ft as a matter of convenience. Temperatures should be taken at the floor, ceiling, and halfway levels, plus within bundles of nursery stock to determine if a uniform ambient temperature prevails throughout the room. By proper use of thermometers, it is possible to gain a high degree of temperature control, which in turn will increase the storage life and maintain the quality of the stored plants.

When placing the plant material into cold-temperature storage, it is desirable to remove the field heat of the plants and to obtain equilibrium between the product temperature and the ambient air of the storage as quickly as possible. This will reduce moisture loss, increase storage life, and maintain the quality of the producct. Under most situations, plant material being placed into cold-temperature storage will be 20–40°F warmer than the air in the storage chamber. Under these conditions, the plant material loses moisture, which could result in desiccation of the plants. Plant material that is more than 10°F warmer than the storage air into which it will be placed should be precooled. This can be accomplished either by placing the plant material in a precooling room and circulating cold air (35–40°F), or by holding the material out of doors overnight (provided that the temperature does not go below the dew point or that which would injure the roots). Also, there should be a low probability of rain if the plant material is to be left out overnight. Wet plant material placed into storage increases the possibility of disease infection. Plant material harvested during periods when cold temperatures prevail can be placed directly into storage without precooling. Storage rooms should also be precooled to the desired temperature prior to loading with plant material. In some situations, particularly with common storage facilities, the storage room air can be cooled by opening the vents during cool night or evening periods and closing the vents during warm daytime periods.

Refrigeration needs for a nursery storage should be based on the storage temperature; the R_t value of the insulation in the walls, ceiling, and floor of the structure; the anticipated heat leakage into the storage while it is being used during the warmest months; and the heat of respiration (HR) of the stored stock. An estimate for HR, based on information for bare-root, dormant rose bushes, is about 3000 Btu of heat by each ton of living plant material per day of storage at 32°–36°F.

A simple practice that can aid in reducing energy requirements in the operation of nursery storages is the planting of evergreen trees on the south and west sides of the structures to shield the walls from the direct rays of the sun. For small structures a hedge planting of arborvitae or a similar type of evergreen is satisfactory. For larger structures, a planting of pine or spruce trees is more appropriate.

Humidity Control

Maintaining proper water-vapor levels within nursery storage facilities is an important factor in the successful storage of plant material. The moisture condition in the air of nursery storage rooms is generally described by relative humidity (RH). This is a ratio of the water vapor actually contained in the air to the amount that it would contain if the air were saturated at the observed temperature. Water vapor functions as a gas and exerts a pressure proportional to the amount present. For physiological purposes, the vapor pressure (VP) is expressed in millimeters of mercury (mm Hg). The moisture diffusion rate, all other factors being equal, is a function of the difference between the VP within the plant and the VP of the ambient atmosphere. This difference is known as vapor pressure deficit (VPD). The smaller the VPD, the slower the rate of moisture loss. For example, plant material in cold storage at 32°F with its intercellular spaces fully saturated has a VP of 4.5 mm Hg, whereas the storage atmosphere at a RH of 90% has a VP of 4.0 mm Hg, producing a VPD of 0.5 mm Hg (which is a small difference). With an increase in temperature to 41°F the VP of the plants (100% saturated) becomes a 6.5 mm Hg and the VP of the storage at 80% RH becomes 5.4 mm Hg, producing a VPD of 1.1 mm Hg, which is two times greater than the previous combination, resulting in a more rapid loss of moisture from the plant material.

Plants stored in plastic structures are subject to considerable variation in VP. If they are exposed to conditions that create a high VPD within the structure, they will desiccate. As previously stated, the orientation of the structure and the type of covering can seriously affect the VP conditions within the structure. When the sun's rays strike the structure in such a manner that they penetrate, they will warm the interior atmosphere, and if they strike the leaves the leaf temperature will be increased substantially. Under such conditions, a high VPD is produced, causing a rapid loss of moisture from the leaves. If the soil is frozen or if the plants are not watered, they will soon desiccate.

It is not uncommon for temperatures in clear plastic houses, oriented in an east-west direction, to reach 60–70°F, and leaf temperatures to attain levels of 100°F or more on clear, sunny days in winter when the outside air temperature may be in the low 30s (Fig. 17–3). If the inside air temperature were 68°F with a RH of 40% and the leaf temperature reached 104°F, the VPD would be 48.5.

	Temp (°F)	RH	VP
Leaf	104	100	55.5
Air	68	40	7.0
VPD			48.5

Plants stored in clear polyethylene houses and oriented in an east-west direction are most prone to this type of injury, whereas plants stored in a house oriented in a north-south direction and covered with milky polyethylene will be exposed to a much lower VPD and generally will survive rather long periods of winter storage. The relationship between temperatures, RH, VP, and VPD is summarized in Appendix L.

Water vapor can be added to the storage atmosphere by various means. In refrigerated structures it is commonly added with the aid of humidifiers or by flooding the floor in concrete structures at periodic intervals. In common storages with dirt floors, it is maintained by placing damp shingletow* about the roots of the plants and wetting the floor periodically during the storage period. In plastic struc-

*Fine, shred-like shavings produced as a by-product in the manufacture of cedar shingles.

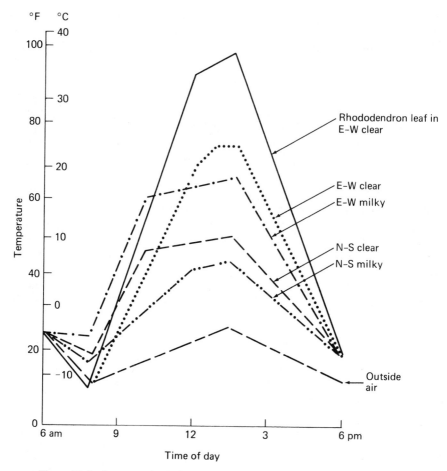

Figure 17–3 Representative leaf and air temperatures occurring on a clear day in winter within plastic structures as affected by structure orientation and type of plastic covering. (From Davidson and Mecklenburg, 1974.)

tures, it can be maintained at fairly high levels by using milky plastic as the outside cover, by spraying a latex paint onto clear plastic, by the use of shade cloth, or by adding water vapor to the enclosed atmosphere. Maintenance of a high RH in storage structures is directly related to maintaining the storage life and plant quality. Therefore, it should be checked periodically. This can be accomplished with the aid of a sling psychrometer, a hygrometer, or with electrical sensors. Instructions for use and calculation of RH are furnished with the psychrometer. The hygrometer and electrical sensors have direct readout of RH.

Air Quality and Movement

Air quality and circulation are also important factors in maintaining the quality of plants in storage. The air must be fresh and free of pollutants that might cause problems to stored plants. The unsaturated hydrocarbons, ethylene and carbon monoxide, have been reported to adversely affect nursery plants in storage. Since fruit, particularly ripe or decaying fruit, generates ethylene, it should not be placed in the same storage with nursery plants.

Loading equipment operated within the storages should be powered either by batteries or propane, to avoid contamination of the air with carbon monoxide and ethylene. Gasoline-powered equipment should be used only in well-ventilated structures, although they can be equipped with a catalytic burner for use in closed structures. The burners are effective only on equipment that operates many hours at a time because they must be hot in order to function efficiently. They are of little value for equipment that is used for only a few minutes at a time.

Air in the storage area must circulate to maintain an even temperature throughout the structure. Good stacking and spatial arrangements within the storage are needed (Fig. 17–4). There should be air passages between the plant material and the walls and ceiling, as well as between stacks, ricks, boxes, bins, or pallets. To assure even air distribution throughout the storage, a horizontal circulator fan should be installed in the ceiling of refrigerated storages and vertical circulator fans on the floor of common storage facilities. The air movement within the storage area should not be too rapid; a rate of approximately 50 linear feet per minute is usually sufficient.

Sanitation

Good sanitation practices within the plant storage structure are essential to assure a high level of plant viability and quality at the time of take-out, following long periods of winter storage. These practices relate to three areas: the structure and related equipment, the plants, and the operators.

The storage structure should be thoroughly cleaned and inspected. It should be free of all forms of organic debris, with all unnecessary openings sealed, the vents should be screened to prevent the entrance of rodents, and the insulation should be inspected and repaired if necessary. All related storage equipment should also be cleaned and repaired as needed. If necessary, the interior of the structure should be painted. Finally, the structure and all related equipment should be either fumigated or sterilized, as appropriate.

Plant material going into long-term winter storage should be fully mature, dormant, and free of insects and diseases. In some situations it may be desirable to spray plants going into storage with a fungicide to minimize loss of quality due to diseases. At no time should fruit or vegetable products be stored in conjunction with valuable woody nursery products.

Finally, workers should enter the storage facility only to perform their duties associated with the operation of the facility. Their clothing, especially their footware, should be clean (free of decaying organic matter, which could be a source of infection). Workers should be instructed to keep the storage area clean and neat at all times and to report to their supervisor any signs of loss in plant quality or changes in the storage environment.

Figure 17–4   Bare-root plants in refrigerated storage. (Courtesy Bailey Nursery.)

PROBLEM AREAS

Five fairly common problems encountered in nursery storages are air pollution, desiccation, freezing, fungi, and rodents.

The *air pollutant* that has caused the most problems in nursery stock is ethylene. It is produced primarily by stored fruits, vegetables, bacteria, and fungi, but it is also produced by decaying plant material and certain woody plants, particularly arborvitae. Woody deciduous plants exposed to 1 ppm ethylene during storage may develop lesions on the stem, abscission, or death of buds and exhibit delayed bud break in the spring following planting. Broad-leaved evergreens may exhibit wilting or dropping of the leaves. Rose plants exposed to 10 ppm ethylene during storage are slow to initiate new growth following planting; flowering is delayed and total growth can be reduced. The ethylene problem can be avoided by storing only fully hardened, disease-free plants within the closed storage facility. Avoid storing fruit and plants in the same closed room. The room should also be maintained in a sanitary condition to avoid sources of ethylene production.

Ammonia gas, which can cause necrosis of foliage, is a potential problem for container plants stored in polyethylene structures. Therefore, ammonium-nitrogen fertilizers should not be used while the plants are enclosed in air-tight structures.

Desiccation of plants in storage can be minimized by maintaining a low temperature and a high relative humidity. Another method used to minimize the loss of moisture from dormant nursery stock, particularly rose plants, is to coat the canes with paraffin wax. The dormant tops are dipped in large baths containing paraffin wax at temperatures between 170 and 175°F. The solidified wax acts as a physical barrier, reducing both the loss of moisture and the rate of respiration. The net effect is the maintenance of quality plants that have a greater chance for survival after planting. Waxing is commonly done at the time of packaging, just prior to shipping to market. Root-wrapped plants displayed for sale are especially vulnerable to desiccation, owing to the high temperatures and relatively low humidities that commonly prevail in retail sales areas. Wax emulsions containing bentonite have been used successfully to spray wax onto dormant ornamental deciduous and evergreen trees and shrubs to protect them from desiccation. A solution should contain 13.8% solids, and the spray must be applied at temperatures above freezing, preferably above 60°F.

To reduce the loss of moisture from herbaceous plants or evergreen seedlings stored at temperatures close to or below freezing, the crates are lined with polyethylene, which functions as a vapor barrier and provides a confined atmosphere with a high RH. This method can also be used to protect small evergreens, especially broad-leaved evergreens, when stored in plastic houses. A thin sheet of plastic laid over the plants and sealed along the edges acts as an excellent vapor barrier, maintaining a high humidity about the plants. It should be used only during the midwinter storage period. The plants should be thoroughly watered prior to covering and checked periodically for dryness, fungi, and for the activities of rodents.

Freezing of roots is the most common form of cold-temperature injury to woody nursery stock during storage. Container-grown and B&B plants left unprotected above ground in cold climates will often sustain root injury due to freezing. Roots are much more sensitive to low-temperature injury than the crowns and should be properly protected. Plants in large containers or with large root balls may not have their roots completely killed, because of the insulation value of the soil. Plants that have suffered root injury normally appear healthy as long as they remain in a cool, humid environment. But when exposed to warmer, dryer conditions they express stress symptoms: evergreens fail to grow and soon desiccate; deciduous species may start to grow but new shoots wilt and the plant dies. Plants that sustain only partial root injury commonly display less vigor than plants without damaged roots.

In places where temperatures below 25°F (-4°C) are expected, it is necessary to protect the roots of sensitive species (Table 17–1) with a mulch such as wood chips, sawdust, or shredded expanded polystyrene. Another practice is to tip small-sized, container-grown plants on their sides, following a thorough watering, and cover the closely packed plants with a thermal blanket (e.g., microfoam). Microfoam is an excellent, lightweight, flexible insulator. Holly, boxwood, fire thorn, and other ornamental plants have been successfully overwintered under a blanket of microfoam. The microfoam should be protected with a covering of polyethylene so that it does not become impregnated with water, which would reduce its thermal properties. The blanket must be removed when ambient air temperature raises to $30°F$ ($-1°C$).

Freezing injury to the crowns of woody plants is not too common in well-operated storage facilities. Occasionally, plants stored in the vicinity of the evaporator in refrigerated storages may be frozen. Also, broad-leaved evergreens (e.g., *Rhododendron, Euonymus*, and boxwood) may be frozen while in winter storage in plastic houses. However, if the cold-temperature killing points were not reached, the plants would recover if left to thaw out gradually at temperatures slightly above freezing.

Fungi can be a serious problem in common and refrigerated storage if the room is not thoroughly cleaned prior to loading or if the plant material is not in a mature condition. Good sanitation must be practiced during the loading procedure and throughout the time the storage is in operation. Prior to loading the storage should be thoroughly cleaned. All sources of mold and disease infection should be removed and the walls, ceiling, floor, and storage bins disinfected. A solution of copper sulfate ($1\frac{1}{2}$–2 lb/100 gal water) is an effective and economical disinfectant for this purpose, although various commercial products can also be used. A good practice is to dust all plants with a fungicide just prior to ricking at the time the plants are graded, bundled, and labeled.

Rodents can cause considerable damage to plants in storage if proper precautions are not taken to exclude their entry or to kill or trap them if they gain entry or are accidentally enclosed within the structure. Mice cause the greatest damage by chewing the bark off plants. Rabbits and other rodents damage plants by cutting off branches and chewing the bark and foliage. The losses caused by rodents can be minimized by screening all vents and doors that must be open periodically for air exchange. Rodenticides and traps can be placed within the storage buildings. If rodenticides are used they should be put into specially marked safety containers.

Methylbromide, $\frac{1}{4}$ lb/1000 ft^3, is effective in killing mice that infest cold storage buildings. Carbon monoxide, 0.07% or more, for 3 hr at 32°F is also effective but should only be used when no plants are in the storage. Considerable caution must be exercised when using chemicals to avoid injury to human beings, domesticated animals, and wildlife.

STORAGE OF CHEMICALS

Chemicals of all types, including fertilizers, insecticides, fungicides, herbicides, rodenticides, and growth regulators, should be stored with care. The materials are not only expensive and need to be protected from the elements to minimize loss and assure proper performance when used, but many of the chemicals are also poisonous.

A chemical storage facility should be (1) located away from areas frequented by people and animals; (2) constructed of fire-resistant materials and have a concrete floor; (3) maintained cool, dry, and well-ventilated; (4) posted as a pesticide storage area when used for pesticide storage; and (5) kept locked, with keys provided to a foreman.

Pesticides and growth regulators should be stored in separate cabinets and appropriately labeled. Chemicals should be kept in their original containers at all times. Containers should be kept tightly closed to prevent volitilization of liquid formulations or the adsorption of moisture by certain fertilizers or wettable powders. If a leak or break is discovered in a container, the contents should be transferred to an identical container. A current inventory should be kept of all pesticides and growth regulators in the storage. Also, containers should be marked with the date of purchase, and identifying materials such as 2,4–D that require special handling can be color-coded. Consult the label for special storage conditions that may be required for a particular pesticide and for information on the proper disposal of empty containers.

SUMMARY

Storage facilities are used by nurserymen to maintain postharvest quality of plants, for winter protection of cold-sensitive species, for the temporary storage of propagation material, to facilitate processing and marketing of nursery products, for the conditioning of plants, and for the storage of seeds, equipment, and supplies. A multiplicity of structures are used to modify the environment and gain control of temperature, humidity, air quality, and various biological organisms. By proper storage management, it is possible to maintain plant quality for extended periods of time following harvest, thus permitting extension of the market season and the radius of the market area. Proper use of storage facilities also ensures against the loss of tender plants due to desiccation or freezing injury and protects supplies and equipment from spoilage, deterioration, and theft.

REFERENCES

ALDHOUS, J. R. 1964. Cold storage of forest nursery plants. J. For. 37:47–63.

ANONYMOUS. 1938. Does freezing injure planting stock? J. For. 36:1244–1245.

————— . 1967. Is palletized storage feasible with general nursery stock? Am. Nurseryman. 126(2):11.

BAILEY, V. K. 1969. Bare root storage of deciduous stock. Am. Nurseryman 130(5):15.

Bradley, K. 1959. Refrigerated storages. Am. Nurseryman 110(5):104.

Chadwick, L. C., and R. Houston. 1948. A preliminary report on the pre-storage defoliation of some trees and shrubs. Proc. Am. Hort. Soc. 51:659–667.

Cook, H. A. 1959. Plastic foam structure for low-cost storage. Am. Nurseryman 109(12).

Cunningham, J. L., and G. L. Staby. 1975. Ethylene and defoliation of ornamental lime plants in transit. HortScience 10(2):174.

Curtis, O. F., Jr., and D. R. Rodney. 1952. Ethylene injury to nursery trees in cold storage. Proc. Am. Soc. Hort. Sci. 60:104–108.

Davidson, H., and R. Mecklenburg. 1974. Overwintering of evergreens in plastic structures. HortScience 9(5):479–480.

Deffenbacher, F. W., and E. Wright. 1954. Refrigerated storage of conifer seedlings in the Pacific Northwest. J. For. 52:936–938.

Dewey, D. H. 1982. Techniques for cold storage of plants, Voice MAN, November–December.

Dilley, D. R. 1972. Hypobaric storage—a new concept for preservation of perishables. Ann. Rep. Mich. State Hort. Soc. 102:82–89.

Dufresne, P. 1970. General information on cold storage of nursery plants in jacket-cooled stores. Proc. Int. Plant Propag. Soc. 20:352.

Dunn, N. P. 1983. Mechanical lifting and cold storage of fruit trees and rootstocks. Proc. Int. Plant Propag. Soc. 33:282–285.

Flemer, W., III. 1970. Cold storage in the nursery. Am. Nurseryman 131(9):7.

Flint, H. L., and J. J. McGuire. 1962. Response of rooted cuttings of several woody ornamental species to overwinter storage. Proc. Am. Soc. Hort. Sci. 80:625.

Gouin, F. R. 1973. Winter protection of container plants. Proc. Int. Plant Propag. Soc. 23:255.

Hall, C. W. 1965. Problems of humidity and moisture in agriculture. Humidity Moisture 2:87–94.

Hartman, H. T., and C. J. Hansen. 1957. Effect of season of collecting, indolebutynic acid and pre-planting storage treatment on rooting of Marianna plum, peach and quince hardwood cuttings. Proc. Am. Hort. Soc. 71:57–66.

Havis, J. R. 1976. Root hardiness of woody ornamentals. HortScience 11(4):385–386.

Hunt, G. M. 1984. Microfoam use for winter protection—your fifth option. Proc. Int. Plant Propag. Soc. 34:418–421.

Krahn, R., and Darby. 1971. The "Filacell" system for refrigerated vegetable storage. Proc. Can. Soc. Hort. Sci. 10:24 (summary).

Larsen, F. E. 1967. Five years results with pre-storage chemical defoliation of deciduous nursery stock. Proc. Int. Plant Propag. Soc. 17:157.

————. 1969. Pre-storage promotion of leaf abscission of deciduous nursery stock with bromodine. J. Am. Soc. Hort. Sci. 95:231.

————. 1969. Promotion of leaf abscission of deciduous tree fruit nursery stock with abscisic acid. HortScience 4(3):216–218.

————. 1971. Pre-storage promotion of leaf abscission of deciduous tree fruit nursery stock with bromodine-ethephon mixtures. HortScience 6(2):135–137.

_____. 1973. Stimulation of leaf abscission of tree fruit nursery stock with ethephon-surfactant mixtures. J. Am. Soc. Hort. Sci. 98(1):34–36.

_____. 1975. Chemical nursery stock defoliant needer. Am. Nurseryman 142(7):12.

LENTZ, C. P., and E. A. ROOKE. 1957. Use of the jacketed room system for cool storage. Food Technical 11(5):257–279.

_____, L. VAN DEN BERGE, E. G. JORGENSEN, and R. SAWLER. 1971. The design and operation of a jacketed vegetable storage. Can. Inst. Food Technical J. 4(1):19–23.

LUMIS, G. P., and E. W. FRANKLIN. 1973. Winter studies show effective use. Am. Nurseryman 137(9):40–43.

LUTZ, J. M., and R. E. HARDENBURG. 1968. Commercial storage of fruits, vegetables and florist and nursery stocks. USDA Agric. Handb. 66.

McGUIRE, H. L., H. FLINT, and E. P. CHRISTOPHER. 1962. Cold storage of Christmas trees. Univ. R.I. Agric. Exp. Sta. Bull. 362.

MILLER, E. J., J. A. NEILSON, and S. L. BANDEMER. 1937. Wax emulsion for spraying nursery stock and other plant materials. Mich. Agric. Exp. Sta. Spec. Bull. 282.

NEILSON, J. A. 1930. Recent information on paraffining nursery stock. Natl. Nurseryman 38(47):5–12.

NYLAND, R. D. 1974. Fall lifting for overwinter cold storage of conifers. Appl. For. Res. Inst. State Univ. N.Y. Coll. Environ. Sci. For. Res. Rep. 22.

PETHERAM, H. D., and H. G. PORTERFIELD. 1941. Cold storage for deciduous planting stock. J. For. 39:336–338.

PRIDHAM, A. M. S. 1952. Preliminary report on defoliation of nursery stock by chemical means. Proc. Am. Soc. Hort. Sci. 59:475–478.

PRYOR, R. L., and R. N. STEWART. 1963. Storage of unrooted softwoody azalea cuttings. Proc. Am. Soc. Hort. Sci. 82:483.

SCHNIEDER, E. F. 1965. Survival of rooted cuttings of three woody plant species after low temperature storage. Proc. Am. Soc. Hort. Sci. 87:557.

SNYDER, W. E., and C. E. HESS. 1956. Low temperature storage of rooted cuttings of nursery crops. Proc. Am. Soc. Hort. Sci. 67:545–548.

TICKNOR, R. L. 1968. Defoliating roses with chemicals. Pacific Coast Nurseryman 17(11): 21–22.

TOY, S. J., and J. P. MAHLSTEDE. 1960. Prolonging dormancy of nursery stock by increasing the concentration of carbon dioxide in the storage atmosphere. Proc. Am. Soc. Hort. Sci. 74:774–784.

_____, J. P. MAHLSTEDE, and F. G. SMITH. 1961. Some effects of coating the canes of dormant rose plants with melted paraffin wax. Proc. Am. Soc. Hort. Sci. 77:583.

UOTA, M., J. M. HARVEY, and R. W. LATEER. 1959 Commercial packaging and storing of bare root rose bushes. USDA Marketing Res. Rep. 308.

VANDERBROOK, C. 1956. The storage of rooted cuttings. Am. Nurseryman 103(9):10.

WELLER, H. A. 1958. Propagation—dollars and sense. Proc. Int. Plant Propag. Soc. 8:54–58.

WORTHINGTON, T., and D. H. SCOTT. 1957. Strawberry plant storage using polyethylene liners. Am. Nurseryman 105(9):13.

ZELENKA, J. 1967. Overwintering evergreens under poly in northern climates. Proc. Int. Plant Propag. Soc. 17:351.

SUGGESTED READING

DE HERTOGH, A., W. CARLSON, L. AUNG, and A. F. G. SLOATWEG. Bulb forcers handbook. Netherlands Flower Bulb Institute, Inc., New York.

GAFFNEY, J. J. 1978. Humidity: basic principles and measurement techniques. HortScience 13(5):551–555.

GRIERSON, W., and W. F. WARDOWSKI. 1975. Humidity in horticulture. HortScience 10(4):356–360.

HEIDEN, R. and A. CAMERON. 1986. Handling bare-root perennials for optimum regrowth quality. Am. Nurseryman 163(7):75–88.

HOCKING, D., and R. D. NYLAND. 1971. Cold storage of coniferous seedlings, a review. App. For. Res. Inst., N.Y. State Univ. Coll. For. Syracuse Univ. AFRI Res. Rep. 6.

MAHLSTEDE, J. P., and W. E. FLETCHER. 1960. Storage of nursery stock. American Association of Nurserymen, Washington, D.C.

SMITH, E. M., ed. 1977. Proceedings of the Woody Ornamentals Winter Storage Symposium Coop. Ext. Serv. Ohio State Univ.

PART IV   Appendixes

A *Partial List of Books and Bulletins Pertaining to Areas of Nursery Management*

ARBORICULTURE

ARBORICULTURE. 1983. Richard Harris. Prentice–Hall, Inc., Englewood Cliffs, N.J.

COMPUTERS

COMPUTERS. 1986. Special Issue. American Nurseryman. Vol. 164, No. 5. American Nurseryman, Chicago.

CONTAINER GROWING

CONTAINER GROWING. 1969. American Nurseryman, Chicago.

CONTAINER GROWING OF WOODY ORNAMENTAL PLANTS IN FLORIDA. 1978. Bulletin 793, Agricultural Experiment Station, University of Florida, Gainesville, Fla.

GARDEN CENTER MANAGEMENT

CARE OF NURSERY STOCK IN RETAIL OUTLETS. 1978. L. W. Kennedy and E. M. Smith. Bulletin 562. Cooperative Extension Service, Ohio State University, Columbus, Ohio.

OPERATING A GARDEN CENTER, 5th ed. 1957. J. J. Pinney. American Nurseryman Publishing Company, Chicago.

PROFITABLE GARDEN CENTER MANAGEMENT. 1978. L. Berninger. Reston Publishing Co., Inc., Reston, Va.

NURSERY MANAGEMENT

ENVIRONMENTAL PLANT PRODUCTION AND MARKETING. 1974. T. Furuta. Cox Publishing Co., Arcadia, Calif.

FOREST NURSERY MANUAL: PRODUCTION OF BAREROOT SEEDLINGS. 1984. M. L. Duryea and T. D. Landis, eds. College of Forestry, Oregon State University, Corvallis, Oreg.

PEST CONTROL

SCIENTIFIC GUIDE TO PEST CONTROL OPERATIONS. 1978. P. Villard. Harvest Publishing Co., New York.

TREE FRUIT AND ORNAMENTAL PESTICIDE GUIDE. 1985. Thompson Publications, Fresno, Calif.

Diseases

DISEASES AND PESTS OF ORNAMENTAL PLANTS. 1978. P. P. Pirone. John Wiley & Sons, Inc., New York.

DISEASES OF FOREST AND SHADE TREES OF THE U.S. 1971. USDA Agricultural Handbook 386. Superintendent of Documents, Washington, D.C.

DISEASES OF SHADE TREES. 1978. T. A. Tattar. Academic Press, Inc., New York.

FOREST NURSERY DISEASES IN THE UNITED STATES. USDA Agricultural Handbook 470, Superintendent of Documents, Washington, D.C.

Insects

A GUIDE TO INSECT INJURY OF CONIFERS IN THE LAKE STATES. 1976. L. F. Wilson. USDA Agricultural Handbook 501. Superintendent of Documents, Washington, D.C.

INSECTS AS PESTS. 1973. H. S. Zinn and G. S. Fichter. Doubleday & Company, Inc., New York.

INSECTS OF EASTERN PINES. 1973. A. H. Rose and O. H. Lindquist. Canadian Forestry Service Publication 1313. Information Canada Center, Toronto, Ontario.

INSECTS THAT FEED ON TREES AND SHRUBS, an illustrated practical guide. 1976. W. T. Johnson and H. H. Lyon. Cornell University Press, Ithaca, N.Y.

Weeds

DIAGNOSIS AND PREVENTION OF HERBICIDE INJURY. 1976. Michigan State University, East Lansing, Mich.

HERBICIDE HANDBOOK. 1974. Weed Science Society of America, Champaign, Ill.

NEBRASKA WEEDS. 1975. Nebraska Department of Agriculture, Lincoln, Neb.

WEED SCIENCE: PRINCIPLES, 2nd ed. 1983. W. P. Anderson. West Publishing Co., St. Paul, Minn.

WEED SCIENCE, PRINCIPLES AND PRACTICES. G. C. Klingman and F. Ashton. John Wiley & Sons, Inc., New York.

PLANT PROPAGATION

GRAFTERS HANDBOOK. R. J. Gardner. American Nurseryman, Chicago.

NERSERY STOCK MANUAL. 1975. J. G. D. Lamb, J. C. Kelly, and P. Bowbrick. Grower Books, London.

PLANT PROPAGATION PRINCIPLES AND PRACTICES. 1975. H. T. Hartmann and D. E. Kester, Prentice–Hall, Inc., Englewood Cliffs, N.J.

PROCEEDINGS OF THE INTERNATIONAL PLANT PROPAGATORS' SOCIETY. Center for Urban Horticulture, University of Washington, Seattle, Wa.

SEEDS OF WOODY PLANTS IN THE UNITED STATES. 1974. USDA Agricultural Handbook 450. Superintendent of Documents, Washington, D.C.

OTHER PUBLICATIONS

COST DATA FOR LANDSCAPE CONSTRUCTION. K. W. Kerr, ed. Kerr Associates, Inc., Minneapolis, Minn. (updated yearly).

SOURCES OF PLANTS AND RELATED SUPPLIES. Current Issue. American Association of Nurserymen, Washington, D.C.

A TECHNICAL GLOSSARY OF HORTICULTURE AND LANDSCAPE TERMINOLOGY. 1971. Horticultural Research Institute, Washington, D.C.

TREE AND SHRUB TRANSPLANTING MANUAL. 1981. E. B. Himelick. International Society of Arboriculture, Urbana, Ill.

B *Addresses of Nursery-Related Organizations**

All-America Rose Selections
P. O. Box 218
Shenandoah, IA 51601

American Association of Nurserymen
1250 I Street, NW, Suite 500
Washington, DC 20005

American Association of Nurserymen's
  Group Insurance Trust
1250 I Street, NW, Suite 500
Washington, DC 20005

American Society of Agronomy
677 South Segor Road
Madison, WI 53711

Associated Landscape Contractors
  of America
1750 Old Meadow Road
McLean, VA 22101

Garden Centers of America
1250 I Street, NW, Suite 500
Washington, DC 20005

Horticultural Research Institute, Inc.
1250 I Street, NW, Suite 500
Washington, DC 20005

The International Plant Propagator's
  Society
Center for Urban Horticulture
University of Washington, GF-15
Seattle, WA 98195

International Society of Arboriculture
3 Lincoln Square, Box 71
Urbana, IL 61801

Landscape Materials Information
  Service
Callicoon, NY 12723

Mail-Order Association of
  Nurserymen, Inc.
210 Cartwright Boulevard
Massapequa Park, NY 11762

National Arborist Association
3537 Stratford Road
Wantagh, NY 11793

*Addresses subject to change.

National Association of Plant Patent
  Owners
1250 I Street, NW, Suite 500
Washington, DC 20005

National Landscape Association
1250 I Street, NW, Suite 500
Washington, DC 20005

Nurserymen's Protective Association
c/o McGill & Son
Fairview, OR 97024

Southern Nurserymen's Association
3813 Hillsboro Road
Nashville, TN 37215

Wholesale Landscape and Retail
  Horticultural Research Institute, Inc.
1250 I Street, NW, Suite 500
Washington, DC 20005

Wholesale Nursery Growers
  of America
1250 I Street, NW, Suite 500
Washington, DC 20005

C *Trade Journals* Related to the Nursery Industry

American Nurseryman
111 N. Canal Street
Suite 545
Chicago, IL 60606

Arborist News
P.O. Box 426
Wooster, OH 44691

Florist & Nursery Exchange
434 S. Wabash Avenue
Chicago, IL 60605

Garden Industry of America
Box 1092
Minneapolis, MN 55440

Grounds Maintenance
1014 Wyandotte Street
Kansas City, MO 64105

Home & Garden Supply Merchandisers
2501 Wayzata Boulevard
P.O. Box 67
Minneapolis, MN 55440

Journal of Environmental Horticulture
Horticulture Research Institute
1250 I Street, NW, Suite 500
Washington, DC 20005

Landscape Architecture
Schuster Building
1500 Bardstown Road
Louisville, KY 40205

Landscape Design & Construction
2048 Cotner Avenue
Los Angeles, CA 90025

Landscape Industry
850 Elm Grove Road
Elm Grove, WI 53122

Lawn/Garden/Outdoor Living
1014 Wyandotte Street
Kansas City, MO 64105

Midwest Landscaping
1706 W. Chase Street
Chicago, IL 60626

*Addresses subject to change.

Modern Garden Center
208 James Street
Barrington, IL 60010

Northwest Garden Supplier
311 Henry Building
Portland, OR 97204

Nursery Business
Brantwood Publications, Inc.
Northwood Plaza Station
Clearwater, FL 33519–0360

Nursery Manager
Branch-Smith Publishing
120 St. Louis Avenue
Fort Worth, TX 76104

Nursery Product News
9800 Detroit Avenue
Cleveland, OH 44102

Pacific Coast Nurserymen & Garden
  Center Dealer
832 S. Baldwin Avenue
Arcadia, CA 91007

Southern Florist & Nurserymen
P.O. Box 1868
Fort Worth, TX 76101

Turf-Grass Times
218 19th Avenue
North Jacksonville Beach, FL 32050

Weeds Trees and Turf
9800 Detroit Avenue
Cleveland, OH 44102

Western Landscaping News
1623 S. La Cienega Boulevard
Los Angeles, CA 90035

D *Approximate Metric Conversions*

Unit		To Metric			From Metric
Length	inches	× 2.5	= centimeters	× 0.4	= inches
	feet	× 30.5	= centimeters	× 0.033	= feet
	yards	0.9	= meters	× 3.3	= feet
	miles	× 1.6	= kilometers	× 0.62	= miles
Area	inches^2	× 6.5	= centimeters^2	× 0.16	= inches^2
	feet^2	× 0.09	= meters^2	× 11.1	= feet
	yards^2	× 0.8	= meters^2	× 1.1	= yards^2
	miles^2	× 2.8	= kilometers^2	× 0.36	= miles^2
	acres	× 0.4	= hectares	× 2.5	= acres
Mass	ounces	× 28,0	= frams	× 0.035	= ounces
	pounds	× 0.45	= kilomgrams	× 2.2	= pounds
	tons (2000 lb)	× 0.9	= tonnes (1000kg)	× 1.1	= tons
Volume	teaspoons	× 5	= milliliters	× 0.2	= teaspoons
	tablespoons	× 15	= milliliters	× 0.007	= tablespoons
	fluid ounces	× 30	= milliliters	× 0.03	= fluid ounces
	cups	× 0.25	= liters	× 4.17	= cups
	pints	× 0.47	= liters	× 2.1	= pints
	quarts	× 0.95	= liters	× 1.06	= quarts
	gallons	× 3.8	= liters	× 0.26	= gallons
	feet^3	× 0.3	= meters^3	× 35.0	= feet^3
	yards^3	× 0.76	= meters^3	× 1.3	= yards^3
Temperature	(Fahrenheit − 32°)	× 0.56	= Celsius	× 1.8 + 32°	= Fahrenheit

E *Rate per 1000 Ft²*
Nomograph

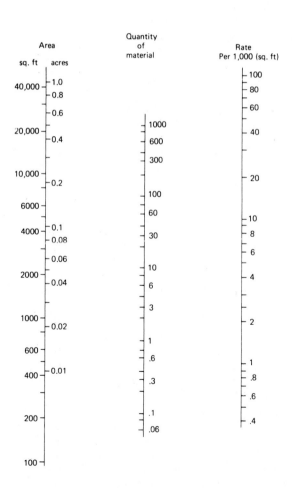

F *Rate per Acre Nomograph*

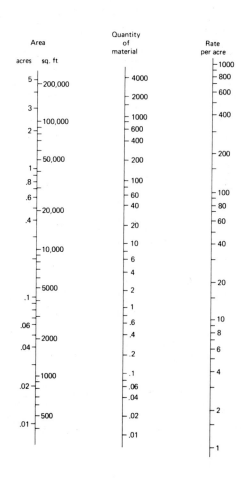

G _Fertilizer Proportioner Nomograph, 100 ppm*_

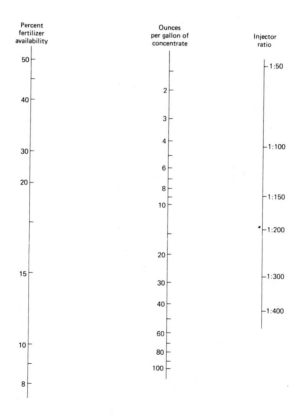

Percent fertilizer availability	Ounces per gallon of concentrate	Injector ratio

*To obtain other ppm concentrations, multiply by appropriate factor. For example, to obtain 200 ppm, multiply ounces per gallon by 2.0; to obtain 50 ppm, multiply by 0.5.

H *Determining the Weight of B&B Plants*

Nurserymen, landscape contractors, and arborists have need, periodically, to determine the weight of B&B trees. They need to estimate weight in order to determine what type of equipment will be necessary to move the plant or plants, estimate cost, and plan transportation routes in accordance with weight restrictions on some roads during the spring-thaw season in certain parts of the country. The weight of B&B plants is dependent upon a number of factors, including the size and species of the plants, the size and shape of the ball, and the soil type, including its moisture content.

The *weight of small plants,* whether they are B&B or in containers, can be readily determined by weighing plants in selected sizes and determining the total weight by multiplying the number of plants within a size class by the averate weight of the class. When a group of selected small plants was subjected to a volume/weight analysis, the results indicated that the weight of B&B plants was directly related to the volume of soil, which was related to the type of root system; shallow-rooted plants weighed less than relatively deep-rooted plants. There was also a correlation between ball size and digging time (Table H–1).

Determining the weight of larger plants is a little more challenging, since the weight must be estimated without the use of scales. This can be done by either calculating the weight of the soil ball plus the weight of the tree or by abstracting the estimated weight from a weight table or graph. Various formulas have been suggested for calculating the weight of the soil ball, including:

(1) $W = \frac{2}{3} (D^2 \times d) \times 110$ (dimensions in feet)

(2) $W = \frac{2}{3} (D \times d) \times 0.075$ (dimensions in inches)

(3) $W = \pi \frac{d}{3}(r_1^2 + r_1 r_2 + r_2^2) \times 110$ (dimensions in feet)

where D = diameter of top of the ball
$\quad d$ = depth of the ball
$\quad r_1$ = radius of the top of the ball
$\quad r_2$ = radius of the base of the ball
$\quad \pi$ = 3.1417

For each formula, certain assumptions are made. In (1) and (2), it is assumed that the volume of the soil approximates two-thirds that of a cube-like block. In (1) and (3) it is assumed that the weight of an ''average'' cubic foot of soil is 110 lb; whereas formula (2) assumes that is it 0.075 lb/in.^{3} (129.6 lb/ft^3).

The weight of a tree can be determined by estimating the volume of the tree and multiplying by the average weight of a cubic foot of wood. The volume can be estimated by measuring the diameter (caliper) of the tree, determining the square-foot area (Appendix I), and this value multiplied by the effective height of the main stem or primary branches. (A subjective assessment must be made as to the effective height.)

The weight of a cubic foot of wood varies considerably from species to species. Wood in the red oak group averages 64 lb/ft^3, whereas northern white cedar is a relatively light wood weighing 28 lb/ft^3. However, on an average the wood of most trees used for landscape purposes weighs approximately 55 lb/ft^3. Thus, a tree 10 in. in diameter, 1 ft above ground level, and 60 ft tall would have an estimated weight of 1800 lb (0.545 ft^2 × 60 ft × 55 lb/ft^3). These calculations are based on the assumption that the total volume of the tree approximates the volume of a cylinder whose caliper and height can be measured.

If these assumptions are valid and since the *American Standards for Nursery Stock* recommends certain minimum depths for balls within a specific size class, it is possible to calculate the approximate weights for balls within these classes and to plot these data onto semilog paper (Appendix J), from which the weight can be read

TABLE H-1   **Volume/Weight/Digging Time Relationship of Selected B&B Evergreen Shrubs**

	Average Weight of B&B Plants (lb)	Average Ball Volume (ft^3)	Proportionate Weight of Soil (%)	Average Time to B&B (min)
Japanese holly, 18–24 in. crown, deep rooted	52.8	0.63	90.6	10.1
Pfitzer juniper, 18–24 in. crown, deep-rooted	50.3	0.63	95.9	8.7
Evergreen azalea, 18-in. crown, shallow-rooted	22.1	0.45	90.1	5.2

Source: After Pease (1959).

directly without further calculations. A second curve can be drawn depicting the combined weight of the tree and soil ball.

REFERENCES

AMERICAN ASSOCIATION OF NURSERYMEN. 1986. American standards for nursery Stock. AAN, Washington, D.C.

PEASE, R. W. 1959. The balled and burlapped pack for ornamental shrubs and trees. W. Va. Univ. Agric. Exp. Sta. Bull, 432, October.

PIRONE, P. P. 1978. Tree maintenance, 5th ed. John Wiley & Sons, Inc., New York.

TREE PRESERVATION BULL. 1, U.S. National Park Service.

FOREST PRODUCTS LABORATORY. 1940. Wood handbook. Superintendent of Documents, Washington, D.C.

I   *Area of Circles in Square Feet*

Diameter in Inches and Half-Inches

$$A \;=\; \pi r^2 \;=\; 1/4 \pi d^2 \;=\; 0.7854 d^2$$

Diameter	0.0	0.5
1	0.006	0.012
2	0.022	0.034
3	0.049	0.067
4	0.087	0.111
5	0.136	0.165
6	0.196	0.230
7	0.267	0.307
8	0.349	0.394
9	0.442	0.492
10	0.545	0.601
11	0.660	0.721
12	0.785	0.852
13	0.922	0.994
14	1.069	1.147
15	1.227	1.310
16	1.396	1.485
17	1.576	1.670
18	1.767	1.867
19	1.969	2.074
20	2.181	2.292
21	2.405	2.521
22	2.640	2.761
23	2.885	3.012
24	3.142	3.275

J Values for Selected Rates of i

Future Value $(1 + i)^n$ and Present Value $1/(1 + i)^n$

	6.0%		6.5%		7.0%		7.5%		8.0%		8.5%	
Year	FV	PV	FV	PV	FV	PV	FV	PV	FV	PV	FV	PV
0	1.0000	1.0000	1.0000	1.0000	1.0000	1.0000	1.0000	1.0000	1.0000	1.0000	1.0000	1.0000
1	1.0600	0.0434	1.0650	0.9390	1.0700	0.9346	1.0750	0.9302	1.0800	0.9259	1.0850	0.9216
2	1.1236	0.8900	1.1342	0.8817	1.1449	0.8734	1.1556	0.8653	1.1664	0.8573	1.1772	0.8484
3	1.1910	0.8396	1.2079	0.8278	1.2250	0.8163	1.2423	0.8050	1.2597	0.7938	1.2773	0.7829
4	1.2625	0.7921	1.2865	0.7732	1.3108	0.7629	1.3355	0.7488	1.3607	0.7350	1.3859	0.7216
5	1.3382	0.7473	1.3701	0.7299	1.4026	0.7130	1.4356	0.6966	1.4693	0.6806	1.5037	0.6650
6	1.4185	0.7050	1.4591	0.6853	1.5007	0.6663	1.5433	0.6480	1.5869	0.6302	1.6315	0.6129
7	1.5036	0.6651	1.5540	0.6435	1.6059	0.6227	1.6590	0.6928	1.7138	0.5853	1.7701	0.5649
8	1.5938	0.6274	1.6550	0.6042	1.7182	0.5820	1.7835	0.5607	1.8509	0.5427	1.9206	0.5207
9	1.6895	0.5919	1.7626	0.5674	1.8485	0.5439	1.9172	0.5216	1.9990	0.5002	2.0839	0.4799
10	1.7908	0.5584	1.8771	0.5327	1.9672	0.5083	2.0610	0.4852	2.1589	0.4632	2.2610	0.4423

K Relationship between T, RH, VP, and VPD

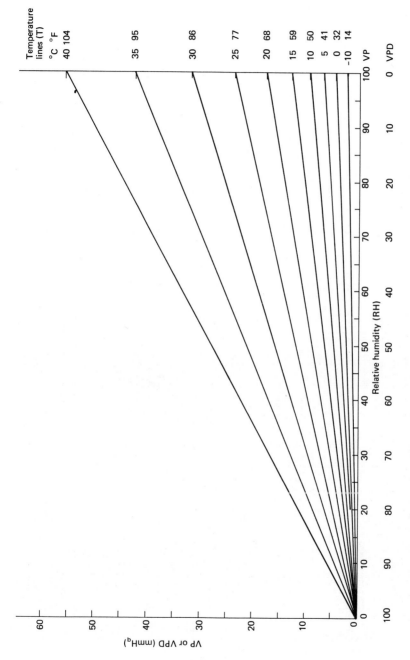

Relationship between temperature (T), relative humidity (RH), vapor pressure (VP), and vapor pressure deficit (VPD). To obtain VP at selected T, read RH scale from left to right. To obtain VPD at selected T, read RH scale from right to left.

L *Approximate Weight of B&B Plants*

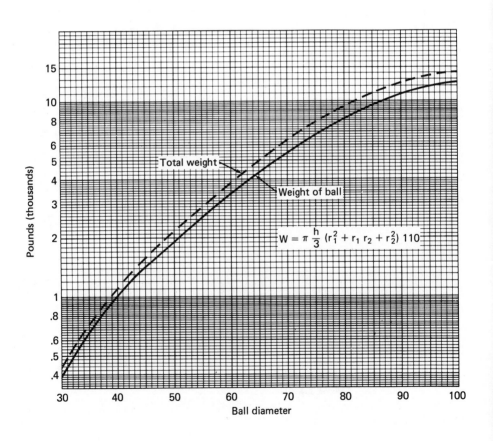

Pounds (thousands) — vertical axis

Total weight

Weight of ball

$$W = \pi \frac{h}{3} (r_1^2 + r_1 r_2 + r_2^2) \, 110$$

Ball diameter — horizontal axis

Index

Accounting:
  accounts receivable, 127
  accrual basis, 115
  cash basis, 115
Acidifying water, 269
Addresses, nursery-related organizations,
  388
Administrative headquarters, 66
Aeration, 286
Air pollution:
  site selection, 60
  storage, 378
Aluminum sulfate, 195
American Standard for Nursery Stock,
  141–148, 174, 178
Animal manures, 216–217
Animal repellents, 297
Antitranspirants, 171
Area of circles, 399
Associations:
  All-America Rose Selections, 28
  American Association of Nurserymen,
    26
  American Association of Nurserymen's
    Group Insurance Trust, 27
  Associated Landscape Contractors of
    America, 28
  Garden Center Symposium, 29
  Garden Centers of America, 27
  Horticultural Research Institute, 29

  International Plant Propagator's
    Society, 28
  International Society of Arboriculture,
    28
  Landscape Materials Information
    Service, 28
  Mail-Order Association of
    Nurserymen, 28
  National Arborist Association, 29
  National Association of Plant Patent
    Owners, 29
  National Landscape Association, 27
  Nursery Marketing Council, 27, 356
  Nurserymen's Protective Association,
    29
  State, regional, and local, 29
  Wholesale Nursery Growers of
    America, Inc., 27

Books, bulletins, list of, 385
Boron, 188, 200, 212, 227, 251
Brake horsepower, 254
Break-even analysis, 107
Broker, 24
Bromodine, 371
Bulk density, 227
Business loans, classification of, 103

Calcium, 187, 200, 202, 211, 236, 240,
  241

Caliper, measurements, 160–162
Cash-flow analysis, 129
Cation exchange capacity, 185, 198–199, 232
Chemical storage, 380
Chloropicrin, 245–246
Circulation and parking, 66
Classification of nurseries:
  function, 17–18
  ownership, 16
  product, 24
  production system, 18–19
Climate, 57
Climatic zones, 95
Codes, 94–97
Companion plantings, 219
Composting, 233, 235–236
Computers, 159, 164, 166, 175–176
Container marketing, advantages and challenges, 22
Container production:
  advantages and challenges, 22
  calcium, 236, 237, 240, 241
  chemical supplements, 23, 187, 237, 267
  containerizing, 349, 354
  containers, 20, 21, 76, 276, 278
  development of:
    cost, 77
    design, 74
    drainage, 75
    growing surfaces, 353
    irrigation, 23, 74
    maintenance, 76
    materials handling, 74, 76
    size, 76
    spacing, 350
    time required, 351
  early history of, 10, 19–22
  fumigants, 245–246
  fumigation, 244, 303, 309, 321
  heat treatment, 243, 305, 309, 321
  ingredients:
    hardwood bark, 232, 235–236
    peats, 231, 237
    perlite, 232
    sand, 231
    sawdust, 232

    softwood bark, 232, 236–237
    turface, 233
    vermiculite, 232
    wood products, 231
  iron, 237
  irrigation, 259–270
  limestone, 238
  magnesium, 240–241
  materials handling, 76
  media. *See also* Container production, ingredients
    aeration porosity, 230
    anchorage and support, 227
    moisture-holding capacity, 227
    nutrients, 227–228
    porosity, 227, 229–230
    reaction, 227, 228, 237
  micro elements, 236–237, 238, 241–242
  mixes:
    Cornell Peat-Lite, 234–235
    John Innes compost, 233
    municipal composts, 237
    other materials, 237
    U.C.-type, 234
  nitrogen, 220, 235, 240–241, 337, 342
  nutrients, 227, 240
  pasteurization, 305, 309
  phosphorus, 227, 235–237, 240–241, 343
  potassium, 235–237, 240–241, 343
  reaction, 227, 238
  soluble salts, 241–242
  spatial arrangement, 74, 81
  sterilization, 243
  storage. *See* Chapter 17
  sulfur, 238
  testing media, 239–243
  water-retention porosity, 230
Control and coordination, 45
Copper, 188, 212, 227
Cornell Peat-Lite mixes, 234
Cover crops, 218

Deer injury, 295
Defoliation, 371
Desiccation injury, 172, 379
Dioecious species, list of, 292

Discounted-cash-flow analysis, 105–107, 124
Diseases:
  control of, 321–328
  early introductions, 13
  monitoring of, 323–324
  prevention of, 319–322
Drainage, 211, 235, 272

Employee:
  evaluation, 51, 52
  motivation, 51, 53, 56
  rewards, 51, 53–55
Environmental Pesticide Control Act, 89
Environmental Protection Agency, 89, 293
Equipment, 164–166
  digging, 11, 12, 20, 356, 357
  injection of fertilizer, 268
  inventory, 164
  lifting and loading, 178
  mechanical planters, 44
  packaging and potting, 22
  planting, 44, 344, 345
  tying, 177
Erosion of nursery soils, 220
Essential elements, 186–188
Estimating, requirements for:
  plant materials, 79, 340
  space in nursery, 80, 350
Ethylene, 378
Evaluation of employees, 51–56
Excess soluble salts, 205–207, 243

Facilities, 64–69
Fair Labor Standards Act, 84
Federal Trade Commission, 90
Fertilizer, 185, 202
  application:
    bark of trees, 214
    foliage, 213
    soil surface, 212, 337, 342
    subsurface, 213
  properties of, 203
  recommendations, 206–212
  types of, 202–205
    inorganic, 202, 205
    organic, 202, 204

Fertilizing via:
  hydraulic displacement, 269
  irrigation system, 266
Field-grown crops:
  crop rotation, 340
  fertilizer recommendations, 206–215, 342–343
  irrigation, 249–272, 345
  market analysis, 332
  organic matter, value of, 215–220
  preferences for selected plants, 190–194
  site, 68
Finance, 99–133
Finances:
  borrowing, 101
  break-even-point analysis, 107
  cash flow, 100
  cash-flow analysis, 105
  cash-flow statement, 130
  discounted-cash-flow analysis, 105
  discretionary spending, 115
  evaluation of alternatives, 102
  negotiating a loan, 107
    limitations, 110
  payback-period analysis, 104
  profit and depreciation accounts, 100
  profit, determining, 116
  profits, nursery, 127
  simple rate of return, 104
  sources of money:
    borrowed funds, 100
    contract growing, 101
    owners' savings, 100
    partnership, 100
  urgency analysis, 103
Flowering, 288–290
Formaldehyde, 245
Freight charges, 182
Frost protection, 270–271
Fruiting, 290
  prevention of, 244
Fumigation, 244, 303, 309, 321
Fungicides:
  classification of, 327
  list of, 328

Garden centers, 25
  beginning of, 7, 8
  location, 7, 61
Gibberellic acid, 281
Goals:
  determining, 38
  evaluating, 39
Green manure crops, 216
Growth and development, 249, 257, 275

Hardwood bark, 232, 235
Harvesting methods, 334, 356–357
Heavy metals, 237
Heterophyllus plants, 215
Highway system:
  effect on nursery industry, 10
  use tax, 180
History, 1–14
Homophyllus plants, 215
Horticultural broker, 24

Inorganic fertilizers, 202, 205
Insects:
  control of, 312–314, 318–319
  early introductions, 12–13
Interest table, selected rates, 401–402
Interstate Commerce Commission,
  179–180
Inventory, 159–169
  computers, 159, 162, 164, 166
  data collection, 160–163
  equipment, 160, 164–166
  field, 161
  flow sheets, 164
  need for, 159
  plant material, 159
  sales, 152, 159
  supplies, 167–169
  systems, 159
Iron, 187, 211
Irrigation, 249–272
  acidifying water, 269
  classification of water for, 250
  container-grown crops, 249, 259
    climatic effects, 265
    container capacity, 265
    excess water, 271
    overhead irrigation, 260

    problems, 262
    subsurface irrigation, 262
    surface irrigation, 262
    water requirement, 264
  distribution system, 255
  drainage, 272
  excess soil moisture, 271
  fertilizer calculations, 268
  fertilizing via, 266, 268
  growth increase, 257
  injectors, 268
  need for, 249
  power, 253
  proportioners, 268
  pumps, 253
  soil moisture determination, 251
  sources of water, 249
  survival rate increase, 249, 257
  systems of, 255
  trickle, 257, 259
  water quality, 250
  water requirement, estimating, 258
  water rights, 250

John Innes composts, 233
Journals, nursery-related, 390

Labeling, production area, 68–70, 160
Labor availability, 60
Land costs, 60
Landscape contractors, 24
Landscape maintenance, 25
Laws:
  federal, 83, 180
  municipal, 62, 92, 180, 250
  state, 92, 180, 250
Leaf analysis, 200–201
Light, effect of, 282–285, 289
Limestone, 196, 236
  neutralizing values, 197
Liner production, 335
Loans, 100–103

Magnesium, 187, 200, 202, 211, 236,
  240, 242
Mail-order nurseries, 7
Maintenance firms, landscape, 25
Maleichydrazide, 292

Management, 36–63
  Bible, excerpts from, 40
  evaluation of:
    balance sheet, 112
    profit-and-loss statement, 113
Manager's responsibilities, 37
Manganese, 187, 211, 227, 236
Map, planometric, 65
Marketing, 135
  analysis, 333
  brokers, nursery, 138
  buyers, 141
  channels of, 149–153
  contractors, needs of, 136
  future sales, projecting, 156
  garden centers, needs of, 138
  mail-order nurseries, needs of, 139
  National Marketing Council, 156
  obtaining information on, 153
  pricing nursery stock, 155
  programs, 157
  sales organizations, 140
  sales representatives, 140
  shipping agreements, 148
  specialization of production, 136
  trade shows, 154
  warranty for plant material, 148
  wholesale units, 147
Massachusetts Bay Colony, 1
Media, 226
Methylbromide, 245
Metric conversions, 92–93
Mice injury, 295–296
Micronutrient mixture, 238
Micronutrients, 187, 211, 238, 242
Migrant Worker's Act, 86
Modifying flowering and fruiting,
    288–293
Modifying growth, 275–295
Moisture-holding capacity, 227
Molybodenum, 188
Monoecious species, 291
Motivation, employee, 51, 53
Municipal compost, 237

Naphthyleneacetic acid, 292
Nitrogen, 186, 203, 207–209, 236, 240,
    242, 267, 337, 342

Nomographs:
  fertilizer proportioner, 395
  rate per acre, 394
  rate per 1000 sq. ft., 393
Nurseries, early, 1–5
Nursery:
  agents, 7
  census data, 8
  classification, 16
  crops, types of, 346–348
  development of, 64
  financing, 100–111
  inventory, 159
  irrigation, 249–272
  marketing of crops, 135–158
  plant materials, quantity of, 77
  planting designs, 69
  production programing, 332–359
  profits, 113, 116–133
  site selection, 57
  soil, 185–222
  space requirements, 80
  storage, 361–381
Nursery centers of production:
  current:
    California, 9, 30
    Florida, 9, 30
    Illinois, 33
    Iowa, 34
    Michigan, 9, 33
    New England, 34
    New Jersey, 9, 32
    New York, 9, 32
    Ohio, 9, 33
    Oklahoma, 34
    Oregon-Washington, 9, 32
    Pennsylvania, 9, 31
    southern states, 34
    Tennessee, 9, 31
    Texas, 9, 31
  early, 2–7
Nursery industry, 16
  beginning of, 1
  brokers:
    horticultural, 24
    nursery, 138
  contractors, landscape, 24
  distributor, 24

Nursery industry (*con't*)
  garden centers, 7
  history of, 1
  landscape nurseries, 18
  maintenance, landscape, 25
  trade practice rules, 91
  United States, 9
Nursery Marketing Council, 156, 356
Nursery stock, 116
  cost of production, 116
    direct costs, 118
    estimating, 125
    indirect costs, 118
    interest, 122
    overhead, 118
    planting, maintaining, and
      harvesting, 118
  determining future value:
    annuity, 111
    invested capital, 111
  determining profitability:
    discounted-cash-flow analysis,
      105–107, 122–124
  pricing, 155
  shipping, 170–184
  value, in-the-field:
    cost of production, 109
    professional appraisal, 109
    wholesale less harvesting and
      selling, 109
Nurserymen, early, 1–6
Nutrient element balance, 199–200
Nutrient element standards, 201

Occupational Safety and Health Act, 85
Organic fertilizers, 204
Organic matter:
  animal manures, 216–217
  bark and sawdust, 219–220
  cover crops, 218, 340
  peat moss, 219
  sod and green manure, 216, 340
Organization:
  function:
    executive, 43
    line, 40
    line and staff, 42

  legal form:
    corporation, 44
    multiple forms, 45
    partnership, 43–44
    proprietorship, 43
  physical facilities, 39, 64–82
Organizations. *See* Associations
Overhead costs, 118

Parcel Post Act, 7
Peats, 231, 238
Perlite, 232
Pest control, 77
Pesticides, 89, 307–309, 314–317,
    328–329
Phosphorus, 186, 209–210, 227, 236,
    240, 241, 267, 343
Photoperiod, 276–285
Pine bark, 232, 236
Planning, by management, 39
Plant growth and development, 275–297
Plant Hardiness Zones, 95
Plant material:
  estimating space requirements, 79
  inventory, 159–164
  response to long days, 284
  shipping, 170–173
Plant Materials Distribution Center, 18
Plant patents, 90
Plant Pest Acts, 87
Plant Quarantine Act, 7, 13
Planting designs, in the nursery:
  considerations, 69
    culture, 73
    economics, 73
  equilateral triangle, 72
  interplanting, 71–72
  rectangle, 71
  row, 69
  square, 69
Policy manual, 46
Pollution, 60
Polyhouses. *See* Storage
Porosity of medium, 229–230
Postharvest care, 359
Potassium, 186, 200, 202, 210, 236,
    240, 241, 267, 343

Price and Services Act, 90
Pricing nursery stock, 155
Production areas, 67
  blocks, 65, 69
  liner beds, 67, 336
  seed beds, 67
Production programming, 77
Production systems for:
  container-grown plants, 74, 349
  field-grown plants, 69, 338
Profit, determination of, 116, 122–127
Profit-and-loss statement, 113
Proportioners, 268
Pruning, 277–280, 347–349, 354
Publications:
  American Standard for Nursery Stock,
    141–148, 174, 178
  Book of Evergreens, 4
  Commercial Storage of Fruits,
    Vegetables and Florist and
    Nursery Stock, 368
  Directory of Registered Plant Patent
    Attorneys, 91
  Federal Motor Carrier Safety
    Regulations, 179
  Fruit Trees of America, 4
  Guide for Commercial Applicators, 89
  Guides for the Nursery Industry, 91
  Magazine of Horticulture, 3
  National Nurseryman, 12
  Nursery Book, 12
  Plant Propagation, 277
  Professional Truck Driver's Handbook,
    180
  Seed and Potting Compost, 233
  Seeds of Woody Plants in the U.S.,
    277
  Storage of Nursery Stock, 368
Pumps and power, 253

Quarantine nurseries, 18
Quarantines, 7, 13, 87–88

Rabbit injury, 295
Ratio analysis, 129–133
Reasonable expectancy, 47–49

Records, 46–47
  financial, importance of, 99
Relative humidity, 374, 404
Repellents, 297
Rewards, employee, 51–54
Rodent injury, 295–297, 380
Root modification, 285, 379
Root pruning, 285
Root systems, 286

Salinity, 206, 239, 241–243, 251
Sanitation, 377
Sawdust, 220
Seedbeds, 67
Shading, 363, 365, 374
Shingletow, 375
Shipping, 170–184
  broker, 179
  cargo insurance, 179
  computers, use of, 175–176
  equipment for, 177
  exempted commodities, 180
  exempted truckers, 180
  facilities, 64, 66
  freight charges, 182–183
  highway use tax, 180
  instructions for, 173–174
  plant material, 170–173
  regulated carriers, 181–182
  regulations, 88
  responsibilities:
    buyer's, 173–174
    carrier's, 179–181
    seller's, 174–179
  title to plant material, 179
  transportation, means of, 176, 179
  truck safety regulations, 179
  unloading plant material, 174
Shoot modification, 275–285
Site selection, 57–63
  air, 60
  competition, 62
  container production, 58
  facilities, 61
  field production soil, 58
  labor, availability, 60

Site selection (*con't*)
   water, 59
   zoning laws, 62
Small plant culture, 336–338
Social Security Act, 83
Sod and green manure crops, 216,
      340–341
Sodium absorption ratio, 251
Softwood bark, 232, 236
Soil:
   field production, 58, 185–225
   losses, 220
   modifying soil reaction, 189–198
   reaction (pH) of, 185, 188–189
      modifying, 189–198
      nutrient availability, 195
      plant preferences, 190–194
   tests, 201–202
Soil conservation, 220–221
Soil Conservation Service, 59
Soil management, 185, 340
Soil moisture, 251–252
Soluble salts, 185, 206, 239, 241, 251
Solu-bridge data, interpretation of, 207,
      243
Spacing, 67, 74, 80, 336, 339, 350
Staffing, 48–49
Staking, 277–278, 347
Standards:
   balling and burlapping, 146–148
   Christmas trees, 144
   deciduous shrubs, 142
   deciduous trees, 142
   evergreens, 142
   fruit trees, 146
   metric equivalents, 92–93, 392
   nursery stock, 141
   roses, 145
Sterilization, media, 243
Storage, 361–381
   chemicals, 319, 380–381
   environment:
      air, 376, 378
      humidity, 374
      temperature, 372
   equipment, use in, 377
   ethylene in, 376

   facilities:
      coldframes, 363
      common storage, 367
      controlled atmosphere, 369
      filacell, 369
      heeling-in grounds, 362
      hypobaric storage, 369
      jacketed storage, 368
      lathhouse, 365
      microfoam tunnels, 363
      polyethylene (plastic) storage, 365,
            366, 375–376
      refrigerated storage, 367, 378
      shade houses, 365
   humidity, 374–376
   physiological condition of plants, 370
   preparation of plants for, 370
   problems:
      air pollutants, 378
      desiccation, 379
      fungi, 380
      rodents, 380
Strip-cropping, 221
Sulfur, 187, 195, 238
Supplies, 167–169

Taper of stems, 278
Temperature, 170, 172, 372, 404
   high, effects of, 287
   killing, 364
   low, effects of, 364, 373, 379
   shipping, 172
   storage, 372
Terraces, 222
Tillage, 221
Time to dig or plant, 50–51
Timing deliveries, 137, 139, 140
Topography, 58
Trade practice rules, 91
Traffic coordinator, 176, 179
Training young trees, 277
Transportation. *See also* Shipping
   national highway system, 10
   rapid truck, 10
   site selection, 64
Trickle irrigation, 257–259, 344
Truck safety regulations, 91

Turface, 233
Turnover, of land, 81

U.C.-type soils mixes, 234
Unemployment compensation, 84

Vapam, 245
Vapor barrier, 367
Vapor pressure, 375, 404
Vermiculite, 232

Warranties Act, 90
Water, 249–272
  acidification, 269
  acre inch, 258
  excess soil moisture, 271
  irrigation, 249
  need for, 172, 249
  quality, 250
  soluble salts, 250
  sources of, 249
  vapor, 375

Weed control:
  analyzing the situation, 303
  band application, 310
  biological, 304
  cleaning sprayers, 310
  cultivation, 304
  environmental, 304–306
  equipment, 308, 311
  herbicides, classification of, 305
    post-emergence, 308
    pre-emergence, 307
  objective, 302
  site situations, 303–304, 309
  vulnerability, of crops and weeds, 303
Weight of B&B plants, 396, 404
Wholesale production nurseries, 17–28
Windbreaks, 66
Winter survival, 293–296
Woody species, responsive to long days,
  284
Worker's Compensation Insurance, 91

Zinc, 188, 227
Zoning laws, 62